PENGUIN BOOKS

T0363588

THE BATTLE FOR LONE PINE

David W. Cameron completed his PhD in 1995 and was awarded an Australian Research Council (ARC) Postdoctoral Fellowship at the Australian National University (School of Archaeology), followed by an ARC QEII Fellowship at the University of Sydney (Department of Anatomy & Histology). He has published a number of books on science and Australian military history, including *'Sorry lads, but the order is to go': The August Offensive, Gallipoli 1915*. He has also published over sixty scientific papers in internationally peer-reviewed journals. David lives in Canberra with his wife Deb and their three children, Emma and twins Anita and Lloyd (and their dogs Mollie and Robbie).

David W. Cameron

THE BATTLE FOR LONE PINE

Four Days of Hell at the Heart of Gallipoli

PENGUIN BOOKS

PENGUIN BOOKS

UK | USA | Canada | Ireland | Australia
India | New Zealand | South Africa | China

Penguin Books is part of the Penguin Random House group of companies
whose addresses can be found at global.penguinrandomhouse.com.

Penguin
Random House
Australia

First published by Penguin Group (Australia), 2012
This edition published by Penguin Group (Australia), 2015

Cover and Text Design by John Canty © Penguin Group (Australia)
Cover image courtesy of AWM (Image #ps1515)
Typeset in Adobe Garamond
Colour separation by Splitting Image Colour Studio, Clayton, Victoria
Printed and bound in Australia by Griffin Press, an accredited ISO AS/NZS 14001
Environmental Management Systems printer.

National Library of Australia Cataloguing-in-Publication data is available.

ISBN 9780143572114

penguin.com.au

Contents

LIST OF MAPS

Prologue

A rush of adrenaline mixed with fear gripped 27-year-old Private Cecil McAnulty, from Middle Park, Victoria, as he and his mate Frank charged across no-man's-land, on a plateau in the hills of the Gallipoli Peninsula not far from the coast, towards the Turkish stronghold nicknamed Lone Pine. As members of the 3rd Australian Infantry Battalion, they were in the centre of the attacking waves sweeping towards the covered trenches on the east of the plateau, on 6 August 1915. Artillery shells exploded all around and machine-gun bullets ripped into their fellow men in khaki scrambling to meet the enemy. Cecil saw men either side of him trip over the thick knotty roots of shredded scrub, while others got momentarily tangled in scraps of barbed wire that littered the killing field; some fell and never got up. Officers yelled orders that couldn't be heard above the deafening sound of exploding ordnance. The paddock erupted into thousands of tiny explosions of dirt as bullets and shrapnel kicked into the dry barren ground. Larger eruptions caused by high-explosive shells sent geysers of earth skyward. Men disappeared in the smoke and dust, or, hideously disfigured and dying, yelled for help, as others charged past, oblivious or terrified, desperate to escape the same fate. Both Cecil and Frank thanked their lucky stars as they reached the Turkish trenches. Cecil later wrote in his diary: 'I can't realise how I got across it, I seemed to be in a sort of a trance. The rifle & machine gun fire was hellish.'[1] However, their troubles had just started, as the front-line trenches were mostly covered with thick timbers and earth. Some stopped to try and dig their way through and drag the heavy timbers aside; however, most, like Cecil and Frank, continued on towards the uncovered trenches to the rear of the Turkish stronghold. The small-arms fire was increasing in intensity as the Turks north and south of the battle poured enfilade and oblique fire into the attacking Australians, caught in the open. Cecil yelled to the others, 'This is suicide, boys! I'm going to make a jump for it.'[2] Frank and three others followed him and jumped for cover behind a Turkish parapet.

Less than fifty metres away, 22-year-old Lance Corporal Joseph Aylward and 24-year-old Private George Hayward, of the 4th Australian Infantry Battalion, were attacking the northern flank of Lone Pine. They were to secure trenches and stop the Turks from across the narrow gully to the north from rolling up the Australian lines. A machine gun to their right was spraying streams of lead across no-man's-land. George lit the fuse of one of his homemade jam-tin bombs with the cigarette dangling from his lips and quickly dropped the hissing projectile into the partly covered Turkish machine-gun pit – the resulting explosion silenced the gun. As George and Joseph pressed on, they realised that they were in danger of heading off the plateau battleground and descending into the gully below. Joseph turned back to see men from the second and third waves of the attack now struggling to reach the enemy trenches, as the Turks on the northern side of the gully awoke to the charge. His small party made an easy target too. Some fell, a crimson patch quickly staining the gritty ground around them. George, Joseph and the others dived into an open communication trench just in front and reluctantly made their way down into the gully, not knowing what awaited them.

On the southern side of Lone Pine, a new arrival to the peninsula, 25-year-old clerk Lieutenant Charles Lecky, set his eyes on a spot on the enemy's front line, where black sandbags were embedded in the trench parapets, and focused on running straight towards it. He didn't hear the exploding shrapnel and swish of machine-gun bullets that swept the plateau. Then he fell, tumbling into a shell crater. Stunned, Charles found a fellow officer in the hole, trying to plug a bullet hole in his arm. The man asked for help to get out. Charles tried but toppled back under the weight of his equipment. The wounded officer, 22-year-old Captain John Pain, was a survivor of the landing four months earlier. He pushed Charles up with his good arm and, in the middle of no-man's-land with shells and bullets roaring all around, Charles pulled the captain out of the crater. They both raced towards the Turkish trenches.[3]

Melbourne solicitor and citizen soldier 38-year-old Lieutenant Colonel Harold 'Pompey' Elliott, commander of the 7th Australian Infantry Battalion, was anxiously watching the charge through a trench periscope just north of the attack, immediately opposite the Turkish lines at Johnston's Jolly, as the position across the gully from Lone Pine was known. The periscope had been carefully wrapped in hessian and fixed against a sandbag parapet, in the hope the camouflage might save it from Turkish sniper fire for a few hours at least. He knew that if the attack failed, his own men were to be thrown against the trenches at the Jolly, which were judged to be more heavily defended than Lone Pine. But even if they were successful, Elliott and his men were not out of the woods – they were slated to reinforce Lone Pine, which itself would be a treacherous task in such conditions. Indeed, so fierce was the struggle ahead of them that, within days, four of his men would be awarded the Victoria Cross for their outstanding valour in the fight to hold Lone Pine.

★ ★ ★

After the first few days of the Gallipoli landings by British Empire and French troops, on 25 April 1915, most had resigned themselves to stalemate. But, with their reputations at stake, the senior British and French commanders at Helles – the southern tip of the peninsula – insisted on trying to break through the Turkish lines. To salvage the campaign, and perhaps their careers, they would expend the lives of huge numbers of their men. About eighteen kilometres further north, below the hills that form the southern end of the formidable Sari Bair Range, on a beach they named Anzac Cove, the men of the Australian and New Zealand Army Corps (ANZAC) had more than enough on their hands just trying to defend their precarious foothold on 160 hectares of Turkish soil. The idea of advancing beyond the coastal ridges and cutting off the southern reaches of the peninsula to Turkish reinforcements was likely far from their minds.

Yet, within months of the landing, that was the objective: to sever the peninsula west to east, isolating the Turkish garrison at Helles and silencing the guns that were blocking the advance of the combined British and French fleets through the Dardanelles.

By June, General Ian Hamilton, commander of the Mediterranean Expeditionary Force (charged with occupying the Gallipoli Peninsula) and his subordinate, Lieutenant General William Birdwood (commander of the Anzac sector), had decided to pin all of their hopes of breaking the Turkish defences on the launch of an offensive immediately north of Anzac Cove, in order to occupy the dominating heights of the Sari Bair Range before pushing east to the Dardanelles. To further assist in future operations, another landing about ten kilometres north at Suvla Bay would be incorporated into the 'August Offensive'.

To help draw Turkish attention and troops away from the northern heights of Sari Bair, a feint was designed to keep the Turks focused on their southern flank. This would be an attack by the men of the 1st Australian Division against the well-entrenched and fortified position known as Lone Pine, on '400 Plateau'. The capture of the Sari Bair Range was to be the first of four phases that would be implemented along the Anzac sector, each pending the success of the former. Lone Pine itself would serve as an important 'jumping off' point for the next phase of the offensive – the capture of Third Ridge and the coastal promontory, Gaba Tepe, a few kilometres to the south. From there, the goal was to sweep across to the eastern shore of the peninsula. Given the failure of this opening stage of the operation, orders for phase two were never drafted.[4]

The battle for Lone Pine, 6–9 August 1915, has rightfully gone down in Australian military history as one of the toughest and most brutal ever fought by Australians in any war. It comprised four days of intense hand-to-hand fighting and bombing in an area covering just a few hectares, with Australian and Turkish trenches often just a few metres apart. Men used anything at hand to gain an advantage in the close confines of the Pine, including fists, bayonets, knives, rifle butts and entrenching tools. Indeed, close to 2800 Australians became casualties during these four days, and Turkish casualties were said to be at least double that number. Unlike most battles in the Great War, casualties at Lone Pine were not dominated by artillery and machine-gun fire, but from small arms, bayonets and homemade bombs (grenades). In the claustrophobic maze of trenches, clogged with the dead and dying, surprise encounters resulting in fierce isolated skirmishes, and the sudden appearance of a bomb, which might be lobbed back and forth several times before it exploded, added psychological horrors to the harrowing ordeal.

Of the nine Victoria Crosses awarded to Australians for the Gallipoli campaign, seven were for outstanding actions of bravery and valour during those four days at Lone Pine. Five were earned in a single day of the fighting, a record in Australian military actions. Many who were there believed a host of others would also have made worthy VC recipients, but the officers who were intent on nominating them died fighting in Lone Pine before they could put pen to paper. Indeed, all of the battalion commanders who took part in the initial attack became casualties, two of whom were killed. It is perhaps fitting that Australia's official commemoration of the Gallipoli conflict is conducted each Anzac Day in the Lone Pine Cemetery, built over what was in 1915 the killing field of the no-man's-land between the Australian and Turkish trenches. The western wall of the cemetery sits on the original Australian front-line trenches at a position nicknamed The Pimple, while its eastern wall rests upon the original Turkish front line at Lone Pine, known to the Turks as Kanli Sirt, or 'Bloody Ridge'.

Given the significance of this tragic battle to Australian military history – Australia's only victory at Gallipoli, at devastating personal cost, amid a wider tactical failure – it is surprising that there has never been a single book focusing on it before now. Only the war correspondent Charles Bean, in his *Official History of Australia in the War of 1914–1918* (Volume II), deals with Lone Pine in any detail. Indeed, this narrative could not have been written without continued reference to his groundbreaking work, along with the volumes of unpublished documentation that he collected over the years relating to the battle, including correspondence from participants (all available at the Australian War Memorial in Canberra). Also, since Bean's monumental work there was a steady increase in diaries and letters donated to the Australian War Memorial and other research institutions, describing actions at Lone Pine as well as in support 'behind' the lines. Thus, in addition to the accounts of the fighting men, from both sides of the conflict, this book draws on the newer material to endeavour to include the important contributions made by non-combatants. This includes senior commanders, sappers, stretcher-bearers, cooks, artillerymen and base nursing staff. Presented here for the first time, then, is a detailed account of Australians' involvement in one of the Great War's most intense assaults, whose tragedy was deepened by being a victorious battle within a defeated campaign.

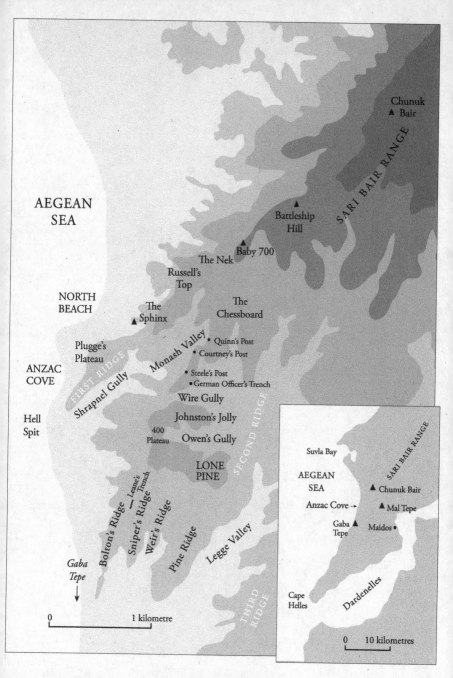

Anzac Sector and (inset) Gallipoli Peninsula

PREPARATIONS

1

'. . . to our last man and our last shilling'

In June 1914, the assassination of Archduke Ferdinand, the heir to the Austro-Hungarian throne, saw the Balkans yet again erupt into violence and war – but this time, nation after nation was dragged into the vortex of destruction. Austria-Hungary blamed Serbia for the assassination, Germany backed Austria-Hungary, Russia backed Serbia, and one by one the dominos of the international alliance system fell. Britain declared war on Germany on 5 August after German troops invaded neutral Belgium.

Few, if any, in Australia took much notice of the small articles that appeared in print about the assassination of the heir and his wife in faraway Bosnia.[1] Certainly no-one suspected that the murder of two people in Sarajevo would lead to the death of 60 000 Australians. Most people in Australia were firmly focused on domestic sporting and political matters. Indeed, a federal election was in full swing.

On 5 August 1914, a cable reached Australia that Great Britain was at war with Germany. With Britain at war, so too was Australia, and the two prime ministerial candidates now went about desperately trying to outdo the other in empire rhetoric.

The then Prime Minister, Joseph Cook, announced during an election rally at Horsham, in Victoria: 'Whatever happens, Australia is part of the Empire to the full. Remember that when the Empire is at war, so is Australia at war.'[2] However, the opposition leader, Andrew Fisher, went further, stating at a similar function in Colac: 'Should the worst happen after everything has been done that honour will permit, Australia will stand beside [the mother country] to help and defend her to our last man and our last shilling.'[3] Fisher went on to win the election for the Australian Labor Party.

The question then was, how many troops did the mother country want? Britain took up Australia's original offer of 20 000 men, which made up one infantry division and one light horse brigade. The idea that ultimately 324 000 men would enlist and serve – not to mention around 3000 nursing sisters of the Australian Army Nursing Service – resulting in 216 000 casualties (a casualty rate of 67 per cent), would have been scoffed at in the early days of the war, if anyone had been mad enough to predict such figures. This from a nation with a population of fewer than five million. These casualty figures do not count the multitude who also suffered psychologically, from 'shell shock' and what would later be diagnosed as post-traumatic stress disorder. Such psychological wounds would turn out to be one of the most widespread of battlefield traumas[4] and become synonymous with those who survived the war. In 1914, however, all of that was in the future.

Senator George Pearce, Defence Minister of Australia, had adopted national peacetime conscription for the first time in 1911, to replace the old state-based militia system. Pearce rejected any notion that compulsory military training amounted to militarism, stating publicly: 'When the people are the Army, the Army cannot be used to oppress the people.'[5] The new system obliged men aged between eighteen and twenty-five years to serve in the infantry militia for drills amounting to a grand total of sixteen days per year, including eight days in an annual camp, which provided the bare basics of military training. The first draftees had begun training in 1912 and in 1914 the militia had around 51 200 men. There was no divisional structure, but officers gained some experience in command of units up to brigade level.[6] The Defence Act of 1903, however, could not force existing militia members to serve overseas. Hence, initial enlistments for the war in 1914 were regionally based and undertaken under mobilisation plans drawn up in 1912. The regular army in Australia was very small and only one unit of the first Australian Imperial Force (AIF) was formed from it in 1914 – the 1st Field Battery. Indeed, the then inspector general of the army, General William Bridges, believed that no viable force could be formed from the militia units, as they were too young and what training they had was based on home defence.[7] Even so, of the 20 000 original volunteers who joined the AIF, 26 per cent were existing members of the militia. A disproportionate number of these men likely provided the initial pool for junior and non-commissioned officers. The great bulk of the remaining volunteers had either no military service (42 per cent) or were former state militia members.[8] The recruits were organised on a territorial basis, with the 1st Brigade (1st, 2nd, 3rd and 4th battalions) consisting of men from New South Wales, the 2nd Brigade (5th, 6th, 7th and 8th battalions) consisting of men from Victoria, and the 3rd Brigade (9th, 10th, 11th and 12th battalions) from the other states and territories.

Unlike in Australia, Britain's 230 000 territorial troops undertook training one or two evenings a week and took part in large-scale exercises annually. In addition, these men could be forced to serve overseas. However, even British territorial training faded when compared to Germany. Every German male, on turning twenty years of age, had to present himself for compulsory military service for a few years, followed by ongoing service in the military reserve until he turned forty-five. Also, those aged seventeen to nineteen could volunteer to sign up before being drafted. By any comparison, the men of the AIF were woefully inexperience and undertrained.[9]

Federation of Australia had only occurred fourteen years before the new nation found herself in a world war. The majority of the recruits likely saw themselves as English first, Catholic or Protestant second, Queenslander or Victorian third and maybe Australian fourth – ties to Mother England were still very strong. State rivalry was still very much a major factor in national politics and states were keen to outdo each other with their contribution to the AIF. It would not take long, however, for the soldiers to see themselves as collectively and uniquely Australian: they wore the same uniform and spoke the same lingo. Indeed, this 'Australian-ness' was soon recognised by newer recruits who reinforced the originals at Gallipoli, as recalled by dental apprentice Private Ben Champion of the 1st Battalion: 'Soon we were the centre of an animated group...Grouped together, they had a sameness which I had never realised before. There was a definite Australian character which is hard to explain, but which was present in every one of them.'[10]

Australians enlisted for many reasons. British patriotism certainly played a part, while for others it was better than unemployment. Some thought it would be a great adventure and a cheap way of seeing the world. Others referred to them as 'six-bob-a-day-tourists', in reference to their exorbitant daily pay. Some recruits eagerly seized the opportunity to be involved in something greater than themselves, to 'be a part of it'. Some likely enlisted to get away from the humdrum of a meaningless daily existence, or to escape family responsibilities. On being asked if he had any dependents, one recruit allegedly replied, 'Yes, two publicans at Gundagi.'[11] Still others believed it was the 'manly' thing to do and reckoned that they wouldn't be able to hold their head high if they didn't enlist, especially if a younger sibling was already in uniform.[12] Recent British arrivals to Australia, like John Simpson Kirkpatrick (soon to become known as the 'man with the donkey'), saw it as a chance to get a free trip back home to see family.

Those seeking family reunions in Britain, however, were to be disappointed. Originally, the AIF and their counterparts from the New Zealand Expeditionary Force (NZEF) had expected to disembark in England, before being sent to France. While at sea, the large convoy transporting the force received a message from London: 'Unforeseen circumstances decide that the Force shall train in Egypt and go to the front from there. The Australians and New Zealanders are to form a Corps under General Birdwood. The locality of the camp is near Cairo.'[13] The unforeseen circumstance was the entry of Turkey into the war on the side of Germany and Austria-Hungary. By siding with the Central Powers, Turkey hoped to recover recently lost territories in the Balkans. The British and French would never countenance Turkey regaining territories that were now independent nation states. It was strongly suspected by the British that the Turks were planning to capture the strategically critical 160-kilometre-long Suez Canal – keeping the AIF and NZEF in Egypt meant that they could be called upon to help defend this vital artery of the empire. Also, Australian Lieutenant Colonel Harry Chauvel, who had arrived in England just as the war broke (and received a telegram that he was to command the newly raised Australian Light Horse Brigade), suggested that it would be better for the Australian troops to train in Egypt, given the cold English winter and the overcrowding of training camps due to the earlier arrival of the Canadians.[14]

The newly appointed commander of the corps, fifty-year-old William Birdwood, had a nervous energy that propelled him to senior command. Birdwood was an Indian Army officer who stood outside the mainstream of the British senior officers then running the war on the Western Front, and was very much a Kitchener man – when that was not necessarily a good thing. Birdwood had seen a good deal of active service during the Second Boer War and along the North-West Frontier of India. By 1911 he was Secretary of the Indian Army Department, and with the coming of the Great War, Kitchener appointed him in late 1914 to command the newly formed Australian and New Zealand Army Corps – ANZAC. Sir Ian Hamilton, who would command the forces during much of the Gallipoli campaign, later described Birdwood as 'the soul of Anzac… if he does not know every soldier in his force, at least every soldier in the force believes he is known to his Chief'.[15] Birdwood was affectionately known to the men of ANZAC as 'Birdie' and his rapport with them made this British general highly respected as a 'digger with stripes'. Sergeant John McLennan, who was aboard the headquarters ship just prior to the landing in April, wrote: 'I am more impressed with General Birdwood. He has drawn his three days' bully beef and biscuits like the rest of us, and carries all his kit in a holdall. If the fact becomes known, and I hope it will, it will make him still more popular with the boys, if it is possible.'[16] Birdwood's relaxed demeanour and genuine concern for the welfare of his men made him an immediate success with the Australians and New Zealanders – they saw his value.[17] Birdwood certainly agreed with their assessment – he was a shameless self-promoter.

In early December 1914, the first of the ANZACs began to arrive in Egypt. The Australians made camp at Mena, close to the pyramids, while the New Zealanders were located some distance away in a desert camp at Zeitoun. Overall, the men were not keen to be taking up residence in Egypt. They were in a hurry to prove themselves against the 'real enemy' – the Germans – before the war ended. They needn't have worried – there were years of slaughter ahead. Even so, they generally made the most of being apparently dumped in the war's backwater, especially the officers who saw it as a great chance to further train their troops and put them through their paces. Reveille was 5.30 a.m., followed by breakfast. Soon after, the men would fall in and conduct a march through the desert, usually with full pack. Water was strictly rationed during these marches and bottles checked. The men returned to camp for tea and lights were out by 9.45 p.m. Sunday, a day of rest, was spent on Church Parade (religious service), after which the camp had to be cleaned – yet again – followed by another parade, with picquet and fatigue duties of all kinds enforced.

The men, however, found ways to let off some steam in camp, usually at an officer's expense. Lieutenant Colonel Harold 'Pompey' Elliott, commander of the 7th Battalion, was a hard taskmaster with a fiery temper, but even so, he was not only universally respected by the men, they worshipped him – they would follow him to hell and back.[18] Still, at times they got their own back on their demanding CO. On one occasion they arranged for one of the local newspaper sellers to stand outside his tent in the early morning hours, declaring: 'Egyptian Times, very good news – death of Pompey the bastard!'[19] This was rather tame compared to the next prank. When Elliott called a parade one day he found that rather than wearing their slouch hats – which he himself favoured – some of his men were wearing the British-style pith helmet. Elliott bellowed that all men were to be wearing slouch hats by next parade, emphasising that he didn't care where they got it from, but any man within the battalion not wearing one would find himself assigned to latrine duty. A few hours later, Elliott was having lunch in the mess tent and removed his slouch hat, placing it on the chair next to him, but when he was ready to leave, it was gone. He spent the day searching for his hat, turning the contents of the men's tents upside down in the process without success. He managed to find a replacement just before the next parade – he was concerned about breaking his own order. However, the only one he could find was too small and the khaki had bleached in the harsh sunlight into a pinkish hue. He valiantly tried to regain his dignity the next day, but sniggering could be heard amongst the ranks during the parade. Elliott neither found his hat or the culprit.[20]

When the men were finally allowed out of camp and into Cairo, their baiting of officers reached new heights. Thirty-four-year-old stockman and Boer War veteran Private William Smith would by war's end be famous, from general on down, as the 'first private of the AIF'.[21] He was universally known within the Australian Corps as 'Smithy'. A private he was, and a private he intended to remain. Smithy had a knack for shattering any pretence of authority when out of the line, but when in the thick of the action all that knew him, including the officers who were frequently the victim of his wit, agreed he was the one bloke you wanted next to you. Smithy had only been in Cairo for a week when he and his mates invaded the plush and very respectable Shepheard's Hotel. Compared to their British counterparts, the six-bob-a-day Australian troops were flush with spending money – the Brits were paid just two bob. Before the colonials arrived in Cairo, there had been no need for British commanders to place well-to-do establishments out of bounds to the rank and file – a serious shortage in coin, but more importantly a structured class system, kept the British Tommy 'in his place', and that was nowhere near Shepheard's Hotel. The Australians had no such impediments, and as ever, authority was fair game for Smithy. In his uniform of a private of the Australian 11th Battalion, he strolled up to British General Maxwell, who was relaxing in the lounge with his staff. One of Smithy's mates recalled after the war what happened next.

Approaching, he saluted smartly, and inquired, 'General Maxwell?'
'Yes, my man! What can I do for you?' was the reply.
'I believe, sir, that you are an eminent archaeologist.'
The general beamed and from his demeanour it was easily seen he imagined Smithy to be a university professor

> serving in the ranks. 'I can lay no claim to eminence,' he
> replied, 'but archaeology is certainly a hobby of mine.'
'You are an authority on Cairo, sir, I believe?' queried Smithy.
'I think I may justifiably say yes to that,' replied the General.
'Ancient and modern?' asked Smithy.
'Yes,' said the general, 'I have made a long study of Cairo,
> both ancient and modern.'
'Then,' said Smithy, 'I wonder if you can tell me where the
> gentlemen's lavatory is in this hotel?'

> Maxwell's staff tried to keep straight faces, but failed. A roar
> of laughter, in which the general joined, rang through the
> room. Smithy's companions decided that a less exalted
> social sphere would suit them better, and escaped into the
> Wazzer [Derb el Wasa, Cairo's red light district]. Smithy
> waited the general's reply, and alone withstood the assault of
> outraged authority...[This] earned him twenty-eight days
> in the citadel. He served twenty-four days only – receiving
> a remission of four days for good conduct – a concession
> he ever after regarded as a most unjustifiable slur upon his
> reputation.[22]

Shortly after, Shepheard's Hotel and similar exulted premises were
placed off limits to all the rank and file.

Meanwhile, Lieutenant Sydney Cook, son of the former
Australian prime minister Joseph Cook, was also busy getting
himself expelled – not from Shepheard's Hotel, but from having
tea with his recent bride, 25-year-old Elsie Sheppard. Elsie had
been amongst the first to sign up for the Australian Army Nursing
Service (AANS), as reported in the Sydney *Sunday Times* on
9 August 1914: 'One of the first nurses in New South Wales to
volunteer from [*sic*] active service was Nurse Shephard [*sic*]...She
is also the fiancée of Lieut. Cook, son of the Prime Minister, who

had also volunteered for active service.'[23] Now in Egypt, it was pretty much an open secret that they had since married. Army regulations, however, stipulated that only unmarried nurses could gain a position overseas – if a nurse married while on active service she had to resign. Syd's father, also a former defence minister, had obviously pulled some strings. Elsie and Syd were having tea in Mena House when Elsie's matron spotted them together. The matron, knowing full well they were married, was put on the spot and was forced to explain to the young officer that it 'wasn't for mere men to intrude there, so Syd soon departed'.[24]

Rightly or wrongly, the Australians were reputed to be an undisciplined, drunken, disrespectful lot. One British officer, Noel Braithwaite of the Manchester Territorials, wrote at the time that there 'isn't much discipline among them as one could get from a lot of maniacs' and that they were generally 'boasting, bragging, uncivilized hooligans'. He went on to add, however, that 'they appear to be made of the right stuff'.[25] Another story from ANZAC training in Egypt, sent home by a New Zealander and likely apocryphal, was about a soldier on sentry duty:

'Halt! Who goes there?'
'Ceylon Planters Rifle Club.'
'Pass, friend.'
'Halt! Who goes there?'
'Auckland Mounted Rifles.'
'Pass, friend.'
'Halt! Who goes there?'
'What the — has that got to do with you?'
'Pass, Australian.'[26]

All was not fun and games, though, as demonstrated by the riot in Cairo that has gone down in history as the 'Battle for the Wazzer'. In early April, a few New Zealanders and Australians complained that they were being overcharged for services rendered in the brothels of Derb el Wasa. A crowd gathered and a riot broke out. A few houses went up in flames and soldiers interfered with a local fire brigade by chopping up their hoses. What actually provoked the riot remains in question, as it has also been said that it started when a Maori was stabbed, which led to beds, mattresses and clothing being thrown into the street and set on fire. Although only a small number of men were involved in the fracas, the next day Cairo was declared off limits to the Australians, who were judged the main perpetrators.[27] It was the publication of this event by Charles Bean, and his reports regarding cases of venereal disease amongst the troops (Bean refused to state it was venereal disease but the context of his reporting makes its clear what he was talking about), that early on made him very unpopular with the Corps and the temperamental Australian public, who would not stomach any criticism of the troops. Bean, however, would redeem himself in their eyes by sharing the dangers of Gallipoli and the Western Front with the men.

An early photograph of Charles Bean, taken by his friend Phillip Schuler while on a transport in late 1914, seems to say it all – a tall, lanky, bookish-looking man, with wire-rimmed glasses, in army-regulation tunic, trousers, puttees and boots, but with his slouch hat disfigured into civilian shape. The black and white photograph can't show his mop of red wavy hair and blue eyes, or his shy conscientiousness, but it does convey a sense of his determination and enthusiasm. For over four years Bean would follow the Australians in and out of the line, recording their stories, not only at Gallipoli but also on the Western Front and beyond. Bean would not only write Australia's official history of the war, but he experienced its horrors firsthand from day one – he was an ANZAC. During the Gallipoli campaign he had been Mentioned in Despatches and official correspondence for his dedication and bravery: he had gone out into no-man's-land on at least one occasion to bring in Australian wounded. But no medals for him – Captain Bean, although officially within the military fold, was a journalist and the Australian Army doesn't award medals to 'civilians'. Indeed, a brigadier at the time warned him against getting involved in such foolery and that if he insisted on doing so he'd be sent back to Australia.

Nonetheless, as an active participant Bean became well and truly acquainted with the tragedy of war and men's differing reactions to it, from the bravest to the most fearful. But he learnt his lesson about keeping negative comments out of official correspondence or newspaper reporting – that would be left for his personal diaries and letters. He wrote in his diary about Australians moving into battle, while others at the same time were falling back, each ignoring the other. He discussed the more 'mundane' aspects of war, including the work of the cooks, engineers, sappers, signallers and others. He concluded: 'Well, this is the true side of war – but I wonder if anyone would believe me outside the army. I've never written higher praise of Australians than is on this page, but the probability is that if I were to put it into print tomorrow the tender Australian public, which only tolerates flattery and that in its cheapest form, would howl me out of existence.'[28]

Another scribe from within the ranks was Private Cecil McAnulty, who enlisted in Liverpool, New South Wales, in February 1915 and was part of the 2nd reinforcement to the 3rd Battalion. McAnulty's service record shows that he was just shy of six feet in height with fair complexion, blue eyes and light brown hair. When enlisting, he filled out his will, leaving all of his property to his younger brother Desmond, but it was to be held in trust by his mother Cecilia until he turned twenty-one. Like Smithy, Cecil apparently enjoyed the odd drink, as he was charged twenty shillings for being 'drunk in camp about 10.30 a.m., found in tent in hopeless condition after reinforcements had left camp – returned to depot'.[29] He liked to play cards, probably while puffing away on his pipe, but most notably jotted down his experiences in a small red diary. By the time he got to Gallipoli, the diary was full and he was forced to scavenge bits of paper, including used envelopes, in order to complete his writings. McAnulty's makeshift diary would turn out to be one of the most poignant of writings during the whole Australian experience at Gallipoli.

While the ANZACs trained in Egypt, the Turks launched a land campaign, not against the Suez Canal as expected (that would come in early February and would be repulsed largely by Indian and New Zealand troops), but against Russian forces in the Caucasus. At the start of this offensive, the commander-in-chief of Russian forces, the Tsar's cousin, Grand Duke Nicholas Romanov, had sent a harried appeal to London requesting that pressure on the Russian Front be relieved by action against the Ottoman Empire. Secretary of War Kitchener, in a letter dated 2 January 1915, informed First Lord of the Admiralty Winston Churchill that the only place a realistic demonstration could be made was against the Dardanelles – the vital sea passage that linked the then Turkish capital Constantinople to the Aegean and Mediterranean.[30] Within days the urgency of the situation from the Russian perspective had changed significantly. Indeed, by mid January Turkish casualties from Russian counter-attacks were truly horrific, with an estimated 90 000 dead and 45 000 captured, leaving a grand total of 12 000 survivors – the Turkish Army in the Caucasus ceased to exist.[31] Regardless, within days a British Naval Squadron bombarded the shoreline defences of the Dardanelles, an attack that ended with a spectacular explosion at one of the Turkish forts guarding the entry to the Dardanelles as a result of a direct hit to its ammunition depot. The assault led Churchill and others to believe that naval power alone would likely succeed in forcing its way through the Dardanelles and the Bosphorus. The original objective to relieve pressure on the Russian Front had now apparently changed to one of knocking Turkey out of the war.[32]

The main opponents of breaking through the Dardanelles with the navy were the admirals and other senior officers at the Admiralty who would have the task of planning and executing the operation. The narrow straits of the Dardanelles were known to be heavily mined and defended by around 200 guns and any number of shore-based torpedo tubes. The Admiralty refused to allow their best ships to be used and, apart from the newly built warships *Queen Elizabeth*, *Inflexible* and *Irresistible*, most of the other ships they sent were due for retirement and manned by reserve crews. The same was true of the French contingent. Even so, it was still a mighty fleet that began its attack on 18 March 1915 – but it failed.[33]

Several hundred lives were lost, three battleships were sunk and another three gravely damaged by mines. In one day Admiral de Robeck lost a third of the battleships committed to the operation with nothing to show for it. Churchill wanted to order the admiral to undertake another assault, but faced with the unanimous opinion of de Robeck and the other naval and military commanders on the scene, the War Council in London was left with little alternative but to abandon the naval attack. This was a wise decision and should have been the end of the 'campaign'. However, it was now concluded that the forcing of the Dardanelles would continue with a combined operation by the navy and army.[34]

A month earlier in London, Kitchener had appointed a Scot, General Sir Ian Hamilton, as commander-in-chief of the Mediterranean Expeditionary Force (MEF). The tall, wiry Hamilton appeared by nature to be more of a poet than a military man – he had a gift when it came to turning a phrase and had published widely. However, he was a warrior whose left hand had been crippled thirty-five years earlier by a Boer's bullet smashing into his wrist at the Battle of Majuba Hill, where he was recommended for the Victoria Cross, though the honour was denied, as he was considered too young.

During the Second Boer War as a colonel, he was again recommended for the VC during the defence of Wagon Hill, but it was denied as it was considered that he was of too high a rank. He also suffered a serious horse fall during active service and smashed one of his legs, which left him with a noticeable limp. His injuries and wounds did not slow him down, however, and during the Russo-Japanese War (1904–05) Hamilton was appointed the official British observer. By 1915 he was one of the most experienced senior officers in the British Army. Indeed, the Germans recognised him as being the most experienced soldier in the world at that time.[35] Aged sixty-two, he still displayed the intellect that propelled him to the position of Kitchener's chief-of-staff during the Second Boer War. After a brief interview with his former boss, Hamilton was given overall command of the MEF and was dispatched immediately to Egypt with a few maps to start planning for an invasion of the Gallipoli Peninsula should the navy fail. He arrived just in time to witness the shattering of the combined British and French fleet operation in March by Turkish resistance.

With the failure of naval operations, the British 29th Division, under the command of Major General Aylmer Hunter-Weston, was slated as the main force to capture the peninsula. In doing so the army would silence the Turkish land-based defences of the Dardanelles and hence make it possible for the combined fleet to penetrate the Dardanelles and lay 'siege' to Constantinople. It was the only regular British division not yet committed to the Western Front and was immediately dispatched to the Mediterranean in mid March. The French, always suspicious of British intentions within the region, also committed a division to the campaign, under General Albert d'Amade. The plan was for the British division to land on a number of beaches around the southern tip of the peninsula at Cape Helles, while the French would initially land along the Asiatic side at Kum Kale as a feint, before later withdrawing in order to support the British right flank. The landing of troops at Helles would enable the army's flanks resting against the Aegean and Dardanelles to be protected by the big guns of the navy, which would assist the troops in a rapid advance north up the peninsula.[36]

Birdwood's ANZACs were also included in the invasion of the Gallipoli Peninsula. The Corps was to land close to Gaba Tepe, a headland on the west coast approximately eighteen kilometres north of the landings at Helles. Behind Gaba Tepe, a relatively flat plain connected the western and eastern shores of the peninsula. Any force that was able to capture the promontory would be able to move rapidly inland, facing little topographical resistance. Hence, Gaba Tepe and the broad expanse of beach just north and south of it were recognised by the Turks as a likely landing place for any invasion, and it was accordingly heavily defended. They were known to be well entrenched, supported by artillery and machine guns, along with strand upon strand of barbed-wire entanglements covering the approach.

While the main objective for the ANZACs was to capture Gaba Tepe, it was also crucial that they occupy the Sari Bair Range, three kilometres further north, to protect their left flank. The heights could readily be approached using the ridgelines that terminated within the southern coastal plain around Gaba Tepe. After accomplishing this, they were to advance further inland to the hill Mal Tepe, which provided a commanding vantage over the plain, from where they could cut Turkish communications north and south. Within days, the British were expected to be advancing up the peninsula to join them.[37]

Things didn't go according to plan – the ANZACs landed on the wrong beach. Rather than arriving close to Gaba Tepe and the surrounding plain, they landed on 25 April at arguably the worst possible place – just below the dominating heights of the Sari Bair

Range, two kilometres too far north. It was no longer a race across the coastal plain, but a much more difficult race up and over the imposing ridges.

At Helles, the British fared no better. They were lucky just to gain a foothold, suffering terrible casualties in establishing a beachhead. At W Beach, at the tip of the peninsula, six VCs would be earnt before breakfast. The flat trajectory of the big guns of the navy had little impact on the entrenched Turks and by day's end the British troops, at great sacrifice, had only managed to penetrate a few hundred metres beyond the beaches.[39]

2

'Goodbye, old chap;
good luck!'

The Australians of the 3rd Brigade, being the first to land, scrambled up the rugged cliffs and gullies leading to the heights. Where the Sari Bair Range reached down to the coast, it split into three ridges. The first loomed immediately above the beach where the ANZACs landed; the second reached further south, ending in an area to be known as 400 Plateau. The third ridge, their ultimate objective, lay another kilometre further inland and terminated close to Gaba Tepe. Within hours on 25 April, the 1st Australian Division had taken the first two ridges, although they were later forced back to the western slopes of the second (as a result of Turkish shelling). The third would never be taken. Later that day, the men of the New Zealand and Australian Division also landed – the ANZAC legend was born. The fighting in the thickly vegetated gullies and slopes was not only physically draining, but psychologically demanding for ANZAC and Turk alike. Many small isolated battles occurred and the fate of the men involved to this day remains unknown. Larger-scale actions by Australians and New Zealanders tried to push the Turks off Baby 700, Battleship Hill and Chunuk Bair to the north (without success), while to the south, at a place later known as Lone Pine, Australians took cover in the available scrub as Turkish artillery positioned on Third Ridge pounded the area with shrapnel, causing many casualties. These men were forced to retire towards the seaward side of the plateau for shelter, leaving Lone Pine in Turkish hands. As the day wore on, any thought of advancing to Third Ridge, Gaba Tepe and Mal Tepe were forgotten: the ANZACs had enough on their hands just clinging to their shallow beachhead. With darkness, the men from both sides dug in and awaited with some anxiety what the morning would bring.[1]

Within days, the wounded from the fighting at Helles and what had been dubbed Anzac Cove started to flood into the military hospitals in Lemnos, Alexandria, Cairo and elsewhere. Sister Elsie Cook was in Cairo at No. 2 Australian General Hospital. She was extremely concerned about her husband, Lieutenant Syd Cook, who was a platoon commander of the 2nd Battalion. Indeed, Lieutenant Cook and his men were fighting for their lives on 400 Plateau, at Lone Pine.[2] Elsie had heard nothing from him and the large number of casualties must have increased her concern. \

As the bulk of the Australian wounded were being cared for in Alexandria at British No. 17 General Hospital, Elsie and eight other sisters were transferred to the port city. She wrote in her diary on 29 April: 'We only had three hours notice to pack up and catch train. Feeling anxious about Syd, [have heard] nothing.'[3] While she continued to worry, her time was quickly consumed with caring for those flooding into the hospital.[4] Elsie soon came across a wounded soldier from Syd's battalion. He told her that Syd had been wounded and was in Alexandria, shot through the thigh. The soldier could not provide any further details and Elsie was far too busy treating the large numbers of casualties coming into her ward to look for her husband. She just hoped that Syd was receiving the same care that she and the other nursing sisters were providing.

Much to Elsie's relief, she soon received a cable informing her that Syd was indeed in Alexandria, at the Deaconesses Hospital. Later that night, she made her way to Syd's side. He was overjoyed to see her and Elsie was relieved that his wound, while painful, was not life-threatening and he was expected to make a full recovery. Unfortunately, that also meant that he would soon be on his way back to Anzac.[5]

After the first twenty-four hours of the landings, trench warfare and stalemate had set in at both Helles and Anzac. Even so, Turkish military doctrine at this early stage of the campaign dictated that the enemy be pushed back into the sea, and they'd spent the last couple of weeks trying to do just that, conducting a series of piecemeal attacks against the ANZAC lines that all ended in failure and death. With the arrival of the Turkish 2nd Division in mid May, the Turkish commanders believed they could finally launch an all-out counterattack against the ANZAC perimeter. Five Turkish divisions would be hauled against the ANZACs, with odds in their favour of three to one.[6]

On 18 May, reports spread amongst the ANZACs that airmen had observed newly arrived Turkish troops massing just behind the Turkish front lines. The ANZACs set about preparing for the inevitable Turkish attack – but at which part of the line were they going to try and force the issue? At 5 p.m. that afternoon, the Turks began a slow bombardment against the whole ANZAC front, apparently attempting to disguise their specific objective(s) – few expected them to attack the entire perimeter.

At this time, Smithy was positioned along the southern flank of Anzac on Bolton's Ridge with the rest of the men from the 11th Battalion. Not far away would have been 24-year-old barber from Western Australia Corporal Thomas McNamara, positioned in a front-line trench. McNamara remembered a deep brooding silence in the lead-up to the Turkish attack that was only broken at intervals by the rattle of equipment or the quietly muttered words amongst the men either side of him. The darkened outline of his mate's head and shoulders 'intensified the unreality of the scene, due to the lines of his body being lost in the darkness of the narrow trench which the faint cold light of the morning stars failed to penetrate'.[7] Finally, word was quietly passed down the line that the men who had been screening the forward trenches had come in and reported that the Turks were on the move. McNamara experienced 'a slight involuntary shiver that might have been due to the chill morning air, a tingling, creeping sensation at the base of the skull which passed down the spine and thoughts which had moved sluggishly now took on a racing pace'.[8] He tried to imagine the Turks slowly, cautiously and quietly creeping up towards his position, hoping to catch him and his mates unprepared.[9]

At 3 a.m., 19 May, most ANZACs in the front line were waiting on their trench firing step after having spent much of the night preparing for the expected attack. Rifle ammunition was distributed along the parapets (the sandbagged front edge of the trenches) within ready reach. Machine-gunners anxiously sprayed a few bullets across no-man's-land to ensure the guns were in good working order. Bombers were waiting with their primitive homemade jam-tin bombs, having lit the hessian of sandbag parapets to a smoulder, enabling them to quickly light their bombs with a blow to make embers, rather than using trembling fingers to strike a match.

Twenty-six-year-old Sydney architect Private Charles Duke, of the 4th Battalion, who would within a few months be fighting for his life in Lone Pine, was blissfully ignorant of the impending attack. He was digging a forward sap (narrow perpendicular extensions dug out from within trenches, for communication or enemy surveillance) from the front line and no-one seemed to have bothered to tell him or his mate, 27-year-old Private George Bell, that they were in danger of being overrun by wave upon wave of Turks whose blood lust was up. Charles and George had earlier been told that their shift had been extended for another two hours and they were not due to be relieved until after 4 a.m. The first inkling that either had that this morning was going to be far from usual was sometime just before 4 a.m., when Charles took a breather and looked up over the parapet. To his amazement, he saw a Turk just metres away. He gave George a nudge and pointed out the interloper, but before they could react the Australian firing line immediately behind them 'broke out as though all hell had been let loose, so Bell and I made our way as quickly as possible through the end of the sap...to the main trench and there joined the boys...in firing as rapidly as possible at the approaching masses'.[10]

ANZAC rifle and machine guns opened up with a vengeance, spraying lead into no-man's-land. Artillery also joined in, exploding behind the now-packed Turkish front lines. In darkness, ANZACs jumped up onto the firing step with their heads clear of the parapet, and a few even climbed into no-man's-land to get a better shot. Officers could be heard directing the men's fire low. Duke recalled: 'It's no exaggeration to say that the constant rapid firing literally charred the rifle woodwork.'[11] Twenty-six-year-old mechanic Corporal Albert Mower, of the 4th Battalion, recalled: 'You didn't have to aim, they came so thick. Just rapid fire and down they went.'[12] He didn't stop to reload his rifle, as the man behind him continuously thrust a loaded weapon into his hand – this man turned out to be Chaplain 'Fighting Mac' William McKenzie.[13] With daylight, the men were forced to keep their heads below the parapet, as it became decidedly more dangerous. Where possible men took up positions behind loopholes (metal plates fixed into the parapet with a small hole for surveillance or a

rifle barrel) and killed the Turks as they continued to charge. The
entrenched ANZAC machine guns, however, remained deadly, as
they continued to pour enfilade and oblique fire across the killing
zone. During the height of the attack there were shrill cries of
'Allah-il-Allah' from the Turks, who also blew bugles or trumpets.
'Most of the enemy got "Allah", all right,' recalled Duke, many
years later.[14]

The Turks attacked the whole ANZAC perimeter, determined
to break it open and sweep away the enemy. Line upon line of
Turks streamed across no-man's-land from The Nek in the north
and Sniper's Ridge to the south. Indeed, waves of Turks could
be seen charging across Legge Valley, in the centre, screaming
at the top of their lungs. Turkish Lieutenant Riza Tevfik Iskin
of the 47th Regiment was with his senior officer, Major Tevfik
Bey, coordinating the effort to push the ANZACs back into the
sea. From the very start of their attack, the darkness of no-man's-
land had been turned into day by a stream of ANZAC flares, each
floating down suspended under a small parachute. Riza recalled
that with the ANZACs 'firing upon us with all their might, our
regiment's commander was walking [above] ... the trenches nonstop and trying to direct every operation personally'.[15] It wasn't
long before Tevfik Bey was hit in the head from a spent bullet,
falling back into his front-line trench, but he climbed back onto
the parapet and encouraged his men to continue the pointless
slaughter. Tevfik Bey (Bey is an honorary title) would survive to
command the Turkish position at Lone Pine at the beginning of
the August Offensive – and there he would not be so lucky.

Within two hours of launching their offensive to push the
ANZACs back into the sea, it was all over. The Turks suffered
around 10 000 casualties and the ANZACs 600, one of whom
was 'the man with the donkey', 25-year-old British migrant John
Simpson Kirkpatrick, who fell prey to a machine-gunner while
ferrying a wounded man on his donkey to the beach.[16] Another

ANZAC legend was born that day, when 22-year-old Albert Jacka singlehandedly retook an Australian position that had been captured by the Turks (the only position they were to capture that day – if only for a few minutes), shooting five dead and bayoneting another two. He was awarded Australia's first VC of the war.

Turkish casualties from the mass assault had been so great that it was a near certainty an epidemic would break out due to the mass of rotting corpses strewn across no-man's-land. The Turks proposed an armistice to bury the dead, accepted by General Birdwood, to take place on 24 May, five days after the slaughter. There were ANZACs too to be buried, most of whom had lain there since the first few days of the landing.

The armistice took force at 7.30 a.m. The weather on the day reflected the men's mood. Rain was falling in the early morning and a low mist was settling in the gullies. Forty-three-year-old former British master mariner, Boer War trooper and now Australian Chaplain Walter 'Bill' Dexter remembered the scene: 'Things very quiet in early morning... The smell is something awful. Some of the bodies have been there lying in [the] heat of the sun for 4 weeks and of course all are unrecognisable. It is only by identification discs that the corpses are known.'[17]

A demarcation line was arranged, running down the centre of no-man's-land. Parties from both armies were allocated to work their side of the line, taking away their dead as well as rifles and ammunition. The enemy's dead were carried in ground sheets, where available, to the centre, where their own men would take charge of them. Enemy rifles in each zone were also given back – minus the bolt. The stench was overpowering and men from both sides dry-retched, not only from the smell but from the sight of the mangled and cut-up corpses strewn in vast numbers, too many to be counted in the narrow confines of the blood-and-bone-enriched fields of no-man's-land. Dexter recalled that many of the missing could finally be classed as dead. The bodies were horrible to look at: 'black and swelled up, stretching out the clothing and in many cases when they were touched falling to pieces... Hundreds of men were engaged in moving them and the work continued without intermission all day. Many of the men, Turks and ours, handling the bodies, had plugs of cotton wool up their nostrils, for at times the smell was overpowering.'[18]

This ceasefire had a profound effect upon the ANZACs, at least. Before this, the appalling wounds that many men had suffered were thought to have been the result of the Turks using expanding dumdum bullets. This had angered many, but now the same men observed similar horrific wounds amongst the Turkish dead. Clearly the effects of mass rifle and machine-gun fire at such close ranges had not been appreciated. One officer recalled that 'one saw the results of machine gun fire very clearly; entire companies annihilated – not wounded, but killed, their heads doubled under them with the impetus of their rush and both hands clasping their bayonets'.[19] They were also able to see their foe up close for the first time in similar circumstance, and not just as either corpses or prisoners. Indeed, a number of ANZACs were very appreciative when during the armistice a Turkish Red Crescent man came amongst them and offered antiseptic wool dipped in perfume to help cover up the stench.

While the men from both sides in no-man's-land were living through Dante's *Inferno*, others more fortunate could for the first time within weeks walk around without the fear of instantaneous death, or worse – a severe debilitating wound or disfigurement. The armistice was to go on until 4 p.m., and these men took full advantage of it. Men bathed in the cove, while others lay on the beach enjoying the few hours of quiet left to them. Chaplin Dexter noticed how strange it all seemed, especially the quietness: 'No explosions and the men getting on the skyline and looking at the Turks through their glasses. There were bathing parades of companies for it was a grand opportunity. No chance of shells from Gaba Tepe on the beach. Our fellows began gathering spent artillery shells for the sailors who prized them highly and gave butter and soft bread for them.'[20]

Just before 4 p.m., the grim reality returned. Both sides retreated into their respective lines. Before leaving, some ANZACs and Turks approached each other along the centre line, as recorded by Lieutenant Knyvett, of Pompey Elliott's 7th Battalion, to farewell their opponents: 'Goodbye, old chap; good luck!' Or, from the Turks: 'Smiling may you go and smiling come again.'[21] Those further down the line, who had for the last few hours been exposing themselves to Turkish observation, including down by the cove and within its cleansing waters, also evaporated back into the rabbit warren of their saps, trenches and dugouts. There appeared to be some hesitation by the rank and file from both sides to restart hostilities, as it took a few minutes before a single shot was fired.

The Turkish assault on 19 May proved that a frontal assault against entrenched enemy positions was suicide – if either side wanted to continue the attack, another avenue had to be found. Birdwood, knowing he had to break the stalemate, looked to the north of Anzac, beyond his outposts in the foothills, for a possible solution to the deadlock. The idea of a breakout away from the confined trenches at Anzac was an attractive one, as there was little sign of any Turkish forces present in any numbers in the tangled mass of gullies and ridges defining the Sari Bair Range immediately to the north. There was a real chance that the Turks were relying on the sheer chaotic nature of the high and rugged terrain to guard their northern flank from attack – this was a logical assessment by any criteria. Nonetheless, seeing no other way to break the deadlock, on 30 May Birdwood and Lieutenant Colonel Andrew Skeen discussed their preliminary plans for an ANZAC flanking manoeuvre to the north with Hamilton. The main thrust of this operation would be against the rugged cliffs and gullies defining the Sari Bair Range just beyond North Beach.[22]

Hamilton had earlier come to the conclusion that attempting a breakout from Helles was a waste of men and resources. It was through no lack of courage on the British and French soldiers' part – charge after charge in broad daylight had already been made against the Turkish forces there, to no avail. His men at Helles remained trapped at the toe of the peninsula with only one way forward – head-on against wire, trenches, machine guns and artillery. The British commander there, Major General Aylmer Hunter-Weston, had been spectacularly and tragically unsuccessful. Indeed, not short of what might be called enthusiastic mismanagement, 'Hunter-Bunter' (as his men called him) had since the first day of the landing ordered numerous bloody and futile ad hoc charges in broad daylight against the Turkish lines, with nothing to show for it but perhaps a few hundred metres at best, soaked in thousands of men's blood. Indeed, just after one of these pointless assaults, Major General Archibald Paris, commander of the Royal Naval Division, was bitterly counting the number of dead and wounded from his division in terms of thousands. He turned to Hunter-Weston and asked about the casualties suffered by the 29th Division. Hunter-Weston's ambivalent reply: 'Casualties? What do I care for casualties?'[23] Soon after, he ordered a British brigade to attack in daylight without artillery support, resulting in one man in three being killed outright. He reportedly described the disaster as 'blooding the pups'.[24]

Fortunately for the survivors of his division, he would be evacuated from the peninsula in late July through illness, along with his golf clubs and two lounge chairs, never to return. Twenty-nine-year-old AANS nursing sister Lydia King, of the Royal Prince Alfred Hospital, Sydney, was on board the hospital ship *Sicilia* and became responsible for the general's care. She found him to be 'a crotchety old man'.²⁵ He would, however, soon reappear on the Western Front, having learnt nothing from his experiences or failures at Gallipoli. He proceeded to bleed another good British division white against German machine guns, artillery and wire.

It would take a different kind of leader, one like General Birdwood, to earn the respect of the ANZACs. Another British senior officer, Major General Harold 'Hooky' Walker, achieved that distinction. Walker was the commander of the 1st Australian Division, and was ably assisted by his chief-of-staff, Australian Lieutenant Colonel Cyril Brudenell White.

A professional soldier, Walker had seen active service in India, the Boer War and Ireland. In November 1914, aged fifty-three, he was appointed brigadier general to the general staff in India. In December, he became chief-of-staff to Birdwood. On the day of the landing he was the first of Birdwood's staff officers to take to the shore and within hours was leading the New Zealand Infantry Brigade, as its commander had become ill. Within days, he was put in charge of the 1st Australian Infantry Brigade, after its commander, Colonel Henry MacLaurin, was killed by a sniper. A week later, Walker was placed in charge of the 1st Australian Division, with the wounding of its commander, Major General William Bridges, under similar circumstances. Bridges was transferred to the hospital ship *Gascon*, but he and everyone else knew his wound was mortal. Before dying, he said: 'Anyway, I have commanded an Australian division for nine months.'²⁶ Later in the war, Walker told Charles Bean that he wouldn't change his command of the Australians for the world. Most of his men remembered him as a good and friendly soldier and a good leader, and appreciated him for not being 'a dugout general'. Few would disagree that Walker was one of the best field commanders at Anzac, if not the whole Gallipoli Peninsula.

Australian Lieutenant Colonel Brudenell White was the son of a prominent grazier, but while still young his family had fallen on hard times. He'd been forced to take up a job as a bank clerk while studying at night, hoping to become a barrister. One weekend he joined a citizen-soldier friend on a local military exercise. It would forever change his life. By 1897, he had been commissioned as a junior officer in a militia regiment. A few years later he was fighting the Boers in South Africa as part of the 1st Commonwealth Horse. After the war he was invited to attend the British Staff College in Camberley – and was the first Australian to do so. With the coming of the war he was appointed General Bridges' chief-of-staff, and with Bridges' death in May, the 39-year-old lieutenant colonel was instated as Walker's chief-of-staff. White wrote to his wife Ethel a few weeks after having landed at Anzac: 'I am obviously not a soldier . . . I confess to any quantity of obsolete notions of peacetime soldiering of which I am no longer proud or boastful! I am not a soldier because I don't like war – modern war. For the successful waging of present day war one wants the courage a lion is believed to possess, the cunning of a serpent and the instincts of a rabbit! A hole in the ground is the only place of moderate safety – I am writing in one now.'[27] However, Birdwood certainly didn't agree, writing later that in White the 'army had no finer soldier'.[28] Indeed, Charles Bean later commented that while White was certainly ambitious, he was too modest to put himself forward. Even so, many, including Bean, quickly came to admire him, and his reputation would continue to grow, not only amongst the senior officers, but amongst the rank and file. Like Walker, White was known to have an eye for detail and was a tireless worker, often working late into the night and the early morning hours. Perhaps the most famous photograph of White during the Gallipoli campaign has him sitting in his dugout, his hair neatly brushed and small moustache carefully clipped, with his pipe firmly clutched between his teeth. He is wearing shirt, suspenders and tie, riding britches and smartly polished boots, and is seated at his small foldout table, eyes down studying reports, a pen in hand ready to correct or simplify.

By mid June, Birdwood's idea of striking north against the Sari Bair Range, outflanking the Turks and finally cutting Turkish communications north and south, had clearly established itself in Hamilton's mind as the only logical way to break the stalemate that had set in at both Anzac and Helles. Hamilton wrote to Birdwood: 'I am gradually forming the conclusion in my mind that Anzac is even more important – and immediately important – than it had appeared in my original concept...we must have a talk soon.'[29] A few days later he recorded: '[Birdwood] wants three new Brigades; with them he engages to go through from bottom to top of Sari Bair. Well, I will give him four; perhaps five! Our whole scheme hinges on these crests of Sari Bair which dominate Anzac and Maidos; the Dardanelles and the Aegean.'[30] However, this grand strategic vision to break the stalemate failed to take into account the tactical considerations on the ground, including the appallingly difficult terrain. Historian Robert Rhode-James correctly describes it as 'mad country'.

> Watercourses change direction, seemingly gentle slopes conceal a precipitous and treacherous surface under the scrub, there is no method in anything. It is very easy to lose one's way, and even with accurate maps on a clear day gets easily confused. One ravine is very much like another, the levels are all wrong, and without a compass or the summits to guide one, it is surprisingly easy to scale a tortuous ravine only to find oneself farther away from the summit than one began.[31]

Another historian, Peter Hart, is succinct when it comes to what was expected of the men: 'It demanded feats of endurance from the assaulting columns climbing to Sari Bair which would have made Hannibal think twice.'[32]

Birdwood's staff set to work on drafting the details of the

ANZAC operation in detail. Officials in London soon informed Hamilton that he was to receive another five British divisions in order to 'finish the thing'. Hamilton was pinning all his hopes on Birdwood and his troops to spearhead an all-out attack. He asked Birdwood how he would use any available reinforcements to progress his planned offensive. Given the small area occupied by the ANZACs, Birdwood knew that a third division couldn't be landed there. It was partly for this reason that another landing about ten kilometres further north at Suvla Bay, by the British IX Corps, was incorporated into the plan. Once the troops at Anzac had succeeded in capturing the northern heights, Birdwood argued, it would be possible for fresh troops to be landed just north of Anzac, along North Beach and beyond.[33]

3

'Rice and meat are
a luxury for him'

In Alexandria, Sister Elsie Cook was trying to cope with the chaos of the hospital ward assigned her at British No. 17 General Hospital. In early May she recorded her despair: 'Had several wards – about 200 patients to look after, simply running all day, dressing washing & feeding them, & yet the awful feeling that they were not getting the right attention – simply impossible... frightfully busy, getting off bandages and dirty blood stained clothes, washing them – the wounds to be dressed, some had not been touched for days.'[1] She also recorded that many of the wounded hadn't eaten for days and were simply starving. When she eventually got back to her quarters late that night she tried unsuccessfully to ring Syd. Not long after, Elsie was called back to her ward as another large batch of wounded had just arrived. She found things in a complete shambles, with 'boots, bandages [and] blood stained tunics... We have got 700 badly wounded men and six sisters and [one] matron.'[2] Elsie eventually took control of the situation, overhauling the procedures, and things later ran as efficiently as they possibly could under the circumstances.

Syd gradually became well enough to visit Elsie using the aid of a walking stick. With the realities of war and the large number of casualties, it appears that the matrons were now taking a more relaxed attitude to male officers mixing with the nursing staff – even one's wife. Elsie recorded in her diary, on 7 May: 'Syd came out for dinner and brought the photo taken of us on the beach, which is splendid. We had dinner in the Summer House, Syd the sole man with so many sisters.'[3] Syd was soon released from hospital and for a week they both resided at the Beau Rivage Hotel. Elsie wrote playfully in her diary on 13 May that his wound had healed, but 'he still limps a good deal and can't run as quickly as I can yet'.[4] Elsie's time with Syd, however, was all too soon over.

On 17 May, word reached Syd that he would soon be on his way back to the fighting. Elsie wrote: 'As Syd is to go away soon Matron has given me tomorrow off duty – a whole day off – Hurrah!'[5] On 19 May, Syd was informed he was to return to Anzac the next day. He arrived at the ward for a final farewell: a 'miserable morning', Elsie recorded in her diary.[6] Within three months, Syd would find himself fighting again at Lone Pine. This time he was to receive what all considered to be a mortal wound – but Elsie would have other ideas.

Twenty-five-year-old Melbourne draughtsman Lance Corporal Cyril Lawrence was a reinforcement for the 2nd Field Company of Engineers. He would keep a detailed diary throughout his time at Gallipoli.[7] On the day that Syd Cook was leaving to rejoin his company at Anzac, Lawrence wrote the first entry in his red leather-bound *Army Book 152 – Correspondence Book (Field Service)*, which served as his Gallipoli diary. He recorded that at about 8.30 a.m. they arrived off Suez, and immediately the order was given to parade in full dress and kit, although it was extremely hot. He and his mates would the next day be on a train for Cairo, a journey that would take about six hours. Up until then Cyril had heard nothing about the landings at Gallipoli, but that would soon change. He was informed on 26 May that he would soon be on his way to Anzac. He and his cobbers had only been in Egypt less than a week and the word was abuzz about the heroic efforts of the Australian and New Zealanders on the peninsula. A few days later he was on board a transport ship, steaming past a 'veritable archipelago – dozens and dozens of small mountainous islands with villages, Greek I suppose, nesting down in the valleys…It has been a glorious day and this evening just before sunset we passed a French torpedo boat going like the devil. The sunset was simply glorious; jingo it was fine. We expect to be in Lemnos early tomorrow morning.'[8]

On 2 June, the lance corporal arrived at Anzac and keenly recorded his first impressions.

> It is daylight about 4 a.m. and the barges are soon alongside to take us ashore. Ever since we have been anchored off the position we have heard the crackle of the rifle fire and soon I suppose we will be in it. We are soon aboard the barge packed like sardines, and, as we approach the shore, what an aspect it opens up before us – valleys and valleys, scrub-covered hillsides, men getting about everywhere and looking for all the world like ants, but above all, the thing that meets, or rather hits, the eye is the number of 'dugouts'. Some are quite palatial; structures made of sandbags and well roofed, even named; others mere recesses in the hillside either covered with a waterproof or a blanket or perhaps they are completely tunneled in like a rabbit barrow. The whole landscape is covered with them. It looks for all the world like a mining camp.[9]

Within days Cyril would be occupying his own small dugout just behind the Australian lines on 400 Plateau, the distinctive broad plateau to the south of Anzac Cove.

In mid June, Lieutenant Colonel 'Pompey' Elliott, who had been wounded and evacuated within the first few hours of the landing on 25 April, rejoined his battalion. Twenty-six-year-old manager Lieutenant Shannon Grills recalled the joys of the men as the 'old man' walked through the trenches: 'Awakened by a tremendous cheer and on looking up found that Col.[*sic*] Elliott had returned. Talk about a commotion. The old boys were extremely pleased to see the Col. return and resume command of the 7th...three hearty cheers rang out...beaming with smiles of delight.'[10] Elliott mingled amongst the men, who were all smiles and were anxious to shake his hand, but he was saddened by the number of faces now missing since his wounding. He wrote to his wife Kate: 'Only about half a dozen of all the Essendon boys left, and only a little over a hundred of all the men I took from Broadmeadows.'[11] Throughout the war he would write a string of letters to his beloved Kate, confiding to her the grim realities of war. He also wrote to their young children, Violet and Neil, explaining to them why he was away – Daddy was fighting 'naughty Germans and Turks', but he would soon be home.

Within days Elliott had settled into the routine at Anzac and had occupied his dugout, describing the scene to Kate: 'You would laugh to see my home. Fancy a place just long enough for me to lie down in comfort, cut out in the side of the hill some eight feet in. My bed is a shelf of earth left some five feet from the top while the remainder is cut some two feet deeper. When the hill falls away near the front it is built up with sandbags.'[12] If he was trying to reassure her that he was safe, he wasn't doing a particularly good job, as he later wrote: 'I went along a trench to see where a shell had burst and to find out if anyone was hurt...when a second shell came and burst in front of me...I wasn't twopence the worse... I had just gone [another] few steps...when a shell came and blew in the whole trench.'[13]

Another to write home describing his new lodgings at Anzac was Lieutenant Colonel Brudenell White, who addressed his wife

Ethel on 30 May: 'My own beloved, I am writing to you from my neat little house dug into the ground and covered with bags filled with sand. My bed is on the floor close into the side, but from my table I look out over the sea on a view which, from my hill some 200 feet high, is perfect...I generally come back after rounds bathed in perspiration. This is rather a nuisance as we cannot get much washing done – except in salt water.'[14] Journalist Ellis Ashmead-Bartlett reported that Anzac was always a pleasure to visit compared to Helles because 'it is the one spot where the army has confidence in its general [Birdwood], who is immensely popular with the men'. He added that 'while the British Tommy [at Helles] carried around with him all his worldly goods, sitting in trenches with his pack on, it was extremely rare to find an Australian or New Zealander in anything more than a pair of shorts'.[15]

Twenty-nine-year-old Lieutenant Hugh Knyvett also recalled that, early on, most ANZACs had decided that their uniforms needed some alteration – the sleeves had to go, so did their puttees, which consisted of khaki strips of cloth wrapped around their calves. Not only were the puttees uncomfortable, but they also afforded a convenient place for lice to breed. Not the types to go by halves, most also ripped their trousers into shorts with their bayonets. Those not wearing slouch hats stitched the spare khaki onto the back of their British-style caps to protect their necks from the sun. As each soldier began to trim his uniform to his 'own idea of comfort, it was soon, in very reality, a "ragtime" army...most everybody decided that a tunic was useless, but some extremists threw away shirt and singlet as well'.[16] It was later said that a Turkish army order had been captured stating that the 'Australians were running short of supplies, as they made one pair of trousers do for three men. Evidently "Johnny Turk" could not understand the Australian disregard for conventionality and his taking to nakedness when it meant...clothes that couldn't be washed wouldn't keep one's body clean and became the home of an army that had no interest in the fight for democracy'.[17]

The Turks were worse off when it came to supplying some of the basics to their men, including uniforms. As one unknown German liaison officer with the Turkish army recalled: 'How difficult it was to fight with no shirt on your back and no shoes on your feet, and how difficult it is to bear the scalding sun...Why should it be a surprise that almost all the sacks sent to be filled with sand and thus fortify the trenches were used by the soldiers as clothing?'[18] Indeed, Lieutenant Ahmet Kemal, of the Scheider Mountain Battery, wrote in May to the Commander at Lone Pine (known to the Turks as Kanli Sirt): 'With the aim [of] covering the cannon (to prevent earth from falling on the cannon as a result of the trembling caused by the firing operation) I had a couple of bodies disinterred so as to recover their overcoats, but there were no overcoats. Sir, if you have them I would pray you send us five empty sacks with the person who has brought you this note.'[19] Given the threat of Allied submarine activity within the Dardanelles, Turkish supplies to the front were increasingly reliant on seemingly endless camel caravans. These 'have been used in the East for thousands of years, and the clumsy and slow carts with wooden wheels pulled by oxen were carrying their load to the front, over newly built roads. As the army was reinforced, its needs increased, and it was not always possible to keep up with this increase,' reported the German officer.[20]

It wasn't just the uniforms that were being altered by the ANZACs and Turks. The waist-high thorny scrub that had covered the slopes before the landing was by early June almost completely gone. War had changed the landscape, not only due to the constant shelling that tore great chunks out of the earth, or the continued *ratatat* of machine-gun fire that ripped apart leaves and stems, but through the more mundane act of men feeding hundreds of camp fires to boil their billies, in order to make a cup of tea or chai, depending on which uniform they wore.

More recently, in the Anzac sector at least, large tracts of the scrub had been removed in constructing terraces within the gullies, which usually required half a spur to be levelled here and half a gully to be backfilled there. These man-made plateaus created order and some degree of regularity – even the meandering trench systems that at first seemed chaotic to new arrivals followed some tactical principle, usually following a ridgeline and terminating to protect a flank that disappeared into a deep ravine. The smaller communication saps, too, were dug with careful purpose and reasoning. It was because of this pattern of tactical necessity that even behind the lines, the unseen living quarters in many places weren't immune from howitzer fire – the gunners from both sides occasionally fished for targets within these rear areas, figuring that they must be full of men and supplies, which they often were. Fortunately for the men, these high-trajectory guns, and just as importantly, their shells, were always in short supply.

When a bloke got the chance he'd crawl into his dugout to take shelter from the heat of the day. Usually no wind stirred and a man would sleep heavily in the heat; it didn't take long for exhaustion and fatigue to take over. Even the swarming flies eventually subsided into the subconscious as a man surrendered himself to sleep. His lullaby might include the sound of an officer yelling for a sapper (as communications were down after some damn fool had tripped over the wire – again!), an NCO storming up and down the line giving orders, or the yell of an enemy soldier, but it always included the crack of a rifle or an exploding bomb or grenade. Just overhead, bullets would fly past and in his sleep the stink of the corpses just yards away would seep into a man's nightmares.

The further back from the front, with its frenetic pace and activity, the more untidy it became. The floor of the rearmost saps and trenches leading to the beach were littered here and there with blankets, greatcoats, bully cans, and picks and shovels untidily rested against the walls. The sign of recent mail from home and perhaps from wounded mates in Cairo was evident, as tobacco tins, eggshells, orange peel and even the odd chocolate wrapping littered the floor, soon to be trampled under boot into the dirt, quickly becoming unrecognisable as foreign material. Most probably preferred the unruly democracy of the front line, even given its dangers, to being in a fatigue party closer to the beach where some semblance of military order and command had reasserted itself.

When the men from both sides weren't on stand-to in the firing line, or in the rear areas digging gun pits, roads, dugouts, trenches or tunnels, they spent considerable time at war with the dreaded lice.[21] Twenty-one-year-old Private William Graham, of the 4th Battalion, who would later fight at Lone Pine, remembered how each night found him back in the line scratching himself crazy because of lice, trying to snatch whatever sleep he could between turns on the fire step. He would long for stand-down so he could, for a short time at least, throw off his equipment and focus on ridding himself of the infestation as best as possible. The army's chosen remedy – Keating's Powder – was bloody useless; the lice seemed to love the stuff. It was a never-ending battle, day after day, night after night.[22]

Food was another of the personal battlegrounds. Since day one, the ANZACs had little chance of getting fresh food. They were mostly given unpalatable biscuits and bully beef, although such delicacies as desiccated vegetables and apricot jam were also on the menu. It hadn't taken the men long to loathe the cans of boiled beef. It was bad enough when 'fresh' but in the heat it didn't take long to spoil – on opening, it was a runny and nauseating mess. Early on, the men had thrown unopened cans of bully over to the Turks in exchange for tobacco, or anything else, but within days this transaction had ceased as the Turks threw back the cans unopened. It was even said that a few Turks took pity on those forced to eat the stuff and had thrown over some small bags of raisins as well. What was supposed to pass for jam wasn't much better.

Men tried to vary the monotony of their diet with concoctions such as bully beef stew, bully beef soup, bully on a rock chewer (an extremely hard army biscuit that many reckoned had been left over from the Boer War fifteen years earlier), apricot jam on a rock chewer, bully and jam together on a rock chewer. Many used a spent shell casing or rock to pound rock chewers into pieces, then mixed them with bully to make 'rissoles', or so they tried to convince themselves. Most soon gave up and admitted defeat, slurping down the contents of the cans while trying to avoid a mouthful of the big black disease-ridden blowflies that loved it. Even this was impossible when it came to the apricot jam. As soon as a tin was opened, thick layers of drowning flies polluted the contents. Twenty-one-year-old painter from Arncliffe Private Leonard 'Len' Barrett, of the 2nd Battalion, recalled there were two main enemies at Anzac – and neither was the Turk:

> The first 'villain' – Fray Bentos – was the meat ration, canned
> in South America, and according to historians and those who
> were forced to eat it, a coarse, stringy beef, with an abundance
> of oily fat, which was partially responsible for the anaemia
> and dysentery which ravaged the ranks of the AIF during the
> summer on Gallipoli. The other 'villain' – Deakin's Jam – was
> an impersonation of apricot. The tin, on being punctured,
> oozed forth a dirty yellow liquid which dripped from bread
> and set a track, onto which immediately rushed a plague of
> corpse-fed flies.[23]

The empty cans came in handy, and not only for making jam-tin bombs. Barbed wire was always in short supply and the men were encouraged to throw their empty tins into no-man's-land – not that space in the trenches allowed the men much choice in the matter. These tins soon completely covered the area and it would have been almost impossible for any Turkish night patrol to approach the parapets without making a hell of a racket – or being cut to pieces from the open cans with jagged, sharp dirty lids attached, resulting in wounds that wouldn't easily heal and would likely result in infection. As Private Barrett wrote after the war: 'So it was that Fray Bentos and Deakin's Jam, although indirectly responsible for sending many hundreds of men to hospital [through dysentery], helped in a small way to guard our lines in the event of Abdul attempting a surprise night attack!'[24]

Despite the appalling conditions, some still managed to find humour in it all. One veteran was seen to be trying to tackle a rock chewer with his false teeth. Twenty-eight-year-old Lieutenant Oscar Tedder, of the 2nd Battalion, from Kingston, New South Wales, had been looking into the next firing recess and spotted the lonely old trooper busy at work. Oscar chuckled to himself and handed the trench periscope to his friend, 25-year-old Lieutenant Charles Lecky, for a look. The old digger was 'busily engaged stamping his false teeth to bits…and the veteran spent the trying period which followed in Egypt having new teeth made. The biscuits were pretty hard.'[25] Not that the Turks had it any better, as recalled by German Colonel Hans Kannengiesser, of the Turkish 9th Division:

Rice and meat are a luxury for him. The emergency ration, if there is one at all, consists of a slice of bread and some olives, the latter wrapped in the corner of a rather dubious looking handkerchief. In the morning he has gruel, late in the afternoon he has another soup, sometimes with meat, but always with oil. His basic dish is Bulgur…squashed wheat cooked mostly in rancid oil and served cold…Clothing of the troops was incredible…summer and winter cloth mixed colorfully, torn and tattered. Footwear was quite varied, often only a piece of hide held together by string. Often string had to replace leather in relation to equipment.[26]

The Turks lacked many things but drinking water wasn't one of them – they were well supplied from a number of natural sources. Water was the most precious commodity for the ANZACs – and there was little of it to be had in their sector. When a man got his lousy ration it tasted vile, as the cans were tainted with a blend of petrol and chloride of lime. It was too valuable, however, to be used for washing, and the long trek to the beach with two petrol tins was something in the nature of a whole day's work.[27] Thirst is 'not a thing to joke about', recalled Lieutenant Knyvett, 'and there were times when the allowance of water was not enough to wash down a half-dozen bites, and the food would stick in one's throat'.[28]

In order to help alleviate the water shortage it was decided to install a water pump at Anzac Cove. In itself it wasn't a bad idea, but instead of ordering and installing a brand-new pump from Sheffield, some reckoned that the officer in charge scoured the backstreets of Cairo for a bargain. Whatever its source, the pump turned out to be a contraption owing more to antiquity than to the present. It took the engineers more than a few days to assemble, and when they stood back to admire their work they couldn't help but wonder why they had so many spare parts lying about. When they fired it up, it worked for about two minutes before whimpering to a stop. Eventually they got it working on a semi-regular basis, but it seldom kept going for long.

Meanwhile, water pipes had been laid, each leading to newly installed storage tanks located just behind the front lines. Each tank had been dragged up the slopes by fatigue parties consisting of over 100 men. They were to be filled by pumping water from the water lighters, massive low-lying hulks anchored just off the beach after arrival from Alexandria. When the pump was working, however, the lighters failed to show up, and when they finally did arrive, the pump had given up the ghost. On the rare occasion when the system might have worked together, the Turks shelled the beach, forcing the pump to be shut down and the lighters to head out to sea.

As a result, water distribution and rationing still relied heavily on water fatigue parties doing the job. A long line of weary tanned and shirtless bodies, in non-issued khaki shorts, with rifles slung across their shoulders, would stand patiently in line, most with a cigarette dangling from their mouths, holding an empty kerosene or petrol can in each hand. Slowly, very slowly, each man made his way to the head of the queue where his cans would be filled. With no time for mooching about, a bloke then made his way back to the firing line. This was no stroll; it involved climbing most of the way, dodging known danger spots and avoiding exploding shrapnel, while trying to keep his rifle from smashing into the cans and his knuckles. Of course, a transient thin snail trail of wet dirt followed behind each man – a small puddle here, a slightly larger one there – though in the heat the telltale signs of such wasted luxury didn't last long. Hopefully, the water carrier would successfully avoid shrapnel or a sniper, but all too often one or both of his cans didn't. He usually only realised it when the slow leak got to the point when the weight made him suspicious, probably halfway up a tortuously steep gully. With that, after a number of expletives, he'd make his way back down to the beach, to the end of the line, cigarette dangling, with a couple of new cans, before slowly, very slowly making his way to the head of the queue.

It was said that it was dangerous to light up after having drunk the precious little water that made it to the front lines, which always smelt and tasted of kerosene, petrol or both. Connoisseurs reckoned that they could tell the brand of fuel that the cans had originally contained just by taking a quick whiff.

Beachside water fatigues meant some took advantage of the opportunity for a cleansing dip, although Lieutenant Knyvett recalled that such a bath was 'pretty unhealthy, for it was practically always whipped by shrapnel and you went in at the risk of your life. Some of the best swimmers used to say it was all right so long as you dived whenever you heard the screech of a shell – that the shrapnel pellets did not penetrate the water more than a few inches.'[29] Most of the Turkish fire originated from the batteries positioned close to Gaba Tepe, which were collectively christened 'Beachy Bill' by the men. Lieutenant Charles Lecky also recalled how some troops 'managed to keep clean by a furtive swim in the Aegean when "Beachy Bill" had his eyes closed. "Beachy" usually slept with one eye open, and many a man paid the supreme penalty for his love of cleanliness.'[30]

It was on a much safer beach, at Alexandria, that Sister Elsie Cook found a way to escape the stress of her nursing duties. Still based at British No. 17 General Hospital, when time and circumstances permitted she would ride a horse along the beach, frequently chaperoned by the hospital's senior surgeon, Captain Bourne, a family friend. Sometimes they would ride in the desert, enjoying the cultivated gardens they discovered.[31] After returning from one of these excursions, she recorded in her diary: 'Several new and very badly wounded men in while I was away – one New Zealander, with shocking abdominal wound, already looks like death'.[32] Elsie soon heard word from Syd, who was back in the line at Anzac – he'd been promoted to Captain. On 26 June, Elsie recorded in her diary: 'At lunch time was called to the telephone, Matron rang up to say that all Australian sisters at No. 17 were recalled and had to return to Cairo.'[33] This was disappointing, as Elsie and the others had finally managed to organise things to their – and the men's – satisfaction. Also, the port city of Alexandria was more pleasant than the squalid conditions of Cairo. Elsie found time for one last ride along the beach before making her way back to the grim realities of the Egyptian capital.[34]

4

'…it looks like a tiny bit on the map'

Birdwood's great offensive to break out of Anzac to the north included a plan to keep Turkish reserves away from the main attack on the Sari Bair Range, by convincing the Turks that Allied intentions were concentrated elsewhere. For an initial assault that would draw the Turkish attention and tie them down, he chose the southern area of 400 Plateau, known as Lone Pine.

Since the landing, the first Australians to reach 400 Plateau had noticed a single pine tree standing on a very slight rise along its south-eastern corner. Thirty-four-year-old engineer from Armidale, New South Wales, Major Athelstan Markham Martyn, of the 2nd Field Company of Engineers, writing under the pseudonym AMM, described it as a 'small ragged pine tree standing out very gauntly and conspicuously in that wilderness of stunted bushes. This was named the Lonesome Pine, and was extended to the position generally.'[1] The tree had reminded many of a then popular song, 'The Trail of the Lonesome Pine':

On a mountain in Virginia stands a lonesome pine
Just below is the cabin home of a little girl of mine

Her name is June, and very, very soon she'll belong to me
For I know she's waiting there for me 'neath that lone pine tree

The tree that lent its name to the position – variously Lonesome Pine, Lonely Pine or Lone Pine, and eventually remembered simply as The Pine – had itself been blown to pieces soon after the landing, although its stump could still be seen from the Australian lines just opposite.

Within days of the invasion the Australians had established their trenches along the western edge of the plateau at their position called The Pimple – so named because the line here was defined by a slight salient jutting out into no-man's-land, which was comparatively narrow and flat, sloping away steeply on either side. The Turks occupied Lone Pine and for some time seemed happy to only lightly hold this position, but gradually they constructed trenches and communication saps running to the rear down into the valley below. Soon the front-line trenches were being covered with local pine logs and thick timbers shipped in from Constantinople and elsewhere. Here, the Turkish trenches were sufficiently spaced apart for the ANZAC artillery to fire shrapnel against their works. The Turks hoped that the cover would provide some protection from shrapnel, but it also restricted observation and the ability to throw bombs against any enemy infantry attack. Fortunately for the Turks, the ANZAC artillery had remained fairly quiet.

The Australians were likewise trenching at The Pimple, but unlike the Turks they were not constructing overhead covers. They were an attacking force, not a defensive one, and commanders wanted to keep the men primed for attack, not digging in and getting comfortable – though it was obvious to anyone that stalemate had already set in. Even if the Australians wanted to cover their trenches they didn't have ready access to the lumber yards in England. A similar complaint was often made about a lack of artillery and shell. As recalled by Major Martyn: 'We were so badly supplied with artillery ammunition and guns that little could be done even to harass the working parties [at Lone Pine], let alone prevent the construction of the trenches.'[2] Indeed, spare parts for the artillery were also a major problem in keeping the guns working. This frequently led to 'cannibalism', the practice of taking spare parts from one gun to repair another.[3]

By late July, the Turkish front-line defences strung along the eastern side of 400 Plateau were considerable. Sandbags, thick timbers, mud bricks and earthen embankments protected the garrisons at 'Johnston's Jolly', at its north-eastern corner, and Lone Pine defined its south-eastern defence. These positions were connected across the broad gully between them, known as Owen's Gully, by communication trenches. Each was defended by a number of front-line and secondary trenches, as well as supporting and communication trenches. The length of the Turkish front line at Lone Pine from Owen's Gully, including a southern spur named Sniper's Ridge, was less than 400 metres. The centre of the Turkish firing line on top of the plateau at Lone Pine itself was set back from both flanks, allowing enfilade and oblique fire to be brought to bear on any attempt to carry the centre of the position, although this may have owed as much to the topography of the terrain as to tactical concerns, as minor gullies cutting into this part of the plateau lent themselves to such a configuration. The southern part of Lone Pine was especially well defended due to its commanding views of Gaba Tepe, Legge Valley and the depression on the eastern side of the plateau, much later nicknamed The Cup by Charles Bean, who visited the area after the war. The Cup was essentially a southern branch of Owen's Gully and was used by the Turks as their main reserve area for the defence on Lone Pine and 400 Plateau generally. The centre of the line at Lone Pine was not as heavily entrenched as the flanks and its main purpose could be thought of as providing communications between each flanking stronghold. In all, the frontage of the Turkish front-line trenches at the Pine atop the plateau was around 250 metres.[4]

The fighting – and dying – on the front lines of the peninsula was being done in close quarters. By far the worst experience for most was the stench and proximity of the dead. The living were always within close range of the stinking, rotting corpses that lay just beyond their trenches in no-man's-land. Even after the burial details of 24 May, many of the hastily dug shallow mass graves didn't remain covered for long. By late June, the troops on the peninsula were swept by a wave of intestinal disease, originating from the ugly blowflies that lived and bred in the corpses strewn across the killing field. These pests would sweep into the trenches as the men tried to eat their meager rations. Attempts to brush the flies away and cover mouths proved fruitless – invariably, a number of the flies were taken in. It made no difference how quick a man was, they rarely got a mouthful that 'hadn't been well walked over, and it didn't do to think where those flies might have been walking just previously'.[5]

Lieutenant Knyvett remembered that there were more 'flies on the Peninsula than there was sand on the shore...We put up sandbags to stop the bullets, but no one had devised a method to stop those winged emissaries of death. Those who died from lead-poisoning were but a score to the hundreds who died of fly-poisoning.'[6] The official medical historian of the AIF, Captain Graham Butler, recorded the devastating effects that dysentery had upon the men:

> The fighting ranks were gravely thinned and, when the crisis of the [August] campaign arrived, a large percentage of the men who remained on duty were fit only for a short-lived effort... The history of disease at Anzac, indeed, in no small measure the history of the flies... their access to food

and to latrines was, for the practical purposes of infection, unrestricted…the efforts to restrict the access of flies to excreta in the latrines [was ineffective]. Few latrines at Anzac were not exposed to direct or indirect fire, and many men were killed or wounded there. The plight of the unfortunate dysenteric, forced to relieve himself every half-hour or so, may be imagined.[7]

Thirty-five-year-old Sydney University physics professor Captain Iven 'the Terrible' Mackay, of the 4th Battalion, suffered the early symptoms of dysentery and managed to get hold of a large jar of castor oil and, unbelievably, a bottle of milk. This was said to be an early basic treatment for dysentery and by early August, if not feeling 'tip-top', he was feeling much better.[8]

Indeed, by early August, the men were well and truly in a bad way. From 1 July to 5 August, an average of seventy-three men per day were reporting sick in the 1st Australian Division.[9] If this represented an ongoing trend, then every ten days Walker's Division was losing one battalion's worth of men due to sickness alone. The point is brought home when it is assessed that throughout the same period, sick cases (2129 men) accounted for 69 per cent of total losses to the 1st Division.[10] Replacements could not make up the differences, as evidenced by the fact that from 6–10 August, during the thick of the fighting, ANZAC had suffered around 5800 casualties (not including sick), but only received about 2000 replacements – just 34 per cent of requirements.[11] Hence, while battalions had a nominal strength of around 1000 on embarkation, in the field battalions were almost always well below strength. In fact, the average battalion size for the four battalions of the 1st Brigade in early August was 725 men. This could not go on indefinitely – indeed, on 6 August, the 2nd Battalion went into the Battle of Lone Pine with just 582 officers and men.[12]

Of course, it wasn't only the living conditions that had resulted in the thinning of the ANZAC ranks – the Turks also played an active part. Just a few days after the landing, Major John Gellibrand, of the 1st Australian Division staff, recalled the decisions a staff officer had to make in regards to snipers: 'The humour of Anzac was not without its trials for some of us [staff officers] and in the very early days it was reckoned a fair thing to warn visitors to the line… "There's a sniper at work". So one had either to run for the amusement of the troops, or walk, with the chance of proving the popular estimate of staff brains to be correct.'[13] Either way, a bloke wasn't safe from fire. In mid May, while laughing at two men whose water bottles had been holed, Gellibrand received a severe wound in his right shoulder and was evacuated to the hospital ship *Gascon* – he would return to Gallipoli just in time for the August Offensive. It didn't take long for all to respect 'Jacko's' snipers, and not only within the front line.

Trooper Ion Idriess, of the 5th Australian Light Horse, had only been on the peninsula a few days and was walking within the reserve area when a man was shot dead in front of him. Idriess recalled how the man killed was just a lad: 'Quite a boy, with snowy hair… He stepped out of a dugout and walked down the path ahead, whistling. I was puffing the old pipe, while carrying a dozen water-bottles. Just as we were crossing Shrapnel Gully he suddenly flung up his water-bottles, wheeled around, and stared for one startled second, even as he crumbled to my feet. In seconds his hair was scarlet, his clean singlet all crimson.'[14]

Private Walter Gifford, aged just eighteen, of the 10th Battalion, had a number of near misses, and not just from snipers. He wrote home about how he'd been in the front line, sniping away for all he was worth, when his lieutenant came along and upbraided him: 'You can't shoot straight.' Taking Walter's rifle to demonstrate how it was done, the lieutenant stood up, exposing himself above the parapet. He immediately fell back dead with a bullet to the head.[15] On another occasion, one of his cobbers had come into some money and was busy sitting in a small cramped dugout trying to lose it as fast as he could playing cards. The card player had been assigned to the water party, but Walter – knowing that at some point the favour would be returned – offered to go in his place. When he came back he found a Turkish shell had landed in the dugout, killing all.[16]

Indeed, it wasn't only Walter Gifford who apparently couldn't 'shoot straight'. Captain Mackay recalled just days before the attack against Lone Pine that some reinforcements came in who couldn't even shoot – most of them didn't know how to fit a clip of cartridges to their rifles. Mackay had these blokes rushed as far away from the firing line as possible, so that they might get a crash course in loading and firing their weapons.[17] Indeed, Lieutenant Colonel White himself was aware of the situation, and wrote: 'No recollection is more bitter than the complaints of the men themselves that they had not had sufficient training to give them a fair chance. That complaint was made to me bitterly before the battle of Lone Pine, and, in such few hours that remained to us efforts were made to remedy the deficiency. But time was not available, and the need of the men great, and ever, in consequence, rests upon our consciences a deep sense of the responsibility incurred.'[18]

Birdwood's break-out offensive would commence on 6 August. The opening salvo of the campaign to occupy the Sari Bair Range, and ultimately the village of Maidos on the other side of the peninsula, would be the attack against Lone Pine, by the men of Walker's 1st Australian Division (a few hours earlier, the British at Helles would launch an attack there to help keep Turkish troops in this sector from being rushed north). Birdwood's original plan for the first day of the August Offensive was to include an attack against Gaba Tepe, but Walker and White had discussed this with Brigadier General Carruthers, temporary commander of the 3rd Australian

Infantry Brigade, who argued that there would be no advantage in capturing Gaba Tepe before the hill Baby 700 and Lone Pine had been captured.[19] Carruthers said that 'the capture of these two points would make the Turkish positions untenable and would, I think, give us the dark [Third] ridge – our original objective'.[20] He believed that capturing both of these positions would mean that the Turks along Second Ridge would be forced to retire, and this in turn would make it difficult for the Turks to hold Third Ridge and Gaba Tepe, as ANZAC artillery and machine guns along Baby 700 would now be in a position to enfilade the Turks entrenched along the eastern side of Second Ridge. In conclusion, he argued: 'to take Gaba Tepe now would only saddle us with another responsibility and another source of casualties without any clear tactical objective'.[21]

Even so, the capture of Lone Pine during the first phase of the new offensive was primarily designed as a feint to draw Turkish attention and reserves away from the objective of the operation – the capture of the Sari Bair Range to the north. The attack against Lone Pine would be made by the 1st Australian Infantry Brigade. Walker had argued strongly against it, noting that it would result, as all feints previously had, in a large number of casualties for little gain.[22] He pointed out bluntly to Birdwood that if the Turkish-held positions along the northern heights, including Baby 700, which dominated Lone Pine, were not captured *before* the attack at Lone Pine then the Turkish artillery would be free to enfilade his men. Walker's concerns made perfect sense if the main objective of the first phase of the offensive was the capture of Lone Pine – but it wasn't. Indeed, Birdwood argued that this would make the feint all the more effective, as the pressure of continuous fighting at Lone Pine would help the main attack at Sari Bair by keeping Turkish reserves away. Walker countered: '[Any advantage] claimed for attacking LONE PINE prior to making an attack elsewhere is that it will draw off reserves. Admitting this for the moment then it must be admitted that, following it to a logical conclusion, the troops allotted to the attack will therefore run considerable risk of failing to retain the ground gained. If they are "outed" before the movement elsewhere is well advanced little is gained and much is lost.'[23] The implication writ large was that his men were expendable – they were to be sacrificed for the greater good of the offensive.

For Hamilton and Birdwood, the attack against Lone Pine was of little consequence in the overall scheme of things – all that was required of it was to keep the Turks pinned down and anxious about their southern flank. Their main objective was breaking the stalemate on the peninsula by a major flanking sweep to the north. Hamilton's perspective is evident in his cable to Birdwood on 30 July: 'The General Commanding wishes your operations to begin … with a strong and sustained attack on Hill 125 (Plateau 400 [Lone Pine]), every effort being made to deceive the enemy as to the locality against which our main effort is to be made, and to induce him to believe that it will be directed against his lines opposite the southern portion of your position.'[24] The overall objective of this new offensive was made clear to the senior ANZAC commanders just a few days before it was launched, in an order sent to them by Birdwood, dated 3 August: 'The Australian and New Zealand Army Corps, with attached troops at Anzac, has been ordered to take part in a combined operation which has for its object occurring a position astride of the Gallipoli Peninsula from the neighbourhood of Gaba Tepe to the Straits north of Maidos.'[25]

Indeed, Birdwood made it clear to the troops on the morning of the attack that the capture of Sari Bair was the first part of the planned offensive. The order read out to the troops concluded with the following paragraph:

There is just one more point I want you all to remember, which is that when we have taken the enemy's position and driven him off it, our work is by no means ended … It is then that our hardest work, and probably the greatest determination will be required, as we not only have to turn the enemy out at present position, but having once shifted him from the front trenches, we have to keep running him out of them as far as we possibly can, capturing we hope everything he possesses, and give him no rest until he is completely defeated here.[26]

Walker and White later explained to their senior officers, who were to launch their men against the Turkish stronghold, that their sacrifice would be a 'prelude to major operations elsewhere... the 1st Australian Division is to take action on its present front with the object of preventing the enemy moving reserves to other areas'.[27] Even so, the planning for the attack against Lone Pine was prepared with a 'thoroughness and skill that had previously been absent during the Gallipoli campaign'.[28]

The flanking movement to the north of Anzac, even without hindsight, was far too ambitious and complex given the lay of the land. Within hours, communications were bound to totally break down between brigade, battalion and company commanders. Most would need to rely on runners, who had no idea of the country they were to traverse. How could they possibly coordinate the complex plan, which required four different columns to make equal degrees of advance from four different avenues of assault? Of even greater concern should have been the condition of the men being called upon to carry out this mad venture. This serious flaw in the plan (and there were many) seems to have been largely ignored and mitigated against success. The ANZACs who would make up a significant component of the attacking force were physically and emotionally spent. The very rough nature of the terrain would have seriously impeded the progress of even the most fit, lightly equipped men in daylight – how could the sick and fatigued ANZACs, carrying rifles, machine guns, ammunition, tools, water and all manner of equipment, in near total darkness, possibly be expected to achieve what was being asked of them? And this was intended as the first of a four-phase operation to capture the township of Maidos and the Dardanelles shoreline of the peninsula. It was madness, given the numbers of men involved (and their physical condition), lack of supplies (including artillery and shell), the nature of the ground to be covered and an overstretched supply line, which would result in a logistical nightmare.[29]

On first hearing of the intended offensive in mid July, 34-year-old British war correspondent Ellis Ashmead-Bartlett, whose later political machinations with Australian journalist Keith Murdoch would have a significant impact on the final decision to evacuate the peninsula, stated that he was 'filled with alarm' and that 'to me it is an utterly impracticable operation of war...which will only lead to fresh reverses and enormous losses. I have never heard of troops being asked to perform such a strange feat of arms before...How can the Australians [and New Zealanders] successfully debouch from...Anzac and storm these hills?'[30]

A few days before the offensive was launched, Birdwood accompanied the officers charged with leading it aboard a destroyer so they might view – using binoculars – the broad expanse of country they were to traverse and the heights they were to climb, attack and capture. Present was British Major Cecil Allanson, who would later somehow lead a mixed force of British and Gurkhas to the very top of Sari Bair, capturing the ridgeline between the peaks of Chunuk Bair and Hill Q for a short time on 9 August. As he listened to Birdwood describing the plan, Allanson turned back to look again at the cliffs and gullies just off North Beach: 'The more the plan was detailed...the less I liked it.'[32] Birdwood at the same time was apparently having second thoughts, recalling: 'It is quite possible, even with the Indian Brigade, I may not be able to effect all I want, as, though it looks like a tiny bit on the map, when you come to look at it from the coast, you realise what a great long stretch of mountain it is.'[31]

5

'It was a ghost, I tell yer'

'Lone Pine', as described by Lieutenant Eric Wren, of the 3rd Infantry Battalion, a 26-year-old clerk from Berry, New South Wales (who had enlisted on his birthday the year before), 'stood gauntly just behind the plateau at the top of White's Gully, [and] was a strongly fortified position, enclosed by rows and rows of barbed wire, and reputed to be one of the strongest positions on the Australian front'.[1] It would be a hard nut to crack. The 250 metres of front-line works to be attacked were heavily defended with strong barbed-wire entanglements and the trenches in some parts covered with thick timbers and layers of earth. Added to this, Turkish machine guns swept the approach, as did artillery batteries entrenched along Third Ridge, just over a kilometre behind Lone Pine. No-man's-land, close to the origins of Owen's Gully, was defined by what had become known as the Daisy Patch. Since the invasion, this cultivated field had stood distinct from the rest of the vegetated plateau, which had at the time been covered with waist-high scrub. The Turkish guns had long since registered the position.

The ANZAC commanders planned for a three-day bombardment before the day of the attack to help destroy the wire and overhead covers that protected the Turkish trenches. This, however, was made difficult by the lack of suitable forward observation posts to direct artillery fire. A partial solution had been found in June, when Australian guns for the first time used aerial observation in counter-battery fire.[2] It had also earlier been realised by mid May that the best way to provide supporting artillery fire at Anzac was with enfilade. Thus the guns of each of the ANZAC divisions – the 1st Australian Division and the New Zealand and Australian Division – covered the troops of the other. This artillery enfilade was exactly the same strategy adopted for the positioning of machine guns, which enfiladed positions to their flanks (and not directly to their front), thus providing a network of interlocking covering fire.[3]

Fifty-two-year-old Colonel Joseph Talbot Hobbs from Western Australia had been an architect before the war, while also serving with the Western Australian artillery as a citizen officer. Landing at Anzac, he was in command of the 1st Australian Divisional Artillery. He spent considerable time surveying the area of 400 Plateau and locating the best positions to provide the infantry with maximum support – greatly risking his life more than once to do so.[4] The three-day 'bombardment' against Lone Pine would turn out to involve a slow rate of fire, with one of the batteries involved allocated a total of just 125 shells for the duration. The final bombardment just before the attack would consist of an hour's intensive shelling by all available artillery – amounting to just eight guns focusing on Lone Pine itself, with around double that shelling the flank and rear positions.[5] However, by Gallipoli standards, this was still a significant number of guns and Hobbs did everything in his power to make every shell count. He recorded in his diary shortly after the attack: 'There is one thing every one of us must never forget – the enormous self-sacrificing assistance the infantry have received throughout from every gun.'[6]

While Birdwood considered the attack against Lone Pine to be a feint, he still expected the position to be captured and held. Indeed, the capture of Lone Pine, while the main force attacked the Sari Bair Range, was critical for the second stage of the offensive – the capture of Third Ridge and Gaba Tepe, enabling a push on towards the Dardanelles side of the peninsula.[7] Operational orders for the second stage would never be drafted, however, as the campaign collapsed.

Walker had only been in temporary command of the 1st Australian Infantry Division, and on 24 June Birdwood appointed an Australian stationed in Egypt, Major General James Legge, to take over. The Australian government had been pushing for an Australian to head the division since General Bridges' death a month earlier. However, Legge was singularly unpopular with his fellow officers. Indeed, on hearing that he was to be transferred to take command, White, who was a firm believer in the British Empire, approached Birdwood, informing him that Legge, a known Australian nationalist, did not have the confidence of the Australian commanders, and that many of them 'would only serve under him with the greatest reluctance'.[8] Birdwood had always preferred Walker and used Legge's unpopularity to transfer him instead to command the 2nd Australian Infantry Division, then training in Egypt. Walker was again placed in charge of the 1st Division and was given one concession in regards to the planned attack against Lone Pine: it had originally been planned for 3 p.m., but it was now to be pushed back to 5 p.m.[9]

The attack would be launched from the Australian lines at The Pimple. Originally, the Australian defences here consisted of just a single front-line trench with a number of communication saps running to the rear. The only rear support had been the wide trench known as Gun Lane, which housed an 18-pounder battery so close to the front-line trench that before one of the low-trajectory guns could be fired, the front-line's sandbag parapet had to be removed. Because there were no support lines, and owing to the nature of the ground, which made it impossible to construct a secondary firing line, it had been decided a few months earlier to construct a firing line in front of the existing front-line trench by tunnelling. This new secret firing line, to remain underground until just before the attack began, was being pushed out in front of The Pimple with the sappers digging up to seven metres a day.[10] Major Martyn wrote that the original front line at The Pimple itself was very deep, with a high parapet consisting of an 'amazing conglomeration of earth and sand-bags and placed in position in the early stages of the campaign when everyone was "sand-bag mad", and when the value of a low parapet and grazing fire was not recognised and the infantry were not happy unless they had a good view of Maidos and a distant view of Constantinople'.[11]

By the time the attack against Lone Pine had been decided upon, the secret underground trench from The Pimple was just about finished. Many recalled that while the entrance of these tunnels was a welcome relief from the heat of the day, the deeper one went into them the more stifling and unbearable they became. Major Martyn recalled that 'instead of coming to the surface and sapping, as was originally intended, a tunnel...with from 3 to 4 feet of cover overhead was driven straight to the front for 30 yards...It must be borne in mind practically no mining tools other than short picks were available, and as we had no means of supplying air other than by blow holes to the surface at intervals, it was impossible to go very far below the surface.'[12] These underground tunnels and the secret underground trench were now an important part of the plan to take and hold Lone Pine. The secret trench would become the staging point for the first wave of the attack.

Since arriving at Anzac, Lance Corporal Lawrence and his men had been working the main tunnel, designated B5, which ran out from The Pimple underneath no-man's-land towards Lone

Pine. He wrote in late July, before heading into B5 to start a day's work, of how a party of five sappers was involved in making jam-tin bombs and were turning out about 200 a day, while nearby a couple of men were 'mucking about with a Turkish rifle to see how far and at what distance a Turkish bullet could penetrate a mock parapet'.[13] Lawrence recorded that these blokes reckoned that at a range of 'thirty to fifty yards, ten inches of sand would suffice and twelve inches of wet clay'.[14]

At the end of B5 tunnel the new underground firing line was being established by Lawrence and his men. The underground trench ran out at right angles from the tunnels, roughly parallel with the Turkish front line about fifty to seventy-five metres away. Lawrence was in charge of four infantrymen who had just about completed their part of the work when he wrote that 'the tunnel itself will be left covered, protecting the men in it from shrapnel and bombs . . . When this firing line is complete it will bring us nearer the enemy by ninety feet . . . Today [Turkish] picking was to be heard very distinctly in tunnels B5 and B6. We have guncotton [a powerful demolition explosive] and details in all readiness.'[15] Major Martyn recalled that unfortunately the Turks got there first and blew in the ends of the B5 and B6 tunnels simultaneously, killing a sapper in each who were engaged in listening at the time. Many encounters 'took place afterwards, but we suffered no further casualties'.[16] It wasn't long before the sappers in B5 and B6 were back at work.

Along with the tunnelling from The Pimple, similar tunnelling and mining operations were also going on further north on 400 Plateau towards the Turkish position at Johnston's Jolly. Captain Iven Mackay and his men were slowly helping the engineers push their works out towards the Jolly and as they mined forward they found that the Turk was equally busy sapping towards them. Men were assigned to listening posts trying to anticipate when the Turks might be close enough to blow a countermine. When the

noise of Turkish picking and shovelling stopped, that was the time
to worry, and the same was true for the Turk: if the enemy had
withdrawn it could only mean one thing – they'd left explosives in
their place. One countermining operation did not go particularly
well for either side. The first explosion by Australian sappers failed
to collapse the Turkish tunnel and the Turks quickly responded
with their own explosion. However, both Australian and Turkish
operations merely resulted in a large crater being formed in
the middle of no-man's-land. The next night men from the 4th
Battalion crept out to inspect the damage, but found the crater
was now occupied by Turks. The new task at hand was to turn
them out. From the Australian trenches, the crater was beyond
the range of the ordinary bomb-thrower, but they had adjutant
Lieutenant Robert 'Jack' Massie, a 'famous cricketer and left-hand
bowler. Massie proceeded to lob jam-tin bombs into the crater
with uncanny precision, and the report of the patrol the next night
was that the crater was unoccupied by the enemy, and looked like
a jam-tin dump.'[17] Massie would soon be called upon to provide
similar services in the furious bombing war that would help define
the battle of Lone Pine.

The work of tunnelling went on day after day, night after night,
in the dark hot, humid, airless passageways. The galleries were a
great drain on candles, which soon gave out. In order to keep the
work going, men and officers used whatever was at hand, and soon
little lamps were sitting on small cutaway shelves in the tunnels,
just a wick of cotton thread dipping into an open or partially
closed can containing the 'fat which we saved from our bacon and
occasionally scanty meat rations', recalled Mackay.[18] The infantry,
under the guidance of the engineers like Cyril Lawrence, did most
of the digging and removing of the spoil to the rear in sandbags,
to bank up and improve the tracks cut into the sides of the hills
in Brown's Dip, the main reserve area just behind the Australian
lines on 400 Plateau.

Private Barrett recalled many years later the digging of B5 tunnel and the terrors encountered, while also having a good laugh at the expense of one of his cobbers. Barrett and a few others were manning the firing step just outside the tunnel entrance. It was close to midnight, when they heard someone stumbling, quickly followed by a curse. A tall lanky figure shot out of the tunnel, dropped his sandbag with a thump, shook his head vigorously and adjusted his cap, picked up his load and with some indignation headed off down the track to the spoil dump. Not long after, the same man re-entered the tunnel, and within minutes he bolted out again and threw down his burden. Barrett and his mates couldn't mistake the figure: 'It was L.G. – known to all as "Long 'Un".' LG again entered the tunnel and soon after came stumbling out again, as white as a sheet. 'What's wrong?' they asked in hoarse whispers to the now rattled LG. 'Ghosts!' he muttered and cursed, going on to explain, 'Every time I pass a certain part of the tunnel me 'at's pulled orf.' 'Don't be balmy,' one of Barrett's mates said. LG knew he wasn't convincing anyone, so he picked up what was left of his load in disgust and headed off for the dump. Barrett and his mates found the whole thing a bit of a laugh and were keenly awaiting the next instalment. It wasn't long before LG came back and reluctantly re-entered the tunnel. As expected, a few minutes passed, and then: '[a] smothered yell and a thumping of size 10 boots. We tightened our grips on rifles. Out shot "Long 'Un". "Not going in that blasted place again."' The men thought he'd probably had more than his share of the rum issue. Now an officer came along to find out what all the racket was about. On hearing LG's story, the officer told him to stop making a damn fool of himself. LG tried to explain in a 'cracked and quaking voice that when he entered the sap and proceeded along to the face nothing unusual happened, but on coming out his cap was clawed off at a certain spot half-way out'. Barrett and his mates watched poor old LG head down the dusty track once more on his way to the dump.

As he returned and cautiously entered B5, the men gathered round to see how long it would be before he bolted out again. Minutes later, 'a babbling figure shot into the trench. "It was a ghost, I tell yer. I struck a match and saw it."' The same officer told LG to stay put while he and Barrett entered the tunnel. They'd gone about thirty or forty metres and stumbled on a sharp rise in the floor. The officer lit a match and they observed a partial roof collapse, and there was LG's ghost: '...a bent arm hanging down, exposed by the dislodgement of earth. When brushed by anything from the entrance end, the arm gave no resistance – it just swung forward, but when brushed from the digging end the arm remained rigid; a clawing hand belonging to the remains of a Turk who had received a hasty shell hole burial during the armistice of May 24. Others who were carrying, being of shorter statue, were not troubled by the "ghost". That was Long 'Un's hard luck. He was six feet three!'[19]

For months now, both sides had watched each other as they dug and expanded their defensive works at Lone Pine and The Pimple. Even so, what lay behind each other's front-line defensive works remained largely a mystery. In July, the ANZAC commanders got their first glimpse at the rear areas of Lone Pine, and a 'detailed' look of the Pine itself, via reconnaissance conducted by British aircraft. This flight – just one of many to take place in the sky above Gallipoli – produced a photograph of the Turkish trench systems at Lone Pine, but even so, interpretation of aerial photographs at this point of the war was still in its infancy. Brigade Major Dennis King, of the 1st Brigade, later recalled that before the attack on Lone Pine he was aware that some of the Turkish trenches were covered over with heavy baulks of timber, but the lack of observation posts made it impossible to get a clear idea of their layout. The photograph eventually reached him but it was 'too hopeless... The attack had to be based on the sketch that we had built up during the previous months.'[20]

Colonel Neville Smyth VC, who was to command the initial attack to capture Lone Pine, was a 53-year-old British professional officer who had been awarded his VC while fighting the Dervishes at Omdurman with the 2nd Dragoon Guards, during Kitchener's conquest of the Sudan in 1898, and later put down an uprising against the British on the Blue Nile. He also surveyed the Sudan, charted the Nile cataracts and fought in the Second Boer War. By the time the Great War came along he was also a proficient airman. With the outbreak of the war he was seconded to the AIF. For a brief time he led the 2nd Australian Infantry Brigade, but before Lone Pine he'd been given the command of the 1st Australian Infantry Brigade. The Australians called him 'Sphinx' while training in Egypt because of his impassive demeanour.[21] Even so, Smyth's courage in action impressed his men, as did his concern for their welfare in and out of the line. Like Birdwood, Walker and White, Smyth was highly regarded by officers and men alike.

Even as news came in every morning that the Turks' few uncovered front-line trenches were being roofed over, Smyth was confident in himself and his men and he believed that when the time came nothing would stop them from capturing the enemy works. At whatever cost, 'they would not be denied'.[22] Smyth also got a copy of the aerial photograph, but even with his flying experience he later admitted at this stage of the war no adequate photographic apparatus was available, and the result was so indistinct that 'little could be made of it, though it established the fact, which was known to us from observations with periscopes ... that the enemy's front trench was roofed over, but could apparently be entered by open trenches and trap doors at intervals'.[23]

From a crude map compiled from this photograph and other intelligence, Walker and White defined the limit of the assault against Lone Pine. The plan was to capture the heart of the position on the plateau. Officers and men were not to be drawn down into the saps and trenches leading off it into the gullies and valley below. At the same time, the central tunnels that led to the ANZAC's secret underground trench would be opened up and extended to the former Turkish front line, supplying communications saps between The Pimple and the newly captured Lone Pine. Details of the Turkish entrenchments, however, still remained agonisingly sparse for those who would be leading the actual attack. Captain Mackay would be leading from the front and later remembered that it was only on 30 July, less than a week before the scheduled attack, that he was approached by the Scottish-born citizen soldier Lieutenant Colonel Charles Macnaghten, 36-year-old commanding officer of the 4th Battalion, who told him that an attack was to be made by the 1st Brigade against Lone Pine and that they'd be in the thick of it. The battalion was still manning the trenches just north of the Pine, opposite Johnston's Jolly. With only a few days to get their bearings, using trench periscopes, officers began to write down their observations. In the 4th Battalion's area, an extra tier of trenches just behind the front line's parados (the rear edge of the trenches, also embanked to provide protection from shelling) was constructed overnight. Mackay later wrote: 'I remember endeavouring to make a detailed plan of the complicated Lone Pine system by the aid of a periscope from this trench, the only one that gave any semblance of overlooking the Turkish trenches, and that to the only very slightest extent.' Word soon reached him and other officers that the 1st Brigade's attack against Lone Pine would be just days away – 6 August.[24]

The Australians of the 1st Brigade would have the honour of leading the initial attack. The men from New South Wales were overall keen, as their two sister brigades had already distinguished themselves – the 3rd Brigade had been the first to land at Anzac just three months before, while the 2nd had distinguished themselves at the Second

Battle of Krithia in the Helles sector.

The small size of The Pimple – even with the secret trench now cutting through the centre of no-man's-land – could not accommodate the whole of the 1st Brigade, and thus, only three of its four battalions would be committed to the initial attack. The assault would be launched in three waves, one following closely behind the other. Each line would consist of around 200 men from each of the three battalions. Hence each of the three lines consisted of about 600 men, which equates to about seven Australians for every metre of Turkish front-line trench to be attacked. The first wave would consist – from north to south – of the men of the 4th, 3rd and 2nd battalions attacking simultaneously along the whole front, with the second and third waves doing likewise, about fifty metres behind them. The first wave would be launched from the secret underground firing line, which would be opened up just before the attack. At its closest point, this trench was less than fifty metres from the Turkish front-line parapets, so these men would be the first to enter the partially covered Turkish stronghold. The second and third waves would launch their successive charges from the front line at The Pimple, around 100 metres from the Pine. Those of the third wave were to bring picks and shovels, along with their standard issue Lee-Enfield 0.303 rifle and fixed bayonet, to help consolidate the position. The 1st Battalion would act as brigade reserve and be ready at extreme short notice to be sent forward into Lone Pine; this also applied to the men of the 7th Battalion (2nd Brigade) and 12th Battalion (3rd Brigade), who would be released from their respective positions at Johnston's Jolly and Tasmania Post upon request from Colonel Smyth.[25]

While most men knew something big was about to happen, the details were unknown. However, the news doing the rounds at Anzac by 5 August was that the '1st Brigade is for it tomorrow'.[26] Lance Corporal Lawrence recorded in his diary that he and his cobbers were done in, and any offensive operation was unlikely to succeed. They thought of nothing else but being relieved. He reckoned that if it wasn't forthcoming soon, they would basically cease to exist as a defensive force – forget any idea of an offensive one. The condition of the men, he wrote in his diary, 'is just pitiful. Surely they won't ask this crowd to do another advance. Anyhow, I don't think that they could do it; they are too weak.'[27] At least Major Martyn's field engineers, who had been digging trenches and tunnels for months now, had reason to be pleased about the coming offensive – they were promised a good rest if it was successful.[28]

Indeed, the associated stress and strain was clearly too much for some men. In early August, just before the August Offensive, Colonel White warned all battalion commanding officers that he had become aware of 'increases of wounded men sent down to the base hospital with the remark "self-inflicted"'.[29] Later, any man presenting himself with a wound to the left hand or left foot fell under suspicion. Others were said to suffer what the medical officers referred to at the time as 'DAH' (Disordered Action of the Heart). This condition had first been recognised during the Boer War fifteen years earlier – a functional disorder related to the stress of combat that can be considered a form of 'shell shock'.[30]

As casualties came in to No. 2 Australian General Hospital in Cairo, Sister Elsie Cook was always keen to hear any news of her husband – the newly promoted Captain Syd Cook. In early July she was told that a casualty from Syd's battalion had arrived in the hospital. Against Army regulations, Elsie 'stole along to see him & find out the news – ran into [Matron] Miss Gould there & was severely "told off" for being in another ward without leave'.[31]

Charles Bean, however, described that as the hour approached for the launching of the great offensive there came over most of the Australian troops, including their young junior officers, whose chances of surviving were significantly less than their men (they were expected to, and did, lead from the front), a 'keenness to make another stroke for the Allies' success... So, as the appointed day, August 6th, drew near, and young British troops in their pith helmets and cotton uniforms began to land by night and camp on the ledges, the ANZAC sick parades diminished.'[32]

It is difficult to assess the reliability of Bean's reporting, as unfortunately there are no figures for the overall sick within individual brigades or battalions, which would include those merely reporting ill as well as those evacuated due to illness. The sick reports for the 1st Division from 1–5 August do not indicate a decrease in the number of men being evacuated sick from the peninsula (99, 100, 84, 111 and 106 men respectively) with a mean of 100 men per day being evacuated sick.[33] There is, however, a decrease on 6 August to just ten men. The previous month, a mean of sixty-seven men per day were evacuated sick. A breakdown of the July figures into weeks, however, demonstrates there is an increasing rate of men being evacuated because of sickness. Between 2–8 July there is an average fifty-four men per day being evacuated; 9–15 July averages sixty-one men per day; 16–22 July averages seventy-three; 23–29 July averages eighty-three; and 30 July to 5 August averages 101 men per day.[34] The available anecdotal evidence suggests there was a progressive increase in the number of men being evacuated as sick at least five weeks before the attack, but twenty-four hours before – when the men first heard that they were imminently going into battle – there was a dramatic decrease in evacuations to just ten men. This, however, may have more to do with logistical arrangements and not reflect the actual (or approximate) number of men reporting sick.

Just before the offensive, Pompey Elliott realised that he was the only one of the twelve original battalion commanders still at the head of his battalion. Day after day of losing his men to snipers and shell fire was also leading to understandable stress. He wrote to Kate in mid July that his men were being blown to pieces by shells buried in their trenches after explosions: '...but Katie, the boys are wonderful. They stick it out and the call for picks and shovels or stretcher bearers never fails to be answered though often another shell sends these willing workers into eternity.'[35] He wrote that one of his men had been hit by a shell, recalling that he had previously seen the lad's face 'set and pale but never shrinking...Our doctor did not give any hope of him being saved at all but news of his death has not reached me, so I am beginning to hope against hope for it was a frightful wound and the poor boy bore it without a murmur...Oh, I do hope his life will be saved.'[36] Within days, Elliott was informed that the soldier, 22-year-old Lance Corporal Ken Walker, had died from his wounds. Even months later the effect of Ken Walker's death was playing on his mind, as he wrote about the prospect of contacting Walker's wife, just after the slaughter of Lone Pine in mid August: 'I suppose poor Lyn is very sad about Ken. I have been intending to write to her since, but feel somehow that I cannot. I think it would break me up completely if I met them. He was such a fine boy and they loved him so much...And when I think of all these things I cannot write.'[37]

Private Joseph Collingwood, of the 2nd Battalion, observed the mood of the men as the time of the offensive drew near. Most knew each other pretty well in their sections and platoons. They'd lived and worked closely together for almost four months, and they felt, given an even break, they could finish the job. If an incentive was needed, it was the thought that 'only a few hundred yards in the rear was the sea. It was frequently discussed among the troops as to what would be the position, should the Turks break through at any point...so the opportunity of placing more distance between themselves and the sea was welcomed'.[38]

6

'... all preparations are going ahead for the coming slaughter'

General Liman von Sanders, the sixty-year-old German officer who commanded the Turkish Fifth Army and who was responsible for the defence of the Gallipoli Peninsula, was increasingly concerned. Ongoing rumours suggested that the Allies were planning a new offensive – nothing new there, but now the reporting began to gain some credibility. Reports arrived via Salonika on 16 July that indicated around 50 000 British Empire troops had landed on Lemnos, with about 140 support and transport vessels now anchored in its harbour for all to see.[1] Further confirmation arrived when, about a week later, General von Falkenhayn, chief of the General Staff in Berlin, sent an urgent cable stating: 'From reports received here it seems probable that at the beginning of August a strong attack will be made on the Dardanelles, perhaps in connection with a landing in the Gulf of Saros (Xeros) or on the coast of Asia Minor. It will be well to economize ammunition.'[2] General von Sanders later recalled how some in the Turkish capital were in a near state of panic, although during July 1915 it is difficult to believe he was so cavalier about the dangers now facing him:

Alarming news from Constantinople about an imminent new great landing...The adjutant of the military mission informed me from a reliable source that the success of this new enemy enterprise was counted on with certainty [and] that already windows were being rented in Pera Street for the entry of the British troops and that the British Embassy was being put in order and the beds newly covered. I merely replied that I requested him to order a window for me too in Pera Street.[3]

The Prussian von Sanders had been singularly unpopular with the German General Staff, who had wasted no time in posting him to far-away Constantinople as a military adviser to the Turks before the outbreak of war. Before the invasion of Gallipoli, however, von Sanders proved himself as he greatly enhanced the defences on the peninsula, with artillery, military hospitals and troop dispositions, and generally raised the morale and effectiveness of his men. By early August, von Sanders held the high ground around Anzac with three Turkish Divisions (5th, 16th and 19th), amounting to around 20 000 rifles and seventy-six guns. Unknown to him, Birdwood would soon have around 37 000 rifles and seventy-two guns. Even so, traditional military doctrine dictates that an attacking force must have an advantage of 3:1 if they are to have any chance of success – Birdwood had nothing approaching that in either men or guns.

On 4 August, two days before the offensive was to be launched, the first of the slow bombardments, which was to destroy the enemy wire and later blow apart Lone Pine itself (and in so doing, totally demoralise the Turks), began. The mission of cutting the wire had been assigned to the New Zealand field artillery. An observation officer at The Pimple with a direct telephone line to the guns helped to direct their fire. The artillery officer reported later to his commanding officer that the wire was largely undamaged by the shelling.[4] The next day, the artillery increased the number of shrapnel shells used, and these were set to burst on percussion against the ground. This was observed by all to be far more effective and the bombardment continued until the wire entanglements had been destroyed to the infantry's satisfaction. These same New Zealand guns did a lot of firing against the Turkish trenches at both Lone Pine and Johnston's Jolly, but the lack of high-explosive shells meant that the heavy overhead covers at Lone Pine remained mostly intact. At the same time, the Turkish batteries retaliated with counter-battery fire and one of the New Zealand guns on Russell's Top protecting the southern Anzac sector was hit and destroyed, and the crew killed. If Lone Pine was to be blown apart, it was crucial that the Allied howitzers had enough ammunition, but like everything at Gallipoli, shells were few and far between. The 'howitzer batteries (4.5 and 5 inch) were limited to a mere 30 rounds per battery on the day before the attack'.[5] By 3 p.m., 5 August, the gunners had fired over 300 shells into Lone Pine itself and against its surrounding barbed-wire entanglements. That night, illuminating red and green star shells were fired around Lone Pine to ensure the Turks were unable to repair whatever damage had been inflicted under cover of darkness.[6]

Some of the Australians now feared becoming caught in their own wire. Even though there was not much of it, it could still result in unnecessary casualties. Twenty-one-year-old labourer from Helensburgh, New South Wales, Private Victor Williams, of the 2nd Battalion, was one of three assigned to bring in the wire on the night of 4 August. For two hours he and two companions crawled along among the Fray Bentos containers and Deakin's Jam tins in no-man's-land, occasionally 'flattening down to get below a machine-gun traverse, or maintaining a death-like stillness while an enemy flare turned night into day; and between times cursing the sharp rattle of the disturbed tins while gathering into a coil the few strands of wire within reach'.[7] With blood still running freely from their hands and faces, with tunics and breeches torn in a dozen places, Victor and his mates quietly returned to the front-line trench of The Pimple. The next night, with two fresh helpers, he gathered in the remaining wire under even worse conditions, as ANZAC artillery was lighting up no-man's-land during the night with star shells.[8]

On 5 August, the Turks at Lone Pine announced to the Australians that Warsaw had fallen to the Germans. They did so by placing a number of placards above the trenches stating that 'Varsaw ash Fallin'.[9] It was hoped this would lower the morale of the ANZACs – but they were to be disappointed. The response they received from one sentry was, 'Let's see if we can't make this bloody notice fall,' as men sought to shoot the supporting poles.[10] The Turks inadvertently helped the Australian cause, as the subsequent Allied bombardment targeting their trench and wire on 5–6 August was misunderstood by the Turks as retaliation for setting up the placards – disguising the real intent of preparing the way for the imminent August Offensive.

On the same day, the infantry battalion commanders assigned to lead the attacks from the front were called to a briefing by their commanding officer, Colonel Smyth. This would be the first time that most were given any details of their roles in the forthcoming attacks – attacks that were to take place the next day. General Ian Hamilton had been obsessed with secrecy to the extent that it seriously impeded the planning abilities for those further down the chain of command – the majors, captains and lieutenants. Colonel Smyth explained that the brigade was to launch its attack against Lone Pine at 5 p.m., about four hours before the main offensive to the north. Their role, besides taking Lone Pine, was to draw as many of the enemy down upon them before the Turks realised it was a feint.[11] The three battalions were to carry out the attack on a frontage of around 100 metres each. The objectives to be taken and held were shown on a map with a coloured line running approximately two-thirds of the way through the Turks' Lone Pine fortifications. Overall, they were to capture the heart of the position on top of the plateau – they were not to enter the gullies and ridges running off it, which would lead to undue exposure. This would leave a thin line of Turks to their front along the very edge of the plateau, which would ensure the Turks could not retaliate with artillery against the Australian position, as they would be in danger of hitting their own trenches. When the time came to push on to Third Ridge, these Turks would supposedly be easily brushed aside. One officer recalled: 'It is well to recall that maps were very scarce throughout the peninsula operations, and those that did exist were for the most part inaccurate, especially with regard to the minor topographical features and contours which are of such vital importance in close and localised fighting.'[12] All attacking troops were to be instructed not to overrun their objective, which meant they were to stay on the top of the plateau. Unfortunately, in many cases this order had to be ignored because on reaching Lone Pine the men realised that their very objectives were actually off the plateau.

On returning to his Battalion Headquarters, 44-year-old Maitland farmer Lieutenant Colonel Robert Scobie, commander of the 2nd Battalion, immediately set to work issuing instructions to his officers, and ordered a company commanders' conference for 3 p.m. that afternoon. Meanwhile, he ensured that all ranks were issued with white calico armbands and white patches that they were to sew onto the back of their tunics, just below the collar. These were for identification purposes – the fighting was expected to be furious and vicious within the small confines of the Pine and it was hoped that this would stop Australians from killing each other. It would also help those further back identify the newly captured positions. After the war, Captain Harold Jacobs recalled that the officers were to dress like the men to avoid being killed by snipers. They, like other ranks, were to wear caps with neck sun protectors. Most officers still wore their metal badges of rank, however, although in a few cases they inscribed their rank insignia with pencil on the shoulders of their tunics.[13]

At 3 p.m., Scobie and his company commanders gathered in his dugout to get the details of the next day's attack. The commanders of the other two battalions would have been providing similar orders to their officers. In the case of the 2nd Battalion, the assault was to be made by B Company, under professional soldier 21-year-old Captain John Pain, C Company under 25-year-old Ballarat schoolteacher Major Leslie Morshead, and D Company under 25-year-old Captain Garnet Brown. The newly promoted Captain Syd Cook led A Company, which was to remain as the battalion reserve. B Company was to lead the assault from the secret underground trench now slicing through no-man's-land, while C and D companies would launch their attack at the same time, but further back in the front-line trenches at The Pimple. The reserve A Company was to move straight up to the underground line as soon as B Company had hopped the bags. Thirty-four-year-old Major Arthur Stevens was to command the three attacking lines. Company commanders were to allocate some officers and NCOs to carry red and yellow artillery signal flags. These were to be planted firmly in the ground to denote limits of flanks and advance for the artillery and to be waved rapidly in case the men came under their own shell fire. Jam-tin bomb sections were to be organised by each company, each consisting of one rifleman in front, followed by one bomb-thrower and one carrier directed by an NCO in the rear, who would be supported by a second bomb-thrower and a second man carrying baskets of bombs. Finally, a soldier with two haversacks full of bombs and fifty rounds of ammunition would be close behind.[14]

On entering the enemy works all wires were to be cut in case they were attached to Turkish mines or bombs. However, officers were also warned that a brigade signal section would be installing telephone communications from Lone Pine to The Pimple as soon as practicable after the assault. All walking wounded were to somehow make their way back to The Pimple and from there to the divisional collecting station beyond Brown's Dip. Only stretcher-bearers were permitted to take the wounded who could not make their own way to the rear. Company commanders were to arrange, if possible, one pick and one shovel for every eight men. Food for forty-eight hours and iron rations for twenty-four hours were to be carried by every man, and they were to roll and tie two sandbags on the back of his belt. Officers' watches 'were to be synchronised at 4 p.m. on the day of attack, and the signal for the attack would be three sharp whistle blasts'.[15] At the conclusion of the conference, all present toasted the battalion – for many, including battalion commander Lieutenant Colonel Robert Scobie, the toast would be their last. Then all immediately set off to provide details, instructions and orders to their NCOs and men. It was going to be a long night.

On hearing for the first time that they would be going into battle the very next day, many men scavenged around for pencil and paper to write what might be their last letter home. Writing materials had been in short supply from day one. Most probably managed to beg, borrow or steal enough to complete at least one letter, setting down their fears and hopes, their homesickness, and expressions of love for their family. Some, accepting that they were going to die, may have used the writing as a form of confession for sins past, and to ask for forgiveness. Others just arrived and ignorant of war may have written home in bravado, expressing the excitement of finally getting the chance to get at 'Johnny Turk'. Some had no-one to write to and wished they had.

Cecil McAnulty had already filled up his first diary and was now forced to use the back of envelopes, letters from home, or any other scrap of paper he could find. He cut these to pocket-notebook size, each carefully numbered at the top of the page. The writing is small, clearly trying to squeeze in as much as possible. One letter from his brother is cut up in this way, but can still be read by turning over and joining the four sheets together. His younger brother concludes: 'Trusting this finds you well and that you will return safe and sound with all the honours of Victory, Your loving brother, Percy.'[16] Many of the empty envelopes – some torn open to be used as sheets of paper – still have stamps affixed and were addressed to: 'Pte McAnulty 3rd Battalion, 1st Brigade – to Secretary for Defence Melbourne'. One was addressed to: '1584 Pte J. P. Sullivan, A Company, 3rd Battalion, 1st Infantry Brigade, 1st Division'. The letter it contained was for James Sullivan, who was killed in action just a few weeks before. Sometime that afternoon Cecil reached in his tunic pocket, took out his bundle of papers and scribbled on a piece of paper he numbered page 36, noting that more troops were arriving, including Lancashires and Gurkhas. The gullies, he wrote, 'are swarming with men now, all nationalities. We are ready to move at any minute. All we have with us now is our equipment, haversacks and water bottles. Each man has a broad strip of white calico sewn along the centre of his back [tunic] and a strip on each arm as the attack will be started in darkness.'[17]

Not far away would have been 24-year-old labourer from Maitland, New South Wales, Private Reginald Donkin, of the 1st Battalion, who had been assigned to help dig the tunnels now leading out towards Lone Pine. During the day of the landing, four months earlier, he'd been fighting with Lieutenant Ivor Margetts along the slopes of Baby 700. Charles Bean notes Donkin's list of injuries in the official history: 'two bullets in his left leg, a third pierced the top of his hat and cut his hair; one ripped his left sleeve; three hit his ammunition pouches and exploded the bullets; [and] another struck his entrenching tool'.[18] He had surely used up a great deal of his allotment in luck. Donkin, like Cecil McAnulty, was a keen diarist, writing that: '[All preparations] are going ahead for the coming slaughter. I hope I will be spared to hop into the Turkey's trenches, but it will be a horrible sight after the bombardment is finished.'[19] Later that night he was busily engaged in the 'task of removing all the sandbag packing and entanglements which had been placed in the underground firing line recesses... and in cleaning out the tunnels generally. Others have been working upon scaling ladders, entanglements, bomb carrying bags and things like that.'[20]

Six sappers were assigned to go 'over the top' with the initial charge. They were to assist the infantry attack by blowing apart any obstructions during the initial assault, including overhead timbers known to be covering the Turkish trenches. They were now very carefully constructing their demolition charges, consisting of slabs of guncotton nailed to a board.[21] Most of the other sappers, however, were still working desperately to complete some underground saps beneath no-man's-land just short of Lone Pine. These would be used to place a number of mines that would be exploded a few hours before the attack. In order to make up the strength of the exhausted sappers, who would also be needed to dig communication trenches to connect The Pimple and Lone Pine, a number of additional men were picked from the infantry and light horse to help make up the numbers – Private Donkin was among them. Major Martyn wrote that two troopers, John Playne and Geoffrey Brockman, had earlier been given commissions and transferred to the 2nd Field Company. Playne, along with fifteen sappers, would go over with the second wave of men from the 3rd Battalion and immediately start sapping back from the captured front-line trench at the Pine towards B5 and B6 tunnels, while others in these tunnels would be digging towards them.[22] Donkin was one of the men assigned to help the sappers dig towards Lone Pine from B5 after the Pine had been captured: 'We have to drive a broad tunnel right through to the enemy trenches. When our chaps charge we will be picking away like old nick, and there will be communications between our lines and the enemy trench, which we all hope will be ours.'[23]

The operational orders of the 1st Australian Infantry Brigade issued on 5 August stated that the men were to leave their packs behind; the only things they were to take with them were their rifles, bayonets, 200 rounds of ammunition, two days' worth of food rations, one day's iron rations, a full water bottle, respirators and two empty sandbags. All battalions' machine guns were also to be taken over to Lone Pine as part of the initial attack, with 3500 rounds.[24] While the total number of bombs allocated to the brigade amount to around 1200, it was known before the attack that this would be insufficient, as shown by an operation order issued on 4 August, stating that 'men should be told to remove the bombs from the dead and wounded whenever possible'.[25] Lieutenant Wren, of the 3rd Battalion, recalled: 'Up to this time, the 1st Brigade had had little or no experience of bombing, beyond the throwing occasionally of a few "jam tin" grenades, the employment of which generally was regarded as a huge joke.'[26] The men, however, would very quickly come to realise how vital these bombs were in holding their captured positions from ferocious Turkish counterattacks. The jam-tin bomb would quickly become anything but a joke. Other ANZACs at Gallipoli, especially at nearby Quinn's Post where the Turks were literally just metres away, had long since come to depend on jam-tin bombs to help defend their position.

The Victorians of the 2nd Infantry Brigade began to move into the front-line trenches at The Pimple to relieve the men of the 1st Brigade so that they might get some rest before their attack. Officers and NCOs were studying plans and attending briefings while the attacking troops prepared themselves – including being allowed the rare luxury of drinking as much water as they wanted. They were also provided with a meal of boiled rice and tea flavoured with rum.[27] Private Charles Duke, of the 4th Battalion, was among them and remembered all hands being busy sharpening their bayonets or making slow-burning matches to light jam-tin bombs. Others were trying to put thread to needle in semidarkness, in an attempt to sew the white square of calico onto the back of their tunic and a broad white strip across its upper sleeve. One of Duke's battalion, as he fixed the calico square, remarked, 'Fancy getting on the field without numbers!'[28] Duke recalled: 'Looking back on Lone Pine now, one can only wonder how it was possible to have emerged alive. My particular chum was Simpson...and if ever a chap had a premonition of death, he had it that night...and sure enough he was killed the next day.'[29] Hunters Hill grazier, 28-year-old Lance Corporal George Simpson was indeed killed in action on 7 August and is today buried at Johnson's Jolly (Special Memorial).

Twenty-two-year-old Lance Corporal Joseph Aylward had been a Sydney cleaner before the war. He, like Duke, was a member of the 4th Battalion and had earlier been assigned the duty of guiding British units to their bivouacs at Anzac in preparation for their attack against the northern heights. With the Lone Pine stunt now on he rejoined his battalion the night before the attack and was disappointed to find that he would not be going into action with members of his section. His mates had been training with jam-tin bombs while he was away and were assigned as a bombing party to attack the northern flank of Lone Pine. As he had no experience lighting and throwing these homemade bombs, he was attached to another section for the attack. His instructions, like many others, were not to attempt to gain entrance into Lone Pine via the front-line trenches, which were mostly covered with heavy sleepers and sandbags, but to continue on and drop into the uncovered support trenches further to the rear, and then make his way back to the covered front-line positions to help oust the Turks with the bayonet.[30]

Captain Iven Mackay, of Aylward's battalion, was busy with his NCOs, ensuring that each man's rifle and ammunition pouch were checked. He paid particular attention to the fresh new reinforcements and provided where necessary a final, exhaustive test in loading a rifle and using a bayonet. He walked amongst the men, encouraging them to keep cool and attack in silence – they should save their breath for the fight ahead. Among the troops, Irish-born 25-year-old Lieutenant Charles Lecky, 2nd Battalion, who had not been long on the peninsula, was trying to get some shut-eye, knowing he and his men had taxing duties ahead. Unknown to him, one of Colonel Alfred Bessell-Brown's 18-pounders had been brought to the front line during the night. While he was probably dreaming of home, the gun unceremoniously commenced registering in a recess just a few metres from him. Wakened with a start, amongst the smoke and smell of cordite, when he came to his senses he raced down the line and grimly asked the nearest sentry where the shell had exploded and if there'd been any casualties. The sentry and a 'dozen companions had been waiting to see the effect on the newly arrived officer, and could not speak for mirth'.[31]

Earlier that night the 3rd Battalion held a special religious service led by Chaplain Dean Talbot in a makeshift church behind the lines of 400 Plateau in Wire Gully, at the head of Shrapnel Valley, close to Brown's Dip. It appeared at first glance a perfect place, as it was relatively safe from Turkish fire. For the same reason, it was also a good spot for the ammunition dump that had been positioned there. With quick improvisation it was turned into an open church, possessing a 'Holy Table on which rested a wooden Cross made by one of the pioneers'.[32] The church was circular, positioned in a small natural amphitheatre, with seats of ammunition boxes now organised one above the other in pews.

The roof was the 'sky overhead, and we looked down the gully to the Aegean'.[33] The chaplain and the men knew that many of them were likely to be casualties the very next day – most fearing, above all else, being maimed. They all celebrated Holy Communion; the service was more crowded than usual. Talbot wrote after the war: 'Would that our churches here were always similarly packed. About 100 received the sacrament, and I still treasure the chalice that I used on that memorable occasion. About half the men who communicated must have fallen the following day.'[34]

Sergeant William Drummond, of the 5th Battalion, was also present, but he and his men had other things on their mind, which were as far from worship as you could get. During the preparation for the attack, Drummond was in charge of a party who were assigned the task of bringing up rifle ammunition and stacking it in the supply dump in Wire Gully. He and his tired men had been hauling ammunition boxes up the hill to the hollow in which Chaplin Talbot and his parishioners were now comfortably ensconced. For a few seconds, Drummond and his fatigue party stood in amazement at the religious service now being performed there. There was nothing for it – as the service was under way, it was punctuated by the thud and rattle of more boxes being slid down a plank into the hollow. The interruption proved so upsetting to Talbot that he loudly informed Drummond 'with no little asperity, that he had "desecrated the first church in Gallipoli". "I'm sorry, sir," replied Drummond, "but," indicating the ammunition with a wave of his hand, "all this is just as necessary for tomorrow as your sermon, isn't it?" The Padre smiled, and supposed that, unfortunately, it was.'[35]

Not far away, Australian sappers were busy in the secret tunnel below no-man's-land, running parallel to the Turkish trenches. They had to break through to the surface before first light, using picks and shovels. Eventually, as they yanked at plant roots dangling above their heads to help speed up the process, the men began to break clear all along the line. ANZAC flares provided some welcome light and occasionally, in the darkness beyond the stars of manganese, infinite stars could be seen lightly flickering.

Meanwhile, down by the beach, around fifty men were busy working around the clock among a pile of old used tins. The jam-tin bomb factory, as it had become known, was the main provider of grenades for the ANZACs. They manufactured improvised bombs with fragments of Turkish shell, cut-up barbed wire, stones, nails and the like serving as shrapnel. The explosive was guncotton, and the bomb would be completed with a detonator and a fuse usually timed for between four to six seconds. The fuses would be found to be far too long, and many in the close confines of Lone Pine would be killed attempting to shorten the period from ignition to detonation.[36] Before the August Offensive, the bomb factory was producing around 200 bombs daily, but at the height of the assault, with the invaluable help of the men from the navy (working on board ship), it would manage to produce 4000 per day.[37]

The night before the big offensive, all appeared normal. From Anzac Cove, in the darkness, looking out across the Aegean past the fleet, small tiny flickering lights could be seen from the Greek islands of Imbros and Samothrace. It looked as if they were a world away from the horrors of the peninsula. This was an illusion. True, a man there could at least get some respite from exploding shells, violent death and the smell of rotting corpses, but they were very much tied to this place. They were the principal supply centres to the campaign, crammed with reinforcements, fatigue parties, tented hospitals and vast stores and ammunition. When the water lighters from Alexandria failed to arrive, the islands would be pumped dry to help provide water to the thirsty army just kilometres across the sea. Their harbours were full of naval ships and commandeered civilian craft of all kinds.

Now, just off Anzac, a fleet of transports bringing in reinforcements and supplies was at anchor. All lights had been extinguished and the only telltale sign that they were there was when one of the large transports slowly moved and blocked out the lights of the Greek islands for a minute or two. The only lights originating from the fleet itself were those from the hospital ships and a couple of destroyers. The white hospital ships, with their large red crosses and green lines running just above the water line, were deliberately lit up for all to see, including any German submarine commander who should by international law leave such vessels alone.

Two destroyers, one covering the northern flank and the other the southern, had turned their searchlights against the lower slopes, sweeping their beams across the terrain, attempting to pick up any Turkish movement threatening the positions. Those onshore protecting each flank looked out into no-man's-land, training their eyes to follow the sweep of bright light as it arced to and fro. Sometimes the column of light would stop, if only for a few seconds, as if sniffing the wind, testing, teasing – when this happened, the ridges and spurs crammed into the bright light threw up eerie shadows.

From the decks of the ships looking back towards the cove, sailors could see thousands of tiny pinpricks of sparkling light. Here and there a small explosion of light lit up the ridges as a grenade or jam-tin bomb exploded. The sound of rifle fire could be heard from a number of directions, disjointed and unrelated. These occasional sounds were all that marked this place out as a battlefield and not some giant jamboree. Further inland from the ridges, dull red glows could be seen. These originated close to the front-line trenches where anxious sentries, usually new recruits from both sides, had lit rags and hessian soaked in petrol or kerosene, and thrown them into no-man's land, sure that they had heard something or someone just beyond the flimsy wire. This would result in a domino effect up and down the line as those close by felt compelled to do the same. Soon a low red-yellow thread of flame snaked along the inland ridges.

However, all eyes on the ships were drawn towards 400 Plateau, and more specifically Lone Pine, by the fireworks provided by the star shells that descended there. Flares of magnesium gently sailed down, suspended by small parachutes, gently swaying this way and that and throwing light in an ever-decreasing arc. These flares would be fired all night long, snipers and artillery observers having taken up positions to make sure that the destroyed Turkish wire and any smashed log-head covers could not be repaired. No Turkish sapper dared move out onto the plateau, as they would immediately be cut down.

The elongated shadows that were thrown out across no-man's-land from the Turkish front line at the Pine were haunting to those few Turks who looked out upon the artificial daylight through their loopholes. For these men, it was the first time that they had a chance to look out into the killing zone for any length of time. They were presented with a light show, a transitory panorama of human wreckage strewn out across the killing field. The fleeting images were embellished by the sharp distinction between light and shadow. Eerie and grotesque images were presented, and just as a man figured out what he was looking at, the scene was plunged into darkness, before almost immediately another area was lit up and the macabre game continued. Usually following three or four flares, there would be a violent explosion and a 'swish' of shrapnel spray across no-man's-land close to Lone Pine or against the works themselves, as ANZAC artillery or a lone British warship let rip a salvo, then silence would resume for another few minutes. The southern destroyer's searchlight would occasionally swing across the plateau, and cut a swath across 400 Plateau, the topography throwing out shadows in all directions.

A week before, the Turks had lost a minor trench work along their southern flank – known to the Allies originally as the Turkish Despair Works. This attack by the men of the 11th Australian Infantry Battalion had been initiated to help further draw the attention of the Turkish commanders to the south in preparation for the August Offensive. The trench lay along the landward side of a major spur running off 400 Plateau, just forward and south of Lone Pine. It had now been incorporated into the Australian front line and rechristened Leane's Trench in honour of Captain Raymond Leane, of the 11th Battalion, who had commanded the attack. The Turks had since turned their attention to recapturing their trench and, in the process, regaining the initiative from the ANZAC commanders. The orders from Turkish Lieutenant Colonel Rushdi Bey to the men of his 48th Regiment, who were assigned the job of taking back their position, were later discovered on the dead body of a Turkish machine-gun officer. They stated in part: 'The 47th Regiment on the left wing will engage the enemy with machine guns and prevent any supports from advancing and will also fire at any of our men who may not stand firm throughout the attack or who may run away.'[38] The Turkish attack on Leane's Trench was to be launched at dawn on 6 August – the day scheduled for the Anzac breakout.

FRIDAY
6 AUGUST
1915

7

'His revolver was
then going strong'

The first rays of morning appeared over Leane's Trench and with them movement and voices were heard in the grimly named Valley of Despair, below. The Australians on stand-to, including Private William Smith ('Smithy'), opened fire, while a few others fumbled with their jam-tin bombs and, if they managed to light them in time, threw them over the parapet into the small valley. Immediately in response, a heavy Turkish rifle and machine-gun fire swept the Australian position from Lone Pine, supported by fire from the southern spurs running off 400 Plateau – Sniper's Ridge and Pine Ridge – both on a higher elevation to Leane's Trench. Quickly added to this was Turkish high explosive and shrapnel from their batteries strung out along Third Ridge. The combination of grenades, shrapnel and high explosive decimated the Australian garrison, especially those manning the southern part of Leane's Trench.[1] One of the Turkish machine-gunners later recalled that he could see their men on the slope below the Australian trench harassed by a 'fierce bomb-fire, which at first appeared to prevent them from climbing over the parapet'.[2] The trench was full of dust and smoke, the survivors found it difficult to see – all was confusion but also determination.

Thirty-nine-year-old engineer from Cottesloe, Western Australia, Captain Julian Aarons, recalled the first rush of the attack: 'Many of our fellows were killed and wounded, but we retaliated with bombs. The old jam-tin affair which had to be lit with a match or a cigarette.'[3] With the lifting of the artillery bombardment, about thirty Turks scrambled out of the gully into what had been their communication saps but which now fed into the Australian front line, although their entrances had been heavily barricaded. They stumbled over the bloated and decaying bodies of their dead – who had been thrown into the saps a week before, after the Australians captured the trench – charging through the open graves to get to the living beyond.

Smithy was immediately ordered back through the southern communication tunnel to get reinforcements. These tunnels were the only way that communications could be maintained between Leane's Trench (along the lower slopes of Bolton's Ridge) and Tasmania Post (on its ridgeline). Open saps were pointless, as the Turks now entrenched along the next inland spurs running off 400 Plateau overlooked the position, and would be able to pour fire into the saps. Smithy pushed upwards through the darkened tunnel; the only light was from the scattered improvised candles. He looked ahead and saw the light flicker in the tunnel exit like morse code, caused by the frantic rushing about of men in Tasmania Post. When he reached the trench, it took a few seconds to adjust his eyes to the bright sunlight. He found a number of men waiting to follow him into the fight and they headed back down the tunnel. Halfway through, Smithy heard the click of a rifle bolt, along with what to him was Turkish gibberish. He and his mates took up a position in a bend of the tunnel to prevent the Turks penetrating any further, while anxiously looking out for the telltale burning fuse of a Turkish bomb.[4] From here, the sound of the desperate fight taking place below was channelled up to them, along with its smoke and dust.

Other parties of Australians from Tasmania Post were also being collected to reinforce Leane's Trench. These were under the command of lieutenants Aubrey Darnell, Ernest Morris and Alexander Robertson. The main focus of the Turkish attack had been against the southern part of Leane's Trench – its centre and northern flank still remained in Australian hands. The reinforcing officers and men were funnelled down the centre and northern communication tunnels to support their cobbers fighting furiously below. Dead and wounded paved the floor. Men struggled to make sense of the slaughter all around them – their confusion heightened by their inability to see or hear clearly what was happening around them, amid the explosions, smoke and dust of battle. Twenty-three-year-old civil engineer Lieutenant Morris later recalled: 'When I got there... the Turks were right up to the edge of the parapet, and a few men had even got into the trench on the right'.[5]

The reinforcing Australians found Leane's Trench a shambles. The sandbags of the parapet had been cut to ribbons by machine-gun fire – sand and gravel poured into the trench. To show a head above the parapet was certain death. While the main focus of the Turkish attack was against the southern end, another group was trying to break into the centre of the Australian position. Turkish hands could be seen above the parapet as they flung their black cricket-ball grenades into the trench. The Australians had only a few jam-tin bombs and no matches to light them with. However, a cigarette lighter was obtained from Captain Aarons, and as the last of the bombs was flung, a further supply of explosives came to hand.[6]

Only a few men were keeping the Turks in the southern part of the trench from penetrating further up the line. They had taken up a position close to one of the traverse bends and continued to fling jam-tin bombs against the oncoming Turks. Twenty-six-year-old Victorian miner Sergeant Albert Wallish was trying to establish a barricade and was pulling down any debris he could find. Nearby, 28-year-old Gippsland geologist Lieutenant Robertson, who just a few years before had narrowly missed out on a Rhodes Scholarship, was emptying his revolver into any Turk that was game enough to show his head. Within minutes, Robertson was killed, one of his men recalling: 'Near as I can make out, he was hit in the head by a piece of bomb exploding in the trench; he then got up on the parapet and emptied his revolver into the oncoming enemy... From the time he jumped onto the parapet there was no hope for him, as Jacko was raining bullets into us.'[7] Meanwhile, Aarons recalled that: 'Wallish [was putting] up a barricade between us, we had a lively interchange of bomb throwing. One bomb hit Wallish, but he stayed on in the trench.'[8]

Nearby, Lieutenant Morris was in the thick of the fighting and remembered how the Turks tried to swarm into the front of his trench section. He discarded his revolver early – he didn't have the luxury of having time to reload its chamber during the intense fight – and quickly got hold of a dead man's rifle and bayonet. At one point he described using a 'trusty iron-shod pick handle [which] did some good work... You cannot imagine what it is like to be running up and down a section of trench, trampling over dead bodies, with men beside you being blown to atoms, the tops of their heads blown off or both arms and feet missing.'[9]

Thirty-one-year-old railway ganger from Bumbleyung, Western Australia, Private Christopher Veitch was with a group of men holding the end of a former Turkish communication sap. Private Albert Boddington wrote that Veitch's rifle did some 'splendid work. All our boys were very cool about it... For about two hours it was a real bomb fight, the enemy bombs doing a lot of damage in our lines, while we were continually giving a leg into eternity... Each Turk seemed to be carrying a number of bombs – both of "cricket ball" or "jam tin" variety. They each had a striker attached to tunic.'[10] Captain Aarons wrote to Charles Bean after the war: 'A bomb fell near me and I covered it with a blanket then with a full sandbag from the parapet before it exploded – a piece of it went into my knee – it also shattered my wrist watch, which then stopped 5.45 a.m.'[11]

Twenty-three-year-old Private Thomas Priestman, of the battalion medical section, set up a dressing station at the northern end of the trench. Among the bombing, shooting and killing he managed to dress and evacuate thirty casualties, despite suffering from influenza. He then stayed to help the wounded until after the battle, but his influenza was considered so bad that he was evacuated from the peninsula later that day. Thomas was Mentioned in Despatches for his actions that day and within weeks was back at Gallipoli.[12]

Even their trusted 'old' cook, 27-year-old Private Andy Graham, was in the thick of it, as recalled by Corporal Hector Haslam:

[We] were all very proud of our cook. He was Andy Graham, a Katanning man, and if ever these pages get near him, I hope he reads these few lines...and learns with what admiration his fellow fighters of the 11th Battalion regard him. While the battalion was fighting its hardest, Andy made some tea and carried it up to the fighting and distributed it to the many wounded and dying pals about – and there were many. He went back for more, and on his return a shell fell near him and buried two soldiers. He put down his tea, and worked until he nearly dropped to extricate the poor unfortunates. He did get them out, but he strained his heart in the doing of it. Undaunted, he picked up his tea and went on with [his] self-appointed job. Many a dying soldier drank of our good cook's tea, many a wounded one, too, and when they were satisfied he gave to the men still fighting. I believe that those who...were in the fighting, will never be able to pass Andy Graham without grasping his hand – no need to say anything – I know I can't.[13]

For almost two hours, Australian and Turk counterattacked, blowing each other apart in a bombing fight – neither side was willing to give an inch. Brigadier General Ewen Sinclair-MacLagan, commander of the 3rd Brigade, had been informed by Lieutenant Colonel Lyon Johnston, commander of the 11th Battalion, that the Turks could not be dislodged from the trench's southern section. The brigadier left his headquarters to take a look from Tasmania Post. Nothing for it, he decided, ordering a counterattack to be launched immediately in broad daylight directly from Tasmania Post – this length of trench had to be retaken. He ordered 21-year-old law clerk Sergeant Tom Louch to collect a party to counterattack the Turks. Just then a shell exploded, seriously wounding Louch in the arm. Louch later wrote: 'It penetrated my right arm near the shoulder, damaging the median and ulna nerves. There was intense pain in my hands and fingers, and I was bleeding like a pig.'[14] Men of the 3rd Field Ambulance were nearby and managed to stop the bleeding and soon had him on his way down to the beach. Even though it would have been a painful wound, he was lucky, as it stopped him from going over the top – which probably saved his life.

Two parties of about twenty-five men each were now organised by lieutenants Charlton Prockter and John Franklyn. Sinclair-MacLagan ordered Prockter's party to charge across the bullet- and shrapnel-swept space of no-man's-land between Tasmania Post and the southern part of Leane's Trench, while Franklyn's men were to stand ready to support the attack.[15] Twenty-four-year-old Prockter, a sheep station manager, must have known that their chances of making it alive to the trench, let alone taking it, were about zero: the Turks along the southern edge of Lone Pine, and those along Sniper's Ridge, looked down on them and had a clear view of the 'paddock' that they were to charge across. Turkish machine-gun enfilade from the southern edge of the Pine, already raking the space, would surely cut them to pieces. Even so, the men lined up along the firing step and waited for the young lieutenant's command. They had about fifty metres to cover, in the bright morning sunlight.

'Now!' shouted Prockter. He and his men scrambled out of the forward trench into no-man's-land. No sooner had they gone over the top than the expected maelstrom of machine-gun and rifle fire tore into their bodies, and they crumbled and fell. A few somehow made it across the space, but most of these overshot the southern part of the trench because of the smoke, dust and confusion, and found themselves in the Valley of Despair – a gully still full of Turks whose bloodlust was up. None of these Australians survived. Only a few wounded managed to reach the trench, still full of Turks, and flung themselves behind the parados at its rear. Charlton Prockter himself almost made it there when a shell exploded 'right alongside him', shattering his left leg close to the trunk and blowing out half his side.[16] Two new reinforcements, 27-year-old Private Ben Johns and 25-year-old Private John Morrison, were seen 'coolly rising and firing rapidly into the trench or the gully and then sheltered again'.[17] Another private, 23-year-old David Roper, was near them, firing in a kneeling position. Sinclair-MacLagan later expressed his admiration for these young citizen soldiers.

Privates Johns and Morrison: On the morning of 6 August, 1915, these men, together with Private Roper, were the only ones of…Prockter's party not killed or wounded in the first assault on the portion of Leane's Trench captured by the enemy. I personally saw them firing rapidly and steadily at the Turks in and behind the works…Each time they fired they had to stand up and expose themselves to a hail of bullets when they might have laid behind the parados in comparative safety. Their action was cool and gallant to a degree…Private Roper…was with the two men mentioned above, but…in the open in a kneeling position [gave] the reinforce signal.

Seeing that all comrades of the assaulting party were killed or wounded, he eventually ran back over the fire-swept ground to explain the situation and was seriously wounded... The coolness and gallantry of these three under particularly severely trying circumstances and very accurate and heavy fire deserves special recognition.[18]

Having observed the slaughter, Sinclair-MacLagan now turned un-hesitatingly to nineteen-year-old draper Lieutenant John Franklyn, ordering him and his small party to re-enact the charge just shat-tered. With this party was Private Albert Facey, who wrote many years later: 'I had seen some hot spots during the campaign but this was terrible. The little strip of land that we had to cross was being swept by machine guns and fire from all angles.'[19] Surely with a combination of fear and adrenaline, from the realisation of what had just happened to Prockter's party, Franklyn and his men climbed out of the trench, and were also quickly cut down. Albert Facey recalled that all of those to his left were killed. An exploding shell mortally wounded Franklyn as he made for the parados of Leane's Trench. Those who reached it stood for a moment, firing down into the crowded bay, then the survivors of both Prockter and Franklyn's parties jumped into the trench. At the same time, the Australians in the centre of Leane's charged over the barricade that had been separating them from the Turks, who were no longer free to bomb them with an avalanche of grenades. Using the bayonet, these Australians stormed in and got stuck into the enemy. No quarter was expected and none was given. After much blood and sweat was spilled, the southern end of Leane's Trench was back in Australian hands. The bodies of the new recruits, Johns and Morrison, were later found amongst the Australian and Turkish dead. Facey later recalled: 'Somehow we recaptured the trench and sand-bagged up the tunnel, blocking in some Turks. They had hand-grenades and had been using them to keep us out. We had grenades ourselves but we had to use these to stop the Turks from climbing up into the trench again as they had done to retake it earlier.'[20]

Twenty-one-year-old Albert Facey was now ordered to get a message back to his commanding officer at Tasmania Post concerning the Turks still in the communication tunnel. The trench was too crowded to make any headway via the central and northern tunnels, so Facey raced across no-man's-land in broad daylight, but was forced to jump into a large shell hole for cover. Spying another crater about ten metres to his left, he jumped up and made a run for it, diving in safely. From here he spotted another about ten metres in front and to his right. Just as he was getting ready to make another dash, a shell landed nearby and the 'whole world seemed to explode. I hadn't moved from cover yet – the hole I was in saved my life... The dust, smoke and earth that showered into the air when it exploded gave me ample cover to run straight into our original firing-line.'[21]

Earlier, before the trench had been retaken, Lieutenant Colonel Johnston had ordered Smithy and the other Australians who had been holding the Turks at bay in the southern tunnel to retire to Tasmania Post. On reaching the main Australian line, they were directed to block the tunnel entrance with sandbags. Johnston later recorded how Smithy fired at the enemy as he 'coolly and courageously kept at least six Turks at bay and erected a barricade keeping them at bay for some time until the tunnel was recaptured... His conduct was cool and gallant throughout.'[22] Smithy organised four men to throw sandbags into the tunnel entrance as he kept them covered. Just as the barricade was near completion, they heard the Turks within yelling. '[A] white rag tied to the end of a bayonet appeared,' remembered Facey, '[and] with that we removed the sand-bags that we had used to block the tunnel and eight Turks came out, one by one. We took their rifles and felt for concealed weapons, then they were put under guard. Several men loaded with grenades were sent along the tunnel to our mates in the [re]captured trench.'[23]

The Turkish prisoners were soon on their way under guard to ANZAC headquarters, close to the beach. Facey later described how the guard detail had been organised with an Australian in the lead, then a Turk, another Australian, then another Turk, and so on, with a corporal at the rear. After passing through the front and secondary trenches, they were approaching headquarters when the Turkish artillery along Third Ridge opened fire with shrapnel. One of these shells suddenly exploded just above this party, killing the first, second and third Turk and badly wounding the fourth. Not one of the Australians in between them was touched, which for Facey was 'one of the miracles of the Gallipoli Campaign'.[24]

The battle, however, was not over yet, as a number of Turks were still positioned in the Valley of Despair, throwing grenades into Leane's Trench, which was now packed with Australian reinforcements. But these Turks were in an extremely precarious position, as the Australians of the 10th Infantry Battalion just north of their position along Silt Spur completely enfiladed the valley, joined by the ANZAC artillery. Only those Turks who had managed to make it into the former communication trenches – now open graves – had any protection from the inferno of ordnance sweeping the valley, which was certainly living up to its name. Nonetheless, even these Turks were soon being picked off one-by-one, as privates Daniel Cocking and Patrick Moran used the loopholes that enabled aimed fire to be brought to bear into what had become death pits. When Turks tried to break off in twos or threes back towards their own lines, the Australians noticed that Turkish machine-gun fire cut them down.[25] Lieutenant Colonel Rushdi Bey was clearly a man of his word.

Within an hour the Australians started to hear the Turks digging beneath Leane's Trench. The men became concerned that the Turks were trying to drive a short mine beneath their position. In reality they were probably trying to dig into the valley wall in the hope of gaining some protection from the lead-swept gully. Indeed, Lieutenant Colonel Leonard Long, commanding officer of the 4th Australian Light Horse, recorded from his position at Ryrie's Post, just south of Leane's, how one of their machine guns 'put some effective fire into the enemy when they were in Leane's Post, and also when they were in their own trenches'.[26]

For over half an hour, the Australians tried to dislodge the Turks by dropping jam-tin bombs into the gully just beyond their front line – but the subterranean digging continued. The jam-tin bombs exploded 'harmlessly' in the valley floor away from the Turks, who had seemingly dug themselves into some cover, and the Australians' small supply of bombs ran dry. Major Henry Clogstoun, of the 3rd Field Company of Engineers, was asked to come over and offer some advice on how to deal with these troublesome Turks. He tried to discover what they were up to by rather foolishly looking over the parapet, and at once was shot through the neck.[27]

On hearing that the Turks were up to something, Brigadier General Sinclair-MacLagan crossed over to Leane's Trench himself using a communication tunnel. Captain Aarons, while wounded, was still in command and recalled the conversation he had with the brigadier:

'How [are] things...going' and I said 'I think they, the Turks, are going to rush the trench. Every time I lift up a periscope...I can see them gathering and before I see much they shoot the periscope out of my hand. I have had six shot that way now and I haven't another periscope in the trench.' 'Alright Boyd' said the general, 'I hope they do come.' I said 'I have only five yards of fire sir'. The general said 'I know – I hope they do come – throw some gun cotton.' Peck said 'Alright Aarons, I'll send you some periscopes.' 'Come on Peck let's get out of here' said the general.[28]

Sappers were brought over to Leane's with a couple of slabs of the high-explosive guncotton, which was fashioned into an improvised explosive device and rolled over the parapet into the valley below. All the Australians made sure they were well below the sandbag parapet and within a matter of seconds a large explosion erupted in the valley – with this, the digging stopped.[29] Dirt, dust and bits and pieces of the odd Turk fell into the trench; a strong smell of the explosive hung in the air.

As the sappers had been preparing their charges of guncotton, an increased crescendo of fire raked the slopes between Tasmania Post and Leane's Trench, signifying to all that another pointless charge had been initiated. Johnston had, unfortunately for all involved, devised his own plan for dealing with these same Turks – yet again, an unimaginative and suicidal charge from Tasmania Post into the valley itself. This was to be undertaken by twenty-five men under the command of 24-year-old bank clerk Lieutenant Sydney Hall. They would attack from the north through the distinct stubbled ground known as the Wheatfield. Hall and his men charged across the paddock with Turkish rifle, machine-gun and artillery fire pouring into them. Again, the Turks were primed and waiting. Hall was hit and flung headlong into the Valley of Despair and a dozen of his men followed him down into the gully. They didn't have a chance – their bodies were never recovered. It was a brave but futile fight, although they had forced some of the Turks in the gully to flee into their own machine-gun fire. Morris recalled: 'Lieutenant Hall, from what I can hear, was last seen standing over the bodies of two of his men who were wounded. His revolver was then going strong.'[30] Only three wounded men of this party survived the charge, by missing the gully and somehow managing to make their way into the northern part of Leane's Trench.

The battle ended at around 10.30 a.m. The few surviving Turks knew it was futile to persist and made their way as best they could to their own firing lines, trying to avoid both Australian and Turkish machine-gun fire. Some fifty-five Australians had been killed and over a hundred wounded. Turkish casualties were thought to be similar: in reality, they were probably significantly higher, as at least forty of their dead lay in open view – most would have been lying within the gully floor, out of sight.[31]

About half an hour after Hall's charge, one of the men in Leane's Trench was looking through a periscope and noticed an Australian slowly and obviously painfully trying to get up. Medical orderly Private Bertram Winzar, of the 11th Battalion, without hesitation shed all his equipment excepting his first aid bag and crept out into no-man's-land. He managed to provide some rudimentary first aid amongst bursting shrapnel shells. All around him the shrapnel was shredding the remaining vegetation as well as the bodies of the dead Turks and Australians scattered on the valley floor. Winzar was lucky, escaping any serious injury. He tied a rope around the waist of the wounded soldier and crawled, dragging his wounded cobber back into Leane's Trench. Winzar received no official recognition for this brave, selfless act, and would perform similar feats while serving on the Western Front.[32]

Leane's Trench, or what was left of it, was a complete shambles. Parapets had been smashed and blown in, and dirt and gravel filled the trench. Dead bodies and wounded lay everywhere and the stretcher-bearers were busy, with the troops, where possible, helping to remove the wounded and dead. Turkish high-explosive and shrapnel shells continued to burst in, around and over the trench, and the surrounding ground was still being swept by rifle and machine-gun fire. A shell exploded right over Lieutenant Morris's head, leaving him dazed. He couldn't recollect much at all during the next few hours, but knew there were mangled remains of his men all round him. He later recalled talking to one of the men: 'I think he had come in with the 6th reinforcements – and we were considering the best means of bolstering up our broken-down parapets, when something burst just above us. I was just deafened for a few seconds, but the other chap had both his legs blown off and the back of his head blown off.'[33]

The dressing station behind the front lines was busy from the results of the Turkish attack. A medical officer and a number of orderlies attended to the men as they came in. The walking wounded were provided with a cup of tea while they were given rudimentary first aid. Most of those on stretchers were sent down the line, given their serious wounds, but those who could be treated at the aid station were taken off the stretchers and placed on canvas sheeting – the stretchers couldn't be spared. There was no remedy for those suffering from shock or a bad case of nerves. They were left to stare into space or quietly mumble to themselves, holding a mug of tea but seldom drinking. Time would see them right – if not, they too would be sent down the line. Even those whose wounds were tended at the aid post were unlikely to fully recover, as infection would soon take hold, leading to what the men called 'the Barcoo Rot'. Sufferers could be seen walking around with gauze saturated in antiseptic solution. It didn't seem to do any good; in fact, it only attracted the damn flies.

Despite the ongoing Turkish barrage, Leane's Trench had to be repaired – not only to be made ready to resist another possible Turkish attack, but also because it was needed to offer supporting fire to the 1st Brigade's attack against Lone Pine that afternoon.[34]

While Birdwood would have been happy to hear that the Turks were focusing their efforts on the southern flank to Anzac, General Walker and the newly promoted Colonel White were gravely concerned on first hearing of the Turkish attack. Was it the sign of an all-out Turkish offensive along their southern sector? Were the

Turks going to beat them to the punch? To their relief, following the Australians' recapture of the trench, the Turks launched no follow-up attacks. It appeared that they had tried and failed to regain their old position and were leaving it at that – stalemate once more. Birdwood, Walker and White of course had other ideas.

8

'...a last handshake'

While the battle for Leane's Trench was finally coming to a close,
the troops of the 1st Brigade, who had been resting in Brown's Dip,
spent much of their time oiling and furbishing their rifles, sharpening bayonets or attending religious ceremonies. That morning,
Captain Mackay made his way to a sniper's position near The Pimple
and took another look across no-man's-land at Lone Pine using a
trench periscope. He recalled that it was 'reasonably flat, rough
country'.[1] Late that morning he remembered how a 'miraculous
cook of ours came up with some quince jam and handed it out to
the men'.[2] Like most others, he wrote a letter home: 'We hear that
Australian mail is hovering around, and I hope to hear from you all
before we go forth to fight... The contemplated work is to be on
a big scale. But I know very little about it, and even if I did, could
not tell you for fear of this letter falling into enemy hands. You will,
however, know plenty before you get this... I hope our move is a
success... As far as we are concerned, today is DER TAG!!'[3] Not
long after concluding this letter, his battalion commanding officer,
Lieutenant Colonel Charles Macnaghten, walked up to him with
a congratulatory handshake, giving him two crowns (one for each

shoulder). Mackay hurriedly scribbled a note to accompany his letter, telling his family that his CO had just promoted him to major, 'which was decent of him... I hope it will not be long before I come back... Look after yourselves till I return... God bless you all.'[4]

Private Donkin, located in Brown's Dip, wrote: 'This is the day of days. Australia is going to do things. Charge! One word enough. Last night Turks fired heavily and attacked the trench taken by the 11th Battalion. They took it back, but our chaps took it again at dawn. Our guns are barking back... [dealing] iron rations to Turkey... the time of the bombardment before the charge is not known.'[5] Private McAnulty recorded in his battered diary of loose papers and envelopes: 'The attack is to take place this evening at 5 p.m. Our instructions are to get our bayonets sharpened and sleep till 4 o'clock.'[6] Some, being so close to the cove, couldn't resist daring a swim – regardless of Beachy Bill's shelling. Those who hadn't already done so sewed on their white calico identification 'badges'. If the patches were lost, there was also a challenge-and-response for identification purposes – 'Walker–Success' had to be met with 'Godley–Success'.[7]

Anglican Chaplain Dean Talbot vividly recalled that morning many years later. While accompanying a party of men carrying provisions to the front line, he had his pockets full of biscuits and 'a pudding in a tin, in one hand, and a bottle of something or other – it wasn't ginger beer – under my tunic, under each arm'.[8] He was soon separated from the party by a Turkish bullet, which grazed him, forcing him to ground. Then all around him Turkish shells began to explode and he crawled the rest of the way, until dropping into a hole that was filled with wounded. He recalled: 'We could scarcely see one another for the smoke of the continually exploding shells.'[9]

Another Chaplain, Ernest Merrington, had just returned from the Greek island of Lemnos, and was touring the lines north of 400 Plateau along Second Ridge. Most troopers of the Australian Light

Horse positioned here would the next morning charge the Turkish entrenchments along the Chessboard, appropriately named, given the complex section of Turkish trenches defending the southern shoulder of The Nek, a saddle that connected Russell's Top to the hill known as Baby 700. The troopers were to storm these trenches in order to support those charging The Nek and Turkish Quinn's, just south of the Chessboard, at the same time. Merrington brought with him as many 'comforts' as he could carry from Lemnos and was happy to have enough to distribute something to every man there. Amongst the most welcome of these presents were envelopes and writing paper. He recalled: 'Many a gallant Anzac trooper was able to write at once to his loved ones in far Australia – and for many it was destined to be the last letter home. Nearly every man said to me "You know we are going over the top tomorrow morning."'[10]

At midday, the company commanders of the 2nd Battalion reported: 'All ready for attack.' Shortly after receiving this report, Lieutenant Colonel Robert Scobie got word from his brigade commander that the attack had been postponed by half an hour to ensure sufficient time for the men to make it to their assembly points.[11] Private William Graham remembered: 'The midday meal was a big one – it might be a long time before we dined again – and after it, with a light breeze tempering this perfect summer day, the men of my company ("D"), 4th Battalion, one-twelfth of the attacking force, all tense and eager, awaited orders.'[12] Within an hour of completing their meal, men from the battalions involved in the attack assembled at numerous 'parade grounds' behind The Pimple, just below the plateau. Officers checked rifles and equipment, called rolls, and issued last-minute instructions.[13] All the men's packs, containing blankets and personal belongings, had been stacked in Brown's Dip – many would remain unclaimed after the battle.[14] Photographs taken of the uncollected packs immediately after the battle remain a haunting image of the desperate struggle for Lone Pine.

It wasn't only those who were assigned to go over the top that were about to face real danger – the sappers had been engaged in their own ongoing war. Private Donkin wrote in his diary: 'Nearly one o'clock and we are off to our little job. But no, the Sgt says remain in our possie till we are sent for. They may have some special jobs for us. One thinks of the old home at times like these.'[15]

By the early afternoon, the dressing stations of the 3rd Field Ambulance had been established just behind Brown's Dip, at the head of Victoria Gully and at Fullerton's Post, halfway along Victoria Gully.[16] Colonel Neville Howse VC was the chief medical officer of the 1st Australian Division. He had been awarded his VC during the Second Boer War for rescuing a wounded soldier in the Orange Free State in 1900. He had grave fears – which would be realised – that the feint at Lone Pine was going to place an enormous strain on the medical units at Anzac. Howse had earlier tried unsuccessfully to order up reinforcements from part of the 1st Field Ambulance on first hearing of the scheduled attack. Birdwood, however, argued that 'adequate arrangements had [already] been made'.[17] So Howse ordered a system of triage to be set up to try and alleviate the chaos that he saw was about to break upon his medical staff. He issued instructions to his medical officers to classify patients as either 'Mudros' (implying that these men would be fit to return to duty after twenty-eight days of recuperation at Mudros, on the island of Lemnos), or 'Bases', for the serious cases, who would be sent to Egypt or Malta. All light or minor cases were to be treated at Anzac. To assist with the expected flood of wounded, five British medical officers were also attached to the casualty clearing station.[18]

At 2 p.m., the attacking infantry marched round to Brown's Dip, the rendezvous point for the attack, before making their way to The Pimple, while the last of the engineers were withdrawing from the short tunnels B26, B27 and B37, now packed with explosives, which led out from the front-line trenches underneath no-man's-land. Within thirty minutes everything was ready and the sappers exploded three mines positioned just short of the Turkish front lines. Major Martyn recalled that the charges for the mines were placed in the three tunnels with about '100 lb. of ammonal being used in each and thoroughly tamped to prevent the explosions damaging the galleries required for the attack'.[19] These mines were not designed to smash the Turkish trenches, but rather to provide some cover for the infantry. No-man's-land was flat and featureless and it was hoped that the craters and resulting debris would break up the surface and provide some cover for the men, who would charge across the field in daylight in three hours' time. However, inevitably, all did not go to plan. While the charges fired successfully and the tamping held firm, it was discovered that fumes from the explosions had filled the tunnels. After removing the sandbags to start work, the men were dragged out overcome by the gas as fast as they went in. It would take at least an hour before the tunnels would be fit to work in.[20]

Walker and White had, the day before, positioned their divisional headquarters at the head of White's Valley, a few hundred metres north of Brown's Dip. Now Brigadier Neville Smyth, commander of the 1st Brigade, set up his headquarters close by. Even though most orders had been issued, White and his staff were still hard at work finalising arrangements.[21] The day before (5 August) an order had arrived from Birdwood emphasising the role of his and Walker's division in the forthcoming battle.

In the event of rapid success of your operation against Plateau 400 before the movement of other columns begins to be felt from the direction of Chunuk Bair, you are to limit your operations to the clearing of Plateau 400 and subsidiary works, and not to press forward across the valley separating Plateau 400 from Gun Ridge [Third Ridge].

You will thus be in a position to cut off the retreat of the enemy from his trenches higher up the valley when driven down by the New Zealand and Aust. Divn [second phase of offensive], and at the same time will be well placed to take immediate advantage of any opportunity of joining hands with the columns from Chunuk Bair when advance down Gun Ridge commences.[22]

From this order it is clear that while the attack against the Pine during the first phase of the offensive was a feint, its capture was intended to play a significant part in capturing Third Ridge when the next phase of the operation commenced.[23]

In Brown's Dip the 1st Battalion also took up their position as the brigade reserve. Companies of men from this battalion now stood around in nervous inactivity, anxiously waiting for the order that would send them into battle. As they stood and chatted, the troops of the three attacking battalions passed by, each battalion taking a separate route to avoid congestion. Soon these men disappeared from sight as the last of them filed up onto 400 Plateau and into The Pimple. It was recalled that the men of the 4th Battalion were apparently keen for the fight, as many took up a call using the slang for 'bugger off': 'It's impshee Turks, now!'[24]

Earlier, as the troops in the attacking force were getting themselves organised, a number of men not assigned to the attack were being ordered by officers and NCOs to clear out if they had no business being there. Some belonged to the 1st Brigade but had been considered too sick to participate and were now trying to sneak back to join their mates in going over the top. Many of these men succeeded, as their NCOs and cobbers turned a blind eye.[25] Birdwood recalled: 'When the troops were forming up, a man came up out of the reserve, seized a man in the firing line, thrust a sovereign into his hand, and said, "You go back there and take my place. My mate is here, and I've got to go with him!" Not quite orthodox discipline, perhaps, but—!'²⁶

This spurt of energy and good humour by the men of the attacking force was momentary and fuelled by ignorance of what lay ahead. Reporter Phillip Schuler was in Brown's Dip and reported a more solemn atmosphere as the men of the attacking force moved up towards The Pimple. Mates from other battalions who realised they were 'for it' dashed out to shake their hands. He wrote that there was a 'warmth about these handgrips that no words can describe. It was the silence that made the scene of the long files of men such an impressive one.'²⁷

The men who had to make their way from The Pimple to the forward firing line, now open and cutting through no-man's-land, were forced to 'worm their way through the tunnels, with seemingly innumerable halts and checks in the darkness, accentuated by the impatient desire to know that they were in position... It was now merely a matter of waiting, and the men stood or squatted quietly by with no apparent signs of nervousness, and thinking those thoughts, never divulged, which come to men about to go over the top.'²⁸

Twenty-two-year-old steelworks smelter from Wollongong, New South Wales, Private Charles Scott, of the 4th Battalion, was with his cobbers in the front-line trench at The Pimple. Scott recalled how the worst thing was being packed in the trenches for an hour and a half while the artillery and naval guns bombarded the Turks' position. He later wrote: 'I can tell you it was no joke waiting to get over to go for your life. It made a chap sort of feel sea sick, as it drew near the time to charge, and to see mates in front with drawn faces having perhaps a last handshake. Every old hand knew that if one out of three got through they would be lucky.'²⁹

The ANZAC artillery began to bombard Lone Pine and its flanks, and the Turks on Third Ridge wasted no time in providing a response with their own batteries. Some of the guns of the navy attempted to provide counter-battery fire. Chaplain 'Fighting

Mac' William McKenzie recorded in his diary: 'The experience of shells walloping our trenches that were full of men was nerve-racking…Many trembled from head to foot.'[30] Not far away, Private Albert Dowse, of the 2nd Battalion, recalled his thoughts while waiting to charge across no-man's-land: 'It is very trying on the nerves when you have to charge a Turk's trench and about four machine guns [are] waiting for you. I have a particular dread of machine guns – they will fairly cut a man in halves if they get properly on him, the bullets come that fast.'[31]

Chaplain McKenzie remembered that as soon as the ANZAC artillery and naval guns opened fire, 'every gun the Turks could command replied and the noise was terrible'.[32] The final and heaviest bombardment started hitting Lone Pine and the surrounding areas at 4.30 p.m., and was to last an hour. Bombardier Arthur Currey was a member of a New Zealand forward observation post. His guns were to smash any remaining barbed wire in front of the Turkish trenches. He saw the effect of Turkish counter-battery fire when a shell 'topped our sandbags, smashed my periscope and knocked it out of my hands. As I stooped to pick it up another shell smashed into our station and blew our walls to pieces . . . two men next to me were knocked out but I still missed injury'.[33] The guns of the British cruiser HMS *Bacchante*, along with other warships just arrived, joined in and fired at the Turkish batteries along Third Ridge. Private Graham recalled: 'For days now the enemy position at Lone Pine had been the subject of attention from our big guns. From our trenches we watch shells bursting on the trenches of the Pine and Johnston's Jolly…saw sandbags and barbed-wire spewed high into the air, and felt just a little sorry for those poor blighters on the receiving end.'[34] Len Barrett was concluding his entry in his diary for that day in one of the front-line trenches, while waiting for the piercing sound of the officer's whistle. As the shelling exploded from both sides, he wrote that he and his mates were 'crouched low and (it sounds incredible) were laughing and cracking jokes'.[35]

Chaplain Merrington wrote that he and most others had never experienced such a barrage on the peninsula before. The Turkish entrenchments were 'very strong and protected by stout-log roofing. Huge lyddite [*sic*] and high-explosive shells dropped and burst upon the whole position, including German Officers' Trench [immediately to the north of the Jolly], and threw out many-coloured fumes and dust. The earth fairly shuddered beneath the hammer blows from the navy, supplemented by our own land batteries.'[36] It seemed to all that no Turk could withstand the destructive power of the bombardment. The lines of Turkish trenches, being partly arranged at right angles to the shore, provided the opportunity for enfilade fire from the sea. Merrington recalled that 'the air was full of sound and fury. The worst faces of the Anzac brightened with pleasure at this solid attack by artillery.'[37] Stretcher-bearer Reynolds, of the 1st Field Ambulance, took out his diary at this time and wrote in his tiny but neat handwriting: 'The incessant crackle of rifle and machine-gun fire commenced and the whole atmosphere in a few minutes seemed to be a regular mad uproar, shells were screaming through the air exploding everywhere with a crash...shrapnel shells began to explode in large numbers lower down the gully over the hundreds of troops sheltering there...casualties were fairly numerous.'[38]

Colonel Talbot Hobbs, commanding officer of the 1st Australian Divisional Artillery, recorded in his diary: 'I will always remember the calm resolute faces of those splendid men of NSW so patiently waiting for the time...determined to succeed. So many of them [going] to their death.'[39] One of his subordinate officers, Lieutenant Colonel George Johnston, of the 2nd Australian Field Artillery Battery, wrote in a letter home:

Some of the Lonesome Pine trenches were within 70 or 100 yards from ours on the 'Pimple'. I was ordered to...prepare the way for our infantry... the scream and bursts of our shells was awful... The Turks seemed to guess that the attack was coming from the 'Pimple' and turned all their guns onto us. My own Brigade was waiting and tried all they know to silence them, but could not succeed... all our telephone wires were quickly cut, and one 8 [-inch] shell landed square on one of the 8th Battery guns, killing or wounding all of the detachment and destroying the gun completely.[40]

In addition, two field guns were run up onto the plateau 100 metres from the Turkish front, where one succeeded in firing a number of rounds directly at the Turkish parapets of the Pine, and the other fired at Johnston's Jolly but was soon put out of action by a direct hit by a Turkish shell from Third Ridge. The Heavy Battery of the Australian Divisional Artillery, consisting of one 4.7-inch gun and two 6-inch howitzers, were able to suppress the Turkish batteries firing from the south of Anzac, but they could not completely destroy them.[41]

Lance Corporal Cyril Lawrence, in Brown's Dip, had his ear to a telephone connected to an Australian battery: 'No. 1 gun fired, Sir. No. 2 gun ready, Sir.' He recalled that every one of the batteries was sending its 'screeching message onto its target field, guns with their roar, howitzers with their mighty rushing sound and mountain battery guns with their bark, a bark too loud for a gun four times their size'.[42] Close by, Private Donkin wrote: 'The Turks are sending in some shells too, now, and I don't feel too safe in our dugout. We got shrapnel in here yesterday – fortunately we were in the sap [digging].'[43] Lawrence wrote that the whole area was defined by exploding shells and the 'whine of flying nose caps and fragments and the noise of empty shell cases travelling everywhere'.[44]

The severity of the artillery barrage on this small patch of the Gallipoli Peninsula was relative, of course. Colonel Neville

Smyth later wrote that the one-hour bombardment, dignified as 'continuous and heavy' in one account, 'after our subsequent experiences on the Western Front...would probably have been described as light shelling'.[45]

This revised assessment is indeed a better reflection of the overall potency of the barrage. Traditionally, artillery support is measured by the ratio of guns per metre, or the number of guns per division (in 1915, ideally thought to be seventy-six).[46] At Anzac, however, they didn't have anything like that number of guns, and there were not enough suitable positions to put these batteries, even if they'd had them. In fact, they only had around 40 per cent of the guns thought necessary, relative to the number of troops involved.[47] Regardless, a more meaningful measure is the number of shells fired, although even this is unreliable, as the guns were notoriously inaccurate, especially the 18-pounder, which was the most common gun in the ANZAC batteries. Indeed, an earlier demonstration in England had shown that just 50 per cent of all 18-pounder shells fired at a range of 2500 metres actually landed within nine metres of its target, with the remainder landing up to forty metres distant. At 4500 metres it was decidedly worse, with the accuracy falling to 50 per cent of shells landing within twenty-three metres of the target, and the remainder up to eighty-two metres away.[48]

The three-day land-based bombardment against Lone Pine (not including the final hour of 'heavy' shelling) turned out to involve a slow rate of fire – the total expenditure of shells by the batteries assigned to cover the 1st Australian Division amounted to the 18-pounder guns firing a total of 211 rounds (only nine of which were high-explosive); the 6-inch howitzers firing seven shells; the 5-inch howitzers firing 157 shells; the sole 4.7-inch howitzer firing thirteen shells; and two Japanese mortars and a few primitive Garland mortars firing a limited number.[49] It must be noted that not all of these shells were fired in support of the attack against

Lone Pine, but also against a number of other targets, including supporting fire for the Australian attack against nearby German Officers' Trench. The naval guns, with their flat trajectory, focused on counter-battery fire against the Turkish guns along Third Ridge and those close to Gaba Tepe. Even if we accepted that all of the land-based artillery fired at Lone Pine alone, which comprised about 40 000 square metres, and that all shells hit their target, this is just one shell for every 103 square metres.

The hour-long 'intensive' bombardment just before the attack amounted to just eight guns focusing on Lone Pine itself, with around double that number shelling the flank and rear positions.[50] Indeed, the total expenditure of artillery shells for the 1st Australian Infantry Division during this one hour of intense shelling amounted to the 18-pounders firing eleven high-explosive shells and 224 shrapnel shells; the 6-inch howitzers eight shells; the 5-inch howitzers 104 shells; and the 4.7-inch howitzer two shells.[51] That is one shell for every 115 square metres. If we refine this further and restrict the bombardment to just the first three trench lines, with an estimated area of 12 500 square metres, it is still only one shell for every thirty-six square metres. A year later on the Western Front, using the same crude statistic, we get one field artillery shell for every 1.9 square metres at Fromelles (approximately 400 000 square metres and 215 000 shells), and it was hardly a success story. While the men at Anzac were impressed with the barrage, these were troops used to just one or two guns firing a couple of shells at a time before falling into silence. By comparison, the bombardment against Lone Pine and nearby positions did appear impressive. However, in reality, the three-day bombardment and final hour of 'intensive' shelling against Lone Pine was ineffectual, especially considering that the bulk of these shells were shrapnel, which, while relatively effective against the enemy wire, would have no negative impact on the covered Turkish works and troops sheltering inside them.

Turkish Captain Ahmet Zeki Bey, commander of the 1st Battalion, 57th Regiment, had been defending Merkez Tepe (German Officers' Trench) for the previous forty-five days, when at the start of the final bombardment of Lone Pine he and his men were finally relieved. After the war, the then Major Zeki Bey would accompany Charles Bean to Anzac, providing details of the Turkish experience. Indeed, he and his men had been among the first to confront the Australian advance towards Chunuk Bair during the morning of 25 April 1915. Bean described Zeki Bey in 1919 as being in his late twenties, with a well-clipped 'slight' (as in small) moustache, 'deep brown eyes and a quick smile...smartly but quietly uniformed...of perhaps slightly under average height', whose 'very quiet voice and reserved manner closely matched his appearance'.[52]

At Merkez Tepe that afternoon, Zeki Bey mistakenly believed that he and his men were about to get some much-needed rest out of the line. Instead, as the only reserves at hand, they would soon be thrown into Lone Pine, fighting for their lives.

Just before leaving the trench with his exhausted survivors, a high-explosive shell had struck one of his positions. He later recalled: 'There was a head cover blown in, and the men lying smashed up and dead. I was very frightened.'[53] He made his way down into the valley, where a refreshing breeze greeted him, momentarily removing the stench of the dead from no-man's-land that he had been forced to endure in the trench along the ridgeline. He made his way to his regimental headquarters, from where he could see 'large and small shells were concentrating on Kanli Sirt [Lone Pine]...My battalion had just come out and was at the moment assembled behind Edirna Sirt [Mortar Ridge, a spur running off Baby 700 into the valley behind Second Ridge], and I ordered the officer-in-charge at once to be ready to reinforce, as they were the nearest reinforcements to Kanli Sirt. From the regimental headquarters at the back of Edirna Sirt you could see

clearly. There was a lot of dust raised by the shells at Kanli Sirt.
I could not see through it.'[54]

In the front-line trench at The Pimple, 29-year-old professional
soldier Major Dennis King, of the 1st Brigade Headquarters staff,
had taken up his position at the opening of the main tunnel leading to the newly exposed front firing line. In one hand he held his
whistle, in the other his watch. He kept the men of the first attacking wave moving into the dark tunnels, lit only by the makeshift
oil candles, in an orderly fashion. At the other end of the tunnel,
at the T-intersection beneath no-man's-land, was Major David
McConaghy, of the 3rd Battalion, also with a whistle. He directed
the men left and right to their assigned places, according to which
battalion they belonged to, signified by their rectangular coloured
shoulder patches: purple over green for the men of the 2nd, brown
over green for those of the 3rd and white over green for the men
of the 4th.

As the Australians took up their positions, most of the
battalion commanders were concerned whether their men,
sick with diarrhoea and strained with lack of sleep and heavy
work, could sustain the prolonged fighting about to commence.
Birdwood himself, rather belatedly, was having concerns about
the men's ability to cope. Days earlier, he was touring the front
lines before the men were aware of the intended offensive when
an ANZAC stated to him with determination: 'No Turk is going
to get past here – I'll see to that. But if you ask me to march a
couple of miles after him, I just couldn't do it.'[55] Birdwood later
recalled with some relief: 'Our greatest anxiety was whether men,
weak from dysentery and strain of many months' heavy fighting,
could answer the enormous calls now to be made of them. We
might have spared ourselves the doubt. Far from shrinking
from the ordeal before them, these great-hearted men seemed

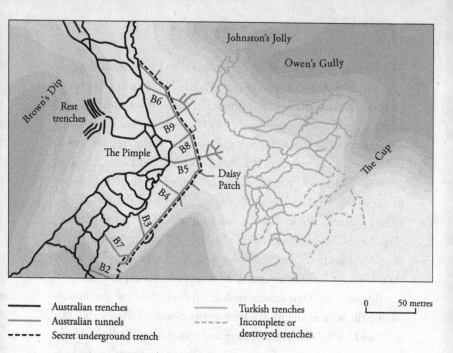

Lone Pine works before the battle

revitalised by the mere prospect of a hard fight.'[56]

Indeed, most officers noticed that as their men entered the trenches, there was a certain amount of excitement that had put new vitality into them. As they waited in the crowded bays, there was not the 'least sign of nervousness in face, speech, or action... Some belated messenger hurried along the trench to find his platoon, and, in passing, recognised a friend. "*Au revoir*, Bill," he nodded. "Meet you over there." "So long, Tom", was the answer. "See you again in half an hour."[57] Now Colonel Smyth turned to one of his officers – it was 5.06 pm: "Inform Division that all battalions are in position, ready."[58]

The shelling from both sides continued as the men readied themselves for the charge across no-man's-land. The trenches shook and shuddered with the bombardment. In the former underground secret trench – now open to the sky – engineers had constructed a number of recesses to form a rudimentary firing step, as well as to help reduce congestion. Private James Holt and Lance Corporal Charlie Allerdice, of the 4th Battalion, were now sheltering in one of these recesses. As the shells exploded around them, Charlie, recalled James, would 'bob his head up' to check on the damage: 'I spoke to Charlie about sticking his head up, and he turned round to me and said, "I'll bet you I'm over at the Turks' trenches before you, anyway."'[59] The two made the wager and shook hands.

Around 600 men tensely looked up from the new trench now slicing through no-man's-land, watching clouds of smoke and dust overhead, as the shelling continued. If others like Charlie had been keen enough – or stupid enough – to raise their heads out to have a peek towards Lone Pine, they'd have seen plumes of dirt and, in a few rare cases, large timbers tumbling into the air, as the ANZAC artillery hit the Turkish line. Turning back, they'd have seen The Pimple, similarly enduring the Turkish counter bombardment. Their part of no-man's-land appeared relatively safe in comparison – they were in the eye of a hurricane. They knew that as soon as the ANZAC bombardment lifted, the officers would blow their whistles and they would charge across fifty to seventy-five metres of open paddock to the Turkish trenches. Troops near their officers no doubt watched them intensely, waiting for any sign of them raising their whistles towards their lips.

As they waited, men shared a smoke and talked, reassuring each other that no Turk could survive the bombardment many believed was tearing Lone Pine apart. Some remained silent in their own private thoughts, just wishing that the waiting would end. One man was heard to ask, 'Can you find room for me beside Jim, here? Him and me are mates an we're going over together.'[60]

Minutes before the whistles blew, Charles Bean had made his way into the heart of The Pimple and recorded in his diary:

> As [I] went along [the] trench, heard an officer telling men, 'Look out for enemy wire' etc., giving last hints. About 5.25 as I reached convenient point in trench S[outh]. of Brown's Dip, after having tried a good many, I arrived at recess near no. 9 [sic] [5] Tunnel. It was crowded with 3rd Bn. Men were chaffing one another – seemed to be quite eager to go out and do something. About five were on the fire step – a little officer crouched in corner [Captain Donald Moore] – and about five or six in trench below. I saw not the slightest trace of nervousness...Presently order came: pull down top bags in recess – so as to make it easier to get over. Whole trench looked suspiciously ragged.[61]

'Five twenty-seven, get ready to go over the parapet,' said Captain Moore, still crouching in the corner of the firing step, staring at his watch through the dust settling around them from the ongoing Turkish shelling. Even above the sound of fire, men could be heard coughing and spitting out wads of irritating dust from their throats. Stretcher-bearers were busy trying to extricate the wounded from the front lines, but given that zero hour was only minutes away, it was crucial that they keep the trenches clear – the pending charge now had priority over the wounded from the Turkish bombardment.

Private Cecil McAnulty of the same battalion was finishing his latest diary entry on a scrap of paper he had managed to scavenge: 'Their artillery are replying now and shells are beginning to rain on us. They are getting the range now, shelling the support trenches. Men are beginning to drop. Howitzer shells are dropping about 30 yards from us, digging great holes where they land. The fumes are suffocating, the shrapnel is pouring all round us getting chaps everywhere. This is hell waiting here...Word given to get ready to charge, must finish, hope to get through alright.'[62]

Lieutenant Wren recalled his commanding officer, 40-year-old professional soldier Lieutenant Colonel Ernest Brown, of the 3rd Battalion, keeping up the men's spirits as he moved rapidly along the line of those crouched behind their sandbag parapet, giving an order here, a little friendly advice there. He paid particular attention to the newly arrived reinforcements with words of encouragement. Brown was a practical leader and loved by his men. Bean had earlier recorded in his diary that when Brown received untrained reinforcements he didn't complain, but merely said, 'Can't shoot, my lad? Well, come along to this loophole and I'll teach you.'[63] Brown had confided to a friend that morning that 'he had a feeling that it would be his last fight'.[64] Wren was standing with Colonel Brown, medical officer John Bean, his brother Charles and a number of officers, and remembered the colonel laughing and saying: '"There won't be a chat alive over there"; throughout the whole bombardment, he kept us amused. I can see vividly that almost cynical little smile of his when he said, "Now Bean – tell us a funny story."'[65] Private Scott was still trying to get over his feeling of seasickness. He later recorded how the men were concerned about showing fear to those either side of them. His officer told them that they were wedged on the firing platform: '"You men are too crowded there. Some of you get in the trench." None of them moved. Nobody would be the first to get down. It meant a lot being down in the trench, because the first over were surely to get it in the neck, because the Turks knew we were coming – the bombardment told them that much.'[66]

Lieutenant Charles Lecky was close by with his friend Lieutenant William Cradick. Both were anxiously awaiting the order to go over the top – as young lieutenants, they would lead their men out. Charles recalled William telling him to 'fix a certain sandbag in the enemy's parapet, make a bee-line for it and run my hardest when the whistle went. Poor old Cradick was killed as we clambered over the top when the whistle blew.'[67]

As the last minute ticked down, Charles Bean recorded: 'Officer took [a] whistle from wrist "prepare to jump out" he said. Put whistle between his teeth...presently he blew whistle...'[68] At precisely 5.30 p.m., the ANZAC bombardment lifted and three blasts from the whistle of Major King could be heard all along the line, announcing the attack. Within seconds, the whistles of the other officers took their cue from King. Further north along Second Ridge, Chaplain Merrington wrote: 'After a moment's pause, every Turkish gunner and machine gun answered, and the enemy shells begun to burst all around our neighbouring posts.'[69] Even among the racket of artillery and gunfire all along the ANZAC perimeter, the high pitch of the whistles from The Pimple, and the newly opened trench in front of it in no-man's-land, could be heard.

'I glanced upwards to see nothing but a sheet of fire'

With a loud chorus of cheers that could be heard above the sound of exploding Turkish shells, three waves of 600 men each, in a scatter of falling sandbags and earth, scrambled from the Australian trenches into no-man's-land. Shells came shrieking – one decapitating a bugler, whose headless body ran on for several yards before it dropped.[1] Red flashes from a thousand rifle barrels erupted. Lieutenant Eric Wren of the 3rd Battalion described the horrific scene: 'Khaki figures that were not moving. Men lying huddled together as if awaiting another signal to move forward. Yes, some were moving – twitching. Others – crawling away – or trying to – maimed – dying. All were perfectly still – a spent wave of dead men. But there were others – they ran – they stumbled – always going forward.'[2] Newly recruited sapper of the 1st Infantry Battalion, Private Donkin, wrote in his diary: 'Our lads charged . . . and from the word "Go!" our lads fell thickly.'[3] Major Martyn recalled that immediately after the men left the trenches, the Turks' rifle, machine gun, and artillery let rip like the sudden opening of a 'terrific hailstorm'.[4] The sound was terrific, and the ground between the two lines of trenches became 'a perfect inferno' of zipping 'bullets and crashing shells, the shrapnel hitting the roofs of the tunnels like hail. The enemy's fire opened so quickly that many men fell back killed or wounded into the trenches they had just left . . . the landscape was soon dotted with prostrate forms, the white armband and patch on the back showing clearly where our gallant lads had fallen to rise no more'.[5]

The 4th Battalion's objective was to capture the northern part of Lone Pine. The newly promoted Major Iven Mackay remembered: 'I had a sandbag step all ready for getting out of our trench, but when the signal was given and I stood on it, it promptly toppled down. I had to throw my rifle over and then vault out . . . expecting every moment to stop one.'[6] Private Charles Duke recalled the first person he saw while charging across no-man's-land was his commanding officer, Lieutenant Colonel Charles Macnaghten, who was blowing his whistle and going for his life just ahead of him. His recollection of the seventy-metre dash to the Turkish trenches remained vivid. The outstanding impression was 'the extraordinary row and noise of the heavy rifle fire that instantly broke out. Indeed, the crackling of the bullets was so thick that it seemed as though one was rushing over brittle twigs.'[7]

Macnaghten and his men crossed the Daisy Patch and presented an excellent field of fire for the Turks, especially for the artillery on Third Ridge, who could clearly see the waves of Australians charging across the area, which was bare of the thick low scrub that covered its flanks.[8] To make matters worse, these men were under complete enfilade from Turks entrenched at Johnston's Jolly to their left, across Owen's Gully. Private Edwin Rider and his mates were 'running like footballers. About half way across I was caught in a barbed-wire trap . . . It was an act of providence for me, as it enabled me to get my bearings. Just in front of me were hundreds of our boys trying to shift the timber, which was on top of the Turks' trenches for overhead cover.'[9] When the whistle had blown, somebody had given Private Charles Scott a leg up and he'd scrambled over the parapet and sprinted across no-man's-land to the second line of Turkish trenches. Within minutes his fellows calmly accounted for the Turks there: 'Nobody near me seemed the least excited. They were standing up over the Turks pumping lead into the trenches as cool as if they were shooting rabbits.'[10]

A few seconds after going over the top, Private James Holt, who had made the bet with Charlie Allerdice, had lost sight of his mate during the charge. It wasn't until approaching the first Turkish trench that he looked down, and there was Charlie. Allerdice had kept his 'word and won the bet, but in doing so had lost his life. It was only a few yards further that I was wounded myself, but managed to get into the trench.'[11] There, James came across a 30-year-old member of his section, Private 'Fred' Catto. Fred's rifle had been completely smashed and on seeing his wounded cobber he began to bandage James's wound. James was still there at 8 a.m., the next morning. He later lamented: 'Poor Fred Catto was killed next morning; so you see, the last man I spoke to before the charge, and the first man I met after I'd got through the charge, were both killed.'[12] Lance Corporal Charlie Allerdice is today buried at the Lone Pine Cemetery, while Private Fred Catto has no known grave and is commemorated on the Lone Pine Memorial.

The 3rd Battalion was to capture the centre of the Pine. They too faced enfilade from the Turks entrenched at Johnston's Jolly. The centre of the Turkish firing line at Lone Pine, however, was set back from both strong flanking strongholds, allowing enfilade fire to be brought to bear on the attackers as they swept past towards the centre of the line. This part of the position wasn't as heavily entrenched as the flanks and for a length of around fifty metres the front-line trench was open with no head cover. Twenty-one-year-old Lieutenant Athol Burrett was leading a platoon and, as he climbed out to no-man's-land, his commanding officer, Lieutenant Colonel Brown, gave him a push. Still smiling, Brown said: '"Go on, give it to them". It was the last time I saw that exceptionally gallant and brilliant officer alive.'[13] Burrett scrambled, using hands and knees to get out of the deep trench, and was then running so hard for the front line that he thought his heart must burst. He wrote: 'Here – there – men staggered, crumpled, pitched forward, sagged sideways. Men shouted, men laughed. Men groaned ... The slaughter commenced from the second we emerged from our trenches. Machine-gun and rifle fire came from the direct front and enfilade fire from both flanks. Men fell thickly on the way over.'[14]

Not far away would have been 22-year-old railway clerk Lieutenant Ernest Litchfield: 'On repeating the whistle blast, I got out and tore like hell over to the Turkish trench, passing some No. 9 men coming out of the holes in the ground [secret trench], they seemed to go down under my feet.'[15] Twenty-nine-year-old Lieutenant Percy Woods later wrote: 'Our boys replied to a man at the signal given. Over the top they went with a rush of fully 60 yards to the Turks' trenches under machine-gun, shrapnel and rifle fire. Some of the unfortunates were knocked. Blown all over the place. But we [kept] going.'[16] Close by, 21-year-old Temora farmer Private Railton MacDonald was eager: 'I immediately jumped over the parapet without waiting orders ... and calling to my mate "Come on Fergy" I rushed on ... and looking back to see Ferguson was following and also trying to skip over the figure 8's of barbed wire which were strewn about the ground.'[17] Charles Bean, watching from The Pimple, recalled seeing the men of the 3rd Battalion tripping amongst strands of barbed wire. Nineteen-year-old labourer from Dubbo Private John Ison was one who got tangled: 'However, I freed myself after having my legs cut about a bit. By jove, the bullets were whizzing close and it seemed a miracle that I was not hit. I advanced about 10 yards and I was flattened out by a concussion of a shell. I lay for a few minutes with shrapnel flying over me like rain.'[18]

The 2nd Battalion was tasked to capture the southern part of Lone Pine. Major Arthur Stevens was in command of the three attacking waves of this battalion. He'd gone over the top accompanied by the men of his signal section, Sergeant William Wass, Corporal John McElroy and Private Albert Townsend. This southern part of the Turkish works was on a slight elevation, and strongly fortified, like its northern flanks, with sandbags, mud bricks, earthen embankments, thick log head covers and at least one machine-gun post. The Australians were open to oblique fire from the south, from the Turks along the upper parts of Pine Ridge and Sniper's Ridge. Corporal Joseph Neal recalled: 'I glanced upwards to see nothing but a sheet of fire or smoke caused by bursting shells of all sorts and machine-gun fire. The next moment I felt a bump and my rifle fell to pieces in my hand.'[19]

Major Stevens and his men charged and stumbled across no-man's-land, the signallers reeling out telephone wire behind them. After finally making it to the Turkish front line they found that the wire had been cut by shelling. Wass had been wounded in the head while crossing the paddock and it was up to McElroy and Townsend to run back across the bullet-swept inferno and repair the line. They did this no less than three times in a matter of hours.[20] Following closely behind Stevens was 36-year-old Sergeant Douglas, who ordered his men to heave at the trenches' overhead timbers.[21] The battalion history records how '[Private Len] Barrett, though wounded, covered this party by firing through crevices at the Turks below. Douglas and others finally succeeded in making openings, and he jumped through one. Immediately he saw that two of his men who had preceded him through another opening had been shot. [Private Stephen] Friel bayoneted a Turk.'[22] Douglas got all his surviving men into the trench and led them away to the right. Meanwhile, others were coming up behind them across no-man's-land, and many of them 'stumbled and fell; some had been hit, others who had merely tripped scrambled up and went on'.[23] Even though wounded in the leg by shrapnel, Private Barrett remained in the thick of the fighting, later writing how the losses on both sides were heavy in the initial assault as well as in the resulting hand-to-hand combat.[24]

Uralla telegraphist Private William Bendrey, twenty-three years old, recalled: 'Talk about shrapnel, it sounded for all the world like blanky hail...the bush...[around] the daisy patch [largely defining no-man's-land] caught alight and showed us up beautifully to the Turkish machine-gunners...The fire was simply hellish, shell rifle and machine-gun fire and i'm hanged if I know how we got across the daisy patch. Every bush seemed to be literally ripped with bullets...our luck was right in.'[25]

Meanwhile, Lieutenant Lecky had taken the advice of his friend and run for one of the black sandbags in the Turkish line. He couldn't remember hearing a sound, although the Turkish machine guns and rifles were firing continuously. Neither could he recall having seen anything except the line of sandbags he was focused on, before he crashed into a crater about halfway across. It was there he came across Captain John Pain, of the brigade machine guns, unable to clamber out after being shot in the arm. When Lecky found himself struggling under the weight of his pack, Pain managed to push Lecky back up with his good arm. Lecky pulled Pain out of the hole and they both reached the Turkish line. According to Lecky, many of the men were 'firing through the logs [loopholes] with which the front line was covered. I called to them to jump into a communication trench which I saw, and jumped in myself.'[26]

Each survivor of the 1st Brigade's charge had his own very personal and vivid recollection, but those behind the front lines had a panoramic view of the surge across no-man's-land to Lone Pine.

Chaplain Merrington, positioned on Second Ridge, remembered a man beside him calling out, 'There are the Australians!' Five hundred metres away from where he stood, Merrington could see the advancing line, as the men in 'slouch hats, with white armlets and patches rushed forward in magnificent style. In the true infantry manner they came on in sprints falling flat on the ground at intervals.'[27] He recalled the charge as being a grand, awful, thrilling sight. His eyes were drawn to the rear of the line, where the dead and wounded lay exposed to ongoing fire, and stretcher-bearers and orderlies were busy at work trying to bring them in.[28] He could see Australians on the Turkish parapets 'bayoneting downwards and jumping into the trench. Others have crossed over the first line, and are making for the second and even the third line of this labyrinth. They are keeping together well, and fighting with invincible stamina.'[29] He especially recalled those trying to break into the covered first- and second-line trenches: 'Can the roof be still unbroken after that terrific bombardment from the sea? And the answer must be in the affirmative. The plateau is about 500 [sic] feet above sea level, and the flat trajectory of the naval guns does not permit their shells dropping down onto level and sunken defences. They burst on the surface and in the air.'[30]

Indeed, Lieutenant John Byrne of the New Zealand Field Artillery, based on the ridge to the north known as Russell's Top, recalled that while many Turks in the rear of the position had been either killed or wounded during the bombardment, the result was 'so inconsiderable as to be of little use to the infantry. After crossing no-man's-land in face of a storm of rifle and machine-gun fire they found the overhead cover practically intact, and the weighty beams defied all individual efforts to remove them. Then came a pause while groups of men bodily lifted the beams and then flung themselves in among the Turks.'[31] Most, however, didn't stop but headed further to the rear of the Turkish works to the open trenches beyond.

Not far from Chaplain Merrington, machine-gun officer Lieutenant Charlie Traill, of the 8th Battalion, was offering covering fire from Courtney's Post, at the centre of the ANZAC line on Second Ridge. He remembered how the men of the 1st Brigade were mown down like 'chaff going across No Man's Land, but when parties got down into the trenches, they went through the Turks like ferrets down a rabbit burrow. There would be parties of Turks that would get trapped and they'd leap out and try to run back to their reserve trenches across open ground. Then it was our turn... It was like potting bunnies in a rabbit plague. I don't think I missed too often.'[32]

Just south of Traill were the men of Pompey Elliott's 7th Battalion, opposite Johnston's Jolly. They too opened up with a fusillade of machine-gun and rifle fire against the Turkish parapets, to help suppress the enemy's fire from the Jolly. Elliott had taken up a position in the front line and watched the attack through a trench periscope. If it failed, he and his men would soon be called upon to charge Johnston's Jolly itself. Elliott wrote to his wife Kate a few days later: 'The Turks had a strong position in front of our line and the First Brigade of NSW men's charge was magnificent and [they] took it. The charge will live forever in history.'[33] South of Lone Pine, along Bolton's Ridge, the troopers of the 7th Light Horse Regiment, and the numerous infantry battalions in the vicinity, including the men of the 11th Battalion at Leane's Trench, also fired into the southern part of Lone Pine.[34]

At The Pimple, Charles Bean observed aspects of the hand-to-hand fighting that was now taking place in Lone Pine. He saw men 'crowded under the parapet of T's [Turkish] trench. Some bayonets in trench... many men started to hop into enemy's trench. Seemed busy over something – thought I saw rifle butts come up.'[35] Close to Bean would have been Major Carl Jess of the 2nd Brigade staff, who wrote: 'Our first line dashed over the front line of enemy trench while the second line engaged [the] front trench, third line reinforcing. Overhead cover was very little hurt so that men were hopping about on top trying to pull the logs off to get into the Turks . . . the whole under shrapnel and rifle fire from the north. Once they got in the slaughter was tremendous.'[36] The Turkish artillery was noticed by reporter Phillip Schuler to be lowering their range from The Pimple, with shrapnel increasingly bursting over no-man's-land as reinforcing troops and signallers with their lines of wire were passing through.

Lance Corporal Cyril Lawrence was still located in Brown's Dip listening to the telephone line when the whistles blew: 'The boys had "hopped out". Golly, how my heart thumped and jumped, did anything but what it was intended for. How were they faring?'[37] The telephone lines were quickly down, cut by Turkish shelling. The rifle and machine-gun fire continued but shortly after the initial charge it noticeably slackened. Lawrence wondered: 'Is [it] because our boys are in their trenches and the bayonet is at work? Yes, it must be . . . it's not until later that a messenger comes back and tells how we've got five trenches and are still holding them, and trying to consolidate our gains, that the horrible feeling of uncertainty passes, only to be followed by the equally virtuous thought – can they hold them?'[38] Close by in Brown's Dip, Private Donkin wrote: 'Our lads . . . took 3 or 4 trenches, at great cost. Our boys in the advanced line of trenches were pelted with bombs.'[39] Donkin also knew that with the success of the initial charge, he and the other sappers would be tasked with digging communication saps between The Pimple and Lone Pine. A decidedly unhealthy objective as far as 'lead poisoning' went, he noted drily. Just before heading off, he finished his entry: 'I'll close for this day now, and write up the attack tomorrow – if there is a tomorrow.'[40]

The troopers of the 3rd Light Horse Brigade, positioned along Russell's Top, saw the infantry charge against Lone Pine, watching excitedly as the figures in khaki appeared to capture the very heart of the enemy's position. They knew that at dawn the next day they were to do the same against one of the most heavily entrenched and defended positions at Anzac – The Nek.[41] Among these men was 33-year-old Northam farmer Lieutenant Hugo Throssell, who heard above the crescendo of rifle fire and exploding shells the cheering and yells of the men of the 1st Brigade as they charged across the Daisy Patch. With him were his older brother Rick and their mates, brothers Ross and Lindsay Chipper. They were sharing a bottle of whisky that they'd pinched from Major Thomas Todd. For many of these troopers, including Ross and Lindsay, it would be their last sunset.[42]

The Turkish garrison at Lone Pine consisted of two battalions of the 47th Regiment, with its third battalion occupying Sniper's Ridge. This ridge was immediately opposite the southern flank at Anzac, directly facing Leane's Trench and Bolton's Ridge. At least 500 men held the front trenches at Lone Pine, with another 500 men in close support in the rear trenches and positioned within the reserve area later known as The Cup. Given the previous days of bombardment, the Turks manning Lone Pine had been ordered to withdraw into their forward tunnels, running underneath no-man's-land, in order to take cover. While the overhead logging could protect them from shrapnel, if hit by a high-explosive shell, the wooden supports would be reduced to timber shrapnel, which could just as easily rip through flesh and bone. Most of the men, except those unfortunates whose turn it was to remain alert on the front-line firing step, were in the tunnels, and now these men were urgently being ordered out to join the others in confronting the attacking enemy.

At the time of the Australians' charge, 53-year-old Turkish III

Corps commander Major General Esat Pasha was located at his headquarters at Scrubby Knoll, the highest point along Third Ridge. He had a perfect view of the enemy's attack. A few years earlier he had distinguished himself as a corps commander in the Balkan Wars, having participated in every major battle in the Thracian theatre in 1913.[43] Up until May 1915, the area opposite the Anzac sector had largely been under the command of his subordinate, Lieutenant Colonel Mustafa Kemal (later dubbed Atatürk, or 'Father of the Turks' – the founder of the modern Turkish Republic), who unwisely went above the head of his Corps commander to write to Enver Pasha complaining about the German General Liman von Sanders' conduct of operations at Gallipoli. With this, Esat Pasha decided that his ambitious subordinate needed closer supervision. Esat Pasha had taken direct responsibility for the Anzac front, leaving Kemal in charge of the northern sector at Anzac along Baby 700.[44] Now, with the Australian attack against Lone Pine, he ordered the 19th Division, under the command of Mustafa Kemal to the north, to throw in its sole reserve – Captain Zeki Bey's 1st Battalion of the 57th Regiment, which had been relieved from Merkez Tepe (German Officers' Trench).[45] Just before receiving his orders, Captain Zeki Bey had climbed onto a higher ledge of Mortar Ridge, above their battalion headquarters, to get a better view of what was happening at Kanli Sirt (Lone Pine). In 1919, Charles Bean reported a conversation he had with the Turkish major about what he saw as the Australian 1st Brigade launched its attack:

> Looking southwards they saw Lone Pine covered with smoke and dust of shells, and at that moment the heavy reports of the guns gave place to a patter of rifles ('as, after thunder, you hear the rain begin,' said one of them later). The regimental observer remarked that he could see men running across no-man's-land…A few minutes later there arrived the order,

telephoned from Mustafa Kemal, for the 1/57th to move to the Pine. The battalion was then ready, and Zeki Bey ordered it to move at the double down Legge Valley, fixing bayonets as it went, while he himself, having told the leading company commander to meet him in Owen's Gully, ran ahead and turned into that valley.[46]

The major and his men would be the first Turkish reinforcements to reach the Pine immediately following the Australian attack, and would bear the brunt of four days of attack and counterattack – killing and being killed.

10

'Bayonets were
bloody – reeking'

Assault of the 4th Battalion, Northern Flank

On reaching the first line of northern Turkish trenches, 26-year-old farmer Lance Corporal Hugh Anderson and his fellows fired in through the loopholes, while others tried to pull the logs apart. Anderson recalled his officer, 'old Dickie Seldon, waving a revolver, "This won't do men! On! On! On!", and running over the top of the trench he came to the second trench and down into it the crowd followed'.[1] With a loud explosion, chunks of Constantinople scrap iron from a shrapnel shell sprayed Seldon, turning one of his eyeballs to pulp, but he ignored it and kept going. Close behind was Private Scott, who dived into a Turkish trench and got a piece of shrapnel in his back. It didn't trouble him at first, so he pushed on further into the heart of the Pine. He made it to the third line and with others he started to make a firing line out of a former communication trench. He was near an officer who noticed 'blood on my back and he told me to "imshi" out of it'.[2]

Meanwhile, 23-year-old Sydney analytical chemist Lieutenant Arthur Giles and his men were the first to reach the northern flank of Lone Pine, which was heavily timbered over. Their job was to secure the northern works from counterattacks by the Turks at Johnston's Jolly. Private Duke had joined up with Giles in a captured trench and saw Turks emerging from another trench less than thirty metres away. He gave a warning yell to Giles, who ordered his men to line the parapet. However, as the men raised their rifles they were met by a burst of Turkish fire. Duke recalled an almighty 'crash right in front of my face which knocked me reeling back into the trench. I knew I was hit as blood was streaming from my forehead into my eyes and over my glasses. I was not knocked out and took my glasses off so that I could wipe them and my eyes sufficiently to look round.'[3] After wiping the blood away he was horrified to see 'every one of those lads who had lined the parapet with me lying still and dead in the bottom of the trench – six of them all hit clean in the head... Fortunately... the attacking Turks [were] wiped out by rifle fire from our chaps further up the trench'.[4]

Charles Bean, still at The Pimple, had seen a number of Australians in the northern part of the line being killed or wounded by a Turkish machine gun positioned just behind the front lines. It was just opposite a crater on a heavy stand and appeared to be mounted behind a trapdoor in the head cover. Bean could see the Turkish crew. A few Australians crossed to the left of the machine gun and, from behind, 24-year-old storeman Private George Hayward slipped three bombs into the opening in the head cover where it was located, smashing the gun and killing the crew.[5] Then, as Hayward was helping Private William Dodd into the trench, Dodd was shot in the head.[6] Hayward could do nothing for him and pushed on with Lance Corporal Aylward. Their objective was to barricade the northernmost section of this trench, to prevent Turks from Johnston's Jolly reinforcing the Pine. The only map that they'd seen had few details, not even including contour lines, and they found themselves reluctantly descending into Owen's

Gully. Turks still held a covered sap running off to their left, which stopped their advance. Here, Lieutenant Giles joined up with them and within minutes a few bombers were throwing jam-tin bombs into the sap entrance. After the explosions, Giles jumped across the junction – a shot rang out and he fell dead. Now 28-year-old station manager Captain Stewart Milson arrived, and Private Walter Back watched as Milson threw bombs 'round the corner quickly with a long right arm. Some of his jam tins certainly got in and frightened the Turks... He was getting bolder and bolder in spite of advice from his men... he tried to rush past [the sap] and was shot as he went by'.[7]

Lance Corporal Anderson was standing next to Milson when the officer was killed: 'I ran, I threw my rifle into the possie and pulled the trigger. I suppose they had never got time to load as I never got hit, but no one followed and I was there alone with no bombs and only my rifle. I shouted to them to come on but they were not having any. I felt a little dickie I can tell you, but I kept firing into the possie from where I was, some of the Turks were firing at me.'[8] Anderson knew there was only one ending to this exchange and when the inevitable happened he felt the bullet hit like a 'sledge hammer on the head and down I went across Milson's body and several Turks, some of whom were only wounded, and groaned and squirmed from time to time. I bled pretty freely and then I got a crack on the shoulder from a shrapnel pellet which hurt badly but did not do much damage.'[9] The Australians continued to throw their jam-tin bombs, and Anderson copped one: '[It] went off near my head, and I got bits of it in the hand and face and was knocked unconscious for a while.'[10] The next thing he remembered was a rush of boots and being trampled on. He lay very still while a lot of shooting and bombing went on all round him, and as the Turks rushed back over him, leaving a heap of dead and wounded. He tried in vain to get his rifle: '[It was] jammed between the bodies. Milson's revolver was handy, and I ought to have used that as I had a good view of the Turk's possie from where I was, but I did not have brains enough at the time.'[11] Private Back recalled how two Turks then threw out their rifles and came out with their hands up – but in the excitement they were shot. Then a Turk shouted out from inside the covered sap and another came out with his hands up. He made signs that they wanted to surrender. They let him go back into the tunnel to bring out the others. In all, seven rifles and two revolvers were thrown out – quickly followed by nine Turks with their hands up.[12]

Moments later, 33-year-old Sydney accountant Lieutenant Richard Seldon arrived, with the remains of his eyeball plastered onto his cheek, and took command. He ordered Aylward, Hayward and a number of others to push on past the sap just captured and clear out any Turks who might still be in the next sap to their left. In so doing, they would be making their way back to the covered Turkish front line. Seldon continued down the trench in which they stood to clear the way of any Turks who might hold up their advance. On reaching the front line, Aylward and his men were confronted by Turks holding a transverse trench under the covered works. The Australians attempted to drive them out by firing around the bend, but they needed bombs, and hunted around for some. When they found a few, they threw them while also firing their rifles, shouting and cheering, trying to sound like the place was occupied by a whole company. The ruse worked and the Turks retreated across the communication trench into Owen's Gully, below.

Aylward and his men continued back into the open trench to rejoin Lieutenant Seldon at the point where Lone Pine descended into Owen's Gully. Here, Aylward and his men came across Seldon's body lying at the head of the trench junction. Carefully peering round the corner, Aylward saw a number of Turks who seemed about to launch a counterattack against their position. As others started to drag down sandbags from the top of the parapet to build a barricade, Aylward quickly cut a niche in the side wall of this trench and commenced firing: 'The sun, glistening on my bayonet, soon gave our position away, and the Turks poured in a hot fire.'[13] By now the low barricade had been completed and Aylward crawled over to Lieutenant Seldon but found that he was dead. He took possession of Seldon's revolver and he and his men placed his body in the sandbag barricade. Lieutenant Richard Seldon is today buried at Johnston's Jolly cemetery.

While Aylward and Hayward were building their barricade, the Turks had taken advantage of the lull in firing to crawl towards their position, but they were discovered in time and driven off by small-arms fire. The trench at this point was about three metres deep, but had no fire step. Setting the others to work, Aylward went to make contact with the rest of the battalion.[14] In doing so, he passed a darkened tunnel and despite the noise of battle heard the distinct sound of foreign voices. He stood at the mouth of the tunnel and ordered the Turks to come out. All he heard in response was a sound like 'Testim, Testim'.[15] (The Turkish for 'surrender' is *teslim*.) This, of course, meant nothing to Aylward, and, convinced that the Turks were wounded and taking shelter in the sap, he perhaps foolishly put his revolver down. He was, however, quickly startled: 'Imagine my surprise when there emerged, not wounded, but seven unwounded Turks, including an officer or NCO. Disarming them after hurriedly regaining possession of my revolver, I ordered them to proceed me towards where I anticipated the battalion HQ would be located.'[16] With the Turks marching in front he didn't get far, as all of a sudden they reversed: 'The whole pack stampeded back on me; guessing that they had run into some of our fellows, I called out, and went ahead of them, and met Sergt. Crawford. The prisoners were handed over to Colonel Macnaghten, to whom I made a request for assistance at the barricade.'[17] No men, however, could be spared and Aylward returned to his small party alone.

About fifty metres south of Aylward were Major Iven Mackay and his men, who had also ignored the front trench and pushed on to the next line of trenches and saps close to the northern edge of the plateau.[18] They ran beside one of the rearward-running saps, shooting at the Turks below, who were making for the rear. Mackay recalled: 'We found the Turks running beneath us in the communication trenches whilst we ran along the top. Most of these Turks were wearing not military boots, but light slippers. We shot a number of these men, firing our rifles from our hips.'[19] However, a few Turks turned and fired back, killing 29-year-old grazier Sergeant Hugh Griffiths and mortally wounding 28-year-old Lieutenant John Merivale.[20] A friend of Merivale, 22-year-old Captain James Osborne, later wrote to Merivale's sister, telling her how he saw John two or three minutes after the charge – he had already been hit and all that he could say was 'I am done for'. Jim bandaged John's wound, but they both knew it was fatal. '[We] shook hands, and then I had to pass on. When I returned about half an hour later he was dead. He was as plucky as possible throughout, and you have every reason to be proud.'[21] Lieutenant John Merivale is today buried in the Lone Pine Cemetery.

Up ahead, Mackay saw a point where the communication sap he was following intersected with another from Owen's Gully below – his objective. Disregarding any potential threat from Turks who might be taking up a defensive position further down the sap, he quickly jumped into it and ran towards the intersection, stopping just short of it. He took a few seconds to gain his breath. Like the enlisted men, he carried a rifle. He now checked his weapon and ammunition, but was interrupted by a number of Turks rushing down a nearby trench. Mackay managed to fire off a few rounds, dropping the Turks. He waited for a short time and as no others appeared he leapt across the intersection, but a shot rang out to his right, the bullet just missing him. One of his men, 20-year-old Corporal Hessel Mills, was not so lucky and was killed when he jumped over the same intersection. Mackay now found himself very much alone. This part of the Pine was clearly a command post, with saps leading from it to all parts of the Turkish position. It was a large, well-constructed, open position about ten metres long and about four metres wide. The sides had been neatly cut with a fire step (which, for the advancing Australians, was facing in the wrong direction). Another two of Mackay's men tried to join him in the post, but they too were killed by the solitary Turk in the side sap who had killed Mills. Now three more Turks, apparently unaware that the post was 'held' by Mackay, appeared from a sap running up from Owen's Gully. Mackay attempted to fire his rifle, but the trigger merely clicked – the magazine was empty – so he 'lunged with the bayonet, and just about scratched the front man's chest as he was jumping back, after which they all turned and ran the way they had come. My men behind, who could see well, said these Turks were unarmed and had come to surrender. I was sorry, but could not help it, and it is things like this, I suppose, which create the impression that we do not take prisoners; certainly these men would be justified in spreading such a report.'[22]

By now, a number of Mackay's men had made their way just short of his position – he had yelled to warn the men of the lone Turk covering the sap to their right. He ordered them to start blocking this sap with sandbags. The Turk kept up a steady stream of fire, trying to keep the Australians from rushing his position. As Mackay's men threw sandbags across the sap, another Turk approached the command post from where his three surrendering comrades had arrived earlier. This time Mackay was ready and shot the man dead. The sandbag barricade was quickly completed and one of Mackay's men took up a position behind it and began to pour fire into the sap occupied by the dogged Turk. There was a short but furious exchange of rifle fire, and with the aid of a few other Australians firing from around the corner at the Turk, the passage was cleared. The Turk had either been hit or sensibly decided that he had 'done his bit' and took cover below the plateau, at least for the time being. Mackay was now joined by his fellows and together they started to block the other sap running down into Owen's Gully, leaving a narrow loophole for defence.[23] It wasn't long before they had built a fire step (facing east) and held the north-eastern angle of the new Australian position in Lone Pine – soon known as Mackay's Post.[24]

At the same time that Aylward and Mackay were establishing their posts, 35-year-old Lieutenant William McDonald and his men took up a position halfway between them. From here they could offer enfilade to the position held by Aylward and his men, while Mackay would be able to offer similar supporting fire to McDonald – if each had been aware of the other's position, which at this stage was doubtful. In capturing this part of the line, McDonald had killed a Turk, but had received a painful bayonet wound. He refused to go to the rear and supervised the barricading of the sap, about halfway along its length. His men pushed sandbags, debris and the dead Turk into the middle of the passage and hunted for additional sandbags and timber to further strengthen the barricade. McDonald went forward beyond the barricade to an angle of the sap to cover the men as they frantically constructed the defensive work. It wasn't long before McDonald was being targeted by Turks further down the line. He returned fire, but his rifle alone was not going to keep them from storming his position for long. McDonald ordered privates Claude Buck, Ernest Churcher and Raymond Benson to throw him jam-tin bombs with the fuses already lit – then caught each of the explosives and threw them towards the Turks. As he did this, the barricade behind him was growing in height and only when he considered it defensible did he scramble over the top of it to his men. The Turks were not far behind him and seeing their chance now rushed forward towards the barricade.[25]

It was about then that Private Duke arrived at the position. Minutes earlier, he was trying to get his breath when from the right end of the traverse a big Turk came 'bolting along the trench. He took no notice of me because close at his heels were two Aussies and as he passed me I raised my rifle and let him have it fair in the middle of the back, almost at the same time as the other two. He went down like a poleaxed bull.'[26] Now with McDonald and his men, he was engaged in a desperate bayonet fight with the Turks trying to push through their barricade. When Duke got his bayonet stuck in a Turk's leather webbing, the Turk instantly raised his rifle to shoot him – just then there was an awful bang alongside Duke's ear, and the Turk crumpled up at his feet. An Australian behind him had put his rifle over Duke's shoulder and shot the Turk dead. Duke remembered that the 'discharge nearly blew my head off'.[27] There was no time to thank his saviour: '[A] dark head appeared round the traverse. I immediately let fly with my rifle from my hip and missed. In reply came two cricket ball bombs. One was kicked by one of my mates round a corner, but the other was behind us.'[28] Duke was seized by a moment or two of uncontrollable paralysing fear: '[I was] utterly helpless with that thing sizzling within a few feet of me. I flattened myself in the side of the trench, clawing at it with my fingers and certainly thought my last moment had come.'[29] By some miracle, none of the Australians were seriously wounded by the explosion, but they were now in serious danger of being bombed out of the newly established position. At the last possible minute, however, they managed to get some reinforcements, which enabled them to keep the Turks at bay. 'It was a hot stop all right, but McDonald was an inspiration to the rest of us.'[30]

Captain Edward Lloyd had reached the Turkish front line just south of where Mackay had crossed. An account of Lloyd's introduction to the Lone Pine trenches, unattributed but most likely penned by Lloyd himself, describes how during the advance he attempted a flying leap over an enemy trench, so that he could get quickly to the rear of Lone Pine, where his company had the job of cutting off any Turkish retreat. But he didn't quite make it. Instead, he tripped and fell into the middle of a trench, which only seconds before had been full of Turks. Fortunately for him, a shell had previously 'landed at this spot, killing and wounding part of the garrison, and causing demoralisation among those who survived'.[31] The unceremonious arrival of Lloyd into their midst caused the Turks to scramble round the corner of the trench. They soon realised, however, that the Australian was alone, and they now poked their rifles around the corner and shot at Lloyd, who returned fire as best he could. He had no illusions as to how this game would end, so the next time a Turk fired he gave out a grunt and rolled over, pretending to be dead. Still puffing from his 100-metre dash across no-man's-land, he was fearful that the Turks would discover his ruse and run their bayonets through him. But apparently their attention was concentrated in meeting the attacks of the oncoming Australians. One of the Turks grabbed Lloyd's rifle from his hand, 'and that he tried to use it against the Australians was made clear later from the discovery of Turkish bullets in the magazine, one of these having jammed'.[32]

For a few minutes Lloyd lay motionless in the trench, as the Turks yelled around him, firing at the Australians and rolling over their dead comrades in the search for ammunition, but nobody bothered Lloyd or trod on him. Once a shell burst just overhead and the case rolled into the trench against his wrist. It was extremely hot, and though he was afraid that a Turk would spot him, he took the risk and gradually worked his hand away from the searing metal. Soon after this, there was a rush of feet, then silence. Seconds later, he heard others pushing their way through. This time, he was noticed, and someone rolled him over. '"Come on, the game is up," shouted one voice, sure that the captive was a Turk in Australian tunic. "Why, it is Capt. Lloyd," another voice broke in, and Lloyd then jumped to his feet, stating that he was not wounded, though his ankle was twisted.'[33]

Assisted by 21-year-old Tennyson clerk Private Tristian Holcombe, Lloyd led the men out of the covered trenches into the open part of the line. To his front and left were two communication trenches, one falling into The Cup and the other into Owen's Gully. At the end of the sap to his left he could see a group of Australians barricading a major intersection: these were Mackay and his men. Essentially, Mackay's sap led down into Owen's Gully and was an extension of the second line trench he now occupied. It would for some reason be called Traversed Trench (it wasn't traversed at all and was a long and straight passageway) and would be occupied by a small garrison under 20-year-old Lieutenant James Osborne. Lloyd and his men pushed for a short distance into the sap to his front, which shortly veered north-eastward and ran just east of Traversed Trench before it too fell into the sides of Owen's Gully. The Turks along Johnston's Jolly completely enfiladed this trench, so at the very edge of the plateau Lloyd and his men set about building a barricade, which would become known as Lloyd's Post. Lloyd placed Private Holcombe in command and painfully hobbled off to make contact with his left. He quickly came across Lieutenant Osborne, who told him that 'Major Mackay had come through all right, and was holding a communication trench on the left'.[34]

At Lloyd's Post, Holcombe was standing near the corner defined by the main trench and the communication trench, when a few Turks appeared. Before he realised what was happening, an Australian shot the Turks dead. Holcombe shook hands with the unknown soldier, who told him that having found himself in the second line with a few of his battalion, he decided to push on. None of the others would budge, so he calmly started off on his own. Holcombe wrote years later: 'What obstacles he met on the way he didn't mention, merely saying it was pretty warm. He was only a boy. After exploring a dug-out and drinking in it, we parted company. I never saw him again. But I'm sure that whatever he did, he did well, for he was of the stuff true leaders are made of.'[35]

When Lloyd returned to his post he set his men to work at clearing the trenches that were partially choked with dead and wounded Turks. They threw the dead Turks out of the trench, while the wounded Turks were 'stowed away in corners as much as possible. Some of them were in a very bad way. Our own wounded we sent back to the rear trench to wait until a communication sap had been opened up with our old trenches.'[36] Lloyd and his men prepared for the inevitable Turkish counterattack, and it wasn't long before Lloyd was sent some reinforcements, though they weren't yet hard-pressed. Lloyd had heard, however, that 42-year-old Sydney agriculturist Major Colin Austin, of the 3rd Battalion, was having a very tough time in the communication trench to his right, so he sent the reinforcements over to him. Lloyd later learned that 'Austin died fighting hard, particularly holding his trench on his own, so I hoped that my reinforcements had arrived in time to give some help, but I heard nothing of them, or their officer, since'.[37] Major Colin Austin is today buried in the Lone Pine Cemetery, and while we do not know the identity of the reinforcements Lloyd sent to him, it is likely they lie nearby.

Close by, Private Rider had scoured round: '[Using] my rifle frequently, I and my mate came across a Turk hiding alongside his [dead] officer. As there was no resistance on the Turk's part, I searched him thoroughly and sent him to the rear.'[38] Not far away was Private Scott, who had been wounded in the back earlier and was ordered to 'impshee'. He approached the former Turkish front line and 'offered to relieve a chap who was guard over a [tunnel] that had Turks in it and thus let him go to the fighting... They got 78 Turkish prisoners out of the [tunnel] I was guarding.'[39]

These Turks had been taking cover in the tunnels during the bombardment of Lone Pine and had not got out in time to meet the Australians as they swept over the front line. Another soldier wrote anonymously: 'The work of consolidating the captured position was greatly hindered by the presence of many Turkish prisoners, who hampered movement in the trenches and were generally a menace to the safety of their captors.'[40]

Assault of the 3rd Battalion, Centre

Those men of the 3rd Battalion who had charged the centre of the line had quickly reached and jumped into the uncovered trenches. This section of the Pine became unduly crowded as men tried to get into the works from this narrow, fifty-metre frontage. Sydney journalist Sergeant Major Paul Goldenstedt, twenty-seven years old, was among the first to make his way to the line, where he saw Turkish rifles pushing their 'nasty snouts out through their openings [loopholes]. I raised mine to fire, only to find my safety catch back, and the shock I got when I discovered this was something to be remembered. Naturally, while it may take minutes to tell, the happening was only a question of a second or two, but I often think that during that second, or, it might have been a split second, I lived through a whole eternity.'[41] He and some of his troops were about to jump into one of the 'uncovered Turk communication trenches, [when] two men dropped beside us with that faint little cough that spells a fatal shot through the heart. Once in the trench there was a rush to find the garrisons which, by now, had retired further back.'[42] Goldenstedt pushed on: 'In front of me two ... [Turks] working a machine gun ... My rifle with ten in the magazine and one in the breach, I fired down those men as fast as I could and remembered ramming in and firing a couple more clips as well. Then I remembered my objective, the fourth trench, and leapt over the first and several cross trenches, firing into them as I passed.'[43]

Meanwhile, the concussed Private John Ison had made his way from the Daisy Patch towards the Turkish front line, and had by now recovered much of his senses. On looking into an open trench he was surprised to find it empty: 'So in I went head first and woke up with a bit of a start when I saw two big Turks not above three yards from me. I thought I was in a tight corner – I was sure of the first fellow but I thought the second may make it quits. However, they never attempted to put up a fight so I took them prisoners.'[44]

Others who entered this part of the line and proceeded down the adjoining communication trenches and saps quickly found that they were descending into The Cup, in Owen's Gully. This was a depression, a deep inlet branching at right angles off Owen's Gully in a southerly direction, which helped to define the rear part of the plateau on which the Turkish trench systems of Lone Pine had been dug. The men had been ordered not to descend into these gullies, but three Australians led by an officer moved quickly down a track towards the Turkish headquarters in The Cup. That was as far as they got – all were killed by a hail of Turkish bullets. It was the furthest point reached by any Australians that day. The identity of these men remains unknown.

Others near the eastern edge of the plateau began to build barricades, while reinforcements behind them followed the trenches and saps along the northern and eastern edge of the plateau.[45] Some remained above the parapets in no-man's-land, firing into Turks who were bolting down the avenues of trenches and saps, heading for the rear. These Australians then clambered into the trenches, turned around and made their way back towards the covered front lines.

Lieutenant Athol Burrett and his men were among those attacking this part of the line: '[We] managed to get down through...holes into the trench. Many of us just rushed over the front line and got into the rear trenches right among the Turks.

Then started probably the most gruesome, bloody and fiercest hand-to-hand fighting of the whole war.'[46] Similarly, Lieutenant Eric Wren recalled that once inside the southern part of the Turkish works the Australian 'bayonets were bloody – reeking. So rapid, so persistent was the advance of those who were at the heels of their faster-flying comrades across to the Pine – those, at least, who survived that first terrible slaughter – that they caught the Turkish garrison as it attempted to vacate its covered trench-shelters.'[47] Australians began to push their way out of the underground chambers into the daylight beyond, having to stumble over the dead and dying of friend and foe. Others continued to fight their way left and right under the covered trenches, hunting down any surviving Turk.[48] Lieutenant Percy Woods later wrote: 'Our men [went] to work with the bayonets, poor Johnnie. We took prisoners where we could, others had to take their chance as we had to push on and there was some gruesome sights.'[49] Neither side can claim that all prisoners remained alive for long. Even so, a few hours later, Colonel White sent a message to Birdwood's staff, just after midnight, requesting an interpreter, as seventy-nine Turkish prisoners from Lone Pine had just arrived under escort.[50]

A critical objective for the men of this battalion was to capture a series of trenches just beyond the front line. One of these was a trench later known as Sasse's Sap and it would help form the central defensive line held by the Australians at Lone Pine. This length of trench lay completely open to Turkish enfilade from Johnston's Jolly, as there were no traverse bends built into it. With their men, 23-year-old Sydney clerk Captain Donald Moore and 31-year-old Maitland school teacher Lieutenant Stanley Garnham approached Sasse's Sap from the covered flanks and were firing into it as Turks tried to escape to the rear. Moore ordered his men into the uncovered trench, and within minutes of its capture a barricade had been built along its northern length. This barricade was short of Lloyd's Post, which lay about fifteen metres further north, and was positioned where a sap from the east ran at right angles to it. This exposed part of Sasse's Sap, between the barricade and Lloyd's Post, remained unoccupied by either side. Any attempts by the Australians to occupy this length of trench resulted in devastating enfilade from the Turks entrenched on the Jolly.

Close by, 23-year-old farmer Private Arthur Belling had made contact with men of the 4th Battalion to his left. He'd earlier heard a call for reinforcements so he moved along the trench and met an officer who was organising for its defence. They were soon joined by 27-year-old Waverley plumber Sergeant Robert Easton, and between them they decided where to position a fire step. Belling stayed with Easton and together they began to build one. When it was completed Easton climbed up to see what sort of field of fire they had when a bullet hit him in the head, killing him instantly.[51] He is today buried in the Lone Pine Cemetery.

Twenty-two-year-old Lieutenant David Brown arrived with his sole surviving machine-gun crew, under the command of 29-year-old Leeton farmer Sergeant Randolph McMahon. They positioned the gun above open ground immediately behind Sasse's Sap. Some of the men occupying Sasse's now climbed out of the trench and took up a position to help protect the gun crew. The machine-gunner, 21-year-old Sydney clerk Private Neil Edwards, had a perfect view across Owen's Gully, only about 200 metres away, to a communication trench on Johnston's Jolly packed with Turks. He squeezed the trigger and his enfilade tore up the trench, leaving it blocked with dead and dying – as with much of Lone Pine, the Turks, for whatever reason, had failed to systematically dig transverse bends here for protection from such devastating fire. Private Railton MacDonald was taking up a position in Sasse's Sap, just as the machine gun opened fire: 'One of the crew noticed me...and yelled at the top of his voice to keep low (a warning needless to say I did not require).'[52] No sooner had the machine gun ceased firing than it became a magnet for the Turks, and most of the machine-gun crew and men around the gun were hit by fire from the Jolly. A Turkish shrapnel shell from Third Ridge finally brought an end to the venture, but not until Edwards had squeezed off over 700 rounds. Brown and Edwards somehow survived and managed to salvage the machine gun, and at the bottom of Sasse's Sap they unsuccessfully tried to repair the damage. Realising the hopelessness of the task, they proceeded to empty its belts of ammunition for distribution amongst the men fighting all around them.

The Turks to the front of Sasse's Sap had not yet given up and were attempting to retake this part of the line. In this short but furious exchange, Private MacDonald noticed Australians not far away in a communication trench digging footholds to enable them to 'secure a better firing position'.[53] MacDonald came across one of his wounded cobbers, 36-year-old Private Edward Smalley, who had been seriously wounded in the chest. MacDonald started to bandage Smalley, but the wounded man told him not to waste his time and with a painful gasp said, 'I'm done.'[54] Just as MacDonald was dragging Smalley to a section in the trench that offered some cover, he received a 'terrific clout from behind which sent me sprawling over the top of him... Picking myself up I recognised one of our Company... nearby. I called for his assistance and together we lifted him and placed [him] down in the fork of the two trenches... here he would be sheltered from machine-gun and rifle fire (I next saw his name in the casualty lists three months later as killed in action)'.[55] Private Smalley was well known and liked in his battalion. Since landing he had taken it upon himself to try and identify those killed to make sure they got a proper burial and that their family knew that their father, son or brother had a gravesite. Sometimes this meant doing it himself, when coming across a corpse long dead. Smalley's burial service ran something like: 'Ashes to ashes, dust to dust. If nobody will bury you, Smalley must.'[56] Private Edward Smalley himself has no known grave and is commemorated on the Lone Pine Memorial.

Later, a Turkish sniper got MacDonald in his sights at Sasse's Sap and put him out of action with a bullet to the thigh. However, the Australians managed to beat back the Turkish counterattack against Sasse's Sap and they hurriedly continued to barricade the communication saps and build firing steps into what had been the rear of the trench.[57] That night, MacDonald somehow made it out of Lone Pine and onto a ship bound for a hospital in Mudros.[58]

At the southern end of Sasse's Sap, and at right angles to it, had been dug a narrow communication trench, heading east towards the edge of the plateau. Off this narrow trench were three additional saps running forward and parallel to Sasse's Sap. As such, they provided a partial screen for any approach to Sasse's Sap. Lieutenant Percy Woods and his men quickly pushed forward and occupied the first of these saps. Midway along, Woods set up a barricade to protect his men from possible enfilade from the Jolly. The Australians occupied the southern half of the sap, leaving its northern half unoccupied by either side. The sap in front of Woods' position was actually a track running up onto the surface of the Pine, but even so a number of Australians took up a screening position. The third sap, which for all intents and purposes now represented the deepest part of the new Australian front line, terminated close to the eastern edge of the plateau looking down into The Cup, and would soon be occupied by Sergeant Major Goldenstedt and his men. This would become a very hot place indeed, as it was well forward of the main Australian lines and looked directly into the Turkish reserve areas. It would become known as Goldenstedt's Post. Sergeant Major Paul Goldenstedt wrote:

After a minute or two I ran into then 2/C (Major David McConaghy)...McConaghy and myself went on a little exploring expedition of our own, following a communication trench until it kind of petered out in the open into Owen's Gully, and behold! – not ten yards from us was the stump of the old tree from which the Pine took its name. Our amazement was cut short in a twinkling, for we immediately received the undivided attention of every Turkish machine gun and rifle in the locality. We both managed to make cover, however – a fact that could hardly be called a tribute to the efficiency of the Turkish shooting.[59]

There were a number of dead Turks in this short sap, including a white-bearded officer. It was likely part of an outlet for mining spoil as it opened into a 'chute' of earth running off the edge of the plateau.[60]

The very end of the eastern-running trench from Sasse's Sap did not run off into Owen's Gully but terminated close to the very edge of the plateau. It was here at this sap, which represented the backbone to the three forward covering saps, that men from the 3rd Battalion, under the command of 23-year-old Cootamundra painter Lieutenant Sidney Pinkstone, established a defensive position by expanding and deepening the trench end. Pinkstone's position, later called Tubb's Corner, now represented the extreme right flank of the 3rd Battalion, and like Goldenstedt's Post was well forward of the Australian main defensive line. Given the tactical significance of Pinkstone's position, a number of men were rushed in to help ensure its incorporation into the Australian lines.[61] Earlier, in pushing into this part of the line, Pinkstone nearly jumped on top of a Turk, who retreated: 'I had two or three pot shots at him with my rifle but he always beat me round a traverse. Then suddenly coming round a bend, I found him nicely spitted on the end of a digger's bayonet. The digger had come in the opposite direction. It was a lucky thing for me that the Turk got there first. Otherwise I might have decorated that bayonet.'[62] Goldenstedt recalled that having just survived Turkish fire near the stump of the original Lone Pine, he now moved down another trench and found one of the three Pinkstone brothers: 'Norman, I think, and a couple of others fighting for their dear lives...in a nearby dug-out the wounded lay in heaps – Turk on Australian, and Australian on Turk.'[63] Lieutenant Pinkstone's younger brother Victor – aged twenty – would soon be killed elsewhere in the fighting for the Pine. He is buried at the Lone Pine Cemetery.

Assault of the 2nd Battalion, Southern Flank

The southern part of Lone Pine was on a slightly higher elevation and its front-line trenches were more completely covered than elsewhere, leaving many of the 2nd Battalion's men exposed to ongoing Turkish machine-gun and shrapnel fire as they searched for a way to penetrate the works. At some point, the Turkish machine-gun post in this area, which had killed or wounded, amongst others, Captain Pain, had been destroyed. Charles Bean later wrote that even so, the 'position of any man outside the trenches was evidently becoming precarious, and the remnant of the crowd by the parapets began to jump into the Pine via the rear-uncovered trenches. Only on the right did a line of men still lie in the open. Not until an hour later did onlookers realise that they were dead.'[64]

Here the fighting was perhaps the most ferocious, due to the labyrinthine trench system. Attackers, individually or in small groups, dug through the overburden of earth and debris covering the timbers, and where possible pried them open and dragged them aside. As they did so, they were hit from Turkish enfilade north and south. The attackers jumped into any opening they could force or find. Those who were the first into the dark holes were often killed immediately by Turkish bullets or gutted by a bayonet. Soon, a number of Australians had made their way into the covered trenches, their eyes unaccustomed to the darkness, giving the Turks a momentary advantage. Even so, Australian numbers began to quickly turn the tide. Many of the Turks were still in their tunnels running underneath no-man's-land, having taken shelter there from the enemy barrage – they were now trapped. Australians penetrated further into the forward and secondary Turkish trenches and communication saps. Frenzied hand-to-hand struggles took place within the darkened galleries. Undoubtedly there would have been cases of Turk killing Turk and Australian killing Australian in the near total darkness and confusion. At this point it was not only rifle and bayonet that was used – facing death, men used knives, spades, fists, feet and teeth if it gave them an advantage. They cursed, swore and yelled uncomprehended insults at each other out of fear and frustration. Flashing, momentary images of friend and foe could be seen in the vertical shafts of light that in some places pierced the darkness from the open roof space, while horizontal flashes of rifle fire sent bullets hurtling out into the darkness – if they didn't smash into bone, they thudded into the trench wall or the timber supports. Sprays of blood and pieces of brain matter covered those in the ferocious melee.

By now Lieutenant Lecky had made it to the southern part of the Turkish works with the wounded Captain John Pain. They jumped into the first uncovered trench they came to and pushed on. As they reached a bend, Lecky would place his cap on the end of his bayonet and hold it forward, and if nobody shot at it he'd poke his head round and advance. He continued this procedure until he thought that they must have covered more than a mile, though he later realised it was far less than that: 'We were only a couple of hundred yards away from the captured Turkish position. The men who followed were ordered to block up the trench with sandbags, and unremitting hard work was carried on to try and secure the position before the counter-attack arrived.'[65] This sap was their main objective and would help define the southern flank of the Australian position at Lone Pine. Parallel with it, and at one point only five metres behind, was a shallow sap, either unfinished or abandoned. The front line from which these communication saps originated was covered in thick timbers and descended abruptly to the south along Sniper's Ridge – still held in strength by the Turks.

Others were still caught up by strands of barbed wire in the open area of no-man's-land – a terrifying experience – 'fortunate if they could tear free in time' before being cut down by a spray of machine-gun fire.[66] Close by, 20-year-old carpenter Company Sergeant Major Walter Host had taken charge of a party whose officers had been killed. On entering this part of Lone Pine he noticed two Turkish machine-gun tripods had been left in position, the crews having evidently rushed the guns away to safety after the initial assault.[67] He must have felt relieved that the gunners had thought the better part of valour was to get the guns out of there.

The first to reach the position later to be known as Jacobs's Trench was Sydney clergymen Lieutenant Everard Digges La Touché and his small party of men. The young lieutenant had signed up as a combatant after not being able to get a position as an army chaplain. La Touché and his men jumped into the sap but were hit by Turkish bullets as they crossed the first transverse bend. The Turks here began to dig in and within the hour would confront Captain Jacobs and his men of the 1st Battalion. Meanwhile, a group with 30-year-old farmer Lieutenant Herbert Youden passed a Y-intersection just north of this sap, encountering no Turks, and continued down a sap close to the head of The Cup as it cut through Lone Pine. As they approached the edge of the plateau, however, a party of Turks stopped their advance with a hail of rifle fire. Youden and his survivors quickly tore down sandbags, mud bricks, dead Turks, and anything else that came to hand, to construct a barricade. This position would become known as Youden's Post, and would soon prove another particularly fierce flashpoint, helping define the south-eastern corner of the Australian perimeter at Lone Pine.

The Turks took up positions close to trench intersections and were warned of any approaching Australian by his fixed bayonet. In several places dead Australians lay four or five deep at these junctions. It didn't take long for the men to realise that they had to keep their rifles upright and close to the body if they were to surprise the Turks. To make matters worse, when approaching a corner or bend, one was never sure that the man beyond was friend or foe. Major Leslie Morshead of the 2nd Battalion was in the southern part of Lone Pine. He was approaching a trench corner when one of his men, believing that Australians were around the next corner, went forward to warn them of their approach. He quickly returned to report otherwise: "'They are Turks, all right," the fellow said quietly, "and they got me [with a bullet] in the stomach.'" After talking for a few minutes he sat down, and shortly after died in great pain.[68]

A little further south, Captain Syd Cook arrived at the same Y-junction that Youden and his men had reached a few minutes before: 'I came across different groups sniping down two different trenches and struggling to build blocks in each.'[69] Seeing that Youden was covering the left sap, Cook and his men headed into the right sap, which soon began to descend into The Cup. Cook made arrangements for the sap to be barricaded a short distance back from the edge of the plateau. Cook organised the construction of parapets and the digging of fire steps along both sides of the trench, as well as one behind the barricade. As they threw Turkish corpses over the parapet they found two in close embrace, one middle-aged and the other quite young, likely father and son. Cook now decided to establish an advanced barricade to help cover his position and provide a warning to any Turkish advance towards them from the valley below. For the time being at least, this made his defensive position relatively secure, even though

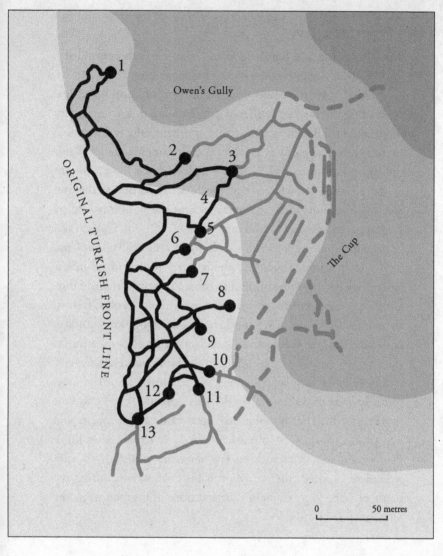

Owen's Gully

ORIGINAL TURKISH FRONT LINE

The Cup

1

2

3

4

5

6

7

8

9

10

11

12

13

0   50 metres

——— Australian-held trenches
——— Turkish-held trenches

1. Aylward's Post
2. McDonald's Post
3. Mackay's Post
4. Traversed Trench
5. Lloyd's Post
6. Sasse's Sap
7. Woods's Post

8. Goldenstedt's Post
9. Tubb's Corner
10. Youden's Post
11. Cook's Post
12. Jacobs's Post
13. Pain's Post

Lone Pine trenches, with Australian posts gained
in the first hour of the battle, 6 August

Turkish sniping and bombing from Jacobs's Trench continued.[70] This position was to become known as Cook's Post.

Even though there was now some form of continuous line connecting the forward parties of 4th Battalion to the north with those of the 3rd Battalion at the centre, the men of the 2nd Battalion to the south were partly isolated from their sister battalions. While the communication saps to their rear linked the three columns of the advance, the closest that the forward parties of the 2nd and 3rd battalions came in contact was at the positions held by Pinkstone at what would become known as Tubb's Corner and Youden in the position named after him, near the head of The Cup. These posts were separated by about thirty metres of no-man's-land. They needed to be bridged to form a forward defensive line. Until then small parties of men, with or without leaders, formed themselves into defensive pockets, establishing low sandbag barricades as best they could. These forward positions were far from secure against any coordinated Turkish counterattack, and if they fell the very heart of the Pine would be lost. The most southern part of the Australian defensive perimeter at Lone Pine was held by the already wounded Captain Pain and his men, who had pushed on and established a post (later named after him). Pain would stay there with his few survivors until he was again wounded.[71] Indeed, the next day, in his final actions during the battle of Lone Pine, Captain Pain and three of his men would be recommended for the VC.

'It was truly an apocalypse,
an apocalypse indeed'

It must have seemed a lifetime ago since the men of the 1st Brigade had launched their attack against Lone Pine. Those who had watches would have been shocked to realise that less than thirty minutes had passed since they had charged across no-man's-land. The three attacking battalions had established themselves in the heart of the Turkish works, holding a communication trench on either flank, and in the centre seven or eight isolated posts in as many communication trenches.[1] An unnamed Turkish officer of the 47th Regiment later wrote home his account of the initial Australian charge:

> The enemy turned all their weapons against us. It was an extraordinary fire, and it lasted for about an hour. Once they had decided that there couldn't possibly be any survivors, they began to attack in waves as previously planned; one wave would collapse upon us like a wooden fence, and then a new wave would immediately appear, and in this way the enemy tried to advance. Can you imagine our Mehmets letting them pass, a new calamity...would incessantly appear, and it would be felled. Unfortunately, the rifles in the hands of

the soldiers overheated. The grease between the wooden and metal parts was sizzling and the mechanisms stopped working. The rifles had to cool, and our enemies profited from this situation. By then the battle was being waged hand to hand, and it was then that I was shot, Sergeant Osman from Silifke carried me on his shoulders to the medical post. The active headcount of our battalion was down to thirty-three, no officers left; the second in command of the battalion from our company, Muhammed Ali the Arab, and the junior officer from the second company, Zahid from Tarsus, had prepared themselves. But then Muhammed Ali was killed at some point during this time. The adversaries took two of our trenches, but could not advance further; I was watching the fighting from the medical post. It was truly an apocalypse, an apocalypse indeed.[2]

The Turks now clung to the rearmost trenches of the plateau, occupying for the most part communication saps that were never designed for defence. Signs of an imminent Turkish counterattack were evident as those Australians who could look down Owen's Gully or Legge Valley using trench periscopes had 'caught sight of Turkish reinforcements coming in continuous stream along the gully-beds, while on the side of the Jolly appeared an experienced officer, who with others, was surveying the Pine through field-glasses and was obviously despatching messengers one after another down the gully'.[3]

As the Australians were capturing the heart of Lone Pine, Captain Zeki Bey reached the inner recesses of Owen's Gully. He recalled to Charles Bean after the war how he came under immediate fire from the Australians holding the positions near the head of the gully. This likely originated from Aylward, McDonald and Mackay's men.

Nearby he came across the battalion commander who had been responsible for holding the front lines at Lone Pine, Captain Mustafa Kemal (not to be confused with Lieutenant Colonel Mustafa Kemal, later known as 'Atatürk'). Zeki Bey asked him: 'What has happened?' But the distraught captain could only reply with: 'We're lost, we're lost!' Zeki Bey replied, trying to sound confident: 'I want you to tell me what the situation is and what you wish me to do.' The captain told Zeki Bey: 'The situation is critical. My whole battalion remained in shelter of the trenches after the bombardment. I'm waiting here for the remnants of it – I have no-one now under my command. If any survive, I'm here to stop them and take them under my command.'[4] Zeki Bey looked around for another officer, but none were to be seen, and clearly he was getting nowhere with the distraught captain. Zeki Bey asked him where his regimental commander was. The agitated officer pointed towards the southern parts of Johnston Jolly – occupied by the Turkish 125th Regiment.

Captain Zeki Bey headed off, soon coming across a half company of Turks lying in the valley, across the route of his battalion, who were now beginning to enter Owen's Gully. These men were clearly rattled and didn't have any idea what to do. They were the survivors of the garrison of Lone Pine. 'They had climbed out of their trenches and got down the gully and were lying there... Fire was coming down the valley from somewhere on the southern side of it.'[5] Zeki Bey pushed on, as he had no time to waste. He came across the regimental commander, Major Tevfik Bey, along the slopes of Johnston's Jolly. The commander was also clearly rattled by the attack and the collapse of his regiment. Zeki Bey tried to reassure him: 'Don't be anxious, Tevfik Bey, I have come with my battalion, which is very well rested and calm. We've come from rest (it was not true of course), and we'll do whatever you want.'[6] Tevfik Bey replied: 'Give me some men.' Zeki Bey asked: 'What trenches do you want them to go into?' Tevfik Bey replied: 'I'll give you some men. They'll take you to the headquarters of the two battalions and the commanding officers will tell you where they want your men to go.'[7]

Captain Zeki Bey climbed down into Owen's Gully, where he again came under fire from the Australians manning the trenches along the northern part of Lone Pine. His battalion was ahead of him. 'It was clear that the trouble was at the head of the branch Gully. That is, the deep, spoon-shaped hollow which here opened out of Owen's Gully on its southern side, and biting more than half-way across the Lone Pine plateau,' he said, describing The Cup.[8] All of the communication trenches from the northern half of Lone Pine ran into the upper slopes of The Cup, which were terraced with bivouac positions for reserves and the regimental headquarters. [9] Captain Kemal wrote a brief report immediately following the battle: 'Major Tevik, commander of the 47th Regiment, which was entrusted with the defence of the said ridge [Lone Pine], had always been a person you could trust. The fact that the trenches were hidden and with protective ditches, and what is more the presence of two lines of trenches, made us reach the conclusion that the eventual attack of the English towards that position would not be successful. We were wrong.'[10]

Most of the Turkish survivors of the 47th Regiment still in the Pine were clinging to the eastern edges of the plateau. Company officers had rallied some of their men and tried to hold the end of saps from the advancing Australians. Zeki Bey climbed up towards The Cup and met some junior officers and the commanding officer of another battalion that had been pushed out of Lone Pine. This officer was 'much cooler than the other had been'.[11] Their headquarters had been on a terrace high up on the side of the valley just behind the trenches, with one battalion at one end and the other opposite. The area had become a magnet for Turkish reinforcements and was becoming crowded with men. If the ANZAC howitzers had shelled the area just behind Lone Pine it would have resulted in a slaughter. Opposite the mouth of the gully, there were some stables partly dug into the side of Kirmezi Sirt (Johnston's Jolly) where horses were still stabled. It was here that the Turkish commanding officer made his command post. Zeki Bey ran up a gully after his battalion and as he reached the top of the plateau he found that his men had been pushed into the front lines by officers of the 47th Regiment.[12] Earlier, as men climbed onto the rear areas of The Cup, officers from various parts of Lone Pine ordered them into the battle. These officers fed Zeki Bey's men into the hastily established and increasingly crowded front line at the very rear of their former position – now represented by just three trenches.[13]

Turks had taken up a position just short of Aylward's Post, along the southern flank of the Australian position at Lone Pine – within easy bombing range. Close by, others were holding the eastern end of the sap, now barricaded by Lieutenant William McDonald and his men, having given up for the time being the capture of this post. Others were in the sap that intersected with the position held by Major Iven Mackay and his men – the same sap from which the Turkish soldier had killed Corporal Mills and others – and the Turks here had constructed their own barricade. Zeki Bey now anxiously approached this part of the line. He later told Charles Bean how he came across 'not an officer but only the Hoja – the chaplain – of my battalion. It being the 1st Battalion of the regiment, he ranked as Mufti – the 2nd and 3rd would have an Imam. He was a very brave man and kept his head very well.'[14] Zeki Bey approached the Mufti, who told him: 'You can't go further up here.'[15] Zeki Bey saw a number of dead and wounded from his own battalion, as well as those who had previously held the line before the attack. It was an old trench-bay, rather knocked about. The Mufti said: 'Behind this place there are English.'[16] Bombs were continually being thrown from both sides, and the situation was finely balanced. Zeki Bey recalled that further to the north an ANZAC artillery piece, located along Russell's Top, was enfilading their men in the upper reaches of The Cup and Owen's Gully. The Hoja Mufti spoke reassuringly to Zeki Bey: 'Don't be anxious about this flank – I'll remain here.'[17] The major realised that the real threat was towards the centre and southern flank, so he left the position in the hands of the capable Mufti and headed south.[18]

The situation at the centre was extremely precarious, as the Australians had managed to push close to the very edge of the plateau. At a corner of a sap Zeki Bey met a young officer who told him that the communication sap just beyond was held by the Australians – they could see their bayonets. Australian jam-tin bombs and Turkish grenades were going over from both sides. Zeki Bey recalled: 'In the trench behind me were dead and wounded, and the soldiers were stepping over them. This increased the emotion of the troops; they were in a state of high strain. I said to the young officer, "You will bar this trench with your fire until we see what is happening elsewhere."'[19]

The captain pushed further south through communication saps crowded with wounded and panic-stricken men. Just above his head, bullets cracked by, thudding into parapets, causing sand and pebbles to pour into the trench. Amid the smoke and smell of cordite, the sound of exploding bombs and men yelling and screaming in anger and urgency was unnerving. This part of the newly established Turkish line was the highest part of their position – and the most important. As he emerged from the main communication sap, Zeki Bey came across an NCO with his men. The major asked: 'What is the position? What has happened?'[20] The NCO replied: 'The English reached even here – see, there are three of their dead here.'[21] Zeki Bey looked down and saw an 'Australian lying beside me'.[22] Unlike the central and northern parts of the line, the Turkish position here was being defended by just a handful of men in disconnected rifle pits. The Australians now occupied all the saps and trenches in this area. Things were clearly critical, as there were just a few saps behind them, which had been for communication purposes, and one cross-trench – none had been built for defence. One concerted attack by the Australians would push through, forcing the surviving Turks off the plateau, whose eastern edge in some cases lay just metres behind them.

An officer approached Captain Zeki Bey, telling him, 'The English have entered our trenches and these men won't go into them.'[23] To encourage them, Zeki Bey replied loudly: 'The trenches aren't empty – we hold enough of them.'[24] He took the young officer to the point that he had just visited, showing him that they had enough troops ready to defend the positions now being held. From the rear of the trenches they looked towards the head of Owen's Gully, where large numbers of Turks were positioned in The Cup and others were entering the northern and central parts of the line. This reassured the officer and his men. Zeki Bey now made his way north through the congested central communication trench back into the centre of their tenuous position. It was there that he observed for the first time the Australians putting up red and yellow artillery marker flags, indicating to the Australian commanders and ANZAC artillery batteries the farthest points gained by their men.[25]

The attack was now at a standstill. Captain Zeki Bey knew that if the Australians tried to push home their advantage, his whole line would disintegrate. The only trench the Turks held that blocked such an advance was a very deep communication trench roughly running along a north–south axis, with three smaller communication trenches running from it off the plateau and down into The Cup. This deep trench, however, had no firing step – it hadn't been dug for defence. He ordered the men to leave 'everything else, and quickly put fire steps in this trench so as to give us a definite line'.[26] With bayonets and entrenching tools, the men set to work. He ordered a nearby NCO and others in this part of the line to provide covering fire to ensure that the Australians kept their heads down. The same thing was being done by other

Turks on their own initiative and a defensible front line was soon established from where the Mufti was located to the north, and to the head of The Cup to the south. The communication trenches were filling with men, ready to join the fight. Seeing that for the moment things were in hand, Zeki Bey headed back to Johnston's Jolly to report the situation. His whole battalion had long since been absorbed into the trenches and he would soon need more men. He wondered why few reinforcements were being sent from Johnston's Jolly and perhaps more importantly why he was not receiving concentrated covering fire from there. To his dismay he would find out all too soon.[27]

12

'...the scrub being alight
in several places'

Though the initial ANZAC charge had undoubtedly put the Turks on the back foot at the Pine, particularly in the north and centre, the level of casualties and the fear of an imminent and powerful counterattack made it inevitable that the men of 1st Battalion would be called upon to reinforce the line. Sometime just after 6 p.m., requests came back from the forward parties across the plateau to Colonel Neville Smyth, commander of the brigade and in charge of the attack, at his command post, next to the entrance of B5 tunnel at The Pimple. He and his staff were barely able to make out the word 'reinforcements' being signalled with a morse-periscope (a tiny blinded window-like device attached to a pole used to flash a message in morse code) under the direction of Major David McConaghy, leading the 3rd Battalion. The device was made useless by the constant pall of smoke and dust, and McConaghy was forced to send the signaller himself across no-man's-land to confirm the need for more men in the central trenches. Meanwhile, reports came from Lieutenant Colonel Macnaghten, of the 4th Battalion in the north, who confirmed that the Australians had 'penetrated 200 to 300 yards from the front trench, but that his left was weak, the Turks were massing to attack it, and reinforcements were required'. Shortly after, Macnaghten sent another report: 'Left safe. Centre wants a few men'.[1] Smyth had to determine how best to deploy the 1st Battalion amid the chaos. Charles Bean later described how Smyth was 'keeping his head most coolly – giving distinct orders to every messenger what to do – sorting out messages – this he answered; that, marked out for Major King'.[2]

Within minutes of receiving Macnaghten's messages, Smyth received another report from the Pine that a large number of Turks from Johnston's Jolly with fixed bayonets could be seen advancing in the communication trenches in Owen's Gully. From The Pimple itself, the bayonets of these Turks could be seen protruding just above the parapets along the southern parts of the Jolly. In reality, however, few of these Turks were likely reinforcing Lone Pine, but instead were being sent to the southern flank of their position at the Jolly to further strengthen it against a possible flanking attack. The threat from the Jolly against the northern flank of the Australian position at the Pine would be an ongoing concern for the Australians that night – almost to a justified point of paranoia. Indeed, a few hours later a note reached Colonel White, informing him that Turks were massing in Owen's Gully – the note requested that artillery shell the gully.[3] A few hours after that, Walker received another request for the guns to light up the gully with star shells as the men believed the Turks were about to mount a counterattack against them in strength.[4] Having now seen for himself the Turks apparently reinforcing Lone Pine from the Jolly, Smyth rush his first reserves forward. Captain Harold Jacobs and his company of the 1st Battalion would have to get across no-man's-land from The Pimple in order to reach the Pine – luckily for them, the enveloping dust and smoke provided some cover, but it would still be a deadly 100-metre dash.[5]

At the headquarters of the 1st Australian Division, Major General Walker and Colonel White were anxiously awaiting news, and quickly reviewed the information as it arrived. It was recorded in the divisional staff diary: 'The attack began... The enemy artillery were quickly onto the opposing parapets, over which our infantry advanced... There appears to be keenest wish to get forward. The men taking the space between the trenches with great gallantry... 4th Bn now pushing forward and well in trenches. Our bayonets visible 30 yards from enemy's position. Enemy artillery fire very severe, the scrub being alight in several places.'[6] Both Walker and White must have been pleased that their men had apparently managed to capture their objectives and they now focused on reinforcing their success with more troops – the Turks were now surely committing their reserves into retaking Lone Pine. Smyth wrote that by 6.30 p.m., he'd committed the whole of the 1st Battalion to battle at the request of the senior commander in Lone Pine.[7]

Charles Bean, close to Smyth, witnessed the battalion's advance: 'Enemy's machine guns always told when our men were going forward. Not a man came back. Attempts to signal – telephone carried by two men came rushing back. Dropped into a hole. They took one line over, another line back. It got cut by shrapnel'.[8] Private Frederick Cherry, from Hillgrove, New South Wales, of the 1st Battalion, was among the last of the battalion to charge across no-man's land. The 20-year-old climbed out of the secret trench: 'I only had a faint idea which way to go so I crawled on my hands and knees for some yards. My rifle in one hand and shovel in the other. I passed the mine crater and there were two of our lads there both wounded. One said to me "Any chance of getting back mate?" and I said "You had better stop [here] till it gets dark".'[9] With this, Cherry pushed on to follow up behind the last of his section. All around shrapnel was exploding and machine-gun bullets swept the field. He was almost across the Daisy Patch, when he felt a 'thump on the thigh and down I went.'[10] He staggered and fell into the former front-line trench at

Lone Pine, which was by now full of wounded men.

Bean's colleague and friend Phillip Schuler recalled seeing 'the signallers creeping over the hill, feeling for the ends of broken wires, trying to link up some of the broken threads, so that information could be quickly sought and obtained'.[11] Twenty-one-year-old Guildford jeweller Signalman James McKinley, of the 1st Australian Divisional Signals Company, knew he was going to have a sleepless night, so he was getting as much rest as he could in his dugout behind The Pimple. Just as he was getting settled, he heard the inevitable cry: 'Linesmen!' He jumped out of his hole, dug into a low-lying spur, and reported immediately to his officer. McKinley and another signaller were ordered to trace the line back to 1st Brigade Headquarters, as it was dead – it clearly wasn't only the telephone lines connecting The Pimple to Lone Pine that were being cut by Turkish fire. McKinley wrote to his mother:

> After a few hundred yards we came to Artillery Road and it was here that our troubles grew fast, for the parapet along the road had been blown in and the Turkish shells were still trying to find our guns there. At one time there had been a dressing station on this road, but it had been blown to pieces . . . In a recess in the side of the road we passed an 18-pounder out of action. Shrapnel had killed the gun crew, who were lying alongside the gun. On arriving at our destination we found that nothing could be done...so we decided to return to our own brigade and run out a new line. While we were at 1st Brigade Headquarters it was being shelled heavily from all sides, and to make matters worse their wounded were returning from the firing line, half of them having little idea where they were making.[12]

In Lone Pine there was no place safe for the wounded. Private Angelo Humphreys, who had put his age at eighteen on enlisting, had attacked the Turkish trenches less than an hour before, but had been wounded in the left thigh and head while fighting in the centre of the Pine. He looked around to see if he knew anybody along-side him and noticed that his cobber, 36-year-old Sydney labourer Private Sidney McClure, was also wounded. McClure had taken the youngster under his wing since training in Egypt, defending Angelo's right to remain a teetotaller. Some of the men had begun to call Angelo 'Molly-coddle', 'Girlie' and half-a-dozen other names, until Sidney put a stop to it. Angelo crawled over to Sidney and began to bandage his wounds but almost immediately felt dizzy from the loss of blood. Angelo later recalled Sidney's instructions to him: '"Lay down, sonny, and when you feel better you can bandage me up". I lay down and he said, "We are fairly safe here". And a shot came past me and killed him instantly.'[13] Sidney has no known grave and is commemorated on the Lone Pine Memorial. Angelo was later evacuated back to a hospital in Egypt and then onto Australia. He was discharged in early 1916, not only as a result of his wounds, but due to a letter from his parents to the Department of Defence after they had heard of his enlistment and wounding, stating that their son was just fifteen years old.[14]

Private Cherry, along with a number of other wounded sheltering in the former Turkish front-line trench, decided that as soon as it was dark they'd try and make their way back to The Pimple – which meant crossing no-man's-land. About an hour later, just before they set off, an officer warned them if any star shells came over to lie flat on the ground. When they were about halfway across, there was a shell burst, vividly remembered by Cherry: '[It was] right over our heads. I stood still and looked around and it was just as if it had been snowing. All our lads lying there dead, it was awful.'[15] The brush fire that had earlier broken out in no-man's-land was intensifying and 'moved remorselessly towards the stricken men. The yells and screams were plainly heard above the din of battle. The mental torture of their mates, forced to look on and listen while bombs and ammunition exploded in the equipment of the dying men was hellish.'[16]

In Brown's Dip, behind The Pimple, Phillip Schuler witnessed the wounded pouring into the dressing station and time and time again he saw stretcher-bearers and wounded being hit by Turkish shrapnel. When a stretcher-bearer was hit he was 'compelled to hand over [his] stretchers to willing volunteers, who sprang up out of the earth... The ground was covered each minute with a dozen bursting shells within the small area I could see. The dirt, powdered, fell on our shoulders.'[17] At the same time, medical officers were treating the wounded as they passed, halting to examine each man, bandages and iodine at the ready for the less seriously wounded. Schuler wrote that the men assessed as being beyond all help 'lay in a heap across the path leading into the sap. It was, after all, just a question of luck. You kept close into a bank, and with the shells tearing up the earth round you, hoped that you might escape. After a time there was so much else to think of, especially for the men fighting, that it was no time to think of the shells.'[18]

Captain Zeki Bey was still in Kanli Sirt (Lone Pine) and was concerned that while some fire from Kirmezi Sirt (Johnston's Jolly) was targeting the Australian position; most men there appeared to be holding their fire. The captain hurriedly made his way back to Kirmezi Sirt to request urgent supporting fire from the commander of the 125th Regiment, Lieutenant Colonel Abdul Risak Bey, whose troops held the trenches there. Risak Bey was clearly more concerned about his own position and told Zeki Bey that the attackers on his front were active, and that some of the enemy sandbags had been removed from the Australian front-line trenches, which usually preceded an attack. Zeki Bey argued that at the moment this was of no major consequence as Kirmezi Sirt was well supported and covered with machine-gun enfilade from Merkez Tepe (German Officers' Trench), a few hundred metres to the north – the immediate threat was to Kanli Sirt. The two officers debated the issue, while the battle for the Pine raged on.

The Australians of the 7th Infantry Battalion opposite Johnston's Jolly were indeed trying to give the impression that they were about to attack. These men poured machine-gun and rifle fire into Abdul Risak Bey's position. Birdwood had earlier informed its commanding officer, Lieutenant Colonel 'Pompey' Elliott, of the unwelcome news that if the assaulting battalions were unsuccessful in capturing and holding Lone Pine, the 7th Battalion would be required to attack the Jolly at dawn the next day. Such an assault could only have one outcome – the slaughter of Elliott's men with no hope of success. Elliott later wrote: 'My task was (with a battalion counting cooks and details, signallers, it did not amount to quite 700 men) to attack a formidable enemy's work known as "Johnston Gully". We knew it was held by a large number of men with machine guns giving three tiers of fire… We have since ascertained that it was held by three complete [Turkish] battalions. You can guess whether my doubts were justified.'[19]

Meanwhile, Zeki Bey was getting frustrated with the ongoing pointless debate with Abdul Risak Bey. Tevfik Bey, who was also present, was writing a report to the commander of the 16th Division, Colonel Rüstü, stating that after the attack, the soldiers under his command had 'retaken the front lines in my position; but they cannot hold on there – they need large reinforcements, and the troops who have gone up there are not enough'.[20] Having just left the trenches it appeared Tevfik Bey was referring to – those running along the side of Owen's Gully – Zeki Bey knew that the Australians had never attacked or occupied these trenches and saps, and sought to correct the misunderstanding. But he was getting nowhere, and grew concerned that his fellow officers seemed more concerned about potential threats, or writing 'propaganda' for their superiors, as opposed to focusing on the very real dangers facing them just a few hundred metres south. He sternly informed Tevfik Bey that he was going back to Lone Pine to help consolidate their extremely tenuous position, adding: 'But you too, on your part, do all you can.'[21]

Lieutenant Colonel Scobie, of the 2nd Battalion, had now arrived in the Pine and took over command from Major Arthur Stevens. The signallers and runners attempted to keep Scobie in communication with Brigade Headquarters back in Brown's Dip. Following closely behind Scobie as he crossed no-man's-land was Alexander 'Doc' Fullerton, of the 2nd Battalion, who had earlier set up his dressing station in Victoria Gully, just behind The Pimple.[22] However, Fullerton soon chose to go in search of the wounded rather than waiting for them to be brought to him. The battalion history states how the fifty-year-old Sydney physician was looking anything but a soldier – more like 'a boy scout in his shorts with hat crushed in New Zealand fashion'.[23] As darkness fell, he went out into no-man's-land looking for men in need of his help. Almost immediately, just beyond the parapet he came across a young wounded soldier and asked him where he'd been hit. When the wounded man told him, Doc responded cheerily: 'Never mind, my lad, you'll get better and live to rear a large family.'[24] Fullerton sauntered on towards Lone Pine, stopping when necessary to render assistance. At one point he was knocked over by a bursting shell, but Private Arthur Barnes was on hand to pick him up, and together the two men entered the Pine to establish their aid post. Doc Fullerton would be conspicuous by his presence throughout the battle of Lone Pine. He believed in treating the wounded as quickly as possible, which meant tending them where they fell – at great risk to himself.

Scobie, now in the centre of the action along the southern flank of the works, placed Stevens in charge of the left sector, while he went straight to the most exposed position, the extreme right flank. He found there a very difficult position, as the trenches were quite straight with no traverses, and along this length of trench small parties of Australians were fighting without knowledge of those on their flanks. Scobie immediately got men to start filling sandbags, which were obtained from the living and dead, and set about constructing low barricades, parapets and fire steps. By now, 26-year-old Captain Harold Jacobs, of the 1st Battalion, who had earlier distinguished himself on the first day of the landing among the fighting for Mortar Ridge, had reached the southern part of Lone Pine with his company. He wrote that the first senior officer he came across was Scobie, who positioned him at a post just south of Captain Syd Cook.[25] Twenty-three-year-old porter Private Clifford Judd, of the 1st Battalion, overheard Scobie saying that he was disappointed that no machine guns had been brought over. Judd turned to the officer and asked for a written authority to get one. Scobie obliged and Judd took off alone over no-man's-land and soon returned with a machine gun.[26] Judd crossed the treacherous paddock of no-man's-land twice more to bring over additional equipment, ammunition and bombs. Jacobs recalled that Scobie 'thought this act so meritorious that he instructed me to give him Judd's name when the action was over. He said he intended recommending him for the VC, adding, "Nothing is too good for a man who would do that".'[27]

It wasn't long before Jacobs and his men were pushing down towards the deep sap (Jacobs's Trench), along the southern flank of Lone Pine. Here the Turks who had stopped Lieutenant Digges La Touché's advance had dug themselves in and began to fire at Jacobs' party. Twenty-five-year-old farmer from New England, New South Wales, Sergeant Archie Barwick, of the 1st Battalion, was likely with Jacobs and recalled one of his men dashed around a transverse bend without hesitation: 'He threw himself fair at them [Turks] and the six fired together and fairly riddled him with bullets. That was our chance and we [went] into them.'[28] Some of the Turks were taken prisoner and as the last of them left under escort, Jacobs was surprised to find two dead Australians and one seriously wounded in the post. On uncovering the face of the wounded officer, he was upset to see his friend Digges La Touché, seriously wounded in the stomach. Jacobs later recorded: 'I intended to let him remain. But he appreciated that he was in the way and asked me to have him sent out. I pointed out that it would be better for him to remain there.'[29] Indeed, moving a man with such a wound was virtually a death sentence and La Touché would have known it. Regardless, he insisted on being moved as he was 'in the way and would interfere with the consolidation of the trench, saying, "It's not me you must consider, but the position".'[30]

It was becoming increasingly obvious that the gap between the 2nd and 3rd battalions had to be bridged – any concentrated attack by the Turks here, at the centre of the Australian line, could shatter their defences. As 24-year-old Sydney wool broker Captain Cecil Sasse arrived at this part of the Pine, with another company of the 1st Battalion, he was ordered to help men from the 3rd Battalion dig a fire trench connecting the isolated posts – Tubb's Corner and Youden's Post. Meanwhile, Colonel Macnaghten had sent another report back to The Pimple: 'Turks were massing in Owen's Gully... Colonel Brown reports Owen's Gully full of Turks.'[31] It was also at this point that Brigade Headquarters was advised: '2nd Bn [Battalion] holds enemy line to top of hill on right. Ammunition and bombs asked for to strengthen our position. Bde [Brigade] advised that we are in touch with 3rd Bn on left and that we have been reinforced by about 50 of 1st Bn.... again asked for... bombs.'[32]

Signaller Albert Townsend of the 2nd Battalion, who had gone over with Major Arthur Smith in the first wave, had volunteered to be Smith's runner between Lone Pine and headquarters. He made several trips across no-man's-land and on one of these occasion was ordered by a brigade officer to take a rest, but he merely picked up the reply and made off, seemingly bearing a charmed life.[33] All the while, his mate Sergeant William Wass, still suffering from a fractured skull, remained in Lone Pine at the telephone, varying signal duty with bombing. Wass would eventually be evacuated out of the Pine on 9 August.[34]

A few hours earlier, the men of the 12th Battalion had received orders to move to their allotted position in Gun Lane, behind The Pimple – they would soon be sent over to Lone Pine to help reinforce the men of the 1st Brigade. Companies fell in by platoons, as later described by Major Denis Lane. Company sergeant majors called the rolls in record time, as shrapnel from counter-battery fire was sweeping the parade ground. Companies moved independently onto Artillery Road where they came yet again under a perfect hail of shrapnel and high-explosive shells, as the Turks tried to destroy the Australian battery there. The men soon reached the relative cover provided along Gun Lane with few casualties. The battalion strength at this point was very weak: 'Companies averaged about 150 bayonets [full strength around 250 men]. While waiting for nearly three hours in Gun Lane, the shell fire was severe, and it was remarkable that casualties were small, as shells repeatedly burst on the parapet along the Lane.'[35]

Twenty-nine-year-old Cootamundra baker Private John Gammage, of the 1st Battalion, was well known for his resentment of authority and was not slow in coming forward, telling any flashy officer what he could do with his spit and polish.[36] Undoubtedly he would have gotten on well with Smithy of the 11th Battalion. Many years later, Gammage bitterly recalled: 'The moans of our own poor fellows and also Turks as we trampled on their wounded bodies was awful. We rushed them out of their 2nd and third line of trenches in half an hour. The wounded bodies of both Turks and our own in the 2nd and 3rd line, especially the third, were piled up 3 and 4 deep.'[37] Bombs continued to be thrown into trenches, and as soon as one man went down another took his place. Besides the Australian wounded, Gammage remembered the wounded Turks 'lying in our trench were cut to pieces with their own bombs. We had no time to think of our wounded... their pleas for mercy were not heeded... Some poor fellows lay for 30 hours waiting for help and many died still waiting.'[38]

In some trenches the Australians developed informal bomb defences among themselves, usually consisting of three men. The first would be a rifleman whose job it was to shoot or bayonet any Turk who presented himself. The second, the 'catcher', was to catch the Turkish grenades and heave them back at the Turks – sometimes this also involved throwing back one of their own jam-tin bombs that the Turks themselves had returned. Clearly, the chances of a bomb exploding on its third throw were extremely high. The third man ran around the trench floor with a half-full sandbag, trying to smother any bomb or grenade that the catcher had missed. It was only a matter of time, however, before the catcher or the smotherer would fumble, with the likely result being that all three would be killed, or perhaps blinded or maimed for life by jagged fragments of metal. Another three would take their place.[39] Twenty-eight-year old carpenter Corporal Riggs, of the 1st Battalion, was put out of action in trying to throw back a Turkish grenade: 'There was an awful explosion and I was knocked to billy-ho. One of their bombs had landed at my feet. I scrambled up but my legs were numb... Again I was lucky. Only my legs were hurt and where others had had arms and legs blow off I was intact.'[40] His wounds were serious enough and he would soon be on a ship back home to Australia.

Lance Corporal Lawrence, back at The Pimple, was fully aware of the dangers his fellow sappers were facing up on the plateau: 'What they have gone through during the last hour has been Hell let loose and as soon as darkness falls, they will be called upon to dig trenches across to those of the enemy that we have just captured – digging away out in the open between the two lines, never knowing when the Turks may counter-attack, up what valley they'll come, nor at what moment one may be singled out by a stray bullet.'[41] When ready, a party would make their way forward, with shells 'flying over in scores', Lawrence wrote in his diary, 'but when these fellows come down again we shall have a better idea of what is going on and what has been done and accomplished'.[42]

Cooks at the rear bivouacs were boiling water for tea and trying, amongst the exploding shells, shrapnel and bullets, to make a decent hot meal for those about to reinforce Lone Pine and for the few coming down the line. This much-needed sustenance would also be carted up to the men in the firing line at The Pimple, and the engineers and sappers digging the communication trenches from the former secret underground trench towards Lone Pine. All greatly appreciated the cup of tea and hot stew – even if the latter consisted mostly of bully beef mixed up with crumbled army rock chewers and the odd piece of onion.

At about this time a single soldier climbed up to The Pimple from the gullies below, ignoring the shelling and stray bullets. He was determined to cross over to the Pine. His commanding officer had given him a vital job – he was to supply rum to the men of his battalion.[43] The lone soldier, carrying a demijohn on his shoulder and his rifle in his other hand, now approached B5 tunnel. Colonel Smyth was at the mouth of the tunnel, receiving messages, and trying to keep the entrance clear to let more urgent traffic through. Charles Bean again recalled seeing Smyth directing reinforcements into Lone Pine tunnels 'as quietly as a ticket collector passing passengers onto a platform'.[44] All had to pass through thirty metres of narrow, pitch-dark tunnel, and from there into the shallow uncompleted saps, and then out over no-man's-land to reach the former parapet of the Turkish works. There were unending lines of men carrying ammunition, water cans, picks, shovels, sandbags and messages, signallers with wire, engineers, stretcher-bearers – all crawling at a snail's pace. The tunnel was 'constantly blocked, while they carried one or two poor badly wounded fellows back... Only those men whose presence was urgently required at the Pine were allowed to go through the tunnel.'[45] The soldier approached the tunnel entrance:

'And what are you carrying, my man?'

'Third Battalion's rum, sir.'

'What?'

'Third Battalion's rum, sir. Colonel put me in charge of it, and told me to see the...'

'Well, put it down here, and stand by.'

'The colonel told me to take it through, sir.'

'Well, put it down here for the present.'

'The colonel told me...'

'Look here! Never mind what you were told; put it down there at once!'[46]

The man put his heavy load down on a fire step, and retired a short distance in annoyance. For a couple of minutes he watched as Smyth dealt with far more important things, but as soon as the colonel looked up in his direction, the soldier stepped forward: 'How about the Third Battalion's rum, sir?' 'Oh, well get along with you,' answered Smyth. The soldier picked up his rifle, shouldered the demijohn of run and disappeared into the tunnel.[47]

In Brown's Dip the chaplains and padres were flat out attending to the dead and dying. Chaplain Dean Talbot witnessed a steady file of wounded, all through the battle, some limping along with the aid of another wounded man, while others came in on stretchers and passed through the dressing stations straight down the gully to the beach, to be taken by tugs and sweepers to the hospital ships. Padre McAuliffe and Chaplain Talbot went together to say a prayer over the dead and buried: '[With no] idea to which religious flock they belonged, and the members of different flocks were all mixed up together, the good priest in such cases blessed the grave, and I, with solemn prayer, committed the bodies to the earth. I remember burying about 19 in one long trench at Brown's Dip.'[48] While in Australia the Catholic and Protestant divide was still broad and influential, the necessities of war gave rise to a less sectarian view in the trenches.

Meanwhile, stretcher-bearer Herbert Reynolds and his mates at the 4th Battalion Aid Post were still located in Shrapnel Gully awaiting orders. They'd expected to go forward where they would be needed. Yet hours ticked by without any orders arriving and they began to think that they'd been forgotten. They became anxious as, every few minutes, howitzer shells would blast nearby, showering them with earth. The shells 'crashed and exploded in the ground at times only a few yards away, one actually crashed among a dozen or more of us, the explosion tossing us in all directions, but fate was kind and only one chap was slightly wounded but the concussion gave everyone a thorough shaking up'.[49] Anything would be better than sitting around waiting for the next shell to tear them apart. It was impossible for them to believe they weren't needed somewhere. '[Taking] risks in performing a dangerous duty is passed by without further notice, but inaction under these circumstances is terribly trying on the nerves,' recalled Reynolds.[50] This state of affairs lasted throughout the night and they 'welcomed the opportunity of taking an occasional casualty down to the C.C. [Casualty Clearing] Station just to relieve the effect of this forced inactivity a little'.[51] He and his mates, however, would soon enough be in the thick of it.

Meanwhile, a message was received at divisional headquarters, at Brown's Dip, from Birdwood: 'Well done, 1st Bde. You have done splendidly.'[52] White sent word to Smyth: 'Message from General Walker to Smyth, "I congratulate your gallant brigade."'[53]

'Christ, won't someone finish me off?'

Captain Zeki Bey was back at the Pine when night fell, as momentary flashes from exploding enemy bombs and Turkish grenades enabled men to see the dead and dying all around them. The half-company of the 47th, which he had first found lying in the valley, had been sent up in disorder, but it had entered the fight.[1] With nightfall, reinforcements from the 13th Regiment, under the command of Lieutenant Colonel Ali Riza, began to arrive. The commanders of the right and centre battalions of the 47th Regiment also came back to their old headquarters in The Cup.[2] Now the men of the 47th and 57th regiments began to establish a limited defensive line consisting of what had previously been narrow communication saps. These saps were expanded into defensive trenches with firing steps and would become crucial in protecting the head of The Cup and their trenches just in front of it, at the rear of the plateau. Zeki Bey observed that the Australians appeared to be digging in, rather than preparing to attack, and wondered why they were not pushing home their obvious advantage.[3]

Major General Esat Pasha now expected that British reinforcements would be thrown against him in order to take Kilid

Bahr Plateau – located between Helles and Anzac. He ordered the 9th Turkish Division, under the command of German Colonel Hans Kannengiesser, currently stationed to his south, to move three infantry regiments with artillery towards the southern flank at Anzac, just behind Gaba Tepe. They were to prepare themselves for an enemy attack against that position, where Esat Pasha's attention was firmly focused. Also now making its way to Lone Pine was the 15th Regiment, which had left the relative quiet and safety of the northern heights to reinforce Anzac's southern flank. By nightfall, Esat had decided to go on the offensive and retake Lone Pine. He ordered the commander of the 16th Division, Colonel Rüstü, who was in charge of the southern sector at Anzac, to launch an immediate counterattack at Kanli Sirt. Given the confusion, however, it would be some time before the attack could be organised, and the commanders at Kanli Sirt knew that it was first crucial that their men be reorganised.[4]

Birdwood would have been pleased to know that the Turkish commander was reinforcing the southern flank of Anzac with men from his 19th Division, who were hence being relocated away from the true ANZAC target – the Sari Bair Range to the north. He would not, however, have been happy to hear that Esat Pasha was also bringing up far more troops than expected from the south, including the 9th Division, with another close to Gaba Tepe on standby to do likewise. These would provide Esat Pasha with a large number of reserves relatively close by, ready to be thrown into any part of his line – including the Sari Bair Range.[5]

From the start of the attack on Lone Pine, Australian sappers and infantry fatigue parties had been digging furiously to push forward from the end of tunnels B5, B6 and B8, before breaking to the surface to open saps that would link up with the Lone Pine trenches. Earlier, the newly promoted Lieutenant John Playne and his sappers dashed forward during the assault and entered the Turkish lines with the job of digging these communication saps, working back towards the ANZAC lines. However, in doing so Playne was killed almost immediately on reaching the Pine. [6] One of those working from the other end – at the former secret trench cutting through no-man's-land – was Private Donkin, fighting off terror and a headache from the concussion of shells exploding above: 'Our old remedy rum does the trick. Also the air is foul from the smell of bodies buried which we continually strike under the surface.'[7] Another engineer, Major Athelstan Martyn, recalled how his sappers worked in a frenzy at the head of the tunnels to break through. Many of these men had to be carried out, overcome by the foul air from the fumes and dead bodies, but the work had to continue at all costs so that those fighting at the Pine could be resupplied and the wounded brought out. Lance Corporal Lawrence wrote in his diary that as a sapper made his way up to the line, the next you heard of him was usually that he'd been either 'killed or wounded by stray shells or bullets and has been taken away. They cannot tell me very much of what has been done; everyone was too busy; there were too many shells and bullets flying about to make the atmosphere anywhere healthy enough to go looking around.'[8] Having finally broken through to the surface, the sappers decided under cover of darkness to speed up the work by digging in the open space of no-man's-land, at great risk.[9] The craters formed by the earlier exploding mines were also made good use of, and saved some digging, but afterwards this was found to be anything but a blessing as 'the broken ground would not stand up, and much revetting had to be resorted to, greatly depleting our stock of sandbags, which was already almost exhausted'.[10]

By 9 p.m., a sap from the southernmost of these tunnels, B5, had been pushed out sufficiently into no-man's-land and an opening made, so that reinforcements, runners and fatigue parties had only a relatively short exposed space to cross in order to reach Lone Pine. By midnight, Private William Graham, of the 4th Battalion, observed that 'one of the open saps, commenced by engineers in our line as soon as the attack was launched, had been driven through to our sector, enabling many of our more seriously wounded to be taken out. And now food and drink were coming through to us from our cooks who were soon to set up their cookhouse in our new home.'[11] By 1 a.m., 7 August, the open sap connecting the B5 tunnel to the Pine was completed. Major Martyn recalled that the sap cut through to a Turkish tunnel running parallel and slightly in advance of the old Turkish front line. This formed a good means of getting into their trenches, as the tunnel was about 2.5 metres wide, semi-circular in section, with 'a portion cut out of the floor in the centre allowing a head room of about 6 feet 6 inches, with a raised ledge on each side on which Jacko evidently ate and slept'.[12] Martyn also wrote that as soon as communications were opened up with the front line of the Pine, the engineers attempted a tour of inspection, but they didn't get far as the trenches were crammed with 'dead and wounded, and packed with infantry, so that moving about was next to impossible. The whole place looked like a regular shambles, and the tunnels were choked with dead Turks, rifles, ammunition, and other impediments.'[13] Indeed, an officer with Martyn recalled that the task of removing the dead was a 'colossal one [so] we gave up the attempt and sealed up the mouth of the Turkish tunnels, leaving the bodies inside'.[14] They had seen enough and headed back to Brown's Dip.

Tunnel B6 was the northernmost and while some progress had been made in connecting it to the Pine, it had to be abandoned due to accurate Turkish fire from Johnston's Jolly, and from some Turks who had crept out into no-man's-land.[15] But with the establishment of communications between The Pimple and Lone Pine via B5 and B8, it was now possible to bring out the remaining Turkish prisoners, who until then had been held in their tunnels. Martyn recalled: 'About midnight a big batch of prisoners came in through B5, and a more motley crowd they were too, but all seemingly very pleased to be out of the strife at last, so pleased that they shook hands with us, and many of them tried to kiss us, but naturally we were not keen on that luxury.'[16]

All along the line, men from both sides were taking matters into their own hands – there was no tactical rhyme or reason for attacking or holding a position. These and other small-scale attacks were the beginning of the first phase of the long and dreadful counterattacks for which the battle of Lone Pine is chiefly famous.[17] Twenty-five-year-old clerk from Tamworth Captain Harold Nash, of 2nd Battalion, was located somewhere forward of the main Australian lines. He sent an urgent message back for grenades: 'For God's Sake send bombs.' This was the last anyone ever heard from him or his men.[18] Harold Nash and his men have no known grave and are commemorated on the Lone Pine Memorial.

Lance Corporal Lawrence couldn't see much of what was happening at Lone Pine, even after taking up a position in the forward trench of The Pimple. He could, however, hear what was going on: 'It was dark and there is almost continually a deafening roar and crackle of rifle fire from both sides. It is only by maintaining a continuous rifle fire that the position can be held. Louder and deeper sounding you can hear the bombs bursting as they are thrown between the trenches.'[19] As he looked over at the Pine, about one hundred metres away, his eyes were continually drawn to the flashes of jam-tin bombs and cricket-ball grenades that lit up the small deadly space.

It was now after 9 p.m. and two companies of the 12th Battalion were ordered into Lone Pine. One was under the command of Major Denis Lane, who, with his men, moved to the northern flank of the Pine and were to be 'prepared to repel any counterattacks the enemy might make from that direction. The ground over which the advance was made was littered with dead and wounded, and gave one some idea of the terrific fire directed at the assaulting troops.'[20] The trenches at Lone Pine were already crammed with troops and the arrival of Lane's men did not help matters. He believed that the earlier bombardment against Lone Pine had caused many casualties among the Turks – in reality, these casualties were likely from jam-tin bombs and some of their own grenades. Lane went on to conclude that 'bayonets of the assault had completed the havoc. The concentrated hostile gun, rifle and bomb fire every minute added to the dead and wounded encumbering the trenches. Wounded were collected in every sap, and communication trench, and owing to the narrowness of these works, it was difficult to get them out.'[21] There was no room available for reinforcements in the newly established front line of the northern part of Lone Pine, so Lane channelled his men as far as possible through the support trenches. They remained there in readiness throughout the night for the expected Turkish counterattack.[22]

Twenty-one-year-old Tanunda station hand Private Allen Thwaites was with Lane as they entered Lone Pine and was hit in the chest by a bullet: 'Oh, it was an awful feeling! It was like a kick, and with that I felt I was in serious trouble. I could feel it had penetrated my lung and come out my back, and blood was coming out of my nose and mouth, and I was in a sorry state.'[23] Like many others who had been wounded, he had to endure the horrors of the Pine while suffering an agonising wound, as there was no way of getting these men out. He took up a position within a crammed dugout with others – they were not evacuated for another two days. While waiting, Thwaites was 'trying to breathe – I only had one lung you see – till the stretcher-bearers came and carried me down to the hospital ship'.[24] Even so, this would be the start of a long and painful journey.

The 2nd Battalion diary recorded how the wounded were 'lying all over the trenches, and are hampering movement. Efforts being made to evacuate them. Our [Medical Officer] Captain A.Y. Fullerton with two of the Bn's AAMC [Australian Army Medical Corps] units followed the last platoon over, and were doing good work. Enemy dead everywhere and we can't avoid walking on them as they are so thick. Star shells being fired by artillery at regular intervals. Picks, shovels and sand bags are badly needed to prepare position for defense…Enemy's bombing causing a number of casualties.'[25] Doc Fullerton was truly in the thick of it: '[His] work was beyond praise; he had established his aid post, but had no hope of coping with the numerous casualties; although those who were fortunate enough to receive his attention were much brightened by his cheery personality.'[26] Indeed, Fullerton plunged into the area with the thickest of the fighting to treat the wounded, doing what he could with bandages to wounds that obviously needed more than he could administer in the shambles of the Pine. Even so, the men's ability to withstand pain without complaint and their eagerness to rejoin their cobbers in the front line never ceased to amaze him.

One of the medical units to be sent to the Pine at this time was a section from the 2nd Australian Field Ambulance. Twenty-two-year-old Melbourne tailor Private Rupert Laidlow, of this unit, recalled his experiences at the time:

> We commenced collecting the wounded at once, and it was awful, we were under a withering shell fire all the time and one of our squads got the full force of a shell, with the result one man was killed and another three wounded, one very seriously as the shell got him in the abdomen. We had to advance right into the trenches to get our men and some of the wounds were awful. Most of them were shell wounds [likely from bombs] and a large number were caused through machine-gun fire. Head injuries were very numerous…we worked through the night and when daylight broke the next

day. We continued our work through the day until 4 pm we were then relieved for some time.[27]

Pompey Elliott was now informed that given the success of the Lone Pine attack, he and his men would no longer be required to attack Johnston's Jolly. He believed that had his battalion been forced to attack the Jolly it would have been 'practically exterminated attempting a...hopeless task'.[28] He was obviously relieved by the news: 'Just as we were making preparations for the attack by making blanket pathways attached to wooden poles to throw over the enemy's wire entanglements as we rushed forward; I was sent for hurriedly, ordered to cease all preparations for attack and move at once to support of the 1st Brigade whose remnants were being pressed at Lone Pine'.[29] Another order soon arrived requesting he send some platoons from his battalion north to assist in the digging of the communication trenches that were needed in the imminent attack against German Officers' Trench, just hours away.[30] Most men were still ignorant that they were about to be fed into Lone Pine, and now that the attack against the Jolly had been cancelled, they had probably started to relax a little, but it would be only a momentary reprieve. Indeed, four VCs would be awarded to men of the 7th Battalion for their actions over the next few days.

The ANZAC artillery was still under pressure to shell the Turkish batteries along Third Ridge. Colonel Talbot Hobbs received constant appeals made to him to fire on this or that part of the Turkish position, from where they continued to fire on The Pimple and former no-man's-land.[31] Lieutenant Colonel Johnston, of the 2nd Australian Field Artillery Brigade, was witness to the continued bombardment: 'Our guns continued to fire until about 9.30 p.m. and the Turks shelled the "Pimple" like mad. Many shells swept "Gun Lane" and cut men down as a scythe. I cannot imagine how I or anyone else lived through those hot hours...

I will never forget that awful walk among heaps of dead or wounded men, with shells bursting all the time.'[32]

Back at Lone Pine, ongoing small-scale Turkish attacks fell upon the Australian posts. These disjointed Turkish attacks, which started sometime after 10 p.m., were part of Colonel Rüstü's long-awaited counterattack to retake the Pine – the conditions, however, were such that a coordinated attack was impossible.[33] Lance Corporal Aylward and his men were still holding the extreme northern flank. In the communication trench that led into Owen's Gully, the Turks were becoming bolder. Aylward gave his men the order to run from one fire step to another, and open fire rapidly, so as to engage the Turks from as many points as possible – hoping that the Turks might think there were at least twice as many of them there as there actually were. Aylward recalled that 'this quieted the Turks for the time being. About this time the adjutant of the battalion, Lieut. Massie, visited us and after complimenting us on gaining the position, said that he would endeavour to obtain a machine gun, which would be needed to repulse any counter-attack, and also some reinforcements.'[34] Word soon reached them that a machine gun was on its way to support them. This brought some relief until the machine-gunner arrived with no machine gun. However, the Turks were now suspiciously quiet. Aylward ordered a strict watch to be kept while he made his way up the support trench. He soon came across one of his friends, 33-year-old Corporal Ernest Stone, who was unaware that Aylward and his party had gained the end of the trench. Aylward asked that the position behind his own be reinforced. With this, he made his way back to his men, but just as he got there he was met by a call from one of the men who had recently joined them, informing him that 'there was movement out in front. On climbing up, it was discovered that a Turk was within a few yards of our position, but after firing a shot, no further movement was seen.'[35]

Not far away, the bombing war at Mackay's Post was intensifying and Mackay and his men were now surrounded on three sides. Reinforcements were brought into the position as many were either killed or wounded. These men nervously lined up along the northern communication trench, each awaiting their turn in the blood-soaked pit – knowing that at any time they too were likely to be blown to pieces, or far worse, maimed. Many who would die in the post might have been saved if only they could have reached the beach and medical attention – but getting out of the post, let alone out of the Pine, was a pipe dream at this point. The communication bay was so large that the Turks couldn't miss lobbing their grenades into the position – even if a Turk couldn't throw, he could literally place his grenade on top of the parapet and let it roll into the Australian position. The Australians tried to either throw back the explosives or smother them with sandbags. But casualties from both dubious methods were reducing the garrison at an alarming rate.

Twenty-nine-year-old electrician from Ryde Lance Corporal Cyril Besanko, of the 4th Battalion, daringly remained shoulder-high above the northern end of the trench bay and kept watch over the slope of Owen's Gully.[36] Mackay later commended Besanko, 'who acted as an observer. Although periscope after periscope was smashed by bullets, he seemed to bear a charmed life and stuck to his post for hours.'[37] He was originally recommended for the Distinguished Conduct Medal, later changed to the VC, but later again changed to the Military Medal. In the end he got nothing, not even a Mention in Despatches.[38]

Mackay was now under a great deal of stress and increasingly concerned that his position 'possessed no importance commensurate to the losses among the men who had to be crowded into it'.[39] He sent an urgent message to Lieutenant Colonel Macnaghten, advising him that the position had to be evacuated. The ongoing avalanche of Turkish grenades made it impossible to hold and was only providing the Turks with helpless victims who could not defend themselves, let alone retaliate. Not long after, Mackay was wounded while throwing a sandbag onto a grenade, the explosion throwing him into the air. On reading Mackay's message and hearing that he had been wounded, Macnaghten sent Lieutenant Robert Massie – who had just arrived from Aylward's Post – to assess the situation and to tell Iven Mackay that he was to seek medical treatment down the line. Mackay refused to leave. Massie was helping a wounded soldier when a Turk held a rifle over the parapet and fired blindly into the pit, knowing he must hit someone in the crowded trench bay. That someone was Robert Massie, who clutched his shattered shoulder with blood seeping through his fingers. Now it was Mackay ordering the young lieutenant out of the post – he staggered out and made his way to the rear. Mackay later commented how this random shot ruined 'the cricketing prospects of Australia's best left-hand bowler'.[40]

The fire trenches here were far too crowded and the communication trenches were even worse. Mackay ordered that the fire trench be thinned of men. There was no chance of clearing the wounded quickly and the 'poor fellows had just to wait where they were till communications could be opened up'. 'Most of our casualties,' he recalled, 'were from Turkish bombs, many of which we nullified by dropping half-filled sand-bags on them before they could harm.'[41] Mackay and many others reckoned that the Turkish cricket-ball grenades had it all over their jam-tin bombs. The bombs were difficult to ignite – sometimes it could take minutes to light one. On the other hand, the Turks had a 'spherical bomb with a fuse, the end of which was prepared as a match tip. All the enemy had to do was rub this tip on his trousers and throw the bomb. If only we had had plentiful supplies of the Mills bomb [the standard British grenade used on the Western Front] at Lone Pine, a different story might have been told.'[42] Nonetheless, dawn would still find the wounded Professor 'Iven the Terrible' Mackay and his few survivors holding the death pit.[43]

Things went no better along the isolated posts established just to the south. Sergeant Major Goldenstedt recalled that his post 'jutted out from what had now come to be the main Australian line along the edge of Owen's Gully, and overlooked from its bottom end Mule Gully, in behind Johnston's Jolly, and some of the fighting we had had that night was the worst in living memory ... out bombed and outnumbered, we hung on until daybreak'.[44] Earlier, as more men from the 12th Battalion were fed into the battle, it became just about impossible for a platoon commander to maintain control of his platoon, and in the inevitable confusion, officers commanded men from a number of companies and even battalions.[45] By 6 a.m. the next morning, White wrote to Birdwood stating that all of the 1st Brigade, along with the men of the 12th Battalion had been 'absorbed in LONE PINE'.[46]

Meanwhile, Captain Sasse and his men of the 1st Battalion were still trying to bridge the gap between Tubb's Corner and Youden's Post. Indeed, the two posts, established by Cook and Youden of the 2nd Battalion, were being heavily bombed by the Turks with grenades. The Turks were positioned within a hollow in the upper parts of The Cup, which meant that any Australian rifleman trying to fire at them had to expose himself well above the parapet. The battalion history records how Australians behind each jam-tin bomb 'thrower and observer kept cutting fuses so that they would light quickly, but as the slow matches issued for lighting the fuses failed to work, pieces of sandbag were kept smoldering for the purposes, although when daylight came, the smoke from these gave away the positions and invited showers of bombs from the Turks'.[47] It was not long before both Cook's and Youden's posts were being attacked from three sides. Given that the Australians were on slightly higher ground, they were able to provide just enough covering fire to keep them at bay – the men here were in an extremely precarious position.

Moonlight now made it possible to identify movement in the former no-man's-land between The Pimple and Lone Pine. Indeed, the stretcher-bearers were risking life and limb carrying their 'broken and suffering comrades across' the open ground.[48] Bravery exists in more than charging an enemy position – it applies in perhaps greater measure to those who provide comfort to men while bullets and shrapnel are flying about, with no way of retaliating or defending themselves.

In the Pine, the dead lay so thick that the only respect that could be paid them was to avoid treading on their faces. The troops were too busy and too weary to carry them to the rear, and nor was there room in the congested trenches to do so. Battalion histories often recalled the pathetic plight of many of the wounded at Lone Pine. They lay in all variety of positions, on the floors of the captured and congested trenches. They were 'trampled upon many times and again by the garrison as the defenders moved hurriedly from point to point to meet and repulse successive and most determined bombing attacks. The victims displayed the greatest fortitude while waiting for their wounds to be dressed.'[49]

At times the wounded men's agony was beyond endurance. New Zealand-born 24-year-old Camperdown bookkeeper Corporal Andrew Haua, of the 3rd Battalion, had suffered an agonising wound. He was screaming, 'Christ, won't someone finish me off?' It would take five days for him to die – he was buried at sea and is commemorated at the Lone Pine Memorial. Somewhere nearby, 27-year-old Lithgow miner Private Robert Dougherty appealed to his officer: 'As long as I've known you, Mr Allen, you've been a gentleman; for God's sake continue to be one and put a bullet through me.'[50] He died from his wounds the next day and is today buried in the Lone Pine Cemetery. Many of the bodies of those killed at Lone Pine were not recovered, even after the battle, and today have no known grave. In several sectors, in order to make space for the living, the dead Australians and Turks were piled in unused communication saps or dugouts until completely full – many of these spaces were then backfilled and the bodies have remained there till this day. Where possible, the wounded were carried out by stretcher-bearers, although to any man wounded in the stomach such movement was usually fatal.[51]

By now, the men were exhausted. Private Rider and his mates of the 4th Battalion were ordered to start to build a new firing line. They worked through the night and Rider recalled his duty consisted of 'an hour observing and an hour deepening our trench. As day-breaked our firing line was completed. So I went to an officer, Captain [Alfred] Shout and got permission to have a sleep.'[52] All night long the ANZAC artillery fired star shells in order to illuminate the columns of Turks who were entering the Pine in preparation for a major counterattack.[53] The wounded Private Len Barrett had stayed in the front line, helping his mates throw back Turkish grenades, but by the middle of the night he was pretty much done in: 'We were being reinforced at about midnight and a new chap took my place and I remembered no more. I "came to" in a bit of a side trench. My leg was very painful and stiff. I crawled to some trenches away from the firing line, and found Mr Phillips badly wounded. We stayed there until 5.30 the following morning.'[54] Both would eventually make their way to the beach and evacuation.

Sometime that night at 1st Australian Divisional HQ, Colonel White recorded in his diary: 'Battle of Lone Pine. Successful attack on enemy trenches. Big losses. Up all night. Great deal of shell fire. Enemy rigorously counter attacked.'[55] With each passing hour, the Turks were massing their reserves to retake Lone Pine.

Further north, the decisive assault against the Sari Bair Range had begun. This was where the fate of the whole August Offensive would be decided. At 10.30 p.m. the Right Covering Force, consisting of the New Zealand Mounted Rifles, began clearing the Turks from the lower slopes of North Beach, including Old No. 3 Outpost below Chunuk Bair. The Aucklanders, under cover of shellfire, took up positions just below the southern slopes of the post and at 9.30 p.m. the shelling ceased. The New Zealanders let out a deafening cheer and took the position. As the Auckland troopers stormed into Old No. 3 Outpost, the Wellington Mounted Rifles had been waiting at the entrance of the Sazli Beit Dere (a large gully with its origins at Chunuk Bair) and now moved up, pushing on past the battle to their left. Their objective was the capture of the Table Top that dominates Old No. 3 Outpost. The troopers stormed and captured the small plateau from the seaward slopes just after 10.30 p.m.[56]

Earlier, the Otago and Canterbury Mounted Rifles advanced northward until they reached the nearest southern spur leading onto Bauchop's Hill. From here they were to climb onto the ridgeline and continue their advance towards the heights. Having seized the lower slopes, the New Zealanders now encountered stubborn Turkish resistance. The troopers needed to clear the way ahead for the infantry, and there was only one thing for it – the Canterbury and Otago troopers charged with the bayonet. Gradually the Turks gave way and the few survivors receded up the hill towards the northern heights. The way was now clear for the Right Attacking Column of infantry to approach Chunuk Bair.[57]

At the northern flank of the offensive, the Left Covering Force, consisting of the British 4th South Wales Borderers and the 5th Wiltshire, had begun their mission of clearing the Turks from the Aghyl Dere (a gully originating from Hill 971) and the dominating spur known as Damakjelik Bair. On approaching the Aghyl Dere, they could see in front the outline of a trench blocking their way. The British charged the position and the few Turks present retreated. By 1.30 a.m., the British Left Covering Force had achieved their objective and occupied much of Damakjelik Bair. The way was now clear for the Left Attack Column to approach Hill Q and Hill 971.

Earlier, the British IX Corps had, at around 9.30 p.m., started to land about ten kilometres north of Anzac, at Suvla Bay. Within thirty minutes they had managed to get four battalions ashore without suffering a single casualty. The landing was a complete surprise and the troops walked ashore facing no opposition. The northern heights and inland hills around Suvla lay open for the taking – but the senior British commanders were apparently not interested, seemingly happy to have just got their men ashore.[58]

The main offensive had started all the way along the line but the Turkish commanders were focused exclusively on reinforcing their southern flank at Lone Pine. Hours later, news reached General Liman von Sanders that columns of enemy troops were making their way north of the Anzac sector. He immediately 'telephoned … the 7th and 12th Divisions at the upper Xeros Gulf, ordering that they be alarmed and made ready to march at once'.[59] At around 1 a.m., orders were issued to both of these divisions to march towards Anzac. It was estimated it would take them from between thirty-six to forty-eight hours to reach the battles breaking out all along the Anzac front, as well as those further north at Suvla Bay. It was now starting to dawn on some of the Turkish commanders that something bigger was taking place and it seemed to be aimed at their northern flank along the Sari Bair Range – or was that just an elaborate feint to distract them from the main assault to be launched further south, at Gaba Tepe? After all, it was there that most expected any future Allied attack to fall. This led to some indecision on the part of the Turkish commanders, which, for a few hours more at least, would work to Birdwood's advantage.

SATURDAY
7 AUGUST
1915

14

'He was not fated to leave from there'

Turkish Lieutenant Colonel Ali Riza Bey, charged with retaking Lone Pine, had divided his position into three sectors and put them in the charge of Captain Zeki Bey, Captain Mustafa Kemal and a third unknown battalion commander. Orders were given to prepare for a counterattack that was expected to take place before dawn.[1] Allied flares of many different colours were falling onto Lone Pine, as well as brilliant white star shells originating from The Pimple. An Australian machine gun was firing from a position almost at the edge of The Cup. Nearby, Australians were throwing their jam-tin bombs to deadly effect. In this confusion and chaos, Turkish officers forced their way through the crowded saps and trenches to try and organise some coordinated movement, but it was taking far too long.[2]

The Turkish defences, especially along the southern part of the plateau, were still mostly rifle pits and hastily constructed low earthen embankments. Zeki Bey approached an officer from the 47th Regiment to get some idea of the layout of the trenches along the very edges of the plateau. When the officer couldn't provide details, Zeki Bey realised that there weren't any saps other than those he'd already passed through. He later recalled to Charles Bean after the war how bombs were being thrown from all sides and, because the main communication trench was too deep, he 'placed men on top in no-man's-land – twenty or thirty were hit there by your fire. So the night passed – nothing done.'³ Overnight, news reached him that some of his men had advanced on their old northern flank, but it was only another version of the old false report – at dawn the position was unchanged.⁴ Turkish losses, especially along the northern and central parts of the Pine, had been heavy.

Sometime during the night, the commander of the 47th Regiment, Tevfik Bey, having been blamed by his superiors for the loss of Lone Pine, ordered a desperate attack against his former front-line trenches. He said: 'Well, I'll take the troops myself and we'll do something, whatever it costs.'⁵ He led from the front and was one of the first to be hit in the pointless attack against Australian mass rifle and machine-gun fire. One of his officers, Riza Tevfik Iskin, recalled seeing his commander in a medical post: 'I spent the night at the seriously wounded section of the medical post. In the morning they brought our regiment's commander, Tevfik Bey, he was totally covered with shrapnel wounds, he was not fated to leave from there.'⁶

All along Lone Pine, Turkish bombing continued and so did the accumulation of Australian casualties. Sergeant Clark and his men, of the 3rd Battalion, spent most of the night and early morning hours returning Turkish grenades '[with] most satisfactory results, although the practice occasionally led to casualties in our own ranks. To give credit where credit is due, it must be related that the Turk was not slow to follow suit, and he returned our jam tins to us.'⁷ To avoid having their bombs hurled back before they exploded, both Australian and Turk either delayed throwing them for a few seconds or, in the Australian cases at least, cut the fuses to a little more than half their usual length – reducing the time before explosion to about three seconds. The results justified the extra risk, although an occasional 'premature' reduced the ranks. 'One...chap was so highly incensed at having his bombs returned that he decided to make the feat impossible with his next. But he cut too low. At the zenith of his swing the bomb exploded and his hand up to his wrist went over with the bomb. Grasping the stump with his left hand, he jumped from the fire step, and with a cheery, "That's the end of this business for me", he set off for the beach,' recalled Clark.[8] Others perhaps took too seriously the name given to the Turkish 'cricket-ball grenades'. One corporal used his rifle as a bat to strike the Turkish grenades as they came over – his lead was said to be taken up by a few others close by.[9] It's likely that this novel approach didn't last long, as one missed strike would have had lethal results.

The Australians waited anxiously for the inevitable Turkish counterattack. Corporal James Rule, along with some of his men from the 12th Battalion, had taken up a position in the hours before dawn just behind the parados of a support trench to help direct fire. Later, with first light, the 22-year-old corporal from Hobart passed the order for his men to get back into the trench, and although some of his men believed he had followed them, he was never again seen.[10] Corporal James Rule has no known grave and is commemorated on the Lone Pine Memorial.

Just north of Lone Pine, the first of the attacks to assist in the capture of Baby 700 and The Nek was about to commence – the Australian attack against German Officers' Trench. The Turkish machine guns here enfiladed no-man's-land at The Nek and Turkish Quinn's, and they had to be silenced before these positions were attacked at 4.30 a.m. The assault from Steele's Post was to be launched from a number of tunnels exiting into no-man's-land.[11]

Just after midnight, the Australians launched their attack. It was a slaughter – the Turks were prepared and waiting. Australian dead and wounded covered no-man's-land, while others completely blocked the tunnel openings. Another attack was organised and, just before 4 a.m., the men charged again, but the end result was never in doubt and a fresh pile of dead and wounded Australians soon lay scattered in front of their trenches. By 4.10 a.m., it was all over.

At the same time as the attack on German Officers' Trench, the Right Attack Column, headed by the New Zealand Otago Infantry Battalion, had been tasked with capturing Chunuk Bair. They had moved towards their immediate objective, Rhododendron Ridge, from which the summit of Chunuk Bair was less than 900 metres away. But the commander of the New Zealand Brigade, Colonel Francis Johnston, called a halt to the advance, insisting on waiting for the arrival of one of his missing battalions before pushing on. His failure to keep the impetus of the attack going was to be felt most tragically by the troopers of the Australian Light Horse, who were at this point about to charge the entrenched Turks at The Nek. After capturing Chunuk Bair, the New Zealanders were to attack the Turks at Battleship Hill and Baby 700 from the rear, while the Australian troopers would charge The Nek, attacking the same positions from the front. However, the Australian troopers were now being called on to assist the New Zealanders in capturing the largely empty summit of Chunuk Bair, through a series of unsupported frontal charges against the heavily entrenched Turks.[12]

Further north, the Left Assaulting Column under Major General Cox's command, led by Colonel John Monash's 4th Australian Infantry Brigade and followed by Cox's own 29th Indian Brigade, had started their approach towards Hill 971 and Hill Q. However, by 3 a.m., these battalions had hardly begun their advance towards the heights, let alone achieved a position to storm them.

At The Nek, Birdwood ordered the attack to go ahead, despite the converging attack by the New Zealanders no longer being possible. The first and second waves of the attack were made by Victoria's 8th Light Horse Regiment. Hundreds of rifles, along with any number of machine guns, were levelled at the 150 troopers as they attempted to bolt across the forty metres or so of no-man's-land. Within five minutes, both waves of Australian troopers had been decimated. The commander of the regiment, Lieutenant Colonel Alexander White, his officers and most of his 300 men, lay dead or dying in the killing field.[13] Most fell dead before making ten metres. Now, the men from Western Australia's 10th Light Horse lined the same front-line trenches. They too were committed to the attack, despite the hopelessness of the situation, and as if to make this even more patently clear, just before the third wave hopped the bags, two Turkish artillery pieces began to fire shrapnel into the Australian trenches, adding to the slaughter. By 5.30 a.m., both regiments effectively existed in name only.

Three hours after these attacks, Colonel Johnston ordered the New Zealanders to take Chunuk Bair in broad daylight. The Turks were well and truly waiting. The charging troops were lost to sight in the dust that was torn up by Turkish machine-gun fire, and almost immediately, mountain guns located on Abdel Rahman Bair, to the north, let loose with a barrage of shrapnel. Johnston ordered another charge, with the same predictable result. He was just about to order a third suicidal charge when General Godley sent out orders that all offensive actions were to cease. The order reached Johnston in time to save the pointless shedding of more New Zealand blood. From his position, the colonel would have seen hundreds of his men lying dead or dying along the upper slopes leading to Chunuk Bair.[14] Birdwood's greatest asset (some might say his only asset) in achieving his objective – surprise – was now well and truly gone. The northern attacks were a bloodbath, with almost nothing having been gained. It was daylight and his men were still nowhere near the heights, let alone capturing them. At this point a halt should have been called to the whole mad enterprise. But too much time and effort had been put into its planning and London was expecting results from its half-hearted commitment to the offensive. It would grind on for another four days – until even 'blind Freddy' would have to admit there was no prospect of success. But by then, thousands of men would lie dead and dying along the slopes of Sari Bair and Second Ridge, and at Lone Pine.

15

'I'd sell my life
for two bob now'

Captain Zeki Bey was in The Cup and, as dawn broke, to his horror he saw Australian trench periscopes looking directly into their
position. On seeing them for the first time, one of his men asked:
"'Aren't those our men?' 'Of course not,' I said. 'Can't you see – we
haven't those things!'"[1] Clearly any attempt by the Turks to mass for
a counterattack from here would be observed by the Australians –
the enemy had to be driven out of these positions. Indeed, Major
General Esat Pasha, from his headquarters at Scrubby Knoll, was
just then being handed a report regarding their position, stating
that the enemy attack at Lone Pine had pushed the Turkish defenders back some 300 metres from the front-line trenches.[2] From his
vantage point he could clearly see this for himself.

The Turks had been pushed so far from their original front
lines by the Australians of the 2nd and 3rd battalions that they
now had their backs to Legge Valley. In the centre of the plateau
they were cut off from their comrades along Sniper's Ridge to the
south by the Australian positions of Goldenstedt's Post, Tubb's
Corner, Youden's Post and Cook's Post. There remained, however,
a possible tenuous line of communication – an unfinished shallow

sap just below the eastern edge of the plateau. Zeki Bey's men immediately began to dig and expand the sap, hoping to link their precarious position to Sniper's Ridge, but no sooner had they entered it when it was targeted by a New Zealand battery positioned along Russell's Top – one shell exploded in their midst. The survivors came tumbling back, leaving two or three dead or seriously wounded.[3] Plans for the expansion of this trench during daylight hours were put on hold.

Zeki Bey told Charles Bean after the war that a continued stream of Turkish reinforcements was arriving at Owen's Gully throughout the early morning hours of 7 August, and he described the horrors they encountered on first reaching the position:

> Kemel Yere [Scrubby Knoll], the headquarters of Esat Pasha, was opposite this sector and saw everything – they didn't want to lose a foot of ground, it was their tactics not to give ground. So they sent troops to push you back... They had to pass up the Valley [Owen's Gully] where Turkish dead were laid out beside the track, four deep. They saw this column of dead men; at the upper end of it were some Australians, including a Lieutenant or Sergeant, a splendid looking fellow of very great stature, lying there – they had got well down into the position – and the sight 'knocked the stuffing' out of the incoming troops. When they got to the top of the gully there were the Australian periscopes looking over at them, and the fight going on – bombs, rifle-shots.[4]

Lance Corporal Aylward and his men were still manning the barricade looking into Owen's Gully at the most northerly point captured by the Australians. The Turks had made a couple of attempts during the night to storm the position, but were repulsed. At some point overnight, Sergeant Spratt and some of his men of the 4th Battalion had constructed a supporting barricade behind Aylward and his men, which was slightly higher and able to provide some covering fire. Sometime before dawn an officer ordered some of Spratt's men to join up with Aylward's party below.[5] As the morning hours passed, the bombing war here increased – it was reaching its climax. Private Back later remembered that at about 10 a.m., the Turks in quick succession threw three grenades into the trench. Private William Kelly picked one up and attempted to throw it back but in the process got his hand blown off, while Aylward was wounded in the legs and wrist.[6] Private George Hayward, unwounded, expected the Turks to attack in force at any moment, and turned to his wounded cobber William Kelly: 'I'd sell my life for two bob now.'[7] Now only Hayward and Back were left unwounded. It seemed that the position must fall, when at the last possible moment reinforcements arrived with a machine gun that was soon in place. The Turks were finally forced to withdraw. Hayward would remain at his post until relieved on Monday, 9 August – he was never more than ten metres away from it, except once when he went looking for his brother – who he didn't know had been wounded.[8] Private Kelly would die from his wounds on 11 August, and like the rest of those who died aboard the hospital ships, was buried at sea and is commemorated on the Lone Pine Memorial.

About fifty metres southeast of Aylward's position, the wounded Major Iven Mackay was still commanding his precarious position in the trench hub, which had long since become a death trap. He renewed his request to Lieutenant Colonel Macnaghten – who had been wounded in the knee by shrapnel and, like all those around him, was utterly exhausted – that he be allowed to evacuate the position. Macnaghten agreed and soon Mackay, weary and half-dazed, began withdrawing the survivors, though only from the hub and not the communication saps leading into it. He ordered that the head of these saps be barricaded and manned, while he alone remained in the trench bay to repel any Turkish advance as the work was progressed. He waited with rifle in hand for the appearance of the Turks, among discarded Australian equipment and dead, while 25-year-old clerk Captain Allan Scott, of the 4th Battalion, and 24-year-old farmer Lieutenant Owen Howell-Price, adjutant of the 3rd Battalion, organised the construction of the barricades behind him.

Earlier, as Mackay and others were barricading the northern end of Traversed Trench, which fed into his former post, a number of men were concerned that they would cut off their only means of escape. Before completing the barricade, Mackay walked along the trench to assure himself and the men that its southern exit was still open and, beyond it, the other trenches still in Australian hands – this was found to be the case. Now back at his original position and with all of the barricades complete, Mackay climbed over one of the barricades into the rear communication saps and arranged for a short firing trench to be driven, to connect the two saps that fed into the rear of his former post.[9] For a brief time things seemed to quieten down: 'We had plenty of water and biscuits to tide us over ... By now hot tea and stew began to arrive, and one man who had only recently arrived, produced a bottle of whisky. This bucked us up tremendously . . .'[10] Mackay had by now received another wound, and upon reporting to Macnaghten was ordered to have his wounds dressed. He recalled feeling 'pretty dizzy, and not good for much, so I went off to the dressing-station'.[11] While there, he heard the latest news of what had been happening at other parts of the Pine.

Just as he was making his way to the rear, somewhere close by some of Mackay's battalion, including Private William Graham and his mates, were beating back another Turkish counterattack, but in doing so had suffered several casualties. These men now focused on consolidating their position with sandbags that had been brought across the previous night. Graham kept watch for enemy movement through a periscope. Men rested, none slept. Rifles and bayonets were 'ever at hand, and no man dared yet remove his equipment. The dead still lay thickly in Lone Pine, for it was not yet possible to remove them for burial. Many of the bodies were thrown into open ground above the trenches, many were packed in open unused saps and gradually congestion was eased.'[12]

Just south of the 4th Battalion, shortly before dawn, the commanding officer of the 3rd Battalion, Lieutenant Colonel Ernest Brown, had ordered all men in Traversed Trench to take up a position along the firing step, as he expected a counterattack at first light. Captain Edward Lloyd later recalled how Brown, while it was still dark, ordered him to follow as he jumped up onto no-man's-land to see the lay of the land. Brown pointed out where Lloyd was to place his men in the open field. Lloyd recalled Brown telling him how it was no good 'trying to beat back the counterattack, which was sure to come from the bottom of the trenches. I must confess that I did not like this scheme, as the Turks held a position on our left, known as Johnston's Jolly, which practically overlooked us.'[13] Nonetheless, Lloyd reluctantly ordered his men out of the trench, while it was still dark, and told them to get whatever cover they could. As they did so they bothered some Turks about ten metres away, who hurriedly scampered back into a trench.

Just as it was getting light, Lloyd's attention was drawn to the north: '[It was the] most wonderful sight I had ever seen. The hills about a mile to our left were one mass of bursting shells. The grand attack [at The Nek] had begun. Just then the Turks on our left opened fire on us, and wounded one chap. This was enough. I passed the word that on my signal we would all jump up and get back into the trench, which wasn't more than ten yards away, so we got back safely.'[14] Brown had good reason to be concerned about the gap between Sasse's Sap and Lloyd's Post, as within hours a number of Turks had managed to creep into the depression between them and let loose a hail of grenades on Lloyd's Post. However, by then, Brown had been killed by shrapnel – he would not be the last battalion commander that the Australians would lose in the battle for Lone Pine. Lieutenant Colonel Ernest Samuel Brown is buried at Beach Cemetery.

At daybreak on Saturday morning, the Turks further decimated the Australian garrison at Lone Pine with a veritable rain of grenades to which they could only make a feeble response, as their supply of jam-tin bombs was limited to a few sandbags' full.[15] Lloyd recalled: 'Turks came at us with bombs, but they wouldn't leave their trenches. As our supply of bombs had run out, we could not drive them off, and the enemy gave us a pretty severe time, wounding several men, so I cleared our trench, with the exception of two men at the barricades – myself and another man.'[16] They remained and managed to hold the position by running to the rear as a grenade landed and exploded – they would then return to the post. Lloyd took up a position near 'a traverse with my man behind me and we watched for bombs. They were only thrown from about five yards away, and any time they might have rushed us, so we had to be ready all the time. This kept on for nearly two hours until we got a fresh supply of bombs and kept the enemy off.'[17]

Nearby, 26-year-old station hand Lance Corporal Charles Nankivell, of the 4th Battalion, was busy saving the lives of his men by throwing sandbags over the enemy grenades and tossing live grenades back to their owners. At one point, he rolled over a body only to find a live unexploded bomb. Without hesitating, he picked it up and threw it out of the trench, saving the lives of his men.[18] Twenty-year-old Enfield machinist Private Norman Pyne, of the same battalion, was also in the thick of it and remembered years later how it was common in the excitement of a Turkish bombing attack to see men arguing among themselves as to how long they should hold a jam-tin bomb until the missile exploded and blew them to pieces. The 2nd Battalion history records the wounded lying in heaps along with the dead: '[The men] fought standing on these heaps of humanity to see where they were.' Gradually the Turkish onslaught seemed to wane – soon there was a protracted period of 'entire calm. All who could dropped down to sleep of exhaustion during the respite, until a sudden shout of "Stand-to" ran along the line, when the position was instantly manned.'[19]

At the headquarters of the 1st Australian Division, in Brown's Dip, Colonel White was dealing with the minutiae of war. At around 6.30 a.m., he sent a message into Lone Pine stating that he was trying to 'organise...a party for carrying food, water and ammunition'.[20] Thirty minutes later he sent another, stating that soon about 250 bombs and 1800 sandbags would be making their way into Lone Pine. He also noted that if required he could send over about six periscope rifles, but that would exhaust all of his reserves.[21] It was bombs that were needed above all else. The jam-tin bomb factory on the beach reported that it comprised '54 men and no room for more to work. We will have 500 more ready by 12 o'clock tonight.'[22] Bombs, rifles and bayonets were keeping the Turks and their fierce attacks from regaining their lost trenches.

During the early morning hours the exhausted troops on the plateau were relieved to see an ongoing stream of reinforcements making their way into the Pine via the communication saps from The Pimple. However, the fresh troops inadvertently choked the arteries of supply. Captain Lloyd approached Lieutenant Colonel Macnaghten and obtained permission to clear the trenches of the wounded. This required that some of the reinforcements withdraw back to The Pimple.

Using a scaled map of Lone Pine, it is possible to estimate that at this point of the battle the Australians held about 950 metres of Turkish trench. It is impossible to obtain accurate casualty figures for the five battalions then in the Pine, but before entering the battle the full strength of these battalions totalled 3925 officers and men.[23] If we estimate that one-third of the men who entered Lone Pine were already casualties, there were 2617 Australians, or 2.8 men per one metre of trench (or about one man per 1.2 square metres), which is close to the preferred figure of three men per metre of front-line trench for the defence of the Anzac perimeter, with about half that number in the support trenches.[24] However, this figure does not take into account the wounded and dead, as well as prisoners, who also crowded the Lone Pine trenches, trench bays and saps, not just in the front line but also in the 'rear' works. Importantly, at such positions as Quinn's Post and Lone Pine, which were so close to the enemy that they endured nonstop bombing wars, the front-line trenches needed to be thinned to avoid casualties, with more men kept in reserve to counterattack any breakthrough. However, there was no room left in the rear 'reserve' trenches at Lone Pine, and three men per metre of trench was just not feasible in the restricted confines of the Pine (or Quinn's) – the active troops, plus the dead and wounded, choked communications, restricted passage and increased casualties from Turkish grenades and small-arms fire.

The reserve companies of the 1st Battalion and two of three companies of the 12th Battalion were now ordered out of the Pine. Those men of these battalions already in the thick of the fighting, however, remained, including Major Lane's company of the 12th Battalion. Thirty-eight-old manager Captain Charles Coltman set about getting things organised, and within an hour most of the congestion in the 4th Battalion's sector had been relieved and the trenches cleared, except for the Turkish dead.[25] Some of the 1st Battalion reinforcements remained to conduct fatigue duties and these men worked hard at clearing bodies from the trenches and parapet, before gradually settling down, prepared for any counterattack the 'Turks might like to send along'.[26]

Along the northern flank of the Australian position, Private Duke was still fighting at McDonald's Post and, like Major Mackay, he lamented the lack of professional arms: '[The Turks] had it all over us with their cricket-ball bombs. Our jam-tin bombs were dreadful, and I often calculate how speedy the result of Lone Pine and the peninsula would have been if we had an adequate supply of Mills grenades.'[27] Several times the men here ran out of bombs. Duke remembered going to Battalion Headquarters for bombs and seeing Macnaghten, left unable to walk by the shrapnel in his knee, sitting on a box with his wounded leg up on another box, 'carrying on serenely, refusing to be evacuated'.[28] The worst part of the whole show, according to Duke, was 'the raging, tearing, unquenchable thirst. I had a jar of rum in that bay, but hardly anyone touched it, and we would have gladly exchanged it for water.'[29]

It was while talking to Macnaghten that Captain Lloyd learned that nearly all the officers of their battalion had been hit, including his mates Milson, Giles, Seldon and MacKinnon. Macnaghten was very upset by the losses.[30] Having cleared the wounded from his post, Lloyd now found his position, as well as the Traversed Trench just to his north, under an intense bombing attack. Lieutenant Osborne, who commanded Traversed Trench, was seriously wounded, and those manning the junction between these two positions were driven back. Lloyd and his men were momentarily pushed out of their post, before launching a successful counterattack. Things then seemed to quieten down and Lloyd left the position in search of the ever-elusive jam-tin bomb supply. Within minutes of his departure, the Turks launched another heavy bombing attack against his men, driving them back down the trench, where they were forced to set up another barricade. Their retirement meant those manning Traversed Trench had now been cut off, with no-one left protecting its southern entrance.[31] Now that Mackay's Post had been barricaded, the men in Traversed Trench were isolated forward of the Australian front line in this sector of the Pine, with both of their flanks completely exposed.

On hearing that the Turks had taken the position, 25-year-old clerk from Wahroonga, New South Wales, Captain Allan Scott, who had been nearby, rushed to the newly constructed barricade just short of the post and called to his fellows, 'Who'll come with me?' Without waiting for a reply, he scrambled over the low barricade, passing the southern entrance to Traversed Trench to his left, and took up a position at Lloyd's original post, further along the line.[32] Following close behind him were a number of men who had taken up the call. Scott was soon confronted by some Turks who had decided to check out the enemy position. He got the better of them, killing three. Other Turks in a nearby trench were still busy throwing grenades into Lloyd's Post – unaware that the post had been vacated. Scott ordered two men to push forward beyond the original barricade, to take up a position just short of the entrance to the trench held by the bomb-throwing Turks, in order to check any Turkish attempt to advance towards Lloyd's Post. As each of these Australians was killed or wounded, another took his place beyond the barricade defence works.

Scott and one of his men were throwing jam-tin bombs across no-man's-land, and when these ran out, they used improvised bombs, including grenades made from 18-pounder shell cases filled with high explosive.[33] The bomb fight continued until one of the Australian bombs finally found its target. All was momentarily quiet and one of the men near the opening took a peek. When the others got his thumbs up, they bolted back over the original barricades of Lloyd's Post. It was then that a Turkish machine gun at Johnston's Jolly opened fire along the length of Traversed Trench, killing many – it was a death trap, and if it couldn't be held, neither could Lloyd's Post. Scott ordered the exposed men in Traversed Trench to try and withdraw as best they could from the southern entrance. As the first attempted to do so, he was ripped apart by a stream of bullets.[34] Scott yelled to those further to the rear (west of the entrance to the Traversed Trench), at the low barricade he had previously scrambled over, to heighten and strengthen it – it would be their new defensive position. He ordered the survivors in Traversed Trench and those at the original Lloyd's Post to make a dash for the new barricade further to the rear as soon as the Turkish machine gun stopped firing. Within seconds, the gun was silent. The men bolted back from Lloyd's, while those in Traverse Trench charged to the exit and threw themselves around the bend – all expected the machine gun to open fire, but for whatever reason it remained silent. With a great sense of relief they threw their rifles and themselves over the barricade defining the newly constructed Lloyd's Post.[35]

With the abandonment of Mackay's Post and Traversed Trench, the Australian northern flank was represented by just four barricaded sap-heads, originally constructed by Aylward, McDonald, Mackay and Lloyd. At each of these posts, the bombing war continued intermittently throughout the next few days, but they were not again heavily assaulted. It became a war of attrition on both sides; the Australians wouldn't budge and the Turks wouldn't directly assault. From now on, the main Turkish attacks would be launched against the centre and southern flank of the Australian positions in Lone Pine.

16

'The trench was
a veritable shambles'

Woods's Post represented the centre of the Australian position, and the Turks located in The Cup, just twenty-five metres away, launched a frontal assault against it. Luckily for the defenders, just a few hours before a machine gun had been set up there and within seconds, the gun, along with rifle enfilade from Goldenstedt's Post, swept away the attack. The Turks didn't try this again, but they did continue to try and force the Australians out of these positions with an ongoing bombing fight.[1]

Further south, the Turks were making their most serious attempts to break into the Australian position. A number had taken up a position in a shallow sap located between Tubb's Corner and Youden's Post. The Australians here began to return fire with jam-tin bombs, but Youden noted that they'd initially left the fuses too long, leaving a real danger of them 'going out before reaching the Turkish trenches, and quite naturally they utilised them by bombing us again'.[2] Indeed, within seconds their bombs were being thrown back. By the time the men realised what was happening, they'd run out of bombs. They tried desperately to get more, but none could be found. Youden send an urgent message to 2nd Battalion Headquarters for just one bomb: 'Even this failed to bring a ready response.'[3] They now had to keep the Turks at bay with rifle fire, but the enemy seemed content not to directly assault them. They continued their bombing, which was thinning the Australian ranks. At some point in the fighting, owing to poor needlework on Youden's part, his white calico armbands came off.[4] Given that previous orders stated that 'any man not answering immediately [sign and countersign] or not wearing armlets and patches was to be treated as an enemy',[5] he was lucky to avoid being shot by his own men. Youden bravely directed the defence of the position until he was wounded by Turkish fire.

About fifteen metres south, at Cook's Post, lines of Turks were seen moving along a shallow trench to the front of the Australians:

[Turkish] enfilade fire was opened from Johnston's Jolly as dawn appeared, and many casualties occurred... Then the bombing attack started. We had no bombs to retaliate with... Despairing appeals were made to Company Headquarters for bombs, but none were to be had. The men caught the enemy's bombs as they fell and hurled them back before bursting. Many were killed, hands and arms being blown off as bombs exploded in the act of being thrown back at the Turks. The trench was now packed with dead and wounded.[6]

Even so, the Australians beat back the attack with accurate rifle fire. Some Turks who had taken cover behind a small knoll near the southern edge of the plateau raised a white flag, but there was no way of accepting their surrender given that these men were closer to their own lines than the Australian position. Consequently, Major Morshead of the 2nd Battalion ordered the firing to continue. Twenty-eight-year-old Woollahra builder Lieutenant Edward Harkness had just arrived on the peninsula and was upset by

Morshead's directive. He tried to argue against the order, but was duly ignored and the firing went on.[7] Sometime later in the day, a Greek from the Turkish group stuck a white flower in the muzzle of his rifle and managed to safely crawl to the Australian lines to give himself up.[8]

The Turks appeared to be making their most determined attacks against the southern flank of the Pine, precisely at the point where Jacobs's Trench bent back towards their original front line. Captains Harold Jacobs, of the 1st Battalion, and John Pain, of the 2nd, had ordered their exhausted men to each take a short stand-to in order to try and keep them awake. At one of the changeovers, a sentry yelled and pointed to a Turkish trench roughly parallel with their own, at a distance of about forty metres. It was 'bristling with bayonets'[9] and almost immediately two lines of Turks charged out towards Jacobs's Trench, but they were quickly repulsed. The surviving Turks either withdrew to their own lines, or took up a position in a short empty section of trench in no-man's-land, just twenty metres from the Australians, where they were effectively stranded.

Things had seemingly quietened down somewhat after the failed Turkish counterattacks along the line. Lieutenant Colonel Scobie and Brigade Major Dennis King took advantage of the situation to inspect their position, making their way to the most threatened positions on their southern flank. They arrived at Youden's and Cook's positions and were concerned that these were still not connected by a firing trench. King ordered that the work on bridging the gap between these two exposed posts be given top priority. It was crucial to incorporate the 2nd Battalion posts into their main defensive line. King promised to help by assigning a party of the 3rd Battalion men to sap from Tubb's Corner to meet them.

Things did not remain quiet for long. Captain Syd Cook, of the

2nd Battalion, was organising the sapping towards the 3rd Brigade when a large number of Turks was seen rushing up the trenches to his right – it looked like they were about to renew their attack against Jacobs's Trench. At the same time, Turkish artillery along Third Ridge – at a location known as The Wineglass – opened fire against the southern flank of the Australian position along Lone Pine. This also enfiladed some of the old Turkish communication saps that led along the southern edge of the plateau. One of these saps was a straight shallow passageway, which neither side held. Only a low barricade had been partially constructed by Australians, as the position was thought to be too exposed for either side to occupy. Earlier, however, Colonel Scobie, passing the position at around 11 a.m., spoke sharply to 27-year-old Lieutenant Frederick Cox, who was in charge of the immediate area, ordering him to get to work building a more substantial defensive position there. Later, while this work was carried out, the Turkish guns from The Wineglass targeted the low barricade, killing Cox and some of his men.[10] Lieutenant Frederick Cox is buried at the Lone Pine Cemetery.

The same guns now enfiladed the communication trenches leading to Cook's and Youden's posts – defining the south-eastern corner of the Australian perimeter at Lone Pine. That they did not target the posts themselves, just the saps behind them, didn't bode well – it indicated that the posts were spared because Turkish infantry were preparing to storm them. By noon, casualties from this fire were appalling. To make matters worse, the nearby Turkish troops also let loose with large numbers of grenades. The Australians had long ago run out of bombs. However, one soldier recalled 'a snowy-headed youth – he could not have been more than twenty – catching the cricket-ball bombs the Turks were throwing and tossing them back. I did not see him at the finish – he must have fumbled a catch!'[11] It was around then that one of Cook's men on the firing step yelled, 'Stand to!' – he'd observed a mass of Turks that looked ready to charge their position.[12] Cook remembered this short but furious attack being the most serious attack against his position to date: '[It was] probably around 12 noon or after... (we had been dealing with constant small groups of enemy rushes throughout the night). The counter attack at mid day came from the parallel trenches at our right and beyond.'[13] The garrison was now being bombed from several directions and had no hope for any kind of defence.[14] Lieutenant Harkness, who had earlier protested Morshead's refusal to take Turkish prisoners, now took a quick look across no-man's-land to determine what the enemy was up to, and was immediately killed with a bullet to the head. Within minutes, Cook himself got up on the firing step to 'size up the position – I was shot in the head and remember nothing more'.[15] Standing close by, lieutenants Herbert Youden and Malcolm Cotton were also wounded in the Turkish onslaught.

Scobie knew there was no way that Youden's and Cook's posts could be held and now ordered the survivors to get out while they still could. Scobie then remained in one of the saps while the men withdrew to make sure none of the wounded was left behind. He also had with him a large improvised bomb, and after having satisfied himself that all of the men were out, he jumped up onto a firing step and was about to heave the explosive towards the Turkish lines when he fell back dead – killed by a Turkish grenade.[16] The Australians had lost another experienced battalion commander. Command now passed to Major Stevens, who was exhausted emotionally and physically, having endured the strain of leading the 2nd Battalion into the initial charge against Lone Pine and organising its early defence.[17]

Stevens ordered Lieutenant Lecky to retake parts of the trench leading into Youden's Post. Many years later he recalled his lucky escape from almost certain death: 'The trench was a veritable shambles... an order was given that the ground in front was to be cleared by a forlorn charge, led by myself. While I was collecting volunteers... Lieutenant Colonel Cass arrived and countermanded the order, as he knew it would have led to the death of every man who obeyed, even before they had got 10ft. away from the trench.'[18]

Just opposite Jacobs's Trench, the Turks launched another attack. Captain Jacobs reported to Stevens that Turks were streaming along a communication trench on his right front,[19] as Turkish reinforcements charged from their rear trench towards Jacobs's Trench. Rifle fire broke up the charge, with the Turkish survivors diving into the shallow sap in the middle of no-man's-land – the same trench the survivors from the earlier attack had occupied. Unlike the previous group, these Turks had grenades and were in easy bombing range and began to bomb Jacobs's Trench and the saps leading back from Cook's and Youden's posts. Pain's men only had one jam-tin bomb, which Pain lobbed into the shallow sap. A number of Australians known to be good with the rifle were posted along the parapet and for a time, at great risk to themselves, forced the Turks to keep their heads down.

Shortly after 1 p.m., the Turkish assault grew more intense and threatening. The Turks who had been held in check before Colonel Scobie's death were now able to advance. At the rear junction of the communication saps, leading into the vacated posts, a small barricade had been built, but the Australians holding it were quickly killed. The Turks pushed on and occupied the junction connecting the posts. Jacobs, just to the south, was unaware that Scobie had earlier ordered the evacuation of Youden's and Cook's posts and was greatly concerned to see Turkish bayonets protruding above the parapets of these two positions. He also observed Turks now pushing down the communication saps, trying to reach their original front line. He hurried with the news to 2nd Battalion Headquarters – it looked as if the southern part of the line must surely fall.

The Turks, in capturing the communication trench leading from Cook's Post and the junction, were now poised to take Jacobs's Trench. An avalanche of Turkish grenades resulted in its eastern end being three deep in dead and dying. The Australians were driven out – there was no barrier across the trench except the bodies of the dead. Having somehow obtained a number of bombs, Jacobs went with 20-year-old Sergeant Alfred Wicks, of the 1st Battalion, to the endangered flank, and began to lob them into the trenches and posts now crowded with Turks, while his men barricaded the trench. This part of the line would become known as Jacobs's Post. As the position was being established, the Australians yet again ran out of bombs, and in spite of the urgency, no more could be obtained. Wicks, however, recalled seeing a supply of captured Turkish grenades in the trench just beyond the barricade being established – he jumped over and went down the eastern end in search of them: '[This] errand would take him, if not among the Turks, at any rate into a curve of the trench in which their bombs were constantly bursting. He nevertheless went forward, and, though wounded, found the grenades, and in three journeys recovered them. This additional supply enabled Jacobs to continue throwing while his men barricaded the trench.'[20]

The high point of the second day's battle was approaching. If these saps fell to the Turks they would be in a position to wrap up the southern flank of the Australian position and from there push their advantage and take the heart of their former works. The Pine would then have to be evacuated as it would be indefensible – the main avenues of supply (and escape) back to the main Australian lines at The Pimple would be in Turkish hands. Major Stevens knew this and urgently sent for their machine-gun officer, the already wounded Captain Pain, ordering him to bring a machine gun into action to support Jacobs's Post. Pain hurried to the nearest machine-gun position.

He found the machine-gun crew lying dead in a heap from an

explosion – but the gun itself was undamaged. Looking around, he ordered the closest men to help carry the gun to its new position. On reaching the trench junction, Pain realised that the situation was critical and decided without hesitation to set the gun up in the open. Standing partially exposed above the parapet, he fired into the Turks crowding the communication trenches.[21]

Major Stevens, anxious about the defence of the position, asked Pain whether the field of fire was sufficient. Pain, like Stevens, knew the precarious nature of their defence and the tactical significance of the saps just in front of him. He looked at his men and they instinctively knew what they had to do – they immediately carried the gun up onto no-man's-land, which commanded an excellent field of fire, but also provided the Turks with an easy target. To further increase the sweep of fire, Pain placed the legs of the tripod of the machine gun on the shoulders of his men, privates William Nichol, James Montgomery and William Goudemey. The Turks opened fire against the exposed targets and it wasn't long before the machine gun's water jacket (its cooling mechanism) was pierced, and Pain himself wounded (yet again). Even so, he continued to squeeze the trigger, firing streams of lead into the Turks in the crowded saps, while hot water from the holed water jacket poured down onto the men, causing them to laugh and swear out of fear and frustration.[22] Private Montgomery was soon hit and the gun was by now too damaged to fire. Pain had managed to fire nearly a thousand rounds. Miraculously, they all managed to get back into the trench, and the wounded officer and private were sent down to the beach. Pain and his men had at the most critical point in the fight brought the Turkish attack to a standstill. The four were recommended for the VC, but for some unknown reason they were denied. Nearly twelve months later, Nichol and Goudemey were each awarded the Distinguished Conduct Medal, while Pain received the Military Cross.[23] Poor old James Montgomery, aged just twenty, didn't even get a wooden cross – he died on a hospital ship and was buried at sea on 11 August, and is commemorated on the Lone Pine Memorial. Within a year, Private William Goudemey would be killed in action on the Western Front.

Meanwhile, Jacobs' men had managed to barricade their trench (Jacobs's Post) at a point about twenty-five metres in advance of Pain's Post, but short of the junction of the communication saps running into Youden's and Cook's posts. These were now firmly held by the Turks, though any further advance had been halted by Pain and his men. Jacobs retired to a dressing station with a head wound and Major Lane took command. The 1st Battalion had been brought back into Lone Pine to reinforce the badly pressed garrison. Some of these men were now positioned just behind Jacobs's Post. Yet again, the situation here was becoming critical. From trenches to the south of Jacobs's, the Turks were massing. The men of the 2nd Battalion, as well as some others, were now trying to deepen a shallow disused trench that ran parallel with Jacobs's Trench and in parts 'almost touched it. By this means, a continuous fire-trench was re-established along the whole southern flank, now reaching from the old Turkish front line to Tubb's corner.'24 Although the saps captured by the Turks at one point were just five metres from Jacobs's Trench, they only defended them lightly, with just a few men. To do otherwise would result in an ongoing bombing fight – a pointless battle that neither side was prepared to wage.

Major Lane recalled many years later that at about 2 p.m., orders were received to reinforce the firing line on the right. The overhead cover of the trenches was in most places still intact. Lane passed through 'a tortuous tunnel, the gloom being accentuated by leaving the bright sunshine. The Turkish dead had not yet been removed, and so thickly carpeted the ground that there was no alternative but to tread along a line of bodies. On arrival in the firing line, the company moved along to ... where the Turks during the morning had counter attacked and affected a lodgment.'[25] The trenches here were extremely narrow and most were not traversed. Australian and Turkish dead lay everywhere, and in some cases Australian wounded were lying at the bottom of the trench. The Turkish position in front was only about twenty metres distant, and they maintained a constant fire. Lane's Company occupied a portion of Jacobs's Post, where they and the Turks made repeated attempts to dislodge each other from their respective position. The main trench bay was completely covered with bodies, which Lane later described as having been 'shockingly blown apart, and presented a spectacle that I would not, if I could, describe. As it was desirable to have us look down the communication trench and also the nature of the enemy's barricade, three men from the floor of our trench directed a rapid fire upon any periscopes appearing. The Turks' barricade was of sandbags, trench high, and could not be carried from our side without scaling ladders, which were not available.'[26]

Twenty-four-year-old Sydney baker Sergeant Donald McLennan, of the 12th Battalion, along with three others, remained in an advance position throughout the afternoon, holding a position close to Jacobs's Post. The Turks hurled a salvo of grenades, which would then be followed by their snipers who would 'instantly appear over [a] traverse and attempt to enfilade our position, while others attacked from around the corner...Our parapet...extended to about 2 feet high, and from this cover an observer with periscope, with sniper by his side, kept down enemy observation'.[27] McLennan's party maintained a continuous bombing war against the Turks, mostly by throwing back Turkish grenades, and repulsed any attempts by the enemy to drive them out.[28] In this fight, Sergeant Don McLeod, who had just arrived, had his hand shattered by a bomb. Holding his 'injured forearm in his sound hand, with the thumb pressed firmly on the artery, he quietly requested another soldier to apply first aid. This was done effectively, and for some hours Sgt. McLeod stood there in the trench, waiting for an opportunity to pass to the rear. He must have been in great pain, but he never murmured or appeared downcast. His bearing was a most inspiring example, at a critical hour, to those about him.'[29]

Sergeant Elgar Hale, also of the 12th Battalion, later wrote to his sister that the Turks nearly got him with a grenade. He had spent some time running along the bottom of a trench chasing bombs as they were lobbed into his trench, dropping a half-filled bag on the hissing ordnance to localise the explosion. He saw one coming through the air and was bending down to pick up his sandbag to drop on it, when it exploded just behind his back and knocked him over. One of his friends who was with him told Hale afterwards that 'he looked for me as the smoke and dirt cleared away and saw me with the bag of sand on top of me and a chap lying across me. All I know is that I struggled out with my eyes & mouth full of sand and my ears buzzing, and very deaf. About half an hour after I was as good as gold again.'[30]

By late afternoon, the Turks were yet again launching a number of piecemeal attacks against the Australians lines. An urgent message was sent from the front line that experienced bombers with bombs were needed. With this, Captain Hubert Jacobs, of the 7th Battalion, and his platoon of trained bombers, totalling thirty-two men, went over to Lone Pine.[31] These men were directed into the crowded Jacobs's Trench, where they found men from the 1st, 2nd and 12th battalions fighting amongst the dead and wounded. The Turks now launched an attack against Goldenstedt's Post, but the men there had recently been supplied with a number of jam-tin bombs. Few of the replacements had ever used the bombs before but they managed to check the attack with them. Sergeant Major Goldenstedt recalled 'a fair amount of misguided enthusiasm, and more than one man lost a limb or was blown to bits as he argued with the man next to him how best to throw it, and how long to hold it after it had been lighted. Had there not been moments of humour during those terrible hours, I am sure no man could have survived.'[32] During the climax of the fighting that Saturday, Goldenstedt's mate Sergeant Campbell managed to provide a tragic laugh for those present at his expense:

'[A] sturdy bullocky of the Third, [he] stuck his head over the lip of the crater at the bottom of the trench and saw Mule Valley below him crowded with Turks... 'Look Goldie! Look, for Christ's sake!' he yelled. 'There are millions of the bastards down here.' His speech was cut short by a sniper's bullet that removed the whole of his front top teeth, which protruded beyond his upper lip as if they had been taken off with a fretsaw. Recovering from the shock, the bullocky in Campbell asserted itself, and there followed the best exhibition of cursing in between the gulping and spitting of mouthfuls of blood it would be possible to imagine. I don't know what the Turks thought, but the dozen or so men left in that trench roared with laughter as the eloquent Campbell beat it to the Beach. I was told later that Campbell hadn't exhausted his vocabulary by the time he had reached the hospital ship.[33]

Indeed, it wasn't only those on the front line who were experiencing humour in the face of adversity. Lance Corporal Lawrence was sitting behind The Pimple in Brown's Dip watching a bombardment of enemy shells slam uncomfortably close by. He decided it was better to stay put – there was nothing to be done about it. A bloke could just as easily run into the path of an oncoming shell in trying to avoid another – better to just sit and wait. He wrote in his diary that a bloke was taking a prisoner down to the beach but hadn't gone more than fifteen metres past him when over came a big shell: '[The Australian] cleared for his life – drat the prisoner. Well, directly the Australian ran, the old Turk ran after him. Down came the shell and burst with a terrific crash right in the centre of the track – just where they had been. The last I saw of them was the Australian going for his life round a bend in the track with the old Turk making good for a splendid second place.'[34] There was a roar of laughter and merriment when the men saw the Turkish prisoner afraid of his life running after his guard: '[It] just shows one the true feelings of these men and their buoyant spirits which it seems are absolutely impossible to quench – and thankful we are that it is so; for in this place one would go mad if it was not for the splendid way in which the men take everything that comes along, and manages to mix a little good humour, jokes, and tomfoolery into it.'[35] As a momentary reminder of this episode, Lawrence and the others now had a hole about two metres long and one metre deep right in the centre of their track.[36]

Major Denis Lane and his men were still in the thick of the fighting along Jacobs's Trench. At dusk their trench was finally barricaded to their satisfaction, but they'd barely finished the job when the Turks commenced another vigorous bombing attack. At first, a couple of grenades landed just behind their barricade, severely wounding the defenders and forcing Lane and his men to retreat further down the trench to get out of range. From a hastily erected barricade they could prevent any Turks from advancing down the trench. No Turks followed, so a few went back to the original barricade, but Turkish bombs fell in perfect succession in and around the barricade. Two or three men managed to escape injury and retired back to their new post. Others were immediately sent back in, but they too were soon either killed or driven out. Lane had no jam-tin bombs to reply with. A bomb screen of chicken wire was sent up from the rear and erected a little in advance of what remained of the original barricade. The men were then withdrawn from the fire recess, as 'two men [were] placed … to prevent any advance down the trench, and those manning the next fire recess ordered to stop any advance of hostile bombers from the communication trench, [and] by this means a brief respite was obtained'.[37]

It wasn't long, however, before Australians here spotted Turks massing in preparation for yet another attack. Indeed, they weren't the only ones to see them. Lieutenant Percy Ross's Australian 7th Battery and the men of the 10th Battalion positioned along Bolton's Ridge also had them in sight. Australian artillery, as well as rifle and machine-gun fire from Bolton's Ridge, now tore into the mass of Turks. Turkish counter-battery fire along Third Ridge replied. The Turks charged across no-man's-land in a brave but futile effort to retake their lost trench. Major Lane recalled that the rifle and machine-gun fire on both sides was incessant and heavy, and the noise of battle swelled louder and louder. More Turks arrived and the attack was renewed. The fire 'redoubled in fury, the men cramming the recesses and leaning well over the parapet to deliver their fire. Away on the right [Bolton's Ridge] the 10th Battalion directed an oblique fire across our front, and the enemy attack wilted … we recovered the portion of the trench we had evacuated "according to plan" (hurriedly conceived on the spur of the moment!) and were "as you were".'[38]

Back behind The Pimple, the officers and men of the 2nd Field Company, like the men fighting in the heart of Lone Pine, were just about done in. These men spent most of Saturday improving communications and evacuating the wounded. It was no easy matter getting the wounded through the narrow and crooked trenches. Twenty-four-year-old Private George Fish, a salesman from Victoria and now a member of the 2nd Australian Field Ambulance, was using a telescope and could see the bodies of the men who had fallen in no-man's land between The Pimple and Lone Pine. He and his mates couldn't reach them because of the ongoing Turkish artillery barrage slamming into the paddock. He recalled how the wounded were coming 'in such numbers [via the saps and tunnels] as to congest the dressing station – the bearers working hard to relieve them…At the beach the Dressing and Clearing Stations were working at full pressure. Doctors and orderlies were going day and night through amputating and dressing the wounded.'[39] Later promoted to sergeant, George would die from wounds while serving in France in late July 1916.

Engineering officer Major Martyn, who had returned from his failed tour of inspection of the Pine, recalled that the dead were mostly left where they fell and a 'dreadful sight it was too'.[40] The Australian dead that could be recovered were taken to Brown's Dip, but the Turkish dead remained, and at the end of the third or fourth day their state was 'dreadful, and eau-de-cologne would have been in great demand if we had had any. Many tunnels were so chocked with dead that we had to fill them in and dig round them.'[41]

Meanwhile, Chaplain Dean Talbot, at Brown's Dip Cemetery, asked a young officer for the list of the dead about to be buried, and recognised the names of several men he knew. One was his friend and colleague Digges La Touché. Talbot later heard (incorrectly) that La Touché had been killed 'just after he leapt over the parapet. Some days later [another] man gave me his prayer book which he picked up at the spot where he fell and died.'[42] Another name on the list was 'Major C. D. Austin, a fine soldier who was always found at his post in the front line trench. I went down into the grave and took a last look at the faces of my friends who had paid the supreme price of their loyalty to Australia and Empire.'[43]

Also in Brown's Dip, General Walker passed by Lance Corporal Lawrence, who was part of Major Martyn's company. Lawrence recorded in his diary how the general was accompanied by 'staff map bearers, periscope carriers, time keepers and all the other "hoboes" that usually accompany generals about. Seeing our Major [Martyn] he grows quite enthusiastic about the manner in which our Company has worked and acquitted itself generally. He shakes the major by the hand, then off he goes…'[44]

Lawrence decided to see the conditions at the Pine for himself, even though he'd been ordered to stay at Brown's Dip: 'The boys up there will surely want a spell somewhere and the boss can only send me back.'[45] The Turks were still bombarding the rear areas with 9- and 11-inch howitzer shells. The worst of it was 'they are not firing at a known target but just lobbing them everywhere and anywhere – searching they call it. One never knows where the next will land.'[46] The first indication that a shell was on its way was when a man heard a faint whistling sound. Gradually it would get louder and a bloke would realise then whether it was going over or falling short. The whistling 'becomes a rushing noise and a black speck appears in the sky. Rapidly it gets longer and the noise increases; someone shouts, "Look out!!" There is a Hell of a loud rush, a thud and an ear-splitting "bang" and up go dugouts, blankets, earth, scrub and what not, and where a few moments before was a clear piece of ground is now a gaping hole; and so it is hour after hour.'[47]

On his way to The Pimple to get a look at Lone Pine, Lawrence and others had to run through about a half-dozen exploding howitzer shells: 'What a different appearance the whole place [The Pimple] has assumed since I saw it last. It is just torn to pieces, sandbags blown to smithereens and parapets just levelled.'[48] He joined up with a party who were assigned to reinforce the Pine and on reaching the tunnel entrance made his way through the passage that he and his sappers had dug for over two months. He reached the former secret underground trench – daylight was now streaming through the opened-up recesses through which the first line had hopped out, and 'lying all along it are the forms of fellows killed even before they had got into the open; lying beside them on the floor of the tunnel are empty shell cases that have come clean through the openings'.[49]

Lawrence now entered the open and shallow sap that had been dug just hours before and began to make his way by crawling towards Lone Pine. As he progressed he noticed 'the smell of dead bodies...getting very strong and unpleasant'.[50] He found himself climbing down into what had been one of the Turkish tunnels whose roof had collapsed. It led directly to the old Turkish front line. In this tunnel were lying dozens of dead from both sides, and amongst them the wounded sat patiently, waiting to be withdrawn to the dressing stations behind the lines and later on to the hospital ships and transports. For many it would be days before they began this slow tortuous trip. These men had been crammed in there all night. Lawrence saw some with truly appalling wounds, yet the men just sat there not saying a word and some had actually fallen asleep despite their pain. One had been 'shot clean through the chest and his singlet and tunic are just saturated with blood, another has his nose and upper lip shot clean away'.[51] Lying beside them, another was asleep. He had been wounded somewhere in the head and as he breathed the blood 'bubbled and frothed at his nose and mouth, truly a most unpleasant sight. Yet all one gave him was simply a casual glance, more of curiosity than anything else. At ordinary times these sights would have turned one sick but now they have not the slightest effect.'[52]

He clambered out of the tunnel back into the sap, which was here about a metre deep with another half-metre of cover from the earthen embankment if he crawled – it was too risky to stand up or even sit and straighten his back. Occasionally he would forget and go to straighten up a little, but 'the way in which bullets hit the bank all round, directly and when the slightest portion of my hat showed up, soon convinced me that it would pay to keep low; but by raising your head cautiously and keeping an eye upon all the cover obtainable it is possible to look back to our late firing line'.[53] No-man's-land was covered with dead bodies, and the scattered equipment that was being rushed across when the men were cut down: rifles, sandbags, bags of bombs and shovels. 'The undergrowth has been cut down, like mown hay, simply stalks left standing, by the rifle fire, whilst the earth itself appears just as though one had taken a huge rake and scratched it all over. Here and there it is torn up where a shell has landed.'[54]

As he pushed through the narrow and shallow sap, he came across 'fourteen of our boys stone dead. Ah! It is a piteous sight.'[55] He lamented that these same men and boys had just yesterday been full of joy but were now lying cold dead, with eyes 'glassy, their faces sallow and covered with dust – soulless – gone – somebody's son, somebody's boy – now merely a thing. Thank God their loved ones cannot see them now – dead, with blood congealed or oozing out. God, what a sight.'[56] A major came upon him and, sitting next to Lawrence, declared: 'Well, we have won.'[57] Lawrence couldn't see any sense in the declaration: 'Great God – won – that means a victory and all those bodies within arms' reach – then may I never witness a defeat.'[58] He had seen enough – his curiosity well and truly satisfied. He and the major began to crawl back and stopped at the point where the sap had broken into the Turkish tunnel, still packed with dead and wounded. Just above, in no-man's-land, he noticed a dead Australian, his head and shoulders hanging into the sap, his blood slowly dripping into the trench. Lawrence sat and watched it, transfixed:

The major has just sat down too on the step into the tunnel and it is dripping on his back. I wonder who this poor devil was. I will look at his identity disc. It is under his chin and his face hangs downward into the trench. Each time I lift up his head it falls back; it is heavy and full of dirt and Ugh, the blood is on my hand – a momentary shudder – but one is used to these sights now, and I simply wipe my hands upon the dirt in the trench. Lying right against the trench (I could get him if it was worthwhile) lies another; his back is towards me, and he is on his side. From the back of his head down his neck runs a congealed line of dark red, but that is not what I notice; it is his hands. They are clasped before him just as though he was in prayer. I wonder what that prayer was. I wonder if it will be answered, but surely it must. Surely the prayer of one who died so worthily (he was right on the parapet of the Turkish trench) could not fail to be answered.[59]

After a short breather, Lawrence realised that the hole in the sap floor needed to be boarded over if the wounded below were to have any chance of getting to a hospital ship. Those in the tunnel could not be got out via the hole; they would need to be brought out of the tunnel through its original entrance in Lone Pine, and from there carried back through the sap to The Pimple. He sent word to the rear that planking was needed. Suddenly, Lawrence was shaken by the major. Turning around he saw the officer staring at something over the bank. All that he could see was a pair of drawn-up knees and a hand: 'The back has been blown out of the hand, it is simply a red hole; but it is the knees. Every few moments they come together; the man must be alive.'[60] They tried to rescue him, but each time they raised their heads slightly above the trench, they were fired upon. A continuous zip and thud was heard as the bullets smacked into the earth around them. 'Now, how can we get him? One can't go out, that's certain. For fully fifteen minutes we throw a rope across the bank to him, shouting out to catch hold of it but each time the rope only comes back; he must be unconscious, and the wounded still remain to be got out.'[61] Soon the man stopped moving and remained quiet. Now the planking arrived and Lawrence began working on the bridge to cover the hole in the sap floor, which was the tunnel's roof. One can only imagine the thoughts of the wounded below as the planking – board by board – closed out the light and 'fresh' air, entombing them in darkness. By the time the planking was fixed and the hole covered it was time for Lawrence to get back to The Pimple. He wrote that night that his hands were 'raw and the smell of blood and death is everywhere. We crawl out along our shallow trench and through B5 tunnel, then along the old firing line of yesterday and so on to Brown's Dip.'[62]

17

'Place like
a charnel house'

With darkness, the Turks had still failed to retake their front-line trenches, but they had routed most of the Australian positions from the head of The Cup. The recapture of these positions was a significant tactical victory, as the Australians no longer had a commanding view into the Turkish reserve areas. Similar views, however, were still available from Goldenstedt's Post, so, for the Turks, this position had to be retaken at all costs. The Australians here continued to throw jam-tin bombs down into the head of The Cup, which exploded murderously among the crowd of Turks waiting to be fed into the battle. The casualties were so severe that some companies normally commanded by majors were now led by NCOs.

Major Ahmed Zeki Bey was keen to press on with trying to retake parts of their former trenches. He approached his men manning the edges of Lone Pine and asked them: 'Why can't you counterattack over the top here?' One of his junior officers replied, 'But can't you see – there are all those men lying on the top who tried to make an attack over the top there. They were caught by fire the moment they got over. You can't go there.' Zeki Bey looked up to the parapet and 'there was a complete line of dead along the top'.[1] Piecemeal frontal charges against the entrenched Australians, without any supporting fire, were no longer an option. Zeki Bey and his CO, Ali Riza, knew that their artillery could not provide sufficient support to assist in an all-out infantry assault, as the trenches were too close together. Another tactic had to be adopted. Zeki Bey ordered snipers and others to take up positions after dark along various points of Lone Pine. He requested similar orders be issued to the men along the southern side of Johnston's Jolly. Zeki Bey and Ali Riza believed that with this covering fire the Australians would be forced to keep their heads down until the moment the mass Turkish assault could be organised. This long-awaited coordinated attack had been postponed until first light the next day, 8 August.

Back at Scrubby Knoll, Major General Esat Pasha was totally focused on retaking his lost works on 400 Plateau, and frustrated by the apparent lack of a coordinated response from his commanders. He was, however, completely ignorant of the chaotic situation facing his officers and men fighting for their lives in the Pine. Everything was a mess and the men still badly needed to be reorganised and their morale restored. Their dead from the first twenty-four hours were moved off the Pine to make room for the living – corpses were laid out beside the tracks leading from the plateau. As reinforcements moved up towards Lone Pine, they had to endure passing rows of their dead comrades, laid out four deep, on their left-hand side. When they reached the summit of the plateau, still overlooked by some Australian periscopes, an officer said they 'were in bad condition and came to a bad situation'.[2]

After dark, Colonel Smyth sent a message to the men defending the captured enemy works across Lone Pine that the Turks were in considerable strength all along the line, but if they try to 'wear us out by continued assault they will not succeed. Yesterday's and today's battles have shown that there are no fighters who can surpass Australians. Every precaution for keeping a good watch will be taken to-night, and the artillery will co-operate.'[3] Undoubtedly, the men would have preferred more jam-tin bombs to platitudes, but above all they needed to be relieved – they had been fighting continuously for over twenty-four hours.

It was not only those fighting for their lives at the Pine who were utterly exhausted. Colonel Neville Howse VC visited the 3rd Field Ambulance dressing station at Brown's Dip, under the command of Captain Henry Fry, and found the stretcher-bearers close to exhaustion and deeply stressed from having to perform their duties continuously since the initial attack, and often under direct enemy fire. Howse ordered up fresh bearers and additional stretchers, and gave instructions that all personnel at the station were to work twelve-hour shifts.[4] Howse did not ask his men to do anything he wasn't prepared to do himself. On 7 August, Howse worked an unbroken shift of twelve hours and personally dealt with around 700 cases who had streamed down to the beach. Working in such exposed areas meant the inevitable happened – on 8 August he was wounded in the shoulder, whether by bullet or shrapnel is unknown. Lieutenant Colonel John Gellibrand, who was next to Howse when he was hit, noted that no great damage was done and certainly none to his reputation. Howse's indifference to danger prompted Sir Ian Hamilton to mention him in despatches shortly afterwards.[5]

The cooks, too, were busy. They are rarely afforded the recognition they deserve in histories of the war. Indeed, Charles Bean later wrote in his diary: 'War Correspondents have so habitually exaggerated the heroism of battles that people don't realise that the real actions [everyday actions] are heroic…There is plenty of heroism in war – it teems with it. But it has been so overwritten that if you write that a man did his job people say: "Oh, but there's nothing heroic in that!" Isn't there? You come here and see the job and understand it and get out of your head the nonsense that is written about it.'[6] One such soldier simply 'doing his job' was thirty-year-old Private Alexander Brims, of the 3rd Australian Field Ambulance, based at Brown's Dip. During the battle for Lone Pine, he was seen around the clock providing men with hot food and a cup of tea, including the wounded passing by, despite frequent bursts of enemy shells around his post.[7] Ordinary work perhaps, but heroic.

During the night, the bombing war continued at Lone Pine, especially at Jacobs's Post, which was quickly becoming this battle's 'Quinn's Post'. Quinn's was reputed to be the most dangerous place on the peninsula because of the closeness of the trenches and the ongoing bombing war fought there day and night. The men at Jacobs's Post were now enduring this horrific experience. Officers and NCOs, including Major Land and Sergeant Wicks, had been seriously wounded. In response, Jacobs, himself wounded, had been summoned back from 2nd Battalion Headquarters, where Colonel Cass had insisted that he rest. Jacobs was quickly in the thick of it again, commanding the men in his former post. The 2nd Battalion Diary records: 'We are sustaining a very large number of casualties from bombs. Two bomb screens have been erected and serving very useful.'[8] The trenches were so packed that men could not dodge the enemy's grenades and as a result its floor was covered with the dead and dying. Those still in the fight had to continue to do so over the bodies of their mates.[9] Jacobs ordered the garrison be reduced to help avoid the pointless casualties. The strong points of the southern flank were defined by a number of forward barricades halfway along a trench or at a trench intersection. Each was defended by two or three men, with the rest further back, taking shelter from the bombs, if possible in the nearest covered works of the former Turkish front line. They moved forward every now and then, from further down the line, in order to be close when called upon to take their turn at one of the barricades. When one man was hit, he was quickly replaced by another.

Finally, during darkness, supplies started to make their way into the captured works, and not just food, water, ammunition and jam-tin bombs, but also materials to help protect the men from the dreaded Turkish grenades, such as chicken wire. Twenty-three-year-old Tasmanian labourer Private 'Viv' Searle, of the 12th Battalion, had been ordered to leave the Pine and bring back some wire to help construct bomb proofs. Along with a few others he had made it back to The Pimple and managed to get hold of some bundles of chicken wire. As they returned, they passed through a communication sap, clambering over the dead and wounded towards the front lines. Searle sent a few blokes ahead of him, while he and 28-year-old Private Albert Smith, from Ballarat, followed behind. As they were about to turn a corner, Searle heard a cry and turning back he saw Smith now on the floor among the other dead and wounded. Searle threw down his bundle and rushed over – a bullet had torn through Smith's windpipe and killed him. Searle grasped the identity disc hanging around his friend's neck, and reached into his tunic pocket and took out his pay book.[10] Albert Smith has no known grave and is commemorated on the Lone Pine Memorial. Just a few weeks later, Vivian Searle was killed by a sniper's bullet. He is today buried in Beach Cemetery.

Lieutenant Lecky was still positioned along the southern flank of Lone Pine close to Jacobs's Trench. Like everyone else, he was badly in need of sleep. He came up to a communication sap and 'felt tempted to sneak down a little way, and have a rest. However, an undaunted chaplain was there administering to the wounded and dying. He looked at me. One look was enough, and I went round to the new position with the survivors, without any more inclination to quit the job. That Chaplain was "Fighting Mac" [Bill McKenzie] the Salvationist.'[11]

'Fighting Mac' McKenzie, aged forty-six, had charged across no-man's-land with his 'flock', taking with him an entrenching tool.[12] Like his men, he was fed up with the brutality of it all. He wrote to his wife shortly after he'd been ordered out of Lone Pine, where he'd been serving amid the carnage for days on end:

> I was there in it all, the trenches were the most awful sight I have ever witnessed. Hundreds of dead Turks and these intermingled with Australia's sons lay tiers deep in some trenches. The dead on top of the wounded and what a terrible struggle to get the wounded out...
>
> Some of the wounds were awful and many must die or be crippled for life. My experiences of getting the wounded out of the trenches over the dead and wounded underneath the dead was sickening. The burials in the tunnels within the trenches too was nerve-wracking as also was the recovery of the dead in the open as the Turkish guns were very busy by day and sometimes by night. When this work was done I buried in all something like 450...I had to leave the graves to retch from the effects of the smells. Burials in Brown's Dip by day were frequently performed under shell fire. Several occasions men were hit and some killed. The experiences of the first week are beyond the telling, the shells, the smells, the sights, the nerve-wracking intensity of the whole fight with its terrible slaughter. The pouring of blood and broken bones was too terrible to describe. I was worked out to a frazzle for days and nights. I was in great pain from neuritis – all my reserved strength was used up and I could hardly crawl around except in pain and with sheer force of will the aid of a stout stick.

The officers urged me to go away but I determined to 'stick it' and see it thro until the regiment was relieved. The bravery of the dashing Australian boys is beyond any cavil. They'd tackle anything. I felt honoured in staying with them and I felt I needed them and they needed me, particularly as I was the only Protestant Chaplain in the Brigade.[13]

Cyril Lawrence concluded his diary that day by describing the Australians' proximity to Turkish bombers, whose deadly arsenal was being lobbed over the trenches in the thousands: 'In one place we were only five yards apart, and one can hear them jabbering away amongst themselves, but the bombs, God they are cutting our fellows out like ninepins... You see the bombs come over and burst in the trench behind the men.'[14] Down on the beach, the jam-tin bomb factory was reportedly now making around 4000 bombs a day, with assistance from the navy. In addition, shiploads of 13 000-odd were being delivered daily from Egypt. Many of the bombs, however, were destined for other parts of the fighting, especially those fighting for the Sari Bair Range to the north. Yet those at the Pine could not keep pace with the Turks. They were throwing over 'twelve to our eleven; it is just real slaughter, but all our communication trenches are through and we can get reserves in quickly in case they are needed, so everyone feels confident that we can hold the ground that we have won'.[15]

All along the northern flank of Lone Pine, intermittent attacks from Owen's Gully kept the men of the 4th Battalion busy, and exhausted, as recalled by Private Graham. The night of 7 August had hardly descended when the fighting once more erupted. But now Graham and his cobbers were feeling a little safer as they'd had time to strengthen their defences, they had been reinforced and Lieutenant Brown had set up a machine gun nearby. With rifle and machine-gun fire they enfiladed some of the Turkish positions on Johnston's Jolly. Their main concern remained Owen's Gully.

From here the Turk still 'sortied from his many strong points, tossing his bombs among us with deadly precision and spraying our posts with rifle-fire. Well into the night at this northern point of the line the fighting continued with unabated fury. But we were holding the Turk and long before dawn he had ceased to worry us. Many Turks had fallen close to our possie but none had reached it.'[16]

At 1st Australian Divisional Headquarters, Colonel White wrote in his diary: 'Operations towards Suvla Bay – Ships guns firing as on 25th April! Progress slow. Lone Pine continually counter attacked. Place like a charnel house.'[17]

Sunday
8 August
1915

18

'…like a battle of savage beasts at the bottom of a pit'

Sunday

8 August
1915

Throughout the darkness of that early Sunday morning at Lone Pine – as elsewhere – there was no rest. All were anxiously awaiting the dawn. 'It came alright,' recalled Sergeant Major Paul Goldenstedt, still located at the post named for him, 'with a hail of bombs that further reduced our now slender garrison to four.'[1] The first of the Turkish coordinated attacks to retake Lone Pine was about to be launched against the Australian post. Captain Ahmed Zeki Bey witnessed the attack against Goldenstedt's Post from the Turkish trenches: 'I saw bombs being thrown and then some young Turks get into the trench with the bayonet… They said they came upon several young Australian dead in the communication trench, with their rifles broken. The Turkish bayonets could be seen advancing ten or twelve yards from the head of the gully… the Australians then lost the [last] position from which their periscopes had stared down the head of The Cup.'[2] Earlier, Lieutenant Owen Howell-Price had visited Goldenstedt's position and recommended that it be evacuated – it was too exposed and couldn't possibly be held. For whatever reason, this hadn't happened and now Goldenstedt was requesting reinforcements from Major Morshead, located about fifteen metres away at Tubb's Corner. The major had none to spare as his own position was under heavy counterattack by the same Turks. Goldenstedt wrote: 'Bombed by overwhelming numbers, the four of us eventually retired to the junction with the main trench, from which position we took part in the general defence of the line now held by the Third [Battalion] and I think, First Battalion, or was it the Second?'[3] He and his men, including Corporal Mark 'Darkie' McGrath, managed to build a new barricade. With Goldenstedt's original post evacuated, and crowded with Australian dead, the Turks wasted no time in occupying it.

While the battle for Goldenstedt's Post was raging, a renewed attack by a half-company of Turks was launched against Jacobs's Trench. As the Turks emerged onto no-man's-land, the Australians poured rifle fire into them. Artillery and small-arms fire from Bolton's Ridge to the south also tore into them, and the attack was easily repulsed. However, a number of men here and elsewhere within Lone Pine were now being hit by Turkish fire, originating from Johnston's Jolly.[4] Captain Cecil Sasse had replaced the wounded and gallant Captain Harold Jacobs and organised the clearing of the Australian dead from Jacobs's Trench, by placing them in nearby unused saps, shelters and tunnels. At first dawn, as this work was progressing, the Turks launched another counterattack. They blew apart the flimsy barricade that had been blocking their approach and began firing into the narrow passage. Sasse hurried to the scene, tore down the sandbag parapets to form a low barricade and proceeded with a rifle to drop any Turk that attempted an advance down the short length of trench. With this, the post was again made momentarily secure.[5]

Similar attacks were launched against other nearby posts, as recorded in the battalion's history. Just north, at Tubb's Corner, Major Stevens got up to look over the parapet 'whence he found himself gazing along a trench full of Turks on the right. Shouting to his men, Stevens got about a dozen of them onto or over the parapet, and, regardless of bullets and bombs, these men poured rapid fire into the massed enemy.'[6] For the moment, at least, this seemed to unsettle the Turks and no advance from this trench was conducted. Indeed, all along the southern flank at Lone Pine there was a brief lull in the fighting. Some of the newer arrivals endeavoured to clear the trenches of dead and wounded, not only to make passage easier, but also for their own health and wellbeing.

Those who had been fighting in the trenches from the start were now too physically and emotionally spent to care about anything. With over thirty-six hours of constant hand-to-hand fighting, they were completely exhausted and slumped into a momentary sleep. There now came across these men the realisation that they were totally done in. One experienced bomber, who had been throwing bombs since the initial assault, 33-year-old Private Joseph Collingwood, of the 2nd Battalion, was so exhausted he couldn't even raise his arm. Colonel Smyth knew it was imperative that he relieve men such as these, especially those from the 1st and 2nd battalions, who had been holding the southern part of the Pine – the fighting there had been the heaviest and the Australians had suffered severely. It was approaching 10 a.m. and Colonel Smyth sent a message to Lieutenant Colonel 'Pompey' Elliott, ordering the 7th Battalion to move forward and relieve the men in the southern sector. Smyth, while acknowledging the stress and strain that the men from the 3rd and 4th battalions had been placed under over the last few days, decided to leave them in the central and northern sectors respectively. They would be supported by men from the 12th Battalion, who had themselves been fighting almost continuously – with the fighting raging along Sari Bair, there were few reserves left.

With the momentary respite from tension and excitement, men began to relax. The problem was it would be nearly impossible for a man to force himself back to renewed effort when required, and this would undoubtedly have been true for the Turks as well, just metres away. The 'nauseating stench and ghastly sights which surrounded them everywhere were sufficient to have dampened the ardour of the freshest and most hardened troops... Lone Pine was a frightful hand-to-hand struggle, like a battle of savage beasts at the bottom of a pit, in which the Australians triumphed in the face of inconceivable difficulties.'[7] Elliott later wrote to Kate about his first impressions of Lone Pine within hours of his 7th Battalion's arrival: 'Found everything in dreadful confusion. Officers and men exhausted and unable to give any coherent account of how things stood. They had sustained violent counterattacks through the night.'[8]

To make matters worse – if that were possible – the constant killing and maiming had resulted in renewed congestion of the trenches, it was as if they had never been 'cleared'. Major Curry, of the New Zealand Artillery, recalled: 'There were all sorts of wounds, one fellow was shot in the neck and with protruding eyes was grasping for breath... Hard biscuits, bacon and jam were the fare, and this had to be eaten in the midst of 700 dead Turks and a lot of our own dead.'[9] Ralph Goode, of the 2nd Australian Field Ambulance, was sent over to help, and wrote in his diary: '[The] Turks have been burying their dead in the trenches & it's like walking on a spring mattress in some parts... rotten things these hand bombs made of nails, slugs & stones put in a jam tin with a stick of dynamite... they make a horrible mess of a chap... practically plug him full of holes'.[10] Twenty-nine-year-old Waverley electrical engineer Sergeant Leslie de Vine wrote: 'Many men wear gas protectors... there has been no attempt up to the present to either remove or bury the dead they are stacked out of the way in any convenient place sometimes thrown up on the parados so as not to block up the trenches, there are more dead than living... [and] we have been too busy to do anything in the matter.'[11]

Somewhere close by was 24-year-old Private William Bendery,

of the 2nd Battalion, who recalled that the dead were piled four or five deep along the trenches: '[They were] lying everywhere, on top of the parapet...in dugouts and communication trenches and saps, and it was impossible to avoid treading on them. In the second line the Turkish dead were lying everywhere, and if a chap wanted to sit down for a spell he was often compelled to squat on one of 'em.'[12] To help alleviate the problem, the Irishmen and Yorkshiremen of the 5th Connaught Rangers were now ordered to conduct the thankless task of helping to remove the dead. Picks and shovels were used to 'prise the dead from the floor of the captured trenches; where many had been literally trampled into the ground during the hand-to-hand combat in the trenches. The bodies were then dragged to an empty saphead and tossed in with no ceremony. The Rangers were only allowed to take care of the enemy dead – the Australians looked after their own fallen.'[13]

Private Donkin, in Brown's Dip, recalled seeing a large 'fatigue party of [5th] Connaught Rangers...digging deep trenches and burying the dead. Horrible sights these are – at 10 this morning there was a row of about 50 lying out when a large shell burst on them and tore the bodies to pieces, the wounded are legion.'[14] Australian Major Gellibrand, who had been assigned to help supervise some of this work, described the smell as being similar to a pork leg left out in the sun for five days.[15] Out of 200 men involved in this thankless task, seven were killed and thirty-one wounded.[16] Those of the Connaught Rangers who may have been disappointed at not being thrown into the battle for Lone Pine wouldn't have long to wait – within two weeks they would be fighting for their lives in the bloodbath at Hill 60. Indeed, Charles Bean wrote of their assault against the hill's slopes in his *Official History*: 'this fine charge called forth the admiration of all who beheld it'.[17]

Further north, below the Sari Bair Ridge, Birdwood and Godley were trying to salvage what was left of their August Offensive.

The crucial aspect of the plan had always been surprise – without it, no troops could possibly hope to climb, capture and hold its summits. Almost thirty-six hours had passed since the offensive had been launched and the Turks were fully awake to the danger and had reacted to it. Hamilton and Birdwood had had one shot at gaining the heights and it had failed. Military logic should have dictated that orders be distributed for the men to withdraw where necessary and occupy defensive positions. However, those in command could not accept failure and were determined to push on regardless of the casualties and the hopelessness of the tactical situation.[18] At this stage, even if the heights could be captured, there were not enough troops left to defend the newly captured positions, and the logistics of supplying the men – even if they could muster enough troops – had been far beyond the ability of the Corps, even before the offensive. With the significant losses suffered since the opening of the offensive, this was even more evident.[19] Along the seaward slopes and gullies of the northern heights, the Empire troops had been awoken at around 2 a.m. The left and right attacking columns set about re-enacting the efforts of the day before. A large number of Turks – with four machine guns – located along Abdel Rahman Bair now opened up with devastating enfilade. The organisation of the Australian battalions was truly in a shambles – communications with platoons, let alone companies, was shot to pieces. The battle for Hill 971 quickly degenerated into a battle of survival along the lower slopes of the northern heights. The Australians were pushed back and very few of the wounded left in Turkish hands survived. Most were either shot or bayoneted outright.[20]

Just south of the Australians, the Indian Brigade was not faring any better. They saw the Australians falling back from Hill 60 and Yauan Tepe. One Gurkha battalion managed to advance up the slopes and gullies a few hundred metres north of them. Led by Major Allanson, they had by 9.30 a.m. advanced to a position just 200 metres below the northern slopes of Chunuk Bair. These troops courageously continued to cling onto this position throughout the day.[21]

South of the Australians and Indians, the New Zealand Wellington and Otago battalions, reinforced with men of the British 7th Gloucestershire and 8th Welsh, had renewed their attack against Chunuk Bair. Leading the assault, the Wellington Battalion pushed on towards the summit, while Auckland infantry strained their eyes in the early morning light to watch their advance, all waiting for the inevitable opening volley of enemy rifle and machine-gun fire. The advance continued up the slope and within minutes their outline could be seen against the crest of Chunuk Bair – the first line quietly disappeared over the summit. In confusion, the Turks had for some unknown reason evacuated the summit in the early morning, just hours before. Chunuk Bair had been captured without a casualty; however, the battle to hold it would be another matter.[22]

Back in Lone Pine, 27-year-old Private Cecil McAnulty, of the 2nd Battalion, was still in the heart of the Pine. At some point during the fighting, he took a minute off to update his diary. He reached into his breast pocket, took out the battered bundle of scrap papers and scribbled:

I've pulled through alright so far, just got a few minutes to spare now. I'm all out, can hardly stand up...when we got the word to charge Frank & I were on the extreme left of the charging party. There was a clear space of 100 yards to cross without a patch of cover. I can't realise how I got across it, I seemed to be in a sort of a trance. The rifle & machine gun fire was hellish. I remember dropping down when we reached their trenches, looked round & saw Frank & 3 other men alongside me. There was a big gap between us & the rest of our men...[who] were behind the shelter of the Turkish parapet ...We were right out in the open...I yelled out to the other chaps, 'This is suicide boys. I'm going to make a jump for it.' I thought they said alright we'll follow. I sprang to my feet in one jump.[23]

His diary entries end here in mid sentence. Private Cecil McAnulty is buried in the Lone Pine Cemetery.

19

'I heard
bagpipes playing'

While individual and heroic efforts were being made in Lone Pine by medical personnel like Doc Fullerton, there was simply no provision for a suitable aid post in the Pine itself during the first few days of combat. Casualties, wherever possible, were removed using the communication saps and tunnels that led back to The Pimple and the beach, demanding sheer courage, endurance and resourcefulness from the stretcher-bearers and medical staff. Within one twelve-hour period during 7 August, these men managed to evacuate close to 800 casualties. However, stretchers were always in short supply and those who could walk out were ordered to do so, while those who were considered hopeless cases had to remain in the Pine. Only those who were considered to have a fair chance of survival, but had to be carried, were assigned to a precious stretcher. Medics and officers were forced to make life and death decisions in the surrounding horrors of the blood-soaked trenches and posts.

The men at Gallipoli fully recognised the Australian and New Zealand nurses as being ANZACs in their own right – they too were often in grave danger, and life on board a hospital ship just off Anzac Cove or North Beach was far from safe. Sister Hilda

Samsing recalled how 'stray bullets pattered on board like rain drips from a shower'.[1] Nurse Madeline Wilson had one of her patients killed by a stray Turkish bullet as she handed him a glass of water.[2] By the end of the war, 388 Australian Army Nursing Sisters would be decorated for courage and dedication to the wounded – seven were awarded the Military Medal for courage under enemy fire. Twenty-five nursing sisters would never return to Australia and are buried overseas.[3]

In the early hours of 8 August, an additional 1500 casualties had made their way to the beach for transfer to hospital ships via flat-topped barges. When a man finally reached Anzac Cove for evacuation, in many cases his troubles were just starting. The cove was absolutely packed with wounded, and there would be a long wait. One medical officer recalled: 'We have 200 (stretcher) cases lying huddled up in traverse: the crowd great, and accommodation and staff so small that it is impossible to do urgent operations or even to dress all the cases that need it.'[4]

Getting aboard one of the hospital ships was often a drama in itself, with many barges being shuffled from ship to ship, as they were found to be full. Of course, it wasn't only the wounded from Lone Pine who had to be accommodated, but also those from the attacks along Second Ridge and from the battles raging further north along the Sari Bair Range. The hospital ships in many cases were merely troop transports with only rudimentary medical facilities. Getting a bunk would have been a luxury – most had to make do with blood-soaked mattresses spread out wherever they could fit. Sister Alice Kitchen, of No. 1 Australian General Hospital, was on board a dedicated hospital ship just off Anzac Cove and wrote in her diary: 'A large lighter full of wounded came alongside, almost 200 patients on it. Never saw such a lot at once before… They say there are hundreds [of wounded] over there lying about everywhere, waiting to be brought down from the hilly places. The stretcher-bearers have lost heavily.'[5] In one tragic episode, a barge was forced back to Anzac as no ships could take on board the wounded at that time, and as morning light broke, Turks believing the barge was full of reinforcements began to shell it, killing many and causing more wounds amongst the survivors.

Disorganisation also prevailed on the nearby Greek islands designated for treating the wounded. Given the restrictions of the harbour on Imbros, further delays ensued that meant after waiting on crowded beaches, the men then waited on crowded hospital ships to be taken ashore. It would take some many days to be transferred from these ships to the makeshift hospitals. Imbros, however, quickly became a major bottleneck in the line of communications for the wounded, and soon Lemnos, which had been assigned as the 'intermediate medical base', was incorporated into the medical planning to try to alleviate the immediate situation.[6] To cope with unfolding events at Gallipoli, two vast tent hospitals were set up around the Imbros harbour, at Mudros. Soon the shortage of water was becoming a major problem, not only for treating the wounds, but simply for giving the men a drink, not to mention complicating and overstretching existing sanitary arrangements. It wasn't long before the medical resources at both Imbros and Lemnos were overwhelmed, further compounding the suffering of the wounded. Many died who might have been saved if appropriate planning and resources had been invoked at the very early stages of the planning for the August Offensive. Hamilton's insistence on secrecy ensured that such planning by the medical staff could not occur in time.

On being taken to a field hospital, the seriously wounded were transferred to fast-moving 'ambulance' destroyers or transport vessels, which ferried them to hospitals in Alexandria or Malta. These so-called 'black ships' – unlike hospital ships, due to time constraints they had not been painted white to indicate that they ferried wounded, and hence were fair game to German U-boats – were hastily fitted out with some very basic hospital facilities and equipment. Australian medical officer Captain Graham Butler, who would later write the official history of Australia's medical services during the Great War, commented that the preparations on these ships were 'gravely inadequate and conditions deplorable'.[7] Many wounded Australians would succumb to their wounds while on board these 'black ships' and would be buried at sea. Private Thwaites, of the 12th Battalion, had no sooner arrived at the Pine than he was hit in a lung and forced to endure being stranded in the works for over forty-eight hours. He eventually found himself, struggling to breathe with one good lung, on a 'black ship' heading for Malta: 'The ship was a sorry plight. There were dying galore there. They'd got all the casualties from Lone Pine and the other attacks. That was very sad, to see some of the poor fellows lying beside you there and the hospital so full with seriously wounded... But it was remarkable, after a couple of days the wound seemed to heal over, and my lung seemed to come back and I was able to breathe.'[8]

The doctors, nurses, stretcher-bearers and orderlies on the Greek islands worked tirelessly under the primitive conditions – their experiences of war were arguably just as bad, if not worse, as those of the men of the front line. While not facing the immediate fear of death or maiming, they had to endure seemingly endless days of stress born of great responsibilities as well as fatigue and the appalling conditions in which they had to work. Others on the islands, however, didn't have it so bad. Indeed, the British officers stationed on the luxury liner SS *Aragon*, anchored in Mudros harbour, were well and truly loathed by just about everyone. They lived in a floating palace, far away from the sounds of the guns, supplied with ice-cream and ice for their drinks, while the medical staff couldn't get any ice for the wounded for love or money. If the troops were disgusted and insulted by the presence of this ship in the harbour, the Australian nurses were just about fed up. Because of the lack of vegetables, the nurses had to drink lime juice to prevent scurvy. Eggs, meat and potatoes were all in short supply. One day, Sister Hell Pike, stationed on Lemnos, was handed a soiled parcel of sacking with blood seeping from it, from one of the men. Inside, to her delight, she found a large cut of steak that the orderly had pinched from the supercilious officers on the *Aragon*.[9]

Amongst the wounded from Lone Pine was Major Iven Mackay. He made his way to the 3rd Australian Field Ambulance, in Brown's Dip. While there, he remembered a medical officer saying to him, 'Jolly close call, this. Must have just missed the old bladder, what!'[10] The officer jabbed a needle in his arm, and he was grateful for it, as he didn't remember much about being shuttled from ship to ship in a barge during the heat of the day, as they tried to find one that would take the wounded aboard. Eventually he was loaded onto a ship and through the blur of morphine he vaguely remembered seeing men swimming in the waters just off Suvla Bay, while close by he recalled hearing from a warship a band playing 'Who Were You with Last Night?'[11] He slept a great deal, believing that at some point he arrived at Lemnos, where he was 'put aboard hospital ship *Dunluce Castle*...I heard bagpipes playing...no recollection of date of sailing'.[12] Mackay spent eight days in a hospital in Malta, which was far from comfortable, recalling how it was 'humid, muggy, enervating...spent the whole time in bed, so could not purchase any lace or curios...Sailed in the naval hospital ship *Somali*...Saw the Eddystone Lighthouse and on August 27th entered Plymouth Harbour.'[13] The only things Mackay now possessed were his cap and boots and the two shillings in his pyjamas pocket, which the Red Cross provided to all wounded men.[14]

Thirty-five-year-old professional nurse Narelle Hobbs had been among the first to sign up for the Australian Army Nursing Service. Nurse Hobbs was based at Malta and noted the terrible conditions for the staff and wounded:

The heat of Malta is disgusting, <u>very</u> moist, the perspiration just pours off you, & the Sirocco [dry, hot wind from North Africa] is rotten, Sydney weather in the middle of summer on a moist day is <u>delightful</u> compared with this. Now, for instance to-day, apparently just to look outside there is a clear blue sky & bright sun shining. & as long as you don't move everything is delightful, move & the sweat runs off you, hot and sticky, & you ache in every joint as though you were just getting flu, & all your boots are two sizes to small...I'm trying to get some letters written I promised to write for my poor and helpless patients, they think so much of any little thing like that.[15]

Another casualty at Lone Pine on 7 August was Captain Syd Cook. He'd been wounded in the head while taking a quick look into no-man's-land, and was carried down to the beach and eventfully taken to Alexandria on board a 'black ship'. He survived the passage – just. On arriving, all believed he was beyond hope. Elsie Cook, at No. 2 Australian General Hospital in Cairo, first heard that Syd had been mortally wounded on 13 August and that he was at No. 19 Hospital in Alexandria.[16] Elsie arranged a transfer to the port city but when she arrived, the hospital admittance records were in a shambles; the system couldn't cope with the numbers now flooding into the already packed wards. Elsie went in search of Syd, and eventually found him lying on a cot on a verandah. He managed a vague smile in recognition before closing his eyes. Elsie was distressed to see him in such a bad condition – his head was wrapped in bandages. In fact, the doctors considered Syd a lost cause, but Elsie managed to convince two of them – one being the well-respected English neurologist Sir Victor Horsley – that all was not lost.[17] Syd's being the son of a former Australian Prime Minister would have helped.

While performing her duties, and continually being rushed off her feet, Elsie used any spare time available to care for Syd. She wrote in her diary on 15 August of her growing concerns:

> Poor old Syd has had headaches continually, sleeps in a heavy drowsy way nearly all day. Feeling very worried about him indeed, don't like the look of him at all and I fancy the other sisters think he is worse, although they do not say anything to me. Sat up with him after I finished my work in the ward tonight and couldn't help shedding some tears in the darkness, it all seems terrible. Went downstairs and wrote a few lines to Mrs Cook to let her know how Syd is, and am going to bed, very tired and very miserable.[18]

With time and care, Syd began to improve. By 18 August, Elsie was feeling a bit more confident about his recovery: 'Syd is improving decidedly cannot speak at all yet but looks better and brighter. His wound looks much the same, perhaps a little cleaner.'[19] It had previously been discharging large amounts of pus. She was extremely happy the next day – their eleven-month wedding anniversary – as Syd whispered his first words since being shot. She recalled how he remembered the '19th, and in a funny old cracked voice for the first time spoke and reminded me of the fact!'[20] He even managed to croakily talk to his neighbour in the next cot. A week later, Syd would be speaking almost normally, but continued to suffer from severe headaches. In September, he was transferred to a military hospital in London and Elsie was allowed to accompany him. Another two years of war in Europe awaited them both.

20

'War is hell, absolute unlimited hell'

Around midday, the wounded Major McConaghy began to supervise the urgent sapping that was required to bridge the gap between Sasse's Sap and Woods's Post. Lieutenant Tallisker McLeod was sent over to Sasse's to supervise the work there, while Lieutenant Percy Woods would do likewise from the post bearing his name. Both officers were in the act of establishing the line to be taken for the digging when McLeod was hit in the head by a Turkish bullet and killed instantly. Within a matter of hours the posts were connected by a firing trench, complete with a firing step. This added significantly to the defence of the centre of the line at Lone Pine. Indeed, the defences of this newly established position were about to be tested and not found wanting.

Just as the work was being completed, someone using a trench periscope observed a number of Turks in broad daylight creeping up from The Cup towards them. Captain Zeki Bey had organised this assault: 'I sent a company to attack and it disappeared altogether; I didn't know if it was captured or killed, or if it got involved in a panic that happened on the left. Possibly they turned round and attacked their own troops by mistake – the trenches were so involved.'[1] Lieutenant Woods certainly knew the fate of the Turkish attack. While at the time he only had a few men with him, he did have a machine gun in position. It was Corporal Mark 'Darkie' McGrath, who had earlier survived the battles for Goldenstedt's Post, who squeezed the trigger and joked and laughed as he swept away the forlorn Turkish charge.[2]

As Darkie McGrath was working his machine gun, Lieutenant Colonel Elliott and his men of the 7th Battalion were replacing the emotionally numb and physically exhausted survivors from the southern posts at Lone Pine. The 1st Battalion had gone into battle with twenty-one officers and 799 other ranks, and of them seven officers and 333 men had become casualties. It was even worse for the 2nd Battalion – it had entered the fight with twenty-two officers and 560 others, and on coming out, no fewer than twenty-one officers and 409 other ranks had become casualties.[3] Beyond these statistics, many of those who walked out of the Pine with wounds were not included in the casualty list, which also failed to take into account the psychological scarring that many would carry for life. Lance Corporal Leonard Keysor was one of those who had managed to physically survive the battle. Even though wounded on 7 August, he remained at his post, throwing back Turkish grenades as well as lobbing jam-tin bombs in amongst the crowded Turkish trenches. The next day, while helping defend Jacobs's Trench, he bombed Turks out of a critical position, allowing Australians to again secure it. He was later awarded the VC for his actions.

Colonel Hobbs and his men of the artillery were now utterly exhausted not only from the physical effort over the last few days, but also from mental strain. Hobbs wrote: 'The difficulty of getting definite information as to enemy dispositions together with the use of our prearranged signals for distinguishing our troops unfortunately led to the loss of several golden opportunities for inflicting heavy losses to the enemy.'[4]

Lance Corporal Cyril Lawrence, of the engineers, was 'relaxing' at Brown's Dip. He scribbled in his diary of another 'glorious Sunday, God's day of rest – Hell, what a mockery!',[5] describing how the air 'fairly quivers with the reports of guns – big, small and indifferent. They have not ceased firing the whole night.'[6] From his dugout, Lawrence could see the Aegean covered with ships of all descriptions: cruisers, hospital ships, transports, torpedo boats, monitors, mine sweepers and barge-loads of men. The rifle fire was incessant, and almost as bad as the 'bursting of the bombs – just dull thuds'.[7] He had heard the reports about the British landings at Suvla Bay, to the north, and saw how the warships were providing them with assistance. Even from his position he could see the shells flying over in the direction of Anafarta by the tonne. Yet, he wrote, 'something seems to brood disaster in that quarter. We only hear rumours of course but we see other things, and it breeds disquiet. The whole thing seems to lack dash.'[8] Indeed, Lawrence was correct in his assessment of the Suvla landings, as recorded by the British *Times* correspondent Ashmead-Bartlett, who was observing the operation: 'The troops were hunting for water, the staffs were hunting for their troops, the Turkish snipers were hunting for their prey.'[9] The Suvla landings had developed into a truly chaotic shambles.

Private Donkin, also in Brown's Dip, wrote in his diary: 'Poor Maj. Scobie is killed. On the left the Indians are attacking with knives and they terrorise.'[10] He was also aware of the landing at Suvla, but mistakenly believed it had been a great success: 'Way out on the [northern] flank an army landed and…are working right around to the rear…They [the Turks] are putting up an obstinate fight for it, but I don't think they will last long when the [British] New Army gets behind them. The view from the heights here of the fleet of war ships and monitors, destroyers and the flotilla of mine layers and troopships, also 6 hospital ships, which I guess will all have a full cargo.'[11] Even in Brown's Dip, he and his mates were still exposed to the ongoing Turkish barrage that was targeting the reserve area: 'Our possie has been banged about and men hit all around us, but we three are preserved so far, thank God. It is horrible sitting in our dugout, waiting, listening. Bang! Close by and swish of pellets all around.'[12]

At 1st Australian Division headquarters, General Walker summarised the offensive's progress: 'Our work during the last few days has been just marvellously splendid. Also we have just received news that mail from Australia has been torpedoed. No one has had a wash or shave for days; half of us don't know how many days have passed. It seems all a blurred moving picture – something doing all the time and going too quickly for the mind to grasp its significance or immensity.'[13] Not far away, Charles Bean had left his dugout. He was keen to get the latest news about the fighting at Lone Pine. The night before he had been hit in the leg by Turkish shrapnel and Colonel Howse had recommended he be evacuated given the danger of tetanus infection, but he refused. Bean was determined to record the significant events unfolding around him. He was limping towards The Pimple along the beach at Anzac when he came across what he later described as a truly disgraceful prank played out against Turkish and German prisoners:

I have just seen as caddish an act as I ever saw in my life. About 100 Turkish prisoners and two Germans were sitting in the pen ... Some chap had poured out a tin of kerosene on the ground in front of it and laid a trail of kerosene ... Some chap put a light to the trail, it flared along and when it reached the kerosene there was a huge flare of fire uncomfortably close – if not dangerously – to the Turks. The wretched prisoners rushed to the far corner of the pen like a flock of sheep rounded up by a dog, and fellows looking on laughed.

There were both Australians and Britishers there amongst the onlookers. I wondered someone hadn't the decency to hit the man who did it straight in the face…

Three Turkish officers are among the lot…[and] were sent off under an Indian sentry to a vacant shell of a dug out in Australian Divisional lines. They were sent there in the morning and absolutely forgotten. No food or water was sent to them. Our divisional interpreter happened to be passing in the afternoon, when these Turks told him. He went to the A.P.M. [Assistant Provost-Marshall] of Army Corps, whose business it was. A.P.M. said he was too busy – would the interpreter get some other officer to do it. The interpreter saw another officer who said he would have bully beef and biscuits sent up. Interpreter said he wouldn't take bully beef and biscuits up – the Turks wouldn't give our officers bully and biscuits if their own officers were feeding better. The officer saw things in this light and sent up a decent meal. The Turks had some tea but no one provided them with any water. Interpreter had to go round for that and couldn't find any. They are there now in a bare dug out, no blankets, no water proof sheet, no comfort of any sort.[14]

By Sunday, Harold 'Pompey' Elliott's 7th Battalion were in trouble – the night before they had sent over their trained bombers to Lone Pine at an urgent request from Lieutenant Colonel Scobie. The few survivors were now scattered all along the line. They would have to make do with the men at hand – most of whom had never seen a jam-tin bomb before, let alone lit and thrown the hissing ordinance. Elliott's battalion was also very much reduced in strength, having entered the works with just thirteen officers and 511 men, as well as a small reserve force under Lieutenant Tubb, still located at Brown's Dip.[15]

Nonetheless, Elliott was a force to be reckoned with and he now moved about his sector assessing the situation. Saps and trenches were still crowded with Australian and Turkish dead and dying. Elliott wrote to a friend about finding an underground cellar apparently used by the Turks for disciplinary purposes: 'I examined it, I found its occupant was a dead Turk chained to a stout post. In the first attack evidently some of our men had entered and in the semi-darkness spotted [him] and run him through with his bayonet...I had over 30 corpses friend and foes alike fitted into this chamber, covered with chloride of lime and the entrance sealed with bags.'[16] It was in many places still impossible not to walk on the dead, and even the veterans found it hard to stomach – not only the sight but the sickening stench that prevailed everywhere. Elliott wrote to Kate: 'In one trench there were 13 dead Turks piled on each other while others lay all around. We were the same...In one charge it was so hot that we had no time to remove the wounded and horrible to tell you we had to tread on these poor dead and dying men lying in the trench to keep the gaps in the line filled.'[17] For Elliott, the battle for Lone Pine was a series of terrible sights. He recalled seeing 'the whole side of this lad's skull ripped out and his brain splashed round',[18] while others lay dying on the floor of the trench suffering terrible wounds, limbs blown off, with their mates trying to help them stem the flow of life from their shattered bodies.

The position in Pompey Elliott's sector was bounded by about ten isolated posts. Elliott divided his front between two companies to enable greater communications within smaller groups. The northern sub-sector, including the newly relocated Goldenstedt's and Woods's posts, were placed under the command of Lieutenant William Symons. Lieutenant Gilbert Dyett would command the southern sub-sector, at Jacobs's Post and Jacobs's Trench. It was

Dyett's positions that had been the focus of Turkish counterattacks attempting to recapture their front-line trenches. Elliott reinforced the three key defensive positions here. The first was defined by the eastern head of Jacobs's Post, which was now finally screened by bombproof wire netting. About fifteen metres back, the post was further strengthened where the original head cover remained (at Pain's Post), while the third position was located at the next transverse of the covered works. All three of these positions gave a clear field of fire over the lower ridges and gullies leading off Lone Pine to the south. The men in this sector were also supported by two machine guns, but their crews were so exhausted that most of the infantrymen were concerned that the gunners were about to collapse – they had been manning their guns for days without end now. It was at the first and third positions that these machine guns were positioned for maximum effect.[19]

Elliott was well aware that the only way to keep the Turks at bay was via the use of the very temperamental jam-tin bomb. Indeed, he later wrote to Kate that they could only respond to the Turkish bombing with 'a limited supply of bombs and they are shaped like jam tins and are not really any good'.[20] Still, after checking the positions were manned to his satisfaction, he sent a message to Brigade Headquarters requesting more bombs, as well as reinforcements for the exhausted machine-gun crews by one of the machine guns of his own battalion. He added: 'Would be glad of engineers' assistance, trenches and bomb screens are being badly knocked about by gun[s] already reported on our right flank [Turkish battery at The Wineglass].' [21] Elliott recorded that the response from Walker was that he must hold his position to 'the last man – that if necessary he [Walker] would come with his staff and take a post in the lines. I assured him that we would hold the place.'[22] As Elliott was writing his reply, the ever-present explosion of Turkish grenades increased dramatically, signalling to him (and others) that another Turkish attack was likely in the offing. Word quickly reached him that the Turks were reinforcing their entrenched works down along Sniper's Ridge, just south of Jacobs's Trench.

Thirty-five-year-old Frankston plumber Sergeant Walter 'Wally' Fisher and 43-year-old Geelong artist Private John Erikson were each commanding one of the recently established posts in Jacobs's Trench and had a clear view to the south. Being the battalion's crack shots, they began sniping for all they were worth at the Turks along Sniper's. Soon, others joined in and a hail of fire from Jacobs's Trench rained against the Turkish positions. Within minutes, the Turks organised a response, with artillery fire from The Wineglass being brought to bear. The Australians in this part of the line were rattled – it was their first experience of being bombarded, as most had only arrived on the peninsula days before. Elliott went amongst the new recruits, steadying their nerves. The 'old man' had the knack of inspiring confidence even in the worse of conditions. He was always in the thick of it, sharing the men's danger – no dugout commander, was Pompey Elliott – which is why he was admired and trusted. He was, without doubt, among the best of the battalion commanders at Gallipoli. Elliott later wrote to Kate:

I had ... to try and keep everybody cool and steady and send reinforcements [that] were only just sufficient and no more, so as to spin them out as long as possible, and when men came to me to implore me for bombs which I hadn't got and for reinforcements I could not spare (or they could not hold out) to tell them to go back and fight with bayonet and rifle until they were dead, and they did that ... I had about 170 raw recruits shoved in just before the fight, most of these fought like demons but a few broke down. I found one fellow wandering about without a rifle, all trembling. I took him to a place which had a dark tunnel in it, and told him to watch that and if he moved an inch I would blow his brains out. It really led to our own lines and there wasn't a Turk anywhere near it, but he didn't know. After about an hour he got alright, and I sent him back to the fight. Another came back trembling all over so that he couldn't hold his rifle. I told him if he couldn't fight to fill sandbags. He went at it like a madman – you never saw a man work like him – but it pulled him round. Later I saw him fighting as well as the rest.[23]

When the artillery bombardment lifted, it was quickly replaced by another avalanche of Turkish grenades falling into Jacobs's Trench, particularly at Jacobs's Post. The dead and wounded from these attacks were heavy and included the snipers, Sergeant Fisher and Private Erikson. Wally Fisher would soon find himself on a ship bound for Australia, while John Erikson took a ship to Egypt but succumbed to his wounds a few days later and is today buried in Chatby War Memorial Cemetery, in Alexandria.

As Elliott was standing in the trench amongst the smoke and dust clouds, organising its defence, a man fighting next to him was hit by a bullet that 'smashed his head like an egg shell'. Elliott was 'splashed from head to foot with [his] blood and brains'.[24] The trenches were crowded with men, all expecting an immediate Turkish charge, each clasping his rifle with bayonet fixed, their supply of bombs just about exhausted. Turkish grenades continued to explode amongst these men, and the wounded, rapidly adding to the casualties. Seeing the result of the overcrowding, Elliott ordered that the position be thinned, placing men in reserve under the covered parts of the former Turkish front lines.

But to everybody's surprise, the bombing attack ceased as suddenly as it had started and no Turkish attack followed.[25] Twenty-one-year-old Private Richard 'Dick' Gardiner, of Elliott's battalion, recalled that when they went in to relieve the men of the 2nd Battalion, the trenches were piled four and five high with dead. Dick and his mates were told that the position was fairly safe, but later in the day conditions changed again: 'We found it decidedly unsafe & also unhealthy. Everything was quiet until about 5 o'clock when Abdul started to bomb us and all the cry was for bombs – more bombs and stretcher-bearers and it lasted until well after dark when things began to quiet down.'[26] Meanwhile, about half a dozen reinforcements joined them and they started to repair the parapets and as the 'stretcher-bearers were busy, we were bandaging the chaps as they came out'.[27]

During the afternoon until dusk, the Turks launched a number of attacks along the whole Australian perimeter at Lone Pine. At around 8 p.m., an order was sent into the Pine from General Walker: 'White armlets ordered to be removed, back patches to be retained.' This likely recognised that many armlets had already come off during the fighting and their absence could no longer be relied upon to denote a Turk. Following closely was another communiqué to the 1st Brigade Headquarters, as noted in its war diary: '20:25 received congratulations for 1st Bn. from Gen. Walker.'[28]

With darkness, it was again the southern flank that was the focus of the Turks, and it was here that the fighting was at its most ferocious. At Jacobs's Post, Lieutenant Dyett had been seriously wounded and was replaced by Lieutenant John West. Dyett was eventually evacuated from Lone Pine and carried down the beach. His lifeless body was placed on the ground awaiting burial – until someone noticed him move. He was soon on his way back to Australia.[29]

It wasn't long before word reached Brigade Headquarters at The Pimple that more men were urgently needed. Lieutenant Fred Tubb and his reserve company of the 7th Battalion at Brown's Dip were now given their marching orders to reinforce the southern sector of the Pine. The Turks were trying to force the issue at the position between Jacobs's and Goldenstedt's posts. It was here that Tubb and half of his company would be positioned, just in time for him and two of his men to take actions that would earn them the VC.[30]

Lieutenant Symons and his men had just taken over from the weary survivors at the newly positioned Goldenstedt's Post, when it was showered with cricket-ball grenades. The veterans of the fighting at Lone Pine couldn't believe the Turks' seemingly unlimited supply of grenades, while they had to carefully husband their tenuous supply of improved explosives packed into jam tins. Symons kept his reserve bombers and other supports in a small dugout nearby to help repulse the expected Turkish counterattacks, which weren't long in coming. The Turkish bombers had taken shelter among thick timber beams from Goldenstedt's original post and they succeeded in forcing their way over the barricade time and again into the new position. Symons' men would counter-charge as soon as the Turks broke into the main position. Hand-to-hand fighting would eventually repel the Turks. The process repeated itself hour after hour – the Turks breaking in and the Australians pushing them out. It wasn't until after 2 a.m. the next morning that the Turks were finally driven out and the position apparently made secure. It is likely one of these fights that Elliott described to Kate in a letter written the very next day: 'The [Turks] came up to the parapet [and] 6 Turks came into the trenches but the boys shot them as they came in and no living Turks got through the line.'[31]

In comparison, the situation along the northern flank had become more stable, as recalled by Private William Graham: '[The pressure from the] enemy in the 4th Battalion's area had begun to wane. Now we could lie out beyond our parapet after darkness had set in and, protected by sandbags, catch him before he came within bomb-throwing range of our position. Rifle and machine-gun fire was now our only worry.'[32]

The stretcher-bearers working in Lone Pine, however, didn't

get such a break from the stress and strain of the fighting. One of these men was Private Charles Bingham, who had long ago lost count of the days:

> On one of the days we evacuated about 600 wounded from Lone Pine, there were a colossal amount of casualties. We had shoulder straps that fitted round the shoulder and into the hand that took the weight on to your shoulders – that's all we had. Most of the stretcher-bearers were pretty strong – didn't smoke or drink. I used to like being on the foot end, instead of the shoulder end which was much heavier, but you couldn't always get away with it. Sometimes you'd come to a bend in the trench, and you couldn't get the stretcher around it, so we'd take the fellow off, carry him round in a sitting position, then bring the stretcher round and put him back in it…We'd carry him through a network of communication trenches, and some of them were rather sharp in that they were about eighteen inches wide, and about six or seven feet deep.[33]

Meanwhile, Private Bendery scribbled in his diary: 'War is hell, absolute unlimited hell. The papers [will] say glorious victory 2nd Battalion capture 3 lines of trench. The real thing should read – We charged in face of murderous fire, took 3 lines of trenches. Losses very heavy.'[34]

Captain Zeki Bey too had been continually amongst the fighting, almost since zero hour of the Australian attack. He was now desperately trying to collect and reorganise what was left of his battalion. However, he also realised that things were improving, at least in terms of their ability to defend their positions. He recalled to Charles Bean in 1919: 'The situation at Kanli Sirt [Lone Pine] was now better, and it was well known that the danger was elsewhere. Indeed, all these days I looked over my shoulder seeing your shells bursting on the rear slope of Chunuk Bair. Although the situation at Kanli Sirt was critical I could scarcely keep my eyes on it – I knew things must be happening at Chunuk Bair...which was more critical by far; and if you succeeded there, what use would be our efforts at Kanli Sirt?'[35] The Mufti and his men had indeed held their ground, as promised, until his battalion was finally relieved on 9 August – it is not recorded whether this brave man survived.

At Chunuk Bair, the New Zealand and British troops had all that morning and afternoon been in a desperate and bloody fight to hold the position – the ferocity of the battle there was equal to that at Lone Pine. By 4 p.m., reports reached Lieutenant Colonel William Malone, commanding the defence of Chunuk Bair, of a continuous line of Turkish troops reinforcing the southern portion of the crest. Malone had all that day led his men from the front in counterattack after counterattack, using the bayonet. New Zealander Major Hastings recalled: 'Twice it looked very bad so with Colonel M [Malone] we joined the lads in front. I had my revolver and a handful of cartridges and Col. M seized up a rifle and bayonet. The Wellingtons seemed to rise up each time from nowhere and the Turks were hurled back. In the first of these attacks the bayonet on Col. M's rifle was twisted by a bullet, so after this he kept it with him; as he said it was lucky.'[36] At one point Malone seemed to accept the inevitable as a mass of Turks yet again charged down the slopes. 'Come on,' he said to his staff, 'they've done it this time – we may as well be in it.' But yet again the Turks were beaten back.[37] Sergeant Stevens recalled: 'There I saw the bravest man I ever saw, Colonel Malone, who was doing the jobs from Lance Corporal to Brigadier General.'[38] At some point, the red and yellow artillery marker flags that had been planted around the perimeter of Malone's position had each been shot down. Seeing no flags, the ANZAC artillery officers took this to mean that the Turks had recaptured the summit, and poured fire into the upper slopes, until the New Zealanders still clinging to the slopes somehow managed to salvage the flags and erect them again, using whatever came to hand, including broken rifles. The shelling from Anzac ceased. The last salvo from this barrage, however, slammed into the hill, tragically killing the gallant Malone.[39] Lieutenant Colonel William Malone and many of his men have no known grave and are commemorated on the Chunuk Bair War Memorial.

At dusk, the New Zealanders and British were still holding their position just below the summit and, with darkness, things eased for the stranded garrison. Parties from The Apex and The Pinnacle were now able to approach Malone's position, bringing up water, bombs and ammunition. At around 10.30 p.m., the exhausted survivors were finally reinforced by the men of the Otago Infantry Battalion and the Wellington Mounted Rifles, under the command of Lieutenant Colonel Meldrum. Losses were appalling – of the 760 men of the Wellington Battalion who went into battle, only seventy unwounded or slightly wounded came out. British losses were just as heavy – the Welsh had lost 417 men and the Gloucestershire 350.[40]

MONDAY
9 AUGUST
1915

'He leaned over the parapet and emptied his revolver into them'

While there was fading hope among the senior Corps commanders that the northern heights might still be carried, the only obvious success of the offensive at this point was the capture of the southern Turkish works at Lone Pine. As such, Lone Pine was no longer just a feint – it had become a rallying point for the offensive, at least in the minds of the senior commanders.

The bludgeoning, bombing, bayoneting and dismemberment that were the reality of the successes at Lone Pine had been escalating over the last three days. Sergeants, corporals and privates had been taking command of groups of men in the absence of slain officers. Countless men from both sides were killed violently in taking and trying to defend just metres of trench. There was no tactical rhyme or reason to the attacks. Men on their own or in small groups decided on bite and hold actions. They gambled and sacrificed themselves in order to chip away at the edges of the enemy's defences. Many had been in the line since day one, grabbing a few hours' sleep at the rear just metres away from the fighting, before getting back into the thick of it.

Lance Corporal Cyril Lawrence awoke early that morning, in Brown's Dip: 'Another glorious day. The smell is getting very strong now. Ugh! It's simply awful; seems to hang to everything, strong and sickly.'[1] It was far worse at Lone Pine. Men there started to report seeing large numbers of Turks advancing from Owen's Gully up to The Cup. All knew that another Turkish onslaught was in the offing. Indeed, soon the Turkish front line was 'full of troops, so much so that some took up positions in no-man's-land just behind the parados of their trenches'.[2] Stretcher-bearer Reynolds recalled how 'the [ANZAC] howitzer and field gun battery on shore woke me early about 5 a.m., when some very severe fighting took place'.[3]

The southern sector, still under the command of Harold Elliott, was by far the largest, and the battalion commander further expanded it from two to three sub-sectors. Twenty-nine-year-old Lieutenant William Symons commanded Goldenstedt's Post, 34-year-old Longwood grazier Lieutenant Frederick Tubb commanded Tubb's Corner and 26-year-old teacher Lieutenant John West commanded Jacobs's Post. During the night, the shallow sap just north of and parallel to Jacobs's Trench had been expanded to provide covering fire to this almost isolated position. This new firing trench was on a slightly higher elevation to that of West's position, and would help cover the position. In addition, a trench bay and firing step was cut into the southern length of the trench to enable concentrated fire to be brought to bear against any Turkish attack from the south. It was only twenty metres or so from the battered and corpse-infested Jacobs's Trench, defining the most southern extent of the Australian advance. Unknown to Elliott and his men, however, this trench bay would also be clearly visible to the Turks entrenched to the north on Johnston's Jolly.[4]

Elliott wrote to Kate: 'At daylight their artillery smashed us. Then...they charged...with the bayonet as we manned the parapet they proceeded with machine gun fire...they caught us pretty hot then.'⁵ Tubb also wrote in his diary, sometime after taking up his position: '0540. Shells are falling thick amongst us…Tired and sleepy, we are all fagged; the strain is wearying. Just lost my Sgt Major Baker from nerves and shock. Pvte Willis also. Another Sgt Major of B Coy outed. It is stiff luck for just as I get the Coy going I lose the men I need most.'⁶

At first dawn, Turkish machine-gun and mass rifle fire swept the Australian parapets. Corporal Richard Gardiner recalled how he went into the firing line and was filling sandbags and fixing loopholes, while also standing to at intervals just before dawn, when 'old Abdul started to make it very unhealthy for us, by showering bombs in us by the dozen, of course that settled the sandbags as far as we were concerned. I devoted my time to keeping the men on their posts and keeping their ammunition up.'⁷ He also recalled how he was 'busy with a blanket and overcoat smothering bombs as they fell into the trench – an overcoat keeps the explosion down'.⁸ Men hastily tried to reconstruct these parapets as best they could. Ali Riza was launching another mass coordinated counterattack, this time focusing on the centre of the Australian positions at Lone Pine.

Under the cover of this concentrated rifle fire, large numbers of Turks left their trenches and stormed towards the southern and central parts of the Lone Pine, while others, separated from the Australians by just a few metres of barricade, began to scramble over them. At the northern flank of their attack, the Turks managed to bomb Australians out of Sasse's Sap, but within minutes the Australians had recaptured it and established a new barricade. Another attack was launched and the Turks, throwing self-preservation to the wind, bravely stormed into the position en masse. They forced their way in, pushing into the very heart of Lone Pine, close to the advanced headquarters of the 1st Brigade and 3rd Battalion.⁹ Lieutenant Wren watched the 3rd Battalion adjutant, Lieutenant Howell-Price, push a periscope over the sandbags at the junction of the 3rd and 4th battalions, to see the Turks heading straight for his position. Howell-Price leaned over the parapet and 'emptied his revolver into them, while his batman [assistant], following his officer's example, did good work with his rifle'.[10] Lieutenant Wren, and a number of men on the firing step, jumped up onto the parapet and fired down into the attackers at great risk, but it seemed to make little difference – masses of Turks were forcing their way through the narrow trenches into the centre of the Pine. Amongst the Australians in this position was Private Norton. Lieutenant Athol Burrett recalled how Norton and Private John Hamilton 'were up on the parapet throwing bombs as fast as they could light them. One burst prematurely in Norton's hands, and blowing both of them to fragments. We sent him back to the dressing station.'[11] The next day the doctor who treated Norton told Burrett: 'Good God! It's wonderful. That man Norton is the gamest thing that ever breathed. After I had finished fixing him up for the beach he said – "Good-bye Doc, old sport. Sorry I can't shake hands".'[12] The fate of this brave private remains unknown.

Howell-Price then rushed into Sasse's Sap, quickly followed by Brigadier Smyth and Major McConaghy, almost colliding head-on with the leader of the Turkish column. One Turk fired at Price, but somehow missed, while another was in the process of throwing a grenade but was shot by Ward. The grenade rolled back and exploded among the dead man's own party – but the Turks kept advancing into the hail of bullets. The centre of the Australian position at the Pine was about to fall. To Lieutenant Burrett it looked desperate, as they were guarding the saps with only a handful of exhausted and, in many cases, wounded men: '[Every] second man faced...We felt that we were there to make a last stand – fighting front–rear in our long straight trench. Every man there was, in the ordinary course of events, due to die in a few minutes. But none hesitated – a long silent line of almost statue-like soldiers waiting – waiting – to fire their last shots.'[13] Athol

Burrett's life was saved by his friend, 21-year-old Paddington civil servant Lieutenant John Harrison, when a bomb fell at their feet. Burrett recalled sadly: 'We were standing together and I did not notice the bomb when it landed. Harrison shouted: "Look out" and pushed me out of the way. Doing so, he got the full force of the explosion himself.'[14] Harrison died from his wounds a month later and is buried at Portianos Military Cemetery in Greece.

Sergeant Major Goldenstedt and his few survivors of the 3rd Battalion were close by. He remembered that Monday morning vividly, writing that the previous day's fighting was a 'Sunday School picnic compared with Monday, when fresh [Turkish] brigades were brought up to finally turn the Australians out of the whole Lone Pine Position. The rifle, bomb and machine-gun fire just after daybreak was something never to be forgotten.'[15] Australians were swept off the parapets by concentrated bombing and gunfire. The 7th and 12th battalions were also taking the full brunt of the Turkish attack. Colonel Smyth issued an order for every man to step down off the parapet and prepare to meet the Turk on the floor of the trench with the bayonet. Goldenstedt was at this time next to Lieutenant Percy Woods, who had earlier been wounded but refused to leave his position. He later admitted that he refused to be placed on the wounded list: 'I would not have my name in the paper as wounded for fear of worrying my wife or people. I bet they worry enough now. What will they think when they get this casualty return?'[16]

Paul Goldenstedt and Percy Woods had been sergeants together. Woods took out a pencil and began to write a few words to his wife on a field service postcard. Having no wife and few relations that he could think of, Goldenstedt scribbled a few lines to her as well. Woods fixed a bayonet to his rifle, while Goldenstedt preferred his revolver. The feeling at that moment 'must be something like what a condemned man feels when the hangman is tying the rope. Anyhow, [all] of a sudden there was a wild cheer, and before we knew where we were the Turks had beat it [back] for their trenches.'[17] Howell-Price sent Lieutenant Burrett to see what had happened. Taking with him 20-year-old Private Frederick Shannon, they pushed through the trench to find only the 'dead bodies of our men who had been holding it. The Turks for some unaccountable reason had retired. Lone Pine had been theirs for the taking, and they had failed to push their advantage.'[18]

A contributing factor must have been due to the heroic actions of nineteen-year-old Private John Hamilton, of the 3rd Battalion. Having been amongst the men with Wren climbing onto the parapet at the first sign of trouble, he had coolly climbed out into no-man's-land and began shooting down Turkish bombers. Hamilton remained in no-man's-land for hours, taking cover behind a couple of sandbags. At one point he also yelled instructions to an officer who was throwing jam-tin bombs at the Turks in the rear, helping to clear the trench. Hamilton survived and for his bravery was awarded the VC.[19]

It was now that the final offensive operation to carry the northern heights was playing itself out. All that morning the New Zealanders were fighting for their lives on Chunuk Bair, after a British supporting assault against the northern slopes of the summit did not eventuate – the British had got lost in the tangled spurs and gullies of the Sari Bair during the hours of darkness. However, on two knuckles further north, the Gurkhas and South Lancashire, under the command of Major Allanson, had the day before gained a position just fifty metres from their objective and during an ANZAC bombardment of the ridge that morning they crept further up the slopes. As soon as the bombardment ceased, Allanson led his men in a charge and took the ridge connecting Chunuk Bair to Hill Q at around 5.30 a.m. – the bombardment had earlier succeeded in driving the Turks off the ridge into the valley below.[20]

No sooner had they taken the ridge than the major looked behind him and saw a flash from a British warship – the navy proceeded to put a number of 12-inch shells into the ridgeline right amongst Allanson's men. They were mistaken for Turks. Then Turkish artillery from Abdel Rahman Bair also fired into them, when it was realised that this area had been captured by the British. Allanson, aware that it was folly to try and hold the ridgeline, reluctantly gave the order to retire. The Gurkhas and Lancashires moved off the ridge and consolidated their position below the saddle. The ridgeline was quickly reoccupied by the Turks.[21]

At Lone Pine the Turkish attack against the centre of the Australian lines had collapsed, but they had not given up on retaking the southern sector of their former trenches. Private William Tope had just returned from one of his 'runs' back to the Australian lines at The Pimple. Since entering Lone Pine he had become the company runner. He made his way into the southern part of the Australian position: 'I thought the best thing would be for me to be down in this trench that had no men in it at all, where these bodies were [corpses], because I felt that the counterattack could come at any time. I'd hardly got into position before an absolute avalanche of bombs fell, puncturing these bodies, and up on top you'd hear the air coming out of the ones up there.'[22] Tope had arrived in the southern sector just as the Turks launched another onslaught to retake their lost trenches. Here, 21-year-old Bendigo engineer Lieutenant Benjamin shot down at least eight Turks while standing clear of the parapet. He continued to fire into the attackers until, inevitably, he himself was killed. Symons too was in the thick of it with his men at Goldenstedt's Post, employing a number of improvised Lotbiniere bombs (made from slabs of guncotton tied to a small board shaped like a hairbrush) to great effect. Having succeeded in stopping the Turks here, Symons was now ordered by Elliott to help

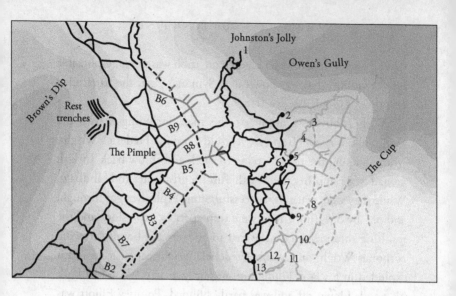

1. Aylward's Post
2. McDonald's Post
3. Formerly Mackay's Post
4. Formerly Traversed Trench
5. Lloyd's Post
6. Sasse's Sap
7. Woods's Post
8. Formerly Goldenstedt's Post
9. Tubb's Corner
10. Formerly Youden's Post
11. Formerly Cook's Post
12. Formerly Jacobs's Post
13. Pain's Post

Lone Pine works after the battle, including
recovered Turkish positions, 9 August

defend Jacobs's Post, while Lieutenant Tubb was made responsible for defending what was now called Symons's Post, the barricaded entrance of Goldenstedt's Trench.

With Tubb was a number of his men, including 24-year-old Corporal Harry Webb and 26-year-old Corporal Frederick Wright, who ran along the trench trying to catch and throw back Turkish grenades, or smother them with Turkish greatcoats and sandbags. While they were generally successful, some explosives got through, and one by one Tubb's men were torn apart by explosions and the resulting shrapnel spray. The first to go were the bomb-throwing corporals Wright and Webb. Frederick Wright caught one and it exploded in his face, killing him instantly. Harry Webb had both his hands blown off and was partly blinded. Pompey Elliott was distressed to see Webb making his own way out of the Pine. He wrote to Kate: 'Fancy seeing a man you knew blinded and with both hands blown off trying to get up on his feet... [with his] bleeding shattered stumps held out in front of him.'[23] Harry Webb died of his wounds shortly after arriving at Brown's Dip.

The Turks, yelling 'Allah! Allah! Allah!', now charged the position, scrambling into the post. They were cut down by concentrated rifle fire, and, just to make sure, a few were bellied with the bayonet. At one point, Tubb stood completely exposed behind the flimsy barricade separating Australian from Turk and proceeded to empty his revolver into the Turks again and again. Soon his men were doing the same, exposing themselves to the Turkish fire in order to try and gain an advantage. 'Good boy!' Tubb was heard to shout at one of his men who stood beside him, above the parapet, firing into the Turks as they charged their position from no-man's-land. The same soldier later admitted: 'With him up there you couldn't think of getting your head down.'[24] Several grenades then exploded simultaneously, killing or wounding four men, and a fifth was blown off the fire step with his rifle smashed. Tubb, already bleeding from wounds to his arms and head, refused to leave.

Things looked bleak. Tubb now only had two survivors with him defending the post from the Turkish onslaught – 21-year-old Ballarat clerk Corporal William Dunstan and 22-year-old Euroa ironmonger Corporal Alexander Burton. Only their adrenaline and bravery were keeping them in the fight. A large explosion soon erupted from a demolition charge of guncotton. It shattered their post, throwing the three men off their feet, as parts of the barricade and parapets collapsed into the trench all around them. Tubb got to his feet and drove the Turks out with his revolver, quickly emptying the chamber, while Dunstan and Burton desperately tried to rebuild the barricade. As the two corporals were doing so, a couple of grenades fell unnoticed between them. They exploded, killing Burton and temporarily blinding Dunstan. It was now that Australian reinforcements arrived, but the Turks had already lost heart and the attack stalled. While they continued to bomb the position, they no longer tried to charge it.[25]

Corporal Frederick Wright was later Mentioned in Despatches, while Corporal Harry Webb was awarded the Distinguish Conduct Medal. Elliott wrote to Wright's sister in 1916: 'I recommended all these boys for the VC…No doubt, had your brother lived, he would have got the DCM if not the VC. There are so many brave deeds that it is almost impossible to receive recognition for them [all]…Why they didn't give anything to your brother I cannot say…Capt Tubb could not speak too highly for the splendid work your brother did for him.'[26] Captain Frederick Tubb and corporals Alexander Burton and William Dunstan were each awarded the VC. Frederick Wright and Alexander Burton have no known grave and are commemorated on the Lone Pine Memorial, while Harry Webb is buried in the Lone Pine Cemetery.

Close by to the south, the struggle to defend Jacobs's Trench was just as fierce. The newly constructed firing position, dug along a slightly higher elevation just north and parallel with the trench, was now lined with men, each keeping their heads below the parapet, ready at a moment's notice to fire at any attack just south of their position. Even so, a Turkish machine gun further north at Johnston's Jolly, located on a slightly higher elevation, could see these men and now had them in their sights. The Australians didn't know what hit them. Elliott recalled how a line of 'dead men with their bayonets still over the parapet held about 20 or 30 yards of trench. In the early morning a machine gun swept that part of the line and killed every man at that spot – the trench slopes forward and as they died, each man so suddenly, that he simply leaned forward on the parapet and in many cases their hats and bayonets could be seen standing steadily behind the parapet and curiously enough that part of the line was avoided by the enemy.'[27] Elliott had supports in the rear ready to rush any Turk who came in, but he didn't replace the dead men as the trench was too exposed to fire from the left rear of the position: 'These men were all shot through the back of the head but apparently the Turks in front of these did not know this nor that they were dead.'[28]

At Jacobs's Trench, Lieutenant John West had been wounded. Elliott recorded: 'I saw John West taken away with a frightful gash on the head...while he was being carried off [he was] warning his men, quite delirious of course – Bombs wanted – tell the colonel we can't hold it unless he sends bombs.'[29] Twenty-three-year-old Shepparton bank clerk Sergeant Richard Gibbs expressed a sentiment held by many: 'Had John not been grazed in the head and knocked out at the height of the show he would have collected a VC.'[30] Elliott now sent 28-year-old Lieutenant Harold Young with six men to reinforce the survivors of West's section. When they got there, they found one man standing holding out on his own, 21-year-old Eaglehawk labourer Private Leslie 'Tim' Shadbolt. But for him, Young later wrote, 'the trench must have fallen, and goodness knows what would have happened [to] my small party then. As it was, we were able to hang on against heavy bombing – with no bombs of our own with which to reply – until in the end we were all casualties, Tim losing an eye…Tim showed such bravery as should have gained him the VC.'[31] Young was hit with a bomb and got a couple of pieces of shrapnel in his elbow and 'some hits on the forehead, three flesh wounds on my leg, and two in right arm'.[32]

At this point, a platoon from the 12th Battalion, under 26-year-old farmer Lieutenant Thomas Woodhouse, was ordered into Jacobs's Trench, but before getting there Woodhouse was killed.[33] The fighting raged on and the Turks – even with the arrival of Australian reinforcements – managed to capture Jacobs's Post and began to press their advantage towards Pain's Post. Elliott sent his adjutant, 20-year-old North Carlton plumber Lieutenant Hector Bastin, to retake the position, and although Bastin was wounded in the attack, he and his men, including Sergeant Major William Smith, succeeded. Elliott wrote: 'My Adjutant had his arm shattered by a bullet after a hand fight with a Turk who jumped into the trench and tried to bayonet him but whom he shot with his revolver in the stomach. As he fell his friends threw a bomb over which burst and blew his head to pieces [the Turk] and so saved further trouble.'[34]

True to form, the Turks launched another attack against the position. A shower of Turkish bombs again decimated the men holding Jacobs's Post. Some tried to keep the attackers back with rifle fire, while others tried to throw back grenades. About twenty metres away, Elliott handed his own revolver to Lieutenant Symons and ordered him to retake Jacobs's Post, saying, 'I don't expect to see you again, but we must not lose that post.'[35] Symons and his men charged out of the covered works into the trench and wasted no time in driving the Turks out. Symons immediately shot two Turks with Elliott's revolver. Still, the Turks maintained the pressure, sensing victory, and were determined to push the

Australians out of the trench. They now attacked the forward post from three sides, vastly outnumbering the Australian defenders, not only in men, but, just as importantly, in grenades. And again it was the Turkish grenades that pushed the Australians back – the post couldn't be held. Symons and his fellow survivors were forced to withdraw to Pain's Post, just underneath the overhead cover, leaving fifteen metres of open trench to the Turks.

Without hesitation, the Turks pushed forward, but time after time Symons led his men out of the covered works in counterattacks that succeeded in driving them back. The Turkish grenades were not as effective against the Australians under the covered works, which gave the defenders some breathing space. At one point, the Turks were able to set fire to the pine log covers, but Symons and his men drove them back and managed to put out the fire. On another occasion, an attempt was made by the Turks to encircle them by rushing no-man's-land just south of their position, but Australian enfilade from The Pimple and Bolton's Ridge – including the men in Leane's Trench – kept them at bay. When 20-year-old Footscray blacksmith Private Harold Schuldt entered this part of the line with a bag of jam-tin bombs, he found the sole survivors of the continuous Turkish assaults were Symons and two of his men. Exhausted and bleeding, they had managed somehow to hold their ground and establish a new post halfway between Pain's and the original Jacobs's Post.[36] Jacobs's Trench remained in Australian hands. A few days later, Lieutenant Symons wrote to his mother:

> Since last writing I have had a rough time…as you will perhaps have heard. The New South Wales boys charged the enemy's trenches, and by dint of hard and strenuous fighting captured them…Two nights after, the Turks attacked and tried to recapture their trench, but were driven out again. Our battalion was sent to assist them and I went in with a

company of 141 men, and the other companies had about a similar number. Anyway, Abdul decided to take his trench at all costs, but in vain… The first attack was at about 3.30 a.m. They came at us in hundreds, and made a special point of my position. I only had about 40 men with me in the firing line, the others being in reserve or else casualties. We had to set our teeth and drive them back, which the lads did with great credit. When I came to muster we had only about 15 left, and I got some of my reserve in and made up the strength again. It was just in time for another attack, which was equally unsuccessful. They were sent away with great loss, but I had to build up again.

By this time the bottom of our trench was filled in some places four or five feet deep with dead and wounded Turks and our brave lads. They were just coming for a third time, when a couple of shells were distributed amongst them by our artillery, and they must have thought discretion was the better part of valour, as they 'imshied', leaving us still masters of the position… I can tell you I was not sorry that they were not game enough for the last attack… I was fortunate to escape practically whole, although losing my other officers wounded or killed. Well, mother, I hope you are all well. As for myself, I feel a little tired, but with a couple of nights' rest I will be fit for them again.[37]

For his leadership during the battle, Lieutenant William Symons was awarded the VC.

22

'...our big battle has come to its standstill'

Earlier in the morning, the remaining reserves of the 12th Battalion were fed back into Lone Pine to help relieve the men of the 7th Battalion. Following closely behind, General Walker crossed over into the captured enemy works. He was informed that the Turkish attacks up and down the line had completely failed. Walker was keen to take advantage of the situation, as the Turks must surely be disorganised and demoralised. He wanted to launch an immediate counterattack and ordered the survivors of the 1st Battalion into the Pine to assist. At some point reality dawned and the proposed counterattack was cancelled – there was no way that the bloodied and exhausted troops could possibly attempt any offensive actions. Even so, the battered survivors of the 1st Battalion were sent back into Lone Pine. Private Donkin, who had been assigned to help the sappers, recorded the plight of his mates from the 1st Battalion: 'The company was withdrawn for a spell, but was urgently needed in the trenches so they had to return to the battle. Poor devils are exhausted.'[1]

The 1st Battalion's Private John Gammage, who took up a position in the front line on his second tour of duty in the Pine, later recalled: 'I got one most daring Turk from 12 yards off who was throwing bombs...We felt like wild beasts but were calm and never fired reckless but deliberate...Bombs all day. Our bomb throwers nearly all dead or wounded...am nearly blinded but men are scarce so I must not throw the towel in. Only scratches from gravel and dirt thrown up by bombs. This [is] an awful place.'[2] At about the same time, the 5th Battalion was also ordered into Lone Pine, to relieve the men of the 12th Battalion, who had been doing battle almost nonstop with the Turks since the 6 August.

Elsewhere, Colonel Hobbs and his gun crews were frustrated by the breakdown in communications: 'The battle still rages...position here is a great hindrance to us due to exposure to enemy artillery fire and problems with keeping in touch with divisional HQ as communication was almost completely severed.'[3] By now the 3rd Battalion had moved back into the reserve trenches behind Brown's Dip. Lieutenant Burrett recalled that he went back to their old trenches. Many had not closed their eyes since Thursday night. Their commanding officer, Major McConaghy, called a muster parade in a little gully behind the old trenches. He tried to speak, but almost broke down. The men were 'dismissed for a meal and sleep. I remember the Dean [Talbot] of Sydney, quite proud of his grazed "little Mary" [slang for stomach] – a really miraculous escape – as he was saved by his...belt [buckle] deflecting the bullet – but very overcome, shaking hands with us officers and saying "Bravo – the thin red line". And I think as we stood there and looked at each other we all saw big tears in the chap's eyes.'[4] In September, McConaghy was invalided from Gallipoli after suffering a nervous breakdown – the stress and strain had been too great and the battle had broken him.[5]

At midday the Turks tried another attack against the centre of the Australian lines and managed to capture parts of Sasse's Sap. Captain

Sasse went in to clear them out, taking a rifle with fixed bayonet and three men carrying filled sandbags. These men were to throw down their sandbags to make a low barricade from which Sasse could take cover and fire into the Turks. The Turks were focused on attacking another part of the line, momentarily oblivious to the threat from Sasse to their left. The battalion diary records: 'Captain Sasse cleared enemy who attacked S.W. angle by communication trench. Captain Sasse surrounded and killed 20.'[6] Sasse's blood was up and he decided to keep the pressure on. Now, joined by Captain Alfred Shout of the 1st Battalion and half a dozen men carrying sandbags and jam-tin bombs, they charged down the trench. Both officers ran abreast, with Shout throwing bombs and Sasse shooting down any Turk who presented himself. The Turks, for the most part, bolted. Sasse and Shout advanced in this same way for several short stages, throwing down a low barricade at the end of each. They had just sighted a suitable point for the final barrier when Shout, 'fighting with a splendid gaiety, lit three bombs at once as a prelude to making the final dash. The third burst in his hand, destroying it and shattering one side of his face and body. Carried to the rear, still cheerful, he sat up and drank a pannikin of tea, vowing that he would soon recover; but his brave life ended on the hospital ship.'[7] Captain Alfred Shout was awarded a posthumous VC for his actions during the battle. He was buried at sea and is commemorated on the Lone Pine Memorial. Shout's commanding officer, Colonel Alfred Bennett, wrote to his widow, Rose:

> I desire to express to you, though quite inadequately, our very deep sympathy with you in the loss of your husband, the late Captain Shout, as a true gentleman and as brave as ever wore the uniform of his king. Numerous acts of conspicuous brilliant conduct had already brought Captain Shout into favourable notice, and he had already, though so short a time in the field, had the Military Cross conferred upon

him. In the storming, capture, and defence of the enemy's stronghold known as Lone Pine, this brilliant officer was again unapproachable in his splendid leadership, and it was while in the act of again bombing the enemy out of their trenches that he sustained the injuries from which he subsequently died. So outstanding was Captain Shout's devotion to duty that I had recommended him for most distinction of the Victoria Cross, before he was wounded, and this recommendation has been approved by the general officer commanding, and, melancholy satisfaction it be, I hope to see his name honoured by enrolment in the band of heroes who have won the VC.[8]

One of Alfred Shout's mates, Lance Corporal Alex McQueen, later wrote: 'Captain Shout said to me before we went over at Lone Pine, "We'll make a name for ourselves tonight Mac". Well I was outed in the early part of the night, but he made a name for himself alright. He was Lieutenant when going in to the charge, made a captain next day, gained the VC the next, and the following eternity.'[9]

Stretcher-bearer Herbert Reynolds, at the 4th Battalion Aid Post, who had earlier feared he had been forgotten as no orders came, was by now well and truly in the thick of it. Reynolds and his mates were still based in Shrapnel Gully: 'Some very severe fighting took place and continued practically all day. Great numbers of wounded came down and we had greatest difficulty to handle them and when relief came about 1 p.m., we were well done up. The 7th Battalion suffered heavily during the morning when the enemy counterattacked their positions and very heavily bombed the trenches but failed to capture any.'[10]

The survivors of the 4th Battalion were finally relieved by the men of the 2nd Battalion, and six officers and 150 troopers of the 7th Light Horse Regiment, just after dark. The history of the regiment records how a portion of the firing line was 'given over to our men and parties were engaged in burying the dead of both sides in the old trenches. The enemy bombarded the whole position, savagely and incessantly, and as the trenches in some places were only 10 yards or less away, bombing was also constant on both sides.'[11] Even so, they would have an 'easier' time of it compared to the veterans of the Pine – although death and horror still awaited them.

Chaplain Talbot was at Brown's Dip as the survivors of the 4th Battalion stumbled along the path leading to the beach. He would never forget the sight of them: 'The men looked like a thin line of spectres. One officer who knew me well stared at me with glassy eyes, and failed to recognise me. We only realised how great the cost had been when we began to bury the dead.'[12] An officer of the battalion wrote: 'The battalion was decimated beyond recognition – a mere handful of men.'[13] Sergeant de Vine, of the 4th Battalion, who also survived the carnage, wrote: 'This was the tightest corner that I have ever been in. Marvelous how I managed to get out without a scratch.'[14] Private Graham described the 4th, following their first roll call after leaving Lone Pine, as 'scarecrows of a skeleton battalion'.[15]

At about the same time, in Lone Pine, the 5th Battalion began to relieve the truly bloodied men of the 12th and 7th battalions. A soldier of the 5th Battalion commented: 'The first person I seen was Pompey Elliott... You could say anything to him in the line, but not a word out... I said to him "Where's this great 7th Battalion?"... He said: "You'll find them lad, they're in there, you'll find them as you go in". They were in there all right, there was nobody alive. They'd blown the end of the trench down and enfiladed them. Dead Australians, all 7th Battalion.'[16] These men lay in mute testimony to the ferocious carnage of the fighting for the Pine. The 5th Battalion war diary provides a similar picture to that provided by the 7th Light Horse history: 'Trenches are [in a] bad state as dead men all over the place and beginning to decompose. Enemy bombing heavily all night.'[17] The 5th Battalion's Captain Robert Hooper was killed in similar circumstances to Captain Shout as he too attempted to bomb Turks out of stubbornly held positions. He is buried in the Lone Pine Cemetery.

Twenty-four-year-old Wynyard teacher Lieutenant Ivor Margetts, of the 12th Battalion, later described the conditions at Lone Pine in a letter to his father just after the 'worse' of the fighting:

> I will try and describe what a captured trench looks like. The trench smelt just like a slaughter house in the cleanest parts...in others it is impossible to describe the smell, in other parts of the trench dead bodies were stacked in heaps in places where there was available room and in other parts where there was no room they were left in the floor of the trench and covered with a thin layer of earth and made a soft spongy floor to walk on. Of course as many [Turks] as we could get rid of were thrown up to help make bullet proof parapets and also to make a barrier to block up communicating trenches leading from Turkish reserve trenches. As some of these bodies had been dead for some days when I went through, and were horribly swollen, remembering that the weather is so hot that one wears as little clothing as possible, it is necessary to try and describe the stench that the men were eating, fighting, and sleeping in. In the trench I counted 7965382165073982 flies who walked first on the perspiring live men and then, so as to cool their feet, they walked on the dead ones.[18]

Earlier that day, at about noon, Private Gammage's second stint at Lone Pine came to an end. He later wrote: 'Am hit again and put out of action. It is not sore but bled freely. My rifle was blown to splinters...Since Friday food was turned off. All I had was taken from dead comrades' haversacks but it's all for a good cause...Today I left some of the best men ever God put breath in.'[19]

The bravest of the brave, the stretcher-bearers, continued to risk life and limb in their efforts to bring in and treat the wounded scattered within and around the Pine. Private Bruce Thomson had just relieved some of the bearers from the 3rd Australian Field Ambulance and remembered his initiation: 'Fell in with stretchers to go to our dressing station for stretcher bearers. Started 7 [a.m.]. Went about...and started work. Big attack on, plenty of wounded and few bearers. Shrapnel flying everywhere. First day on Peninsula never to be forgotten.'[20] Private Robert Bates, of the 7th Battalion medical section, was far from new to the goings on and for his devotion to the wounded for days on end would be awarded the Military Medal for his efforts during the battle. He would be awarded a bar to his military medal for similar devotion during the horrific trials of Pozières, where he again brought in his wounded cobbers, day and night.[21]

Behind The Pimple, Lance Corporal Cyril Lawrence added to his diary that the men were still holding what they had gained, but at an awful cost – most casualties had simply been cut to pieces by bombs: 'Soaked in blood, perhaps half a leg blown away, a hand or jaw missing, and yet one just looks and forgets all about it. The hospital ships only stay here about a couple of hours now, whereas before this a week or a fortnight passed before they moved off.'[22] The newly captured trenches at Lone Pine 'are just full of dead still, whilst others lie on or just over the parapets. In one place we have had to build a parapet of bodies; it's horrible but necessary and one does not seem to realize the awfulness of what he sees or what he does, nor what he hears. It's just one dream.'[23] Nearby, Private Donkin was also writing in his diary: 'Our trenches are in a horrible state. We cannot remove the dead...and men must man the trenches at all costs...We are beginning [to be] shelled from the right flank now the left flank is in our hands, but still we are steadily driving them trench by trench, to the honour of old Australia be it said.'[24] While this may have been the case during the initial assault on 6 August, it was now the Turks who were doing all of the attacking at Lone Pine, reclaiming some of their former works.

Meanwhile, in the trenches, Captain Leslie Morshead and Private James Bryant were unknowingly about to become part of the photographic history of Lone Pine. The image taken is perhaps the best known from Anzac, if not the whole Gallipoli campaign. They had survived. It is daylight and Morshead is looking up at the parapet covered with Australian dead. One man's leg is protruding into the trench. Morshead, wearing an officer's cap, has a bewildered look on his face. A bayonet has been thrust into the side of the trench wall, the men's equipment hanging off it. Morshead's exhausted men are sitting on a firing step – one looks straight into the camera almost accusingly. All seems quiet – no weapons (except for the bayonet) can be seen anywhere in the image. Standing next to Morshead, wearing a slouch hat and also looking straight into the camera, is the tall, lanky 24-year-old farmer Private James Bryant. Both would survive this world war to fight in the next.

After four days of slaughter on both sides – killing up close and personal – the battle for Lone Pine came to an end, though the fighting would go on for months. At a terrible cost, the Australians had secured a dominant position in the works on 400 Plateau, but would now await the success of the main offensive before further plans were enacted. With night, the Turkish high command sent out orders that the men were to focus on consolidating their positions. The real danger of the British assault was now recognised – the battles for the Sari Bair Range and Suvla Bay. Captain Ahmed Zeki Bey and his men had been fighting at Lone Pine for the last four days without rest and were finally withdrawn. They were to take up a bivouac position behind Mortar Ridge, where they had originally camped on the afternoon of 6 August after having manned German Officers' Trench for over a month without a break – just hours before the opening of the battle for Lone Pine.[25]

Harold 'Pompey' Elliott, now finally out of Lone Pine, scratched in the battalion diary: 'Back in bivouac at Phillips Top. Men and officers who survived are utterly exhausted.'[26] He also wrote to a close friend that the ongoing attacks by the Turks were such that the men were prevented from attending properly to the wounded, which also meant they were unable to remove the dead. The weather was 'hot and the flies pestilential. When anyone speaks to you of the glory of war, picture to yourself a narrow line of trenches two and sometimes three deep with bodies and think too of your best friends for that is what these boys become by long association with you mangled and torn beyond description by the bombs and bloated and blackened by decay and crawling with maggots.'[27] He also stated how they had to live amongst the dead for days 'in spite of taking advantage of every night to work with respirators endeavouring to remove them this is war and such is glory – whatever the novelists may say'.[28] He now also concluded his letter to Kate: 'After 24 hours we were relieved by the 5th Battalion... I must end now dear. I fear I am wandering a bit I think you will excuse me.'[29]

Close by, behind The Pimple, over half of the packs that had been left behind before the men stormed Lone Pine days before remained unclaimed. John Gammage believed 'their owners lay at Lone Pine, and the maggots dropping from their bodies there were swept up by the bucket full'.[30] Private Donkin recalled: 'A great collection of our equipment from dead and wounded indicates our losses, and in the captured trenches the dead are chucked out over the parapet.'[31] The next day he added: 'The pile of cast off equipment grows bigger and the grave-diggers still dig, and men still wait patiently for whatever is to come to them.'[32] Sergeant Major Paul Goldenstedt (who came out of the battle a lieutenant) had somehow survived the battle and wrote how he would never forget the sight of the 'unclaimed packs that lay piled up on the little parade ground below Battalion Headquarters that overlooked the track down Shrapnel Gully'. He recalled their first muster after coming out of the battle: 'I have to this day my Field Service Pocket Book with the carbon copies of the "B" Company parade state before the "hop-over" on the Friday.'[33] The men present on the afternoon of the attack against Lone Pine on 6 August who made 'ribald jokes about all manner of things, numbered five officers and 166 other ranks. "B" Company came out of the Pine without a single officer, and with only 49 men.'[34]

At dawn the next day, 10 August, British troops who had replaced Malone's men at Chunuk Bair were swept off the summit, as thousands of Turks poured over and retook Chunuk Bair, The Pinnacle and The Farm. The August Offensive had failed – defensive operations all along the line commenced. This failure was soon apparent to all. Charles Bean awoke on the morning of 11 August to an astonishing sight, given all of the activities of the last few weeks and especially over the last few days. He wrote in his diary: 'Woke up to find everything perfectly quiet. Sea glassy smooth. One hospital ship here... and two hospital ships off Suvla Bay... Evidently our big battle has come to its standstill.'[35]

The 1st Australian Division's battle for Lone Pine resulted in 2277 Australian casualties, and over 800 killed outright. Two battalion commanders were among the dead, while another received a serious wound earlier on in the fight and an acting battalion commander suffered a nervous breakdown shortly after the battle. Most physical wounds were the result of hand-to-hand fighting, including grenades, bayonets and small-arms fire. Unlike in most battles of the Great War, few casualties at Lone Pine were from artillery fire. The percentage breakdowns of Australians killed or wounded in the battle per battalion have been calculated at: 1st Battalion (42 per cent), 2nd Battalion (74 per cent), 3rd Battalion (67 per cent), 4th Battalion (64 per cent), 5th Battalion (19 per cent), 7th Battalion (51 per cent) and 12th Battalion (16 per cent). The Turks themselves lost far more men in the battle for Lone Pine, with the 16th Turkish Division's casualties estimated at around 7200, with 1520 killed, around 4750 wounded, 760 missing and 134 captured.[36]

In his third despatch to the British Secretary of State for War, General Sir Ian Hamilton wrote the following in regards to the Australian attack against Lone Pine:

> [They] had firmly resolved to reach the enemy's trenches, and in this determination they became for the moment invincible. The irresistible dash and daring of officers and men in the initial charge was a glory to Australia. The stout heartedness with which they clung to the captured ground in spite of fatigue, severe losses and the continued strain of shellfire and bomb attacks may seem striking to the civilian – it is even more admirable to the soldier.[37]

Aftermath

A week after the battle, conditions in the trenches and saps in the Pine hadn't improved much. Trooper Ion Idriess and his mates of the 5th Australian Light Horse Regiment recalled how they stumbled in their approach through the communication saps towards Lone Pine in near total darkness. The floor was uneven with puddles of putrid water. He remembered the trenches as being like a 'cavern dug in a graveyard, where the people are not even in their coffins. We are right in Lone Pine now and the stench is something awful; the dead men, Turks and Australians, are lying buried and half buried in the trench bottom, in the sides of the trench, and built up into the parapet. They have made the sand bags all greasy. The flies hum in a bee-like cloud... Dead men, sun-dried, lie all between the trenches... bullets hum ceaselessly.'[1] The conditions just opposite weren't much better, as recalled by Lieutenant Mehmed Fasih of the Turkish 47th Regiment. He and his captain toured the front-line trenches, which were still a shambles. As they walked, they collected spent cartridge cases and bits of shrapnel. At one point, they picked up a cartridge and disturbed a swarm of flies. They continued to poke around and more flies took off. Fasih concluded that it was obviously a breeding ground for flies. They then discovered the 'sloppily covered grave of one of our soldiers. His flesh is rotting and covered with maggots. We moved on. In this world, woe is to be found everywhere!'[2]

Private Reginald Donkin, who had spent much of his time during the fighting digging and sapping his way towards Lone Pine, as well as helping to shore up its defences, requested a transfer back to his section in the infantry. A week after the battle, he was allocated to Captain Sasse's machine-gun section. He wrote in his diary the next day: 'Finish 7. Breakfast 7.30 must get some sleep. No I won't. I'll shave and go down to Jimmy Rowe to the old sappers' possie for a game of 500. Poor old "G" Co. [his original company before being transferred to the sappers]. Still suffers. Our old comrade Archie Hood killed in Lone Pine . . . yesterday . . . Enemy 75[mm] guns are playing havoc with us today and fragments are tearing . . . near me as I write.'[3] He'd earlier written, just after the battle for Lone Pine: 'I feel a relief to write this rubbish, but I hope it will find its way home to be read there, so they may know what their boys have done here. But I hope to take the old diary back myself, God grant that I can.'[4] The day after transferring to Sasse's section, Donkin made his way into the front lines of the Pine. He was killed within hours of taking up his position. Reginald Donkin has no known grave and is commemorated on the Lone Pine Memorial.

About a month after the battle, Major General Walker, who was against the attack, would himself become a casualty of Lone Pine. Chaplain Dexter remembered approaching the front lines after the thick of the fighting and coming across Walker. He had just been wounded by a machine-gun bullet through the shoulder and another remaining in the thigh. Dexter wrote a few weeks later: 'He is very brave and went off to the Hospital ship where the bullet was taken out. He will not be back to us for at least a month.'[5] Indeed, he would not recover in time to return to Anzac before it was evacuated, but later took command of the 1st Australian Infantry Division on the Western Front.

On 12 September, the men of the 23rd and 24th battalions, 2nd Australian Infantry Division, took over from the men of the 1st Division at Lone Pine. The weary and battered men of the 1st and

2nd Brigades made their way to the beach and boarded a number of barges, which proceeded to take them to Lemnos for a well-earned rest. They gradually built up their strength and after a few weeks even began playing sport. Just before they were to head back to Anzac, the 7th Battalion played the 8th in a game of cricket. The festive spirit was increased with the attendance of around thirty Australian nurses from the nearby hospital. Major McCrae noted that 'they all turned up and we had quite a jolly afternoon'.[6] Shortly afterwards, the men from the 7th Battalion got the news that corporals Burton and Dunstan, and lieutenants Symons and Tubb, all from their battalion, had been awarded the VC for their action during the fighting at Lone Pine – Burton's being awarded posthumously.

Back on the peninsula at Lone Pine, the defences were so formidable that the war went underground. The Turks were using the now covered old Traversed Trench to dig tunnels underneath the Australian front line. These tunnels had first been identified just before the men of the 1st Division were rotated out of the line. Immediately, men of the 23rd and 24th battalions (2nd Division), who replaced them, began to countermine. In mid September, this digging enabled a charge to be laid near Jacobs's Post by the 2nd Field Company. The resulting explosion failed to collapse the Turkish tunnel and merely resulted in creating an opening. Turkish rifle fire from within immediately broke out. It is difficult to assess who was more surprised – the Turks or the Australians. Quickly both sides threw up barricades in defence – each posting sentries to avoid a repeat. About a week later, countermining by Australian sappers close to Mackay's Post broke into a Turkish gallery, and in the fighting the Turks managed to hold the opening between the two tunnels. Two days later, they were driven back by a number of jam-tin bombs thrown down the Turkish tunnel – again barricades were constructed by both sides, and stalemate set in.

Lieutenant Ted Gaynor recalled years later the trials and

tribulations in negotiating passage through the labyrinth of saps and tunnels that defined the Lone Pine defences: 'Here there is a murky tunnel running off the sap. About 100 yards long, it seems endless. A movement, you instinctively grasp your revolver. False alarm and you breathe once more freely. But no, a creep – you stop – listen, not a sound – you move – it moves – you grasp your revolver a little tighter: What foolish fears have grasped me. There is no chance of a Turk in this tunnel but the bravest of the brave will quail.'[7] Gaynor made his way about fifty metres, which to him seemed like kilometres, and after carefully and gingerly making his way another twenty metres, the 'familiar and welcome "Halt, hands up, State your business," is heard. Welcome, I say if you have good ears, but the antithesis if you are a little hard of hearing, because I had previously warned my patrol to shoot if he gets no reply.'[8]

Some of the men were truly fed up with underground battles, as recalled by Private Charles Mehlert: 'Still sapping. Abdul shelling all morning. It is simply like living in hell. We are longing for an attack to be able to get some of our own back. I got a piece of shell in the arm.'[9] Clearly, at this point Private Mehlert was new to the goings-on of war. This tunnelling battle went on until the very last day of the campaign, with a spider-web of tunnels being pushed below each side's lines, the scene of exploding mines and terrifying hand-to-hand combat in near total darkness.

As the tunnelling and underground fighting continued – and winter set in – above ground, the Turks celebrated the Islamic sacrificial feast of Kurban Bayrami (19 October). This requires every Muslim man of means to slaughter a sheep or some other animal, for distribution of meat to the poor, in memory of the ram sacrificed by Abraham in place of his son. ANZAC intelligence officers were aware of the significance of this feast and feared that the Turks might, in religious fervour, launch an attack against the Anzac perimeter. But most Turks just wanted to take a break from the war – if only for a day. Lieutenant Mehmed Fasih noted in his diary that the enemy shelling was unusually heavy that day:

> In dug-out, have some coffee. Feeling very tired, stretch out without intention of sleeping. Shelling starts. Howitzer shells explode to our right. One impacts ten paces to right of my dug-out. Decide I better move to second-line. Lieutenants Kazim and Ahmet, comrades from 3rd Battalion are there. Join them in their bunker. Whizzing by with loud rustling, howitzer shells land nearby. Our second-line trenches are in fairly good condition. They have been freshly dug. Haven't been damaged yet. Shrapnel is hitting entrance to our bunker. Shells explode and roar, fifty paces from where we are…Exchange 'Bayram' wishes with colleagues. Some privates and NCOs join us. We also exchange wishes with Battalion Commander. Am very hungry. Did not have morning tea. Food arrives. Four comrades and I eat with gusto.[10]

Evacuation was in the air. The great offensive had failed and, with winter, many trenches would soon be waist-deep in water, if not totally flooded out. After a conference on Mudros, in mid November, a telegram from Birdwood arrived telling Colonel Brudenell White to prepare plans for a possible evacuation of the peninsula.[11] White now set about ordering his first of many ruses to fool the Turks that he and his men were digging in for winter. He immediately ordered extended periods of inactivity so that the Turks would become accustomed to the idea that they were bunkering down. It was hoped that this would go some way to fooling them should the final decision be made to evacuate Anzac: the Turks would by then be familiar with the relative quiet and be less inclined to believe that the enemy were actually being evacuated beneath their noses. These extended periods of silence would begin on 24 November, starting at 6 p.m., with two days' cessation of fire along the whole Anzac front.

Some men at Anzac mistakenly believed the plan was meant to have the very opposite effect – that it was to indicate a withdrawal from the peninsula, while the troops would in fact remain, holding the sector through the oncoming cold months. Sapper Edmonds wrote in late November: 'The ruse to make the Turks think we are evacuating commences from tonight. Not a single shot is to be fired for three days and nights. All fatigue parties are to cease and men are to remain in their dug-outs during daylight. To-morrow's water ration is being drawn tonight.'[12]

Twenty-six-year-old Melbourne optician Lieutenant George McIlroy, of the 24th Battalion, recalled that during the second day of the enforced inactivity the Turks could no longer control their curiosity. Early that morning a sentry noticed a Turk carefully poke his head above the parapet. After a cautious look around, the Turk became more game, climbing out of his trench and crawling across the narrow space of no-man's-land towards the Australian trenches, just metres away. The sentry was spellbound, not believing what he was seeing. He excitedly whispered to his NCO, positioned next to him: 'Hey! Corp! Is that a live target?' That is, was he authorised to fire? It was quickly decided that such a target came 'within the meaning of the Act'. The muzzle of a rifle was placed just outside the loophole and when the Turk, after much care, 'glued his eye to the hole to investigate, he did not have time to realise what hit him'.[13] Not long afterwards, and to the surprise of the same sentry, another Turk commenced to 'crawl forward to see what held his "cobber" gazing spellbound into the loophole. In due course, he ranged himself alongside and peered into the other hole, but as neither he nor his cobber had any inclination to return and report to their comrades, no doubt, the latter suspected there was a catch in it, and things soon settled down again to an unbroken silence.'[14]

Such incidents notwithstanding, however, the historian of

the 16th Battalion recalled that the Turks quickly became more comfortable with the quieter conditions. They were walking about in front of the battalion as though they 'owned the place, strolling along trenches and exposing heads and shoulders in what was practically an invitation to shoot'. This began to annoy some of the ANZACs, who found it difficult to let such easy and frequent targets pass by without being able to take a shot. However, as the battalion history notes, 'Orders were orders…and the 16th obeyed them. At the end of the second 48 hours every man was itching for the word to recommence firing, and when the time did expire most of them had a Turk balanced on the foresight for the first shot.'[15]

On 26 November, the weather became cold and rainy, and the next day was marked by the first blizzard of snow. Colonel Brudenell White ordered that the period of silence be extended by another day – now to end at midnight of the 27th. Following this, the troops would revert back to 'normal' activity. Two days and nights of a continuous freezing wind followed, and on 28 November the thermometer did not rise above freezing point. Those who did not have the luxury of a dugout, cut into the slopes of Anzac, had to make do with lean-tos constructed with tarpaulin roofs and whatever else they could lay their hands on. With the weight of a few hours of snow, these lean-tos could quickly unravel and collapse, dumping their freezing load on the men. This was especially tragic for the men of the 7th and 8th battalions who had just returned from Lemnos and were bivouacking in the open with no shelter at all. A small issue of rum was released but didn't help much. Those in the front-line trenches awoke to icicles hanging down from the parapets, while those further back and lower down had to try and negotiate through the rivers of mud that now filled the gullies, the mud eventually becoming frozen and covered with snow and thin layers of ice, which made negotiating these natural pathways extremely slow and dangerous – more than a few must have slipped and broken a limb or two in the circumstances.

The final straw for the Australians came on 29 November, when, at around 9 a.m., the Turks began a massive bombardment against Lone Pine. The fears of the Allied commanders that the Turks might soon be heavily reinforced with heavy howitzers and shells from Germany and Austria-Hungary had become a reality. The men of the 24th Battalion were at the time passing through the saps leading to the Pine, to relieve the men of the 23rd Battalion. They were suddenly being blown apart by high-explosive shells. The Turkish artillery soon shortened their range and shells began to pound the Pine itself.

The ANZACs had never experienced such devastating artillery fire before. Until now, howitzers and their shells had always been in short supply – apparently, for the Turks at least, this was no longer the case. The combination of high-explosive shells and their steep trajectory tore the Pine apart. Parts of the front literally ceased to exist, especially the northernmost areas where trenches were smashed in, filled in, or both. After the bombardment, medical officer Joseph Fogarty, of the 21st Battalion, went in search of his brother Christopher, who with his men had been near the front line. All that he could recover from his brother's last known position was part of a lower limb.[16] At least a dozen other men, including Major Frederick Johnson – who had set up an aid post in Lone Pine – were buried alive. Only a few were dug out. It was later recorded: 'Major Johnson, who had been inspecting the Pine when the bombardment started, and who had at once established an improvised aid-post, was smothered, along with the men whom he was tending.'[17] Major Frederick Johnson is buried in the Lone Pine Cemetery.

The combination of the appearance of the heavy-howitzer batteries, a developing freezing winter and a renewed desire in London to fight the 'real enemy' on the Western Front (as opposed to 'side shows' like Gallipoli) spelt the end of the campaign. The decision had finally been made – the men were to be evacuated as soon as possible. Cyril Lawrence, like many others, had heard the talk: 'There is great consternation and indignation in Anzac. It has been rumoured that we are going to evacuate the Peninsula…Oh, it couldn't be; how could we leave this place now…And after the blood of brothers and fathers that has been shed in making it OURS. How could we leave those comrades who have paid the price and now lie sleeping under the sod in the cemeteries tucked away in the valleys?'[18]

White had just about finalised his evacuation plans for Anzac during the first week of December. At Lone Pine, the men led by 25-year-old Prahran draper Lieutenant Stanley Savige, of the 24th Battalion, were assigned to hold the position until the very end. Having been informed of the evacuation at a conference, he and the others couldn't believe they were leaving after the men of the 1st Division had suffered so much in taking the Pine, and the men of the 2nd Division had suffered in holding it. He recalled: 'We left that conference with feelings too deep for speech. We were stunned and broken in spirit, if not broken-hearted.'[19]

Most of the men would be taken away before the night of 18 December, with only a few thousand ANZACs to remain during 19 December, and then this would reduce to just a skeleton force of a few hundred during the final few hours on 20 December – they would be facing over 20 000 Turks alone. It did not bear thinking upon what would happen to these men if the Turks cottoned on. Consequently, those who were to be amongst the last to be evacuated were christened the 'diehards'. Many men volunteered to be part of this force, especially the veterans of the campaign who had been there since the beginning – they reckoned it was their right to be amongst the last to leave. It was for this very reason, however, that these men tended not to be chosen, as they were the most weakened by their brutal duties. Only the more recent and hence most fit reinforcements were likely and 'lucky' enough to get the nod, though a few veterans did manage to be picked because experience was also required.

On hearing that the evacuation withdrawal was going ahead, Chaplain Walter 'Bill' Dexter, went 'up the gullies and through the cemeteries scattering silver wattle seed. If we have to leave here I intend that a bit of Australia shall be here. I soaked the seed for about 20 hours and they seem to be well and thriving.'[20] It was a nice gesture, but none of the plants would survive the winter.

It was just before midnight of 19 December and the final deception had to last another three hours. The Anzac perimeter was now being held on average by one man for every ten metres, with each moving along the front line and firing out into no-man's-land from a number of different loopholes, trying to keep up a normal rate of fire and bomb-throwing. As remembered by Lieutenant Savige, they were to each command around ten to fifteen fire bays. This demanded great 'individual activity, as each man, though able to fire from only one bay at a time, must maintain a regular fire from all. This fire must be maintained by firing from irregular bays, and not bay after bay in succession.'[21] Given the poor physical condition of the men, even though they represented the fittest of the men available, it was indeed a great ask. The plans, while not overly difficult in making, were extremely difficult in execution, as the average distance between the Australian and Turkish lines at Lone Pine especially were extremely close – within just metres at some points.

Lieutenant George McIlroy in the heart of Lone Pine recalled that it was a still and quiet night, with a bright moon overhead. It was a scene so peaceful 'one could hardly associate it with war, and the mind found leisure to wander off to far Australia and imagine something of the surprise which would be caused by the newspaper headlines on the morrow'.[22] All remained quiet in front and everything was working like clockwork. McIlroy gave himself the luxury of contemplating the 'hitherto very remote possibility of our getting away with it altogether. It was a great satisfaction to know that most of the troops were already clear, and it was beginning to look like a sporting chance for us, although time enough for quite a lot of things to happen yet.'[23] McIlroy remembered vividly his men quietly and confidently going about their duties without any trace of nervousness. A little after midnight, he and the other officers were jolted back into the precariousness of their position with a phone call reporting that a Turkish patrol had been observed pushing up Wire Gully to their left. If this 'meant a general move forward, we could expect trouble very shortly, while our isolated party might easily be cut off in the rear'.[24] If this was indeed the case, they were in serious trouble, as their orders clearly stated that their position within the Pine must at all costs be held, until at least 3 a.m. Nothing was said to the men, except a warning to be alert. Finally the time arrived for the next group, including the machine-gunners, to evacuate Lone Pine, while the phone and wires were disconnected and also taken away, leaving three officers and thirty-four other ranks now feeling very much alone. However, just before the phone was dismantled and removed, the diehards got a welcome message: 'Embarkation of the main body having proceeded faster than scheduled, our time would be reduced by 20 minutes. As we considered the last half-hour might be the most trying for the men on the posts, this information was passed onto them.'[25]

Lieutenant Savige recalled that the order to move finally arrived at 2.40 a.m. On receiving the final order, all but those who were to set the drip rifles (an Australian-designed weapon that fired a single bullet automatically via a system of counterbalances, dripping water and string tied to the trigger) collected their gear. Savige recalled the 'strange eerie remoteness of the situation was experienced as we each collected our packs in the deserted corners usually so full of men. This strangeness was intensified by the blanketed trenches and padded boots. I remember the little shiver that ran down my spine at that moment.'[26]

Savige and McIlroy's men now had just thirty minutes to reach Watson's Pier on Anzac beach, where the last boats awaited them. En route, they managed to destroy five artillery guns with explosives. Savige recalled that time had been lost and, to make matters worse, the strips of blankets around their boots – used to help muffle the sound of 'marching' men in the quiet early morning hours – were now coming apart and unwinding, further impeding progress. There was no time to fix the problem – they had to push on.

Even though they were keen to put as much distance between themselves and the Turks, as they passed the cemetery at Brown's Dip, where the dead from the battle of Lone Pine were buried, McIlroy recalled: 'One could not help but feel a little ashamed that we were deserting those comrades and leaving undone the job they had started.'[27]

Once they were clear of the trenches and Turks, the adrenaline that had kept them going was fading. Fatigue now began to set in, worsened by the heavy load of full packs and rifles, and some began to drop out of line. All that these men wanted to do was sleep – stuff the Turks. Most pushed themselves forward on their own accord, but McIlroy recalled that for some, persuasion was useless and time was slipping away. There was nothing for it but to 'ply the boot to the fleshy part of the anatomy. We literally booted some of them along to, and onto, the last boat, but thank God, we got them all aboard.'[28]

McIlroy and his men, the last Australians to occupy Lone Pine, would also be among the last to leave Anzac. The young lieutenant recalled with some pride many years later:

We began to link up with [other] parties converging from the centre of the line…At the beach we found a sentry, who warned us to hurry past, as 'Beachy Bill' was dropping his 'pills' regularly every few minutes. We crowded on to the barge lying alongside the jetty and between decks was soon filled with a mass of unshaven, haggard and dirty looking Diggers all talking at once, and the air thick with tobacco smoke. After the recent strain and the prohibition on smoking for fear the lighting of matches might arouse suspicion, one can imagine the clamour which broke out – everybody at once trying to tell the other fellow his experiences. I will always remember those men – probably the pick of the whole Force, and they looked it, despite their ragged appearance; some with full beards, while the lean cheeks of the others were covered with several days' stubble.[29]

Still at Lone Pine in the early morning darkness of 20 December, at around 4 a.m., Turkish Lieutenant Mehmed Fasih, not yet knowing that he had survived Gallipoli, was recording in his diary:

Tonight there is much grenade activity on both sides. The front is very noisy. This continues till midnight…I spot a halo of seven colours around the crescent moon. Point it out to Nuri. He says this is a miracle and can be considered a good omen. At that moment, an enemy plane is in the sky, above us. After a while, the halo gradually fades away. Inspect the trenches and supervise repairs. Continue reading the novel. Niyazi drops in a few times to see me. Nuri goes to bed.

22.30 hrs – Am terribly tired. Last night had no sleep.
23.00 hrs – Issue my orders and go to bed.
3.30 hrs – Get up. Tea is ready. Wake up Nuri. We have tea together. The front lines are extremely quiet. No grenades.
3.35 hrs – A dumdum [mine] explodes to our left. Nuri and

I have tea. Battalion commander arrives…Offer him tea. [A] patrol is readied. He asks me where it will emerge from our lines. Explain it will move into no-man's land from the spot where the mine was detonated.[30]

This was the last entry in Lieutenant Mehmed Fasih's Gallipoli diary. The peninsula was again wholly in Turkish hands.

Epilogue

Within days of the initial assault against Lone Pine on 6 August, word of the great offensive at Gallipoli had made its way back to Australia. The first news read by the Australian public was on 11 August, in a brief and vague note published by Sydney newspaper *The Sun*. There was no mention of the battle of Lone Pine, only of significant gains in an attempt to carry the enemy heights.[1] As the days passed, more information was slowly being provided to the newspapers – passed through the military censors. All news was of praise; no mention that the offensive had been a disaster. *The Sun* was the first to publish an account by General Sir Ian Hamilton that specifically mentioned the attack by the men of the 1st Australian Brigade: 'The Australian troops have again done splendidly in the recent prolonged and very heavy fighting. The charge of the 1st Infantry Brigade and the capture by them of an enemy strongly protected [by a] labyrinth of trenches was magnificent.'[2] Towards the end of August, however, not even the military censorship could hide the large casualty lists being printed, which reflected the true nature of the slaughter. Readers of *The Sun* were left in no doubt about the toll being taken in an article published on 23 August under the heading 'HEAVIEST LIST TO DATE – OVER 700 CASUALTIES'. These figures would have included those who fought at Lone Pine.[3] The news read: 'It is one of the longest lists issued since the fighting commenced on the peninsula, and it contains the names of 109 officers and 601 men who have suffered either death or wounds...

or are amongst the missing. The officers have suffered more severely than on any previous occasion, and New South Wales is harder hit than any of the other states.'[4]

The first news to reach the public specifically mentioning Lone Pine in any detail was written by Charles Bean and appeared in a number of Australian newspapers on 25 August. Bean recorded what he had witnessed on the afternoon of 6 August, while positioned in the front-line trenches at The Pimple, waiting for the initial charge of the 1st Brigade against the Turkish stronghold. His despatch began:

> Since Friday night the battle which started in the Australian right [flank] at Anzac, with the magnificent capture of Lonesome Pine trenches by our first infantry brigade, has rolled away to the north... The battle actually started with the bombardment of Achi Baba and an attack at Helles about 4 p.m. on Friday. Then came a magnificent assault by the first infantry brigade at Lonesome Pine at 5.30. This was practically finished by 7.30.[5]

'Practically finished by 7.30' – hardly. The real human cost of the August Offensive was finally made clear to the Australian public on 30 August, when the casualty list was published in the Melbourne newspaper *The Age*. 'The losses so far sustained almost equal the strength of the First Australian Division when it went into action close to four months ago.'[6] It also soon became clear that Lone Pine was not a direct attack to break through the Turkish lines and thus lead to victory – it was revealed as a feint. In the eyes of many, especially those who received the news that their husband, father, son or brother had become a casualty of the battle, these men had seemingly died and suffered in vain, and it clearly impacted on Australian Army recruitment figures. War was no longer seen as a great adventure – it equated to waste, death and suffering. During the heady days of 1914, the national monthly recruitment average was around 10 500. This figure peaked at 36 600 in July 1915. In August 1915, this figure, while still remaining high, dropped to 21 700. After the news of August, the figures dropped to 16 600 in September, and in October, for the first time since the landing, the figure dropped below 10 000.[7] The highest fall in enlistments occurred in New South Wales, the home of the 1st Brigade, which suffered so terribly in the fighting at Lone Pine.[8]

While censorship was enforced, not all of the soldier's letters from Gallipoli could be screened, given the enormous amount of mail. Hence, while the military did its best to censor unwanted news, some letters from the front often made their way into the local and state newspapers. Even so, while some civilians, such as Pompey Elliott's wife Kate, received letters from the front that were descriptive and more detailed than those published in the newspapers – which tended to self-censor, as required by government guidelines set up in 1914 – such letters were generally personal and not widespread. As a result, the Australian public still remained largely unaware of the true horror and carnage of the battle for Lone Pine.[9]

Of course, to those who had loved ones on the casualty list, including those listed as missing, the effects of Lone Pine were far more personal and all too often tragic. George and Sara Irwin had been informed that their 19-year-old son, Private George Roy Irwin, from the 4th Battalion, went missing during the fighting for Lone Pine in early August. After receiving the news, they met every boat arriving in Sydney with sick and wounded members of his battalion, seeking any information about their son.[10] They searched the casualty lists and questioned whether the 'G. Irwin' listed might actually be their son. In January 1917, George was officially declared as having been killed-in-action sometime between 6–9 August in the battle for Lone Pine. Even so, Sara refused to believe her son had been killed and wrote to the authorities in

August 1917, stating that there was no evidence of George's death – and pleading that if they had such evidence could they send it to her. She also wrote of eyewitnesses who had seen George wounded and lying in a trench in Lone Pine, just before the Turks recaptured it – some of his mates reckoned he may have been taken prisoner. It is unlikely, however, that these same witnesses told her that George had been shot through the stomach – then an almost certain mortal wound. The suggestion of his possible capture was undoubtedly conveyed to her with the best of intentions, but ultimately it led to a false sense of hope.

In additional correspondence to military authorities, Sara questioned an official letter quoting George's regimental number as being 3145 when in reality it was 2145 – hoping this might signify a clerical error in reporting George's death. Additional information from the Red Cross could neither confirm nor deny George's death or capture by the Turks. This led to a chain of ongoing correspondence between George's parents and military authorities throughout the war – all preserved in George's military file at the National Archives Australia. George's parents were, not surprisingly, hoping against hope that he had been taken prisoner by the Turks and was somewhere safe in Turkey. At the end of the war, however, they had to face the reality that George had been killed in action in the trenches at the Pine. But their anguish did not finish here, as the Australian War Grave Service Unit at Anzac could not locate his body. Sara provided details of the likely personal effects he would have gone into battle with, including photographs and letters, hoping that this might help them identify her son – but to no avail. In 1921, Sara and George were informed that their son could not be identified and was officially listed as having no known grave.[11] Five years later, George and Sara made the then difficult and expensive pilgrimage to the Gallipoli Peninsula and the Lone Pine Memorial which bears George's name, and while there they made a precious rubbing of his name listed on

Panel 22.[12] This is just one story from a family of one of the 60 000 Australians killed in the Great War.

One of the many questions that remain about the fighting for Lone Pine is why, of the seven VCs awarded during the battle, almost all were awarded for actions on the last day of the battle, overlooking those who took the Turkish works itself. While Lance Corporal Leonard Keysor was awarded his VC for his heroic actions between 7–8 August, the remainder were allocated for actions on 9 August. Surely there were similar heroic efforts in the intense hand-to-hand fighting that originally took the position on 6 August? There must have also been others beside Keysor that deserved special recognition between 7–8 August. It couldn't be that all officers who witnessed such actions were killed and thus couldn't report the brave acts of their men, although in some battalions they came close to it – the 2nd Battalion lost over 70 per cent of its officers in the first twenty-four hours.[13] On two occasions Lieutenant Colonel Scobie asked Captain Jacobs to remind him to put Private Clifton Judd up for the VC after the battle, but Scobie was killed before being able to do so. Jacobs reported Judd's actions to his new commanding officer: 'I reported it to my own CO, unfortunately he did not see the act and did not therefore appreciate its merit.'[14] This must have been an all too common occurrence. Even so, it's difficult to understand how the well-documented actions of Captain John Pain and his men, privates William Nichol, James Montgomery and William Goudemey, were overlooked. After all, at the most critical point of the battle, when the Turks were about to retake Jacobs's Trench, Pain stood in no-man's-land, completely exposed, firing a Vickers machine gun resting on the shoulders of his three men, and repulsed the enemy's near breakthrough – surely action worthy of a VC. Yet they were passed over.

Similar arguments could be made regarding the actions of

Major Iven Mackay, holding the blood pit that was named after him. Indeed, Mackay was recommended for the VC but was also overlooked. The same applies to Sergeant Major Paul Goldenstedt, Captain Harold Jacobs, Private Tim Shadbolt and many other individuals whose well-documented actions deserved special recognition for bravery and for turning the tide of battle at a most critical point. This is not to argue that those who were awarded the VC at Lone Pine were not deserving – they clearly were – but to wonder why only seven, and why all but one during the last day of the battle. Many at the time pondered this and after the war more than a few discussions and articles were devoted to the question, especially in returned service men's journals, such as *Reveille*. Elliott himself tried to address the issue, suggesting that when Walker visited Lone Pine on 9 August the general informed Elliott: 'I will see that your battalion is not forgotten.'[15] Walker was clearly a man of his word. Indeed, Elliott recalled how the divisional commander 'judged by the number of [7th Battalion] wounded streaming by his Head Quarters that we were getting a warm time… He saw with his own eyes the trenches choked with the dead and dying trodden on by their comrades because they could not be removed from the narrow trenches, and torn to pieces by the bombs and shells the enemy were hurling.'[16] Maybe if Walker had entered the works earlier, others too (or instead) may have been awarded the VC. But as Paul Goldenstedt wrote as a journalist after the war, Walker and Smyth had intimate knowledge of the difficulties, struggle and desperate nature of the combat waged in taking and holding Lone Pine. They were in 'close touch with the whole of the operations of the 6th, when the Pine was captured by the 1st Brigade… and on the 7th and 8th, when it was held against counter-attacks of such intensity that Captain Bean… rightly describes them as "titanic"'.[17]

Elliott's experience as a solicitor probably helped when it came to drafting his recommendations. He knew how to construct a case and he obviously wrote very convincingly about the brave actions of his men, justifying with every phrase why his nominations should be approved. Others, perhaps, wrote less forcefully in their recommendations and while the efforts of their men were recognised, they just didn't quite read like VC material. Still, it's difficult to understand how Pain and his men could be passed over, even if represented by the most awkward piece of prose.

In 1919 peace had been declared – the war to end all wars was finally over. Charles Bean, along with his small team of seven, consisting of Captain Hubert Wilkins (photographer), Honorary Captain George Lambert (painter), Sergeant Arthur Bazley and Lieutenant John Balfour (personnel assistants) and Lieutenant Hedley Howe (Gallipoli veteran of the landing), along with Lieutenant Herbert Buchanan and Sergeant George Rogers (engineers – draughtsmen), were now given their final orders – return to Anzac. Bean had been pushing for this for some time. In order to enhance the official status of his team's visit – as he would be dealing extensively with the military – he adopted the title 'Australian Historical Mission'. Bean's primary role was to inspect the Australian graves and offer advice to the Australian government regarding the establishment of official war cemeteries on the peninsula. They were also to collect artifacts for the intended war museum (later to become the Australian War Memorial). Added to this, Bean had since been charged by the government with writing the *Official History of Australia in the War of 1914–18* and hoped to solve some historical questions – riddles, he liked to call them – which he felt could only be addressed by walking and surveying the 'old' battlefields. A few weeks later, Bean and his team had finally returned to Anzac. It was now February 1919 and they eagerly began to scour the war-scarred terrain:

[I] rode on with Lambert and Wilkins up a road which

wound from Legge Valley on to Pine Ridge (a southern spur of the plateau) and hence on to the level summit of 'the Pine' and into the heart of the Old Anzac position... Reaching the plateau it led over part of the maze of trenches, which still deeply fringed the whole summit of the Second Ridge. We found the trenches worn by rain and a little overgrown but otherwise almost unchanged except that all wood – whether supports or roofs or other fittings – had been taken from them. This reticulation, still six or eight feet deep, and so intricate that Lone Pine looked like an anthill, would have made riding there (as indeed on most parts of Second Ridge except along no-man's-land) impossible if the road had not crossed the trenches on bridges of pine trunks... Those men of both sides who fell in No-man's-land... still lay [there] in 1919, very thickly in some parts... Lambert and Wilkins were deeply moved. 'Much the most impressive battlefields I've seen,' said Wilkins. 'At one place,' wrote Lambert next day, 'a perfect rabbit warren, and too ghastly for me to people with the image of fighting.' [18]

Bean later advised the Australian government that there were two options in terms of Australian graves and the human remains that presently could be found in large numbers among the gullies and ravines. He urged that the government should 'as soon as possible express its wish as to whether graves should be retained in their present positions, and men's remains be buried where they lay, or whether graves and remains should be concentrated in a few of the large existing cemeteries'.[19] Bean recommended the first option, with the important caveat that the 'whole of that area [must be] vested in the Imperial War Graves Commission'.[20] This came to pass with the signing of the Treaty of Lausanne in 1923 and Bean's recommendation was endorsed, at least for the area now officially recognised as Anzac. The treaty obliged that the new Turkish Republic grant to the governments of the then British Empire, France and Italy '[in] perpetuity the land within the Turkish territory in which are situated the graves, cemeteries, ossuaries or memorials of their soldiers and sailors who fell in action or died of wounds, accident or disease, as well as those of prisoners of war and internal civilians who died in captivity... The land to be granted by the Turkish Government will include in particular, as regards the British Empire, the area in the region known as Anzac.'[21] Fifty years later, the sector officially known as the ANZAC Area was incorporated into the Turkish National Park Service, consisting of around 5900 hectares. With the rediscovery of the detailed Sevki Pasa maps drafted by the Turkish High Command in 1916, it became clear that many historic sites relating to the 1915 campaign were beyond the then park boundaries. Consequently, with the establishment of the Gallipoli Peninsula Peace Park by the Turkish Government in 1996, the boundaries were expanded to include over 33 000 hectares.[22]

Today, the Lone Pine Cemetery is the venue for the annual Australian commemoration held each Anzac Day, 25 April, at Gallipoli. Lone Pine is the largest Australian cemetery on the peninsula. It has 1167 graves (471 of which are unidentified), as well as the memorial that commemorates the 4221 Australian and 709 New Zealanders without a known grave, and the 960 Australian and 252 New Zealanders who were buried at sea.[23] In 1919, and later, the men buried in Brown's Dip were exhumed and reinterred at the newly established cemetery. The cemetery itself is orientated along an east–west direction and occupies the former no-man's-land – the Daisy Patch. The western end of the cemetery lies on what would have been in 1915 the heart of The Pimple, while the eastern end lies over the former Turkish trenches at Lone Pine, close to where Sasse's Sap would have been. Running in a north–south orientation directly through the centre of the cemetery would have been the secret underground trench, from which the initial charge was made. An aerial photograph taken in June of 1923, when the cemetery was being constructed, clearly shows the former trenches and saps. The cemetery is rectangular in plan and is outlined by the scrub-choked gullies and spurs surrounding it: Army-issue regularity among nature's chaos. Clearly seen in the photograph, along its western and eastern edges, are the spiderweb-like orientations of the former trenches, emanating from the cleared cemetery, while the faint outline of the secret sap running through no-man's-land can just be made out. Just to the north a number of workmen's huts can be seen as well as a new road that runs along the southern part of the plateau. The Cup can also be clearly seen in the upper left-hand corner of the photograph, with Legge Valley and the lower slopes of Third Ridge beyond.

Today, the remains of the former front-line trenches at the Pine are mostly gone. One has to go behind the eastern wall of the memorial to find collapsed trenches, here and there a piece of rusted wire and, more disconcertingly, the odd fragment of bone – usually too small to identify precisely, but clearly bone and almost certainly human. In 2003, the author conducted a preliminary archaeological survey of the Anzac battlefields at Gallipoli and recorded in relation to Lone Pine that the whole area was covered in low scrub, though again the complex trench system could still be seen. The vegetation in many cases had yet to be established. While some natural backfilling had occurred, other trenches were exposed and subject to ongoing erosion.[24]

Standing on the plateau in 2003 was certainly an emotional experience. The author's great-uncle is commemorated on the Lone Pine Memorial – Private John Tunks, who signed up as John Thompson, 4th Battalion, and who landed on the afternoon of 25 April and was killed somewhere near Lone Pine four days later. As far as is known, I was the first of his relatives to visit the spot. First, sadness overcomes you as you stand in the cemetery – all those names and potential – then there is a feeling of almost contentment. Anzac is hauntingly beautiful, and surprisingly small. Looking south, you can see Bolton's Ridge; somewhere close by lies Leane's Trench. To the immediate north, what appears to be a stone's throw away, lies Johnston's Jolly, with the positions along Second Ridge – German Officers' Trench, Steele's, Courtney's and Quinn's posts – not much further away. The Nek, Chunuk Bair, Hill Q and Hill 971 lie further still. For eight months in 1915 it was hell. But now, almost 100 years later, the memories and the landscape have weathered, and it is a place where people commemorate and contemplate the meaningless slaughter of war.

Anyone who visits the Australian War Memorial in Canberra is usually first drawn to the Gallipoli boat at the entrance and, after entering the Gallipoli Room, to the Lone Pine diorama. This diorama, sculptured between 1924 and 1927 by Wallace Anderson and Louis McCubbin, portrays the initial charge of the 1st Brigade, as they attempt to penetrate the overhead timbers of the front line. A central figure is captured forever frozen in time, throwing up his left arm, while his right hand is about to drop his rifle, having been hit. Men either side of him are tearing at the timbers, firing down into open spaces, while others are lowering themselves down into the Turkish trenches. Australians can be seen inside the trench, underneath the pine log-covered trench, hunting down Turks. Above ground, at the rear of the diorama, a painted glorious sun is setting against the nearby Greek islands (in reality, the setting sun was a few hours away). The diorama is dramatic and compelling; you are drawn to it, reflecting on the heroism and brutality of it all. Years before, in the 1930s, it was almost too much for a tired veteran, who saw the diorama for the first time while it was in display in Sydney. He was reduced to tears. 'It's that Lone Pine model,' he said. 'I've got to get out. It's too much for me. My pal was killed there beside me.'[25] Today, lying on the floor below the diorama, almost seemingly as an afterthought, are original timbers from Lone Pine, collected by Charles Bean in 1919.

Lone Pine is now very much a part of the Australian vocabulary, and images similar to those depicted in the diorama appear automatically to the mind when the battle is mentioned. Around Australia, public places from streets to nature reserves are named 'Lone Pine', in remembrance. A great many schools have a 'Lone Pine' tree growing in their grounds – perhaps seeded from a number of kernels collected from Gallipoli over the years. Go to any plant nursery in Australia and you can purchase a 'descendent' from the original Lonesome Pine, or a purported close relative.

Lone Pine does not belong to the past – it is still very much with us, although those who served and suffered in that charnel house have passed. The sacrifice they made is still very much embedded in the Australian experience of war.

What happened to...

(Note: All ranks listed are those at the time of the battle for Lone Pine, unless stated otherwise.)

Aarons, Julian (11th Battalion) Captain Aarons suffered a bomb splinter to his knee while throwing a sandbag and himself onto a Turkish grenade in Leane's Trench during the morning of 6 August. Aarons was ferried to the 1st Australian General Hospital, Heliopolis. He recovered from his wounds and fought with his battalion on the Western Front until the Armistice, returning to Australia in 1920 with the rank of major.

Anderson, Hugh (4th Battalion) Lance Corporal Anderson was initially wounded, while his Commanding Officer Captain Stewart Milson was killed, as both tried to drive Turks out of their covered works in the northern flank of Lone Pine. Anderson survived the battle, as well as Gallipoli, but was killed in France in May 1917, at the second Battle of Bullecourt. He has no known grave and is commemorated at the Australian National Memorial, Villers-Bretonneux, France.

Aylward, Joseph (4th Battalion) Corporal Aylward was wounded in the legs and wrist on 7 August while defending the post that was to be named after him. He returned to Australia in late 1916 after being hospitalised for his wounds. The last correspondence in his

AIF file is dated 1967 – a request for the Gallipoli medal.

Bastin, Hector (7th Battalion) Lieutenant Bastin was sent into Jacobs's Trench as the Turks broke into the position. He was seriously wounded in this action, but recovered from his wounds to fight on the Western Front, returning to Australia in 1918 with the rank of major.

Bates, Robert (7th Battalion) As a stretcher-bearer in the heart of Lone Pine, Private Bates was lucky to have survived and for his bravery was awarded the Military Medal (MM). Indeed, he would somehow survive the bloodbath of Pozières a year later, being awarded a bar to his MM for devotion and bravery. He returned to Australia in 1920 with the rank of sergeant.

Bean, Charles (official Australian government war correspondent) Charles Bean wrote the first six volumes of the *Official History of Australia in the War of 1914–18* and edited the remaining six. He collected a large number of artifacts during the war for what would later become the Australian War Memorial. In 1919, on his way back to Australia, he returned to Anzac to advise the government on the Australian war cemeteries scattered around the gullies and slopes. He also conducted historical research, including the interviewing of Turkish participants, principally the then promoted Major Ahmed Zeki Bey. He was a long-time director of the Australian War Memorial in Canberra. Bean was admitted to Concord Repatriation Hospital in 1964, dying there in 1968, amongst other members of the AIF.

Bean, John (3rd Battalion – Medical Corps) Captain John Bean was Charles's brother and served as a medical officer in the 3rd Battalion at Anzac. He also served on the Western Front, including at Pozières. In 1917, he was transferred to a military hospital in Britain, returning to Australia in 1919. He died in 1969.

Bendrey, William (4th Battalion) Private Bendrey was in the initial charge to take Lone Pine. He survived the battle, but was wounded in action eight months later on the Western Front, losing an eye. He returned to Australia in late 1916.

Besanko, Cyril (4th Battalion) Lance Corporal Besanko was instrumental in defending Mackay's Post during the first twelve hours of the battle for Lone Pine. He was recommended for the Victoria Cross (VC) but was somehow passed over. In 1916 he was serving on the Western Front and was wounded in the chest and arm while bringing in a casualty under heavy fire. He was awarded the Distinguished Conduct Medal (DCM) and returned to Australia in late 1916.

Birdwood, William (commander ANZAC) Lieutenant General Birdwood went on to command the 1st Anzac Corps on the Western Front. However, with the formation of the Australian Army Corps in 1918, command was passed over to an Australian, Lieutenant General John Monash. Birdwood toured Australia and New Zealand in 1920 and then returned to the Indian Army, becoming commander-in-chief in 1925. He had hoped to retire as the Governor General of Australia, but by then only Australians were being considered for the position. He died in Britain in 1951.

Brim, Alexander (3rd Australian Field Ambulance) Private Brim, a cook based at Brown's Dip, provided around-the-clock hot meals and tea to the troops despite Turkish shells continually falling close to his 'kitchen'. In 1916, while serving on the Western Front, he was promoted to lance corporal, but resumed the rank of private at his own request. Brim obviously later had second thoughts, returning to Australia in 1919 as a sergeant. He died in 1951.

Bryant, James (2nd Battalion) Private Bryant was in the thick of the fighting in and around Jacobs's Trench/Post, surviving Gallipoli and, with Captain Morshead, figured in one of the most iconic photographs of Anzac. He served on the Western Front, being awarded the MM in 1918. He also served in the Second World War as a lieutenant, but spent most of his time as a prisoner of the Japanese in Changi Prison.

Cherry, Frederick (1st Battalion) Private Cherry was wounded while crossing the Daisy Patch during the night of 6 August. He suffered a severe shrapnel wound in his back and was evacuated to Malta and then onto London. On recovering, he was reassigned to the 53rd Infantry Battalion and fought on the Western Front. He returned to Australia in 1918.

Clogstoun, Henry (3rd Field Company of Engineers) Major Clogstoun was shot through the neck during the battle for Leane's Trench on 6 August. He spent some time in England recovering from his wound and later served with distinction on the Western Front, before returning to Australia in 1919.

Cook, Elsie (Nursing Sister, AANS) – see Cook, Sydney

Cook, Sydney (2nd Battalion) Captain Syd Cook was severely wounded in the head during the battle for Lone Pine. His wife and Australian Army Nursing Sister, Elsie, nursed him back to health in Cairo. He eventually recovered and served on the Western Front, as did Elsie. They sailed back to Australia together in 1919 and took up residence in Perth, and then Sydney. In later years, their grandchildren would run their fingers over the groove on Syd's scalp left by the Turkish bullet that had nearly cost him his life. Syd and Elsie both died in 1972.[1]

Dexter, Walter 'Bill' (Chaplains Corps) Chaplain Dexter survived

Gallipoli and went on to serve on the Western Front. He returned to Australia in 1919 as the most highly decorated Chaplain of the AIF, having been awarded the Distinguished Service Order (DSO) as well as the MM.

Duke, Charles (4th Battalion) Private Duke helped defend McDonald's Post and survived Gallipoli as well as the Western Front. He returned to Australia in 1919 as a captain of the 5th Pioneer Battalion, having been awarded the Military Cross (MC).

Dunstan, William VC (7th Battalion) Corporal Dunstan was awarded a VC for his actions defending Symon's Post, but was badly wounded and blind for some time. He survived the war, but pieces of shrapnel were continually removed from his body for many years afterwards.[2] His son later recalled: 'He had shrapnel permanently in his brain, and for the rest of his life he suffered from terrible headaches. When the headaches came there was no sleep, and as children we were told to move very quietly about the house. The entire household was aware of his suffering.'[3] He died of a heart attack in 1957.

Dyett, Gilbert (7th Battalion) Lieutenant Dyett was seriously wounded defending Jacobs's Post and was sent down the line and given up for dead, until someone noticed him moving. He was returned to Australia in 1916. Dyett played a significant part in recruitment and in 1917 was promoted to captain. In later years he became a voice for the veterans and was elected president of the Returned and Services League (RSL). Sir Gilbert died in 1964.

Elliott, Harold 'Pompey' (7th Battalion) Lieutenant Colonel Elliott survived Gallipoli and went on to command a brigade along the Western Front. He was clearly distraught after the Battle of Fromelles, in 1916, when his brigade's survivors stumbled back into their lines after suffering devastating casualties. Elliott had tried to get the attack cancelled, but to no avail. Later in the war, many, including Pompey, believed he should have been given command of one of the five Australian Divisions, but his outspokenness cost him any chance of this. In battle he proved to be an excellent, inspirational leader and led his men right through to the final battles against the Hindenburg Line. In January 1919, he received the fondest of farewells from his brigade. But Elliott, like many others who survived the Great War physically intact, had not survived emotionally. He went on for the rest of his short life to suffer bouts of depression, but still managed to battle for the rights of his men after the war, inside and outside the federal parliament. In 1931, Elliott was checked into hospital suffering a nervous breakdown. Although watched by the staff, he managed somehow to obtain a cut-throat razor and, during the early morning hours of 23 March 1933, a nurse discovered Elliott with blood everywhere. The razor was 'embedded in a deep gash near his left elbow; the peace and release he craved had come swiftly. All Pompey Elliott's battles and worries were over.'[4]

Facey, Albert (11th Battalion) Private Facey, with his mates of the 11th Battalion, was in the thick of the fighting at Leane's Trench during the morning of 6 August. Both of his brothers, Roy and Joseph, were killed while serving at Anzac. Facey survived the war to write late in life the Australian classic *A Fortunate Life*.

Fasih, Mehmed (Turkish 47th Regiment, 2nd Battalion) Lieutenant Fasih had been wounded during the Turks' mass attack against the Anzac sector on 19 May. He returned to his regiment in mid October and kept a detailed diary of his time at Kanli Sirt (Lone Pine). Fasih survived the war, but was wounded during the War of Liberation in 1922. He was later promoted to lieutenant general and died of a heart attack in 1964, aged seventy.

Fullerton, Alexander 'Doc' (2nd Battalion) Doc Fullerton was conspicuous for his bravery in treating the wounded at Lone Pine and was twice recommended for the DSO. He was also recommended for the French Croix de Guerre. None of these recommendations were forthcoming, although he was twice Mentioned in Despatches. Shortly after Lone Pine, Fullerton fell ill to dysentery and biliary colic and was evacuated first to Mudros, and then Britain. He was returned to Australia in 1916 and set up a practice in Lismore. He died in 1946.

Gammage, John (1st Battalion) Private Gammage, who, like Private Raymond ('Smithy') Smith had no time for any flashy NCO or officer, was wounded at Lone Pine but soon recovered and saw active service during the Palestine Campaign, returning to Australia in 1919 with the rank of corporal.

Goldenstedt, Paul (3rd Battalion) Sergeant Major Goldenstedt received no medals for his actions during the battle, but was Mentioned in Despatches for his actions during 6 August. He survived Gallipoli and later served in the Middle East in the 15th Australian Light Horse Regiment. He was wounded in action in 1917 and returned to Australia in 1919 with the rank of major.

Goudemey, William (2nd Battalion) Private Goudemey, with his mates, helped Captain Pain with the machine gun at the height of the battle for Jacobs's Trench. He was nominated for the VC for his actions during 8 August. For his actions at Lone Pine he was awarded the DCM. Lance Corporal William Goudemey was killed in action in July 1916 and has no known grave. He is commemorated on the Australian National Memorial, Villers-Bretonneux in France.

Graham, Wally (11th Battalion) Private Graham had been the cook at Leane's Trench during the morning of 6 August. He survived the war and returned to Australia in 1919 with the rank of lieutenant and the MM plus bar. Within three weeks of making it back home, Wally was dead, having fallen from a building scaffolding.

Graham, William (4th Battalion) Private Graham was in the thick of the fighting along the northern flank of Lone Pine and remained in the fight to the end. He was wounded in France in 1916 and 1917, as well as suffering from being gassed. He later joined the 56th Battalion and returned to Australia in 1919 with the rank of lieutenant. The last correspondence in his AIF file is dated 1964 – a request for a replacement for the 1914/15 Star Medal.

Hale, Elgar (12th Battalion) Sergeant Hale, who wrote to his sister explaining his miraculous escape from a Turkish bomb, was not so fortunate during the Battle of Passchendaele in 1917. Then a lieutenant, Hale was killed in action on 5 October and is buried at Tyne Cot Cemetery, Passchendaele, Belgium.

Hamilton, John VC (3rd Battalion) Private Hamilton survived Gallipoli only to fight in some of the worst battles involving the AIF, including Pozières and Mouquet Farm during the 1916 Somme Offensive. In 1918 he had reached the rank of captain and was returned to Australia after the Armistice. During World War Two he saw active service in New Guinea and Bougainville. He was the last surviving member of the seven Australians awarded VCs for actions at Lone Pine, dying in 1961 from cerebrovascular disease in the Concord Repatriation Hospital in Sydney.

Hayward, George (4th Battalion) Private Hayward, along with his mate Joseph Aylward, was heavily involved in defending Aylward's Post. Hayward was still there days later, after all of the other original defenders were either dead or wounded. By 1917 he had been promoted to warrant officer, but a year later reverted to private. He returned to Australia in 1919. The last correspondence in his AIF file is dated 1941.

Hobbs, Talbot (Artillery – 1st Australian Division) Colonel Hobbs commanded the Australian artillery during the battle for Lone Pine. He then commanded the Australian Artillery in France in 1916 and later that year took command of the Australian 5th Infantry Division, participating in the battles of Second Bullecourt, Peronne and Villers-Bretonneux. Indeed, the Australian triumph at Villers-Bretonneux can largely be put to Hobbs's planning. After the war, in 1919, he took command of the Australian Corps from Monash. In April 1938, Hobbs left for France to attend the unveiling of the Australian war memorial at Villers-Bretonneux, the design competition for which he had adjudicated. He suffered a heart attack at sea and died on 21 April. Hobbs's body was brought back to Perth for burial with state and military honours.

Howell-Price, Owen (3rd Battalion) Lieutenant Howell-Price helped Major Mackay construct barricades at Mackay's Post during the morning of 7 August, as well as helping to repel the Turkish near-breakthrough along Sasse's Sap on 9 August. He survived Gallipoli and was awarded the MC for his actions at Lone Pine. He took over command of the 4th Battalion from Mackay in 1916, but was killed with a shot to the head while checking out a machine-gun position in November 1916 at Flers. Lieutenant Colonel Howell-Price is buried at Heilly Station Cemetery, France.

Ison, John (3rd Battalion) Private Ison survived the initial charge and fighting at Lone Pine, and went on to fight on the Western Front. He was killed in action at Passchendaele in November 1917. He has no known grave and is commemorated at the Ypres (Menin Gate) Memorial in Belgium.

Jacobs, Harold (1st Battalion) Captain Jacobs was wounded while defending the trench and post that bears his name. While still wounded he went back into the front-line trenches to help stem the Turkish onslaught against Jacobs's Post. He survived Gallipoli and was Mentioned in Despatches for his actions during the battle for Lone Pine. In October, Jacobs was evacuated from the peninsula with enteric fever. He was promoted to second in command of the 61st Infantry Battalion in December 1916, with the rank of major. Jacobs was wounded in action in 1918 and returned to Australia in 1919.

Judd, Clifford (1st Battalion) Private Judd crossed no-man's-land three times to bring over a machine gun and ammunition. Lieutenant Colonel Scobie planned to put Judd up for a VC but was killed before being able to do so. Judd returned to Australia in 1919 as a lieutenant, having been awarded the DCM and the MC.

Keysor, Leonard VC (1st Battalion) Lance Corporal Keysor was awarded the VC for his actions during the battle for Lone Pine. He was soon promoted to lieutenant and survived Gallipoli, but suffered wounds while serving on the Western Front. He returned to Australia in 1918. He died from cancer in 1951, aged sixty-four.

Knyvett, Hugh (7th Battalion) Lieutenant Knyvett survived Gallipoli and was transferred to the 59th Battalion as an intelligence officer, with the rank of captain. He fought on the Western Front and returned to Australia in 1917, where he wrote the book '*Over There*' *with the Australians*. The book was used as a rallying cry for the United States to join the Great War. He died in the US in 1918, a victim of the flu pandemic.

Lane, Denis (12th Battalion) Major Lane was in the thick of the fighting to hold the extreme southern flank of Lone Pine, defined by Jacobs's Trench. He survived Gallipoli and was later promoted to command the 12th Battalion on the Western Front, returning to Australia as a lieutenant colonel.

Lawrence, Cyril (2nd Field Company of Engineers) Lance Corporal Lawrence survived Gallipoli and the Western Front. He returned to Australia in 1919 with the rank of sergeant. His detailed day-by-day account of his experiences while serving on the peninsula was published in 1981. Lawrence's sense of humour is evident – according to his daughter, Margaret (who informed the author), he wanted his Western Front correspondence to be published as *French Letters*. They were published after his death in 1981, under the more banal title *Sergeant Lawrence goes to France*.

Lecky, Charles (2nd Battalion) Lieutenant Lecky had taken the advice of his friend to focus on a specific position during the initial assault against Lone Pine. He fought and survived along the southern flank of Lone Pine. While serving as a major in the 54th Battalion in 1917, he was wounded in action, suffering gunshot wounds to a leg and arm. He returned to Australia in 1917, having received the Distinguish Service Order (DSO) for his actions in France and was also Mentioned in Despatches by General Haig.

Lloyd, Edward (4th Battalion) Captain Lloyd played possum after 'falling into' an occupied Turkish trench in the initial assault, and later established and defended the post that was to bear his name. After Lone Pine, he suffered a severe case of enteric fever and was shipped to Cairo for treatment. He was later sent back to Australia to recover. In early 1917, he returned to active service, fighting on the Western Front as a major in the 36th Battalion. He returned to Australia in 1919, having been Mentioned in Despatches.

McAuliffe, Edward (Chaplains Corps) Padre McAuliffe returned to

Australia in 1916, but soon rejoined his men on the Western Front and did not return to Australia until late 1918. He was appointed parish priest at Kensington in Sydney, a position he held until his death in 1964.[5]

McConaghy, David (3rd Battalion) Major McConaghy took over command of the 3rd Battalion after the death of Lieutenant Colonel Brown during the battle for Lone Pine. A month later, he was invalided from Gallipoli after suffering a nervous breakdown. He recovered to fight with his men on the Western Front, but was killed in action in 1917, having three times been Mentioned in Despatches and awarded the DSO. He is today buried in Namps-Au-Val British Cemetery, France.

McDonald, William Thomas (4th Battalion) Lieutenant McDonald and his small band of men held back the Turkish onslaught along the northern flank of Lone Pine. The position was later named McDonald's Post and he was wounded while defending it, but refused to leave. He survived Gallipoli only to be killed a year later at Pozières. Lieutenant William McDonald is buried at Courcelette British Cemetery in France.

McGrath, Mark 'Darkie' (3rd Battalion) Corporal McGrath helped Sergeant Goldenstedt defend the original Goldenstedt's Post and was one of the few survivors there during the early morning hours of 8 August. He returned to Australia in 1918 with the rank of sergeant and having been Mentioned in Despatches.

McIlroy, George (24th Battalion) Lieutenant McIlroy was not only among the last to leave Lone Pine during the final evacuation, but also from Anzac itself on 20 December 1915. He was promoted to captain and for his actions at Pozières in 1916 was awarded the MC. After Pozières he was considered medically unfit for further active service and returned to Australia in 1917.

McKenzie, 'Fighting Mac' William (Chaplains Corps) Chaplain McKenzie made his reputation at Gallipoli with heroic efforts in the front lines. He went on to do likewise on the Western Front. McKenzie was awarded a Military Cross for 'distinguished service in the field', which was presented to him by Birdwood. It was also rumoured that three times 'the fighting Salvationist' had been recommended for the VC. After the war he became a feature of Anzac Day marches. It was said that his hand was often bleeding after a march because so many man were anxious to grasp him in greeting. He died in 1947.[6]

McLeod, Donald (12th Battalion) Sergeant McLeod had his arm shattered while defending Jacobs's Post and refused to leave until the post was secure. He recovered and served on the Western Front. He was promoted to captain and in 1918 would be Mentioned in Despatches and twice recommended for the MC. He returned to Australia in late 1918.

MacDonald, Railton (3rd Battalion) Private MacDonald had been wounded during the first hour of the battle for Lone Pine at Sasse's Sap. He recovered from his wounds, but in 1916, at Pozières, he was among the 23 000 Australian casualties. He was sent to England suffering from severe wounds and his arm was amputated from the shoulder. He returned to Australia in 1917 and later spent twenty-nine years recovering from his wounds in Concord Repatriation Hospital, where he died in 1953.

Mackay, Gifford Iven (4th Battalion) Major Mackay became the commanding officer of the 4th Battalion and fought with his men at Pozières and other battles on the Western Front. He later became the brigadier general of the 1st Brigade. He returned to Australia in 1919, having been awarded the DSO with bar and the French Croix de Guerre. He returned to the University of Sydney, but was in uniform again seeing active service in the Second World War as a lieutenant general. He died in 1966, aged eighty-four.

Margetts, Ivor Stephen (12th Battalion) Lieutenant Margetts survived the worst of the fighting at Anzac from day one to the evacuation without suffering a wound. However, he was killed in action on the Western Front a year later, at Pozières. He has no known grave. Captain Ivor Margetts is commemorated at the Australian National Memorial, Villers-Bretonneux, France.

Martyn, Athelstan Markham (2nd Field Company of Engineers) Major Martyn survived the war with the rank of lieutenant colonel, and served as a senior officer of the AIF headquarters staff, before returning to Australia in 1919.

Massie, Robert (3rd Battalion) Lieutenant Massie had before the war represented New South Wales in cricket, as a left-handed batsman and left-arm fast-medium bowler with a very respectable bowling average of 18.3. His cricketing career, however, came to an end on 6 August while at Lone Pine in Mackay's Post, when he was shot in the left-hand shoulder while helping a wounded soldier. He continued to serve on the Western Front, returning to Australia in 1919 as the lieutenant colonel of the 3rd Battalion, with the DSO and having been Mentioned in Despatches for his actions at Lone Pine and in Europe. Massie's only son, John, was killed in action during the Second World War. Massie died in 1966, at the age of seventy-five.

Merrington, Ernest (Chaplains Corps) Chaplain Merrington survived Gallipoli and stayed with the Australian Light Horse, serving throughout the Palestine Campaign. He returned to Australia in 1919.

Moore, Donald (3rd Battalion) Captain Moore was left for dead while in Lone Pine, but was found alive by his friend Lieutenant Woods. After receiving treatment for his wounds in England, Moore fought on the Western Front and survived the war, returning to Australia in 1919 with the rank of lieutenant colonel and highly decorated.

Morris, Ernest (11th Battalion) Lieutenant Morris was in the thick of the fighting at Leane's Trench during the morning of 6 August. Within a month, he would come down with a near-fatal case of pneumonia and was invalided back to Australia in 1916.

Morshead, Leslie (2nd Battalion) Captain Morshead survived Gallipoli and went on to command the 33rd Battalion on the Western Front, returning to Australia in 1919. He served in the Second World War as a lieutenant general and commanded Australian troops in 1941 at the crucial battles and siege at Tobruk. He was approached by Prime Minister Curtin to become commander-in-chief of Australian forces, but turned him down. Sir Leslie Morshead, one of Australia's greatest soldiers, died in 1959.

Nankivell, Charles (4th Battalion) Lance Corporal Nankivell was engaged in the fighting along the northern flank of Lone Pine. He saved a number of his men by returning Turkish grenades as they came across. He was promoted to sergeant just after the battle of Lone Pine. However, within a year he was killed at Pozières. He has no known grave and is commemorated at the Australian National Memorial at Villers-Bretonneux, France.

Nichol, William (2nd Battalion) Private Nichol, with his mates, helped Captain Pain with the machine gun at the height of the battle for Jacobs's Trench. He was nominated for the VC for his actions during 8 August. He survived the war and was twice Mentioned in

Despatches while serving on the Western Front. For his actions at Lone Pine he was awarded the DCM.

Pain, John Henry Francis (2nd Battalion) Captain Pain and his men – privates William Nichol, James Montgomery, and William Goudemey – were nominated for the VC for their efforts in stemming the Turkish advance close to Jacobs's Trench on 8 August. While completely exposed in no-man's land, they fired a machine gun into the oncoming Turks. Pain was forced to leave Lone Pine when he was wounded for a third time. He survived the war, returning to Australia in 1919 as a major, having been Mentioned in Despatches three times and awarded the DSO and the MC for his actions at Lone Pine. He died in 1941.

Reynolds, Herbert (stretcher-bearer) Private Reynolds was evacuated from Gallipoli due to sickness. On recovering, he rejoined his unit and was wounded in action while serving on the Western Front. He returned to Australia in 1919.

Sasse, Cecil Duncan (1st Battalion) Captain Sasse was awarded the DSO for his actions at Lone Pine and later a bar to this medal for his actions on the Western Front. By the end of the war, he commanded the 4th Battalion as its lieutenant colonel. He died in 1934.

Scott, Allan (4th Battalion) Captain Scott, with a few others, retook Lloyd's Post, which allowed the Australians in the Traversed Trench to escape their hopeless position. He was awarded the DSO for his actions at Lone Pine. He commanded the 56th Battalion on the Western Front and was Mentioned in Despatches three times before being killed in action in 1917. He is buried at Buttes New British Cemetery in Belgium.

Shadbolt, Leslie John (7th Battalion) Private Shadbolt lost an eye while defending Jacobs's Post at a most critical time on 9 August. Many believed he should have been awarded the VC – in the end, he received nothing for his heroic actions that day. He was returned to Australia in late 1915. He was killed in a car accident in 1949.

Smith, William Raymond 'Smithy' (11th Battalion) Private Smith became famous during the war for his antics and was known, from generals down, as the 'first private of the AIF'. After the war he disappears from the historical record. His best mate, Snowy Howe, recalled that the last time he heard from Smithy he was kangaroo shooting on the Murchison during the Great Depression. In 1941, the body of a man who had suffered a brain haemorrhage after receiving a number of blows to the head was found in an old hut on a property at Leigh Creek, Victoria. The body was identified as a war pensioner of 'no fixed place of abode', William Raymond Smith. One of Smithy's mates – an NCO of the 11th Battalion – described him as a 'brilliant soldier' when in the line.[7]

Smyth, Neville Maskelyne VC (1st Battalion) Brigadier General Smyth took his brigade to France and in late 1916 was given command of the Australian 2nd Division. With the formation of the Australian Corps in 1918, he was transferred back to the British Army, taking command of the British 58th Division. He died in 1941.

Stevens, Arthur Borlase (2nd Battalion) Major Stevens commanded the 2nd Battalion during the initial charge against Lone Pine and, after the death of Lieutenant Colonel Scobie on 7 August, commanded the battalion throughout the battle for Lone Pine. He was Mentioned in Despatches and returned to Australia in 1919, having commanded the battalion as its lieutenant colonel.

Symons, William VC (7th Battalion) Lieutenant Symons was awarded the VC for defending Jacobs's Post and was wounded during the battle. Soon after, he contracted enteric fever and was evacuated to England, having been reduced from twelve to eight stone. He would survive the war – being seriously gassed on the Western Front – returning to Australia in 1918. He died in London in 1948 after suffering from a brain tumour.

Talbot, Dean Albert Edward (Chaplains Corps) Chaplain Dean Talbot suffered a slight wound while in Brown's Dip during the battle for Lone Pine. He returned to Australia in 1916 and died in 1936.[8]

Tope, William (12th Battalion) Private Tope was Captain McPherson's runner and often had to cross parts of no-man's-land with messages. He survived Lone Pine and returned to Australia due to illness, with the rank of lieutenant, in 1917.

Townsend, Albert (2nd Battalion) Signaller Townsend continually crossed no-man's-land between the Pine and The Pimple, to fix cut wire or deliver messages by hand. He was Mentioned in Despatches and remained with the battalion throughout the war, returning to Australia in 1919.

Tubb, Frederick VC (7th Battalion) Lieutenant Tubb was awarded the VC for his leadership at Symons's Post and went on to see action on the Western Front. While Tubb survived Gallipoli, the newly promoted major would be killed fighting in Belgium in September 1917. Lady Waring, with whom Frederick Tubb had spent his last leave as a guest at her home, wrote: 'The manner of his death came as no surprise to those who knew his gallant spirit, and I, for one, feel certain it is the death "Tubby" would have desired.'[9] He is today buried in the Lijssenthoek Military Cemetery in Belgium.

Walker, 'Hooky' Harold (1st Australian Division) Major General Walker suffered a wound while visiting Lone Pine after the battle.

The evacuation of the peninsula took place before he had a chance to recover, so he never returned to Gallipoli. He led the Australians in numerous battles, including at Pozières in 1916 and through to the Hindenburg Line in 1918. Walker, who had served his men well for four years, was among the last British officers to leave the AIF, following the formation of the Australian Army Corps in 1918, relinquishing command of the 1st Australian Division to Major General Thomas Glasgow. Walker was soon back among the fighting, leading a British division on the Western Front until the Armistice. After the war he returned to Britain and died in 1934.

Wallish, Albert (11th Battalion) Sergeant Wallish courageously barricaded the southern part of Leane's Trench during the morning of 6 August, as the Turks tried to force their way into the central parts of the trench. He was wounded, but continued to fight until a Turkish grenade shattered his leg. It was later amputated and he returned to Australia in 1916, having been awarded the DCM for his actions that day.

Wass, William (2nd Battalion – signaller) Sergeant Wass suffered a fractured skull during the initial charge into Lone Pine, but refused to leave his post. He survived the battle and Gallipoli, only to be killed in action during the Battle of Fromelles in France in 1916, fighting with the 54th Infantry Battalion. He was awarded the MM and was Mentioned in Despatches. Wass's identity tags were eventually passed on to the Australian government by the Germans via the International Red Cross – he has no known grave.

White, Brudenell (1st Australian Division) Brigadier General White went on to become a prominent figure in Australian military history, serving with distinction on the Western Front. In 1918 many considered that he should have taken control of the newly established Australian Army Corps, but that honour went to Monash.

With the end of the war, White was placed in charge of demobilisation and repatriation of the AIF. He was promoted to lieutenant general. For his services after Gallipoli, he received five foreign decorations, was appointed aide-de-camp to King George V and Mentioned in Despatches five times. He returned to Australia in 1919 and was instrumental in the reorganisation of the Australian Army between the wars.[10] With the outbreak of war in 1939, White, who had retired, was called back to serve in 1940 as chief of general staff. While keen to return to active service, he admitted that he felt 'like Cincinnatus called from his farm'.[11] On 13 August 1940, the then Prime Minister, Robert Menzies, recalled with great concern and regret: 'A knock came on my door, and somebody walked in. There had been a dreadful air crash, almost within sight of my windows…the most scholarly and technically talented soldier in Australian history, Sir Brudenell White…was dead…I shall never forget that terrible hour.'[12]

Wicks, Alfred Ernest (1st Battalion) Sergeant Wicks helped stop the Turkish capture of Jacobs's Post during the afternoon of 7 August by retrieving captured Turkish grenades from a recently evacuated trench exposed to fire. He ventured into this trench on a number of occasions but was eventually wounded in doing so. Wicks remained at his post until receiving a more serious wound a few hours later. He returned to Australia in 1918 having been awarded the DCM and Mentioned in Despatches for his actions on the Western Front.

Winzar, Bertram (11th Battalion) Private Winzar, at great risk to his own life, brought in a wounded man stranded in the Valley of Despair during Turkish shelling, on the morning of 6 August. He was soon invalided back to Australia suffering bronchitis. In 1916 he was discharged as permanently unfit and some uncaring little bureaucrat denied him a pension, arguing that his heart trouble was pre-service in origin. In 1917 he re-enlisted in the 11th Battalion and fought on the Western Front. Winzar returned to Australia after the Armistice, and died young from a 'diseased heart'.

Woods, Percy (3rd Battalion) Lieutenant Woods, with Sergeant Major Goldenstedt, prepared for a last-ditch fight at Lone Pine on 9 August, when at the last minute the Turkish mass attack was repulsed. He later served as the commanding officer of the 55th Battalion on the Western Front, having been Mentioned in Despatches numerous times, awarded the DSO (with bar) and the MM. He returned to Australia in 1919 with the rank of lieutenant colonel.

Youden, Herbert Alexander (2nd Brigade) Lieutenant Youden was seriously wounded during the afternoon of 7 August, while defending the position that bears his name. He recovered from his wounds and towards the end of the war led the 2nd Battalion as its lieutenant colonel. He returned to Australia in 1919, having been awarded the DSO and Mentioned in Despatches.

Zeki Bey, Ahmet (Turkish 57th Regiment) Captain Ahmet Zeki Bey survived Gallipoli and later served as staff officer in the Turkish 2nd Corps and 48th Division as chief-of-staff. During 1918–19 he was the chief-of-staff for the 3rd Army Corps. The then Major accompanied Charles Bean on his return to Anzac in 1919. Ahmed Zeki Bey fought with distinction during the War of Liberation in 1921 and was promoted to major general in 1927. He retired in 1934 and died in 1957.

Acknowledgements

It would be impossible to approach any history of Lone Pine without continually turning to the writings of Charles Bean, not only in his *Official History of Australia in the War of 1914–1918: Vol. II*, but also his correspondence with participants who fought there, Australian and Turk.

A big thankyou must also go to those who published their battalion histories in the 1920s and '30s, listed in the bibliography. They provide a wealth of material, some humorous, some very tragic. More recently, a number of other researchers have contributed to writing detailed battalion histories, including Ron Austin, James Hurst, Neville Brown and Ian Gill.

Also of significance have been the writings of the diggers themselves, in returned servicemen's journals such as *Reveille* and *Stand-to*. Some historical purists may question the use of such material; I unashamedly embrace the importance of these writings by the men who experienced war at the sharp end. In almost all cases, they provide historical gold dust, which has been all too often ignored. It must also be remembered that at the time these men were writing (1920–30s), their peers were reading, which provides a great, self-imposed editorial mechanism.

I would like to thank Dr Peter Stanley and Dr Rhys Crawley for reading early draft chapters of the manuscript. Their suggestions greatly improved the manuscript. Of course, any errors remaining are totally the responsibility of the author.

Like all researchers, I am indebted to those soldiers who not only kept a record of their experiences, but also unselfishly donated their precious documents, writings and 'curios' to numerous research institutions for others to study. This also applies to relatives who have provided similar valuable records. For those copyright holders I was unable to locate, I trust that the material quoted meets with your approval.

I am especially indebted to Dr Margaret Heese, the daughter of then Lance Corporal Cyril Lawrence, for allowing me to quote from her father's diary. His diary (held at the Australian War Memorial) and published by Melbourne University Press in the early 1980s, is a detailed account of one man's experience during the Gallipoli Campaign. A big thankyou also to Mr Hartley Cook, grandson of Syd and Elsie Cook, Mr Mark Derham QC, grandson of General Brudenell White, and Ms Jan McCombe, relative of General Harold 'Pompey' Elliott, each of whom allowed me to publish excerpts from their relative's writings.

Another thankyou goes to Professor Haluk Oral, who allowed me to quote from his book *Gallipoli 1915: Through Turkish Eyes*. Not only does it provide a wealth of important and new information, but it surely is one of the most beautifully produced books ever published on the Gallipoli Campaign, if not military history in general. Further thanks to Dr Michael McKernan for giving me permission to quote from his fascinating book *Padres: Australian Chaplains in Gallipoli and France*.

I would also like to thank the following institutions for supplying and/or permitting me to quote material in their care: Australian National Library, libraries at the Australian National University, the Australian War Memorial, and the National Achieves of Australia. Thank you also to the NSW Returned and Services League (RSL) for allowing me to quote from their outstanding journal *Reveille* – keep up the good work.

At Penguin, I would like to thank my publisher, Ben Ball, for taking time to hear my proposal and agreeing to publish this book. A huge thankyou also to my editor, Michael Nolan, whose contribution to getting the rambling manuscript into a publishable form cannot be overestimated.

Finally, I thank my wife, Debbie, for her encouragement, support and advice, as well as Emma, Anita and Lloyd who, seemingly at the right time, bring Dad back to twenty-first century.

Notes

PROLOGUE
1 McAnulty, C., Diary (AWM 1DRL042)
2 ibid
3 Lecky, C.S. (1932) 'Inferno of Death: 2nd Bn. Losses', *Reveille*, August, p.29
4 See Crawley, R. (2010) 'Our Second Great [Mis]adventure: A critical re-evaluation of the August Offensive, Gallipoli, 1915', PhD dissertation, University College University of New South Wales, Australian Defence Force Academy; and Crawley, R. (2010) 'The Myths of August at Gallipoli', in Stockings, C. (ed.) *Zombie Myths of Australian Military History: the 10 Myths That Will Not Die*, New South, Australia, pp.50–69

CHAPTER 1
1 Smith, D.J. (2008) *One Morning in Sarajevo, 28 June 1914*, Weidenfeld & Nicolson, London
2 Souter, G. (1976) *Lion and Kangaroo: Australia 1901–1919 The Rise of a Nation*, Fontana, Collins Australia, p.210
3 ibid, p.210–11
4 Harris, K. (2011) *More than Bombs and Bandages: Australian Army Nurses in World War 1*, Big Sky Publishing, NSW; Tyquin, M. (2006) *Madness and the Military: Australia's Experience of the Great War*, Australian Military History Publications, Sydney; Bean, C.E.W. (1937) *Official History of Australia in the War of 1914–18. Vol I: The Story of Anzac—from the outbreak of war to the end of the first phase of the Gallipoli Campaign, May 4 1915*, 7th ed., Angus & Robertson, Sydney
5 Quote from Connor, J. (2011) *ANZAC*

and Empire: George Foster Pearce and the Foundations of Australian Defence, Cambridge University Press, Australia, p.27
6 See Robson, L.L. (1970) *The First A.I.F.: A Study of its Recruitment 1914–1918*, Melbourne University Press, Melbourne; Mallet, R. (1999) 'The Interplay Between Technology, Tactics and Organisation in the First AIF', MA dissertation, University of New South Wales, Australian Defence Force Academy; Connor, J. (2011) *ANZAC and Empire: George Foster Pearce and the Foundations of Australian Defence*, Cambridge University Press, Australia
7 Kenneally, T. (2011) *Australians: Eureka to the Diggers*, Vol. 2, Allen & Unwin, Sydney
8 Mallet, R. (1999) 'The Interplay Between Technology, Tactics and Organisation in the First AIF', MA dissertation, University College, University of New South Wales, Australian Defence Force Academy, pp.13–14
9 Strachan, H. (2001) *The First World War, Volume I: To Arms*, Oxford University Press, pp.159–60; Rawson, A. (2006) *British Army Handbook 1914–1918*, Sutton Publishing, United Kingdom, p.7; Passingham, I. (2003) *All the Kaiser's Men: The Life and Death of the German Army on the Western Front 1914–1918*, Sutton Publishing, United Kingdom, pp.7–8
10 Quote from Robertson, J. (1990) *Anzac and Empire: The Tragedy & Glory of Gallipoli*, Hamlyn, Australia, p.174
11 Quote from Stanley, P. (2010) *Bad*

Characters: Sex, Crime, Mutiny, Murder and the Australian Imperial Force, Pier 9, Australia, p.46

12 Scott, E. (1936) *Official History of Australia in the War of 1914–18, Vol. XI: Australia during the* War, Angus & Robertson, Sydney; Robson, L.L. (1970) *The First A.I.F.: A Study of its Recruitment 1914–1918*; Gammage, B. (1972) *The Broken Years: Australian Soldiers in the Great War*, Penguin, Australia

13 Bean, C.E.W. (1938) *Official History of Australia in the War of 1914–18. Vol II: The Story of Anzac—From 4 May, 1915, to the Evacuation of the Gallipoli Peninsula*, 6th ed., Angus & Robertson, Sydney; Birdwood, W. (1941) *Khaki and Gown*, Ward, Lock & Co. Ltd., London; Hart, P. (2011) *Gallipoli*, Profile Books, London, UK

14 Hill, A.J. (1978) *Chauvel of the Light Horse*, Melbourne University Press, Australia

15 Hamilton, I. (1920) *Gallipoli Diary, Vol. 2*, Edward Arnold, London, p.98

16 McLennan, J.H., Diary (AWM 1 DRL 454)

17 Aspinall-Oglander, C.F. (1929) *Military Operations, Gallipoli: Inception of the Campaign to May 1915*, Vol.1, Imperial War Museum, London; Bean, C.E.W. (1937) *Official History of Australia in the War of 1914–18. Vol I: The Story of Anzac—from the outbreak of war to the end of the first phase of the Gallipoli Campaign, May 4 1915*, 7th ed., Angus & Robertson, Sydney

18 Austin, R. (2004) *Our Dear Old Battalion: The Story of the 7th Battalion AIF, 1914–1919*, Slouch Hat Publications, Victoria, p.77

19 McMullin, R. (2002) *Pompey Elliott*, Scribe Publications, Melbourne, p.96

20 Howe, H.V. (1934) 'The Senior Private of the A.I.F.', *Reveille*, February, p.7; Hurst, J. (2005) *Game to the Last: The 11th Australian Infantry Battalion at Gallipoli*, Oxford University Press

21 Quote from Rees, P. (2008) *The Other ANZACS: The Extraordinary Story of Our World War One Nurses*, Allen & Unwin, Sydney, p.4

22 Cook, E., Diary (AWM PR82/135)

23 McAnulty, C., Service Record, Series

B2455: First Australian Imperial Force Personnel Dossiers, 1914–1920 (SERN 1406 1803)

24 Quote from Stanley, P. (2010) *Bad Characters: Sex, Crime, Mutiny, Murder and the Australian Imperial Force*, Pier 9, Australia, p.33

25 ibid

26 Hurst, J. (2005) *Game to the Last*, p.23

27 See Stanley, P. (2010) *Bad Characters*; Harper, G. (2011) *Letters from Gallipoli: New Zealand Soldiers Write Home*, Auckland University Press, New Zealand

28 Bean, C., Diary (AWM38 3DRL 606, item 17) – Censorship. (Entry 26 September 1915); also see Fewster (2007) *Bean's Gallipoli*, Allen & Unwin, Sydney, p.206

29 McAnulty, Service Record, (SERN 1406 1803)

30 Erickson, E.J. (2001) *Ordered to Die: A History of the Ottoman Army in the First World War*, Greenwood Press, Connecticut; Erickson, E.J. (2001) 'Strength Against Weakness: Ottoman Military Effectiveness at Gallipoli, 1915', *Journal of Military History*, 65(4): 981–1011; See also Meyer. G.J. (2006) *A World Undone: The Story of the Great War 1914–1918*, Delacorte Press, New York; Ford. R. (2010) *Eden to Armageddon: World War I in the Middle East*, Pegasus Books, New York; McMeekin, S. (2010) *The Berlin-Baghdad Express: the Ottoman Empire and Germany's bid for world power*, The Belknap Press of Harvard University, Massachusetts

31 ibid

32 Aspinall-Oglander (1929) *Military Operations* Vol. 1

33 The Mitchell Report: Report of the committee appointed to investigate the attacks delivered on the enemy defences of the Dardanelles Straits. CB1550. 1919. (AWM51) Part 1; Aspinall-Oglander C.F. (1929) *Military Operations: Gallipoli* Vol 1. Imperial War Museum, London; Bean, C.E.W. (1937) *Official History of Australia in the War of 1914–18. Vol. I: The Story of Anzac—From the Outbreak of War to the End of the First Phase of the Gallipoli Campaign, May 4 1915*, 7th ed., Angus

& Robertson, Sydney; Travers, T. (2007) 'One More Push: Forcing the Dardanelles in March 1915', *Journal of Strategic Studies*, 24(3):158–176

34 ibid

35 Lee, J. (2000) *A Soldier's Life: General Sir Ian Hamilton 1853 – 1947*. Pan Books, London; Lee, J. (2004) 'Sir Ian Hamilton, Walter Braithwaite and the Dardanelles', *Journal of the Centre for First World War Studies*, Vol 1(1): 39–64

36 Steel, N. & Hart, P. (1994) *Defeat at Gallipoli*, Papermac, London; Steel, N. (1994) *Gallipoli*, Battleground Europe Series, Leo Cooper, Yorkshire; James, R.R. (1999) *Gallipoli*, Pimlico, London; Mitchell Report (1919)

37 Bean, C.E.W. (1937) Official History Vol. 1; Cameron, D.W. (2007) *25 April 1915: The Day the Anzac Legend was Born*, Allen & Unwin, Sydney

38 ibid

39 Rodge, H. & Rodge, J. (2003) *Helles Landing: Gallipoli*, Pen and Sword, South Yorkshire

CHAPTER 2

1 Bean (1938); Cameron (2007)

2 ibid

3 Cook, E., Diary (AWM PR82/135)

4 Rees, P. (2008)

5 ibid

6 Travers, T. (2001) 'The Ottoman Crisis of May1915 at Gallipoli', *War in History* Vol. 8(1): 72–86; Travers, T. (2001) *Gallipoli, 1915*, Tempus, South Carolina, p.115

7 McNamara, T. (1936) 'Memories of Gallipoli', *Reveille*, June, p.28

8 ibid

9 ibid

10 Duke, C.R. (1934) 'Reminiscences of Gallipoli', *Reveille*, May, p.20

11 ibid

12 Quote from Chapman, I. (1975) *Iven G. Mackay Citizen and Soldier*, Melway Publishing Pty Ltd, Melbourne, p.38

13 ibid

14 Duke, C.R. (1934) *Reveille*, May, p.20

15 Oral, H. (2007) *Gallipoli 1915: Through Turkish Eyes*, translated by Amy Spangler, *Turkiye Is Bankasi, Kultur Yayinlari*. p.246

16 Curran, T. (1994) *Across the Bar: The Story of 'Simpson', The Man with the Donkey – Australia and Tyneside's great military Hero*. Ogmios Publications pp.358–59

17 Quote from McKernan, M. (1986) *Padre: Australian Chaplains in Gallipoli and France*, Allen & Unwin, Sydney, p.85

18 ibid

19 Herbert, A. (1919) *Mons, Anzac and Kut*, Arnold, London, p.138

20 Quote from McKernan, M. (1986), p.85

21 Herbert (1919) p.138

22 Bean (1938); Pugsley, C. (1998) *Gallipoli: The New Zealand Story*, Reed Publishing, Auckland; Cameron (2011)

23 Quote from Moorehead, A. (1956) *Gallipoli*, Pan Books p.220

24 Quote from Carlyon, L. (2001) *Gallipoli*, MacMillan, p.326

25 Quote from Rees, P. (2008), p.88

26 Quote from Bean (1957), p.74

27 Quote from Derham, R. (2000) *Silent Ruse: Escape from Gallipoli: A record and memories of the life of General Sir Brudenell White KCB KCMG KCVO DSO*, Oryx Publishing, St Kilda, p.13

28 Birdwood (1941), p.277

29 Quote from Travers (2001), p.115

30 Hamilton, I. (1920) p.288

31 James (1999), p.237

32 Hart (2011), p.282

33 Bean (1938); Pugsley (1997); Cameron (2011) *The August Offensive at Anzac*

CHAPTER 3

1 Cook, E., Diaries (AWM PR 82/135)

2 ibid

3 ibid 7 May, 1915

4 ibid 13 May, 1915

5 ibid 17 May, 1915

6 ibid 19 May and 20 May, 1915

7 Lawrence, C., Diary (AWM PR86/266), 20 May, 1915

8 ibid, 28 May, 1915

9 ibid, 2 June, 1915

10 Elliott, H.E., Personal Papers (AWM, 2DRL/3328)

11 ibid

12 ibid

13 ibid

14 Quote from Derham, R. (2000), p.15

15 Quote from Brenchley, F. & Brenchley, E. (2005) *Myth Maker: Ellis Ashmead-Bartlett, the Englishman who Sparked Australia's Gallipoli legend*, Wiley & Sons Australia, p.150

16 Kynvett, H. (1918) *Over there with the Australians*, Charles Scribner's Sons, New York, pp.67–68

17 ibid

18 Quote from Oral, H. (2007), p.210

19 ibid p.214

20 ibid p.210

21 Keown, A.W. (1921) *Forward with the Fifth: The Story of 5 Years' War Service*, Speciality Press, Melbourne, p.121

22 Graham, W.A. (1967) 'Lone Pine', *Stand–To*, October–December, p.26

23 Barrett, L.H. (1932) 'Lone Pine: Tin Can Defences', *Reveille*, August, p.37

24 ibid, p.66

25 Lecky, C.S. (1932) 'Inferno of Death: 2nd Bn. Losses', *Reveille*, August, p.29

26 Kannengiesser, H. (1927) *The Campaign in Gallipoli*, Hutchison, London, p.133

27 Anon., from Glen Innes (1930) 'All Misery: Soldiering at Gallipoli', *Reveille*, May p.25

28 Kynvett (1918), p.68

29 ibid

30 Lecky (1932), p.29

31 Rees (2009)

32 Cook, E., Diaries (AWM PR 82/135), 31 May, 1915

33 ibid, 26 June, 1915

34 Rees (2009)

CHAPTER 4

1 Athelstan Markham Martyn [writing as AMM] (1920) 'Lone Pine', *Journal of the Royal Military College of Australia*, Issue 7, Number 13 pp.13–14

2 ibid

3 Aspinall-Oglander (1932)

4 Bean (1938)

5 Knyvett (1918), p.69

6 ibid

7 Butler, A.G. (1938) *Official History of the Australian Army Medical Services 1914–1918*, Vol. 1, Australian War Memorial, Canberra, p.228 & p.241

8 Chapman, (1975)

9 Data from Unit War Diary – 1st Australian Division – August 1915 (AWM4 1/42/7 Part 3)

10 Data from Unit War Diary – 1st Australian Division – July 1915 (AWM4 1/42/6 Parts 2 to 10); Unit War Diary – 1st Australian Division – August 1915 (AWM4 1/42/7 Part 3)

11 See Crawley, R. (2010)

12 Unit War Diary – 1st Australian Division – August 1915 (AWM4 1/42/7 Part 3)

13 Gellibrand, J. (1931) 'Humorous Interludes: Anzac Campaign', *Reveille*, March, p.20

14 Idreiss, I. (1932) *The Desert column*, Angus and Robertson, Sydney, p.19

15 Quote from Laffin, J. (1989) *Damn the Dardanelles! The Agony of Gallipoli*, Alan Sutton, UK, p.110

16 Chapman (1975)

17 Quote from Laffin (1989), p.110

18 White, C., Papers 'Some Recollections on the Great War', (AWM, 3DRL6549, item 66), 1 April 1921

19 See Bentley, J. (2003) 'Champion of Anzac: General Sir Brudenell White, the First Australian Imperial Force and the Emergence of Australian Military Culture, 1914–18', PhD dissertation, University of Wollongong

20 War Diary, 1st Australian Division, August 1915 (AWM4 1/42/7 Part 3), Notes on proposed operation including Kabe Tepe and intervening ridges in defensive line

21 ibid

22 Bean, C.E.W. (1957) *Two Men I knew: William Bridges and Brudenell White – Founders of the A.I.F.*, Angus & Robertson, Sydney, p.103

23 Note on proposed attack by 1st Australian Division (undated) War Diary, 1st Australian Division, August 1915 (AWM4 1/42/7 Part 3)

24 Hamilton I., (1920), p.325

25 Army Corps Order No.16 dated 3rd April 1915 –War Diary, 1st Australian Division (AWM4 1/25/5 Part 3 – Appendix 5)

26 Birdwood communiqué to the troops – War Diary, 1st Australian Division (AWM4 1/25/5 Part 3 – Appendix 17)

27 War Diary, 7th Australian Infantry Battalion, August 1915 (AWM4, item 23/24/6)

28 Bentley (2003), p.233

29 See Crawley (2010), pp.50–69

30 Ashmead-Bartlett, E. (1928) *The Uncensored Dardanelles*, Hutchinson & Co., London, p.151

31 Quote from James (1999), p.256

32 Birdwood, W., Papers (AWM 3DL/3376 item 11/5)

CHAPTER 5

1   Wren, E. (1935) *Randwick to Hargicourt: History of the Third Battalion A.I.F.*, Ronald G. McDonald, Sydney, p.97
2   Cubis, R. (1978) *A History of A Battery, Royal Australian Artillery*, Elizabethan Press, Sydney; Smith, A (2011) *Do Unto Others: Counter Bombardment in Australia's Military Campaigns*, Big Sky Publishing, Australia
3   War Diary, 1st Australian Division, July 1915 (AWM4 1/42/1) Conference report dated 11 May
4   Coombes, D. (2007) *The Lion Heart – Lieutenant General Sir Talbot Hobbs: An Australian Commander in World War One*, Australian Military history Publications, Victoria
5   Bean, (1938)
6   Hobbs, J., Papers/Diary (AWM PR82/153, 1/3)
7   See Crawley, (2010)
8   Birdwood Papers, item 31; see also Bentley (2003), p.218
9   Bean, (1938)
10 See Mallet, R. (1999) 'The Interplay between Technology, Tactics and Organisation in the First AIF', MA dissertation, University College University of New South Wales Australian Defence Force Academy, p.45
11 AMM (1920), p.14
12 ibid
13 Lawrence, C., Diary (AWM PR86/266)
14 ibid
15 ibid
16 AMM (1920), p.14
17 MacKay (1932), p.14
18 ibid
19 Barrett (1930), p.24
20. Lone Pine (AWM38 3DRL/8042 item 19), Bean papers
21 Bennett, S. (2011) *Pozières: The Anzac Story*, Scribe Publishing, Melbourne
22 Smyth (1932), p.7
23 ibid
24 Mackay (1932), p.14
25 Bean (1938)
26 Schuler, P. (1916) *Australia in Arms*, Fisher Unwin, London
27 Lawrence, C., Diary (AWM PR86/266)
28 AMM (1920) *Journal of the Royal Military College of Australia*, p.15
29 Quote from Stanley, (2010), pp.49–50
30 Tyquin, (2006)
31 Cook, E., Diaries (AWM PR 82/135), 9 July, 1915
32 Bean, C.E.W. (1952) *Anzac to Amiens*, Australian War Memorial, pp.142–43
33 Data from War Diary, 1st Australian Division, August 1915 (AWM4 1/42/7 Part 3)
34 Data from War Diary, 1st Australian Division, July 1915 (AWM4 1/42/6 Parts 2 to 10); War Diary, 1st Australian Division, August 1915 (AWM4 1/42/7 Part 3)
35 Elliott, H.E., Personal Papers (AWM)
36 ibid
37 ibid
38 Collingwood, J.J. (1931) 'Lone Pine: 1st Brigade in Epic Fight', *Reveille* July, p.13

CHAPTER 6

1   Von Sanders, L. (1927) *Five Years in Turkey*, 1st English edition, Bailliere, Tindall & Cox, London
2   Von Sanders (1927), p.81
3   ibid p.82
4   War Diary, 2nd Australian Infantry Battalion (AWM4 23/19/6)
5   Byrne (1922) *New Zealand Artillery in the Field, 1914–18*, Whitcombe and Tombs Ltd, Auckland, New Zealand, p.72
6   Taylor, F.W. & Cusack, T.A. (1942) *Nulli Secundus: A History of the Second Battalion, A.I.F, 1914–1919*, Sydney
7   Barrett (1932), p.66
8   ibid
9   Bean (1938, p.524
10 ibid
11 Taylor & Cusack (1942), pp.122–23
12 ibid
13 Quote from Stanley, (1984), p.24
14 Taylor & Cusack (1942)
15 ibid., pp.124–25
16 McAnulty, C., Diary (AWM 1DRL042)
17 ibid
18 Bean (1937), p.298.
19 Donkin, R., Diary typed manuscript (AWM 2DRL/0069)
20 ibid
21 War diary, 7th Australian Infantry Battalion (AWM4 23/24/6)
22 AMM (1920), p.16
23 Donkin Diary, August 6
24 Operational Order No. 3 War diary dated 5 August – 1st Australian Infantry Brigade (AWM4 23/1/8 Part 2)

25 War diary, 7th Australian Infantry Battalion (AWM4 23/24/6)
26 Wren (1935), p.105
27 Taylor & Cusack, (1942)
28 Quote from Chapman, (1975), p.53
29 Duke (1934), p.20
30 Aylward (1937) 'With the 4th at the Pine', *Reveille*, August, p.66
31 Lecky (1932), p.29
32 Talbot (1932) 'Lone Pine: A Padre's Memoirs', *Reveille* August, p.32
33 ibid
34 ibid
35 See Graham, W.A. (1967) *Stand-To*
36 Robertson, J. (1990) *Anzac and Empire: the tragedy and glory of Gallipoli*, Hamlyn, Australia
37 Lawrence, C., Diary (AWM PR86/266), 28 May 1915
38 Translation of diary of Turkish Machine gun officer in Lone Pine (AWM 3DRL/8042, item 15)

CHAPTER 7

1 Belford (1940)
2 Bean (1938), p.490
3 Aarons J., Papers (AWM 3DRL8042 item, 15), letter to Bean, June 12, 1922
4 Bean (1938)
5 ibid; Hurst (2005), p.151
6 Bean, (1938)
7 Quote from Hurst, (2005), p.153
8 Aarons J., Papers (AWM 3DRL8042 item, 15), letter to Bean, June 12, 1922
9 Quote from Hurst (2005), p.153
10 ibid
11 Aarons J., Papers (AWM 3DRL8042 item, 15), letter to Bean, June 12, 1922
12 Priestman, T., Service Record, Series B2455: First Australian Imperial Force Personnel Dossiers, 1914–1920 (SERN 396)
13 Belford (1940), p.139
14 Quote from Olson, W. (2006) *Gallipoli: The Western Australian Story*, University of Western Australia Press, Perth, p.212
15 Bean (1938)
16 Hurst (2005), p.155
17 Bean (1938), p.492
18 Belford (1940), p.140
19 Facey (1981) *A Fortunate Life*, Penguin, Australia p.345
20 ibid
21 ibid
22 Report of Colonel Johnston, 11th

Battalion AIF – War Diary 3rd Australian Infantry Brigade (AWM4 23/3/3 Part 1)
23 Facey (1981) p.346
24 ibid, p.347
25 Aarons J., Papers (AWM 3DRL8042 item, 15), letter to Bean, June 12, 1922
26 Holloway, D (2011) *Endure and Fight: A detailed history of the 4th Light Horse Regiment, AIF, 1914–1919, Gallipoli, Sinai and Palestine, France and Belgium*, The 4th Light Horse Regiment Memorial Association, Victoria, p.80
27 Bean (1938); Belford (1940)
28 Aarons J., Papers (AWM 3DRL8042 item, 15), letter to Bean, June 12, 1922
29 Bean (1938); Hurst (2005)
30 Quote from Hurst (2005), p.161
31 Bean (1938)
32 See Hurst (2005)
33 Morris, E., Service Record, Series B2455: First Australian Imperial Force Personnel Dossiers, 1914–1920
34 Bean (1938); Hurst (2005)

CHAPTER 8

1 Quote from Chapman (1975), p.52
2 ibid
3 ibid
4 ibid
5 Donkin, R., Diary typed manuscript (AWM 2DRL/0069), 6 August
6 McAnulty, C., Diary (AWM 1DRL042)
7 Bean, C., Diary (AWM38, 3DRL/606, item 11/2)
8 Talbot, (1932), p.32
9 ibid
10 Quote from McKernan (1987), p.110
11 Taylor & Cusack (1942)
12 Graham (1967), p.27
13 Wren (1935)
14 AMM (1920); Graham (1967)
15 Donkin, R., Diary typed manuscript (AWM 2DRL/0069), 6 August
16 Austin, S. and Austin, R. (1995) *The Body Snatchers: The History of the 3rd Field Ambulance, 1914–1918*, Slouch Hat Publications, McCrae
17 Quote from Tyquin (1999) *Neville Howse: Australia's First Victoria Cross Winner*, Oxford University Press, Melbourne, p.62
18 Austin & Austin (1995), p.55
19 AMM (1920), p.16
20 ibid

21 Quote from Derham (2000), p.17
22 Communique from War Diary, HQ
    ANZAC (AWM 4/1/25/4, Part 3), 5
    August 1915
23 See Crawley, R. (2010)
24 Schuler (1916), p.226
25 Moorehead (1956)
26 Birdwood (1941), p.272
27 Newton L.M. (1925) *The Story of the
    Twelve: a record of the 12th Battalion,
    A.I.F. during the Great War of 1914–1918*,
    12th Battalion Association, Hobart, p.63
28 Schuler (1916), p.226
29 Quote from Austin, R (2007) *The
    Fighting Fourth: A History of Sydney's
    4th Battalion 1914–1919*. A Slouch Hat
    Publication, Victoria, p.69
30 Quote from McKernan (1986), p.117
31 Quote from Robertson (1990, p.120
32 Quote from McKernan (1986), p.117
33 Quote from Pugsley (1998), p.271
34 Graham (1967), p.26
35 Maitland, G. (2000) *The Battle History
    of the Royal New South Wales Regiment,
    Volume 1: 1885–1918*, Simon and
    Schuster, Australia, p.58
36 Quote McKernan (1986), pp.110–111
37 ibid
38 Reynolds, H.V., Diary (AWM
    PR00039)
39 Quote from Coombes (2007), p.79
40 ibid
41 Crawley (2010)
42 Lawrence, C., Diary (AWM PR86/266)
43 Donkin, R., Diary typed manuscript
    (AWM 2DRL/0069), *6 August*
44 Lawrence, C., Diary (AWM PR86/266)
45 Smyth (1932), p.7
46 See Griffith, P. (1994) *Battle Tactics of
    the Western Front: the British Army's Art
    of Attack 1916–18*, Yale University Press,
    United States; Griffith, P. (2010) *The
    Great War on the Western Front: a Brief
    History*, Sword and Pen, UK
47 See Crawley (2010), p.189
48 ibid, pp.204–205
49 War Diary, 1st Australian Division,
    August 1915 (AWM4 1/42/7 Part 4),
    Artillery Daily Report 3rd to 5th
    August 1915 1/42/7 Part 3
50 Bean (1938)
51 War Diary, 1st Australian Division,
    August 1915 (AWM4 1/42/7 Part 4),
    Artillery Daily Report 3rd to 5th
    August 1915

52 Bean (1952), p.125
53 ibid, p.183
54 ibid, p.184
55 Birdwood (1941) Khaki and Gown,
    pp.269–70
56 ibid p.272
57 Bean (1938), p.502
58 Quote from Chapman (1975), p.53
59 Quote from Austin (2007), p.71
60 Quote from Pedersen (2007), p.89
61 Bean, C., Diary (AWM38, 3DRL/606,
    item 14/2) – August fighting;
    McCarthy, D. (1983) *Gallipoli to the
    Somme: The story of C.E.W. Bean*, John
    Ferguson, Sydney
62 McAnulty, C., Diary (AWM 1DRL042)
63 Quote from Austin (2007), p.69
64 Lecky (1932), p.29
65 Wren (1935), p.100
66 Quote from Austin (2007), p.69
67 ibid
68 Bean, C., Diary (AWM38, 3DRL/606,
    item 14/2) – August fighting; Quote
    from McCarthy (1983), p.171
69 Quote from McKernan (1986), p.111

CHAPTER 9

1   Wren (1935), p.101
2   ibid
3   Donkin, R., Diary typed manuscript
    (AWM 2DRL/0069), *6 August*
4   AMM (1920), p.17
5   ibid
6   Quote from Chapman (1975), p.53
7   Duke (1934), p.20–21
8   Bean (1938)
9   Quote from Austin (2007), p.70
10 ibid
11 ibid, p.71
12 ibid
13 Wren (1935), pp.100–01
14 ibid
15 Litchfield, E.N *A Prelude to Lone Pine*
    (AWM 3DRL3520, item 131, pp.3–4)
16 Woods, P.W., Papers (AWM,
    PR00050), letter
17 Lone Pine (AWM38 3DRL/8042 item
    19), MacDonald letter
18 Harrison, L. (1995) *Dear Da ... Dubbo*,
    NSW, p.28
19 Quote from Robertson (1990), p.121
20 Taylor & Cusack (1942), p.130
21 ibid pp.128–29
22 ibid
23 ibid

24 Maitland (2000)
25 Quote from Gammage (1974), p.69
26 Lecky (1932), p.2
27 Quote from McKernan (1986), p.117
28 ibid
29 ibid
30 ibid
31 Byrne (1922), pp.72–73
32 Quote from Austin, R. (1997) *Cobbers in Khaki: The History of the 8th Battalion, 1914–1918*, Slouch Hat Publication, Victoria, p.97
33 Elliott, H.E., Personal Papers, (AWM 2DRL/0513, items 7–9), letter to Kate dated 8 August 1915 (Note: likely written on August 9)
34 See Hurst (2005); Richardson, J.D. (1923) *The 7th Light Horse Regiment, 1914–1919*, Radcliff Press, Sydney; Emery, M. (2008) *They Rode into History: the Story of the 8th Light Horse Regiment Australian Imperial Force 1914–1919*, Slouch Hat Publications, Victoria; Browning, N. and Gill, I. (2011) *Gallipoli to Tripoli: History of the 10th Light Horse Regiment AIF 1914–1919*, Quality Books, Western Australia; Holloway, D (2011).
35 Bean, C., Diary (AWM38, 3DRL/606, item 14/2); See also Fewster (2007) *Bean's Gallipoli*, Allen & Unwin, Sydney, p.183
36 Jess (IWM DOCS)
37 Lawrence, C., Diary (AWM PR86/266)
38 ibid
39 Donkin, R., Diary typed manuscript (AWM 2DRL/0069), 6 August
40 ibid
41 See Emery, M. (2008); Browning, N. and Gill, I. (2011)
42 Olson (2006); Cameron (2011)
43 Hall, R.C. (2000) *The Balkan Wars 1912–1913: Prelude to the First World War*, Routledge, New York; Erickson, E.J. (2010) *Gallipoli – The Ottoman Campaign*, Pen and Sword, UK
44 Mango, A. (1999) *Ataturk*, John Murray, London
45 Kemal. M. (un-dated) *Atatürk's Memoirs of the Anafartalar Battles*, Imperial War Museum (undated), K35413
46 Bean (1938), pp.527–28

CHAPTER 10

1   www.australiansatwar.gov.au (Lance Corporal Hugh Anderson at Lone Pine)
2   Quote from Austin (2007), p.73
3   Quote from Hart (2011), p.302
4   ibid
5   Bean, C., Diary (AWM38, 3DRL606/192)
6   ibid
7   ibid
8   www.australiansatwar.gov.au (Lance Corporal Hugh Anderson at Lone Pine)
9   ibid
10 ibid
11 ibid
12 Bean, C., Diary (AWM38, 3DRL606/192)
13 Aylward (1937), p.37 & p.43
14 ibid
15 ibid
16 ibid
17 ibid
18 Mackay (1932), p.87
19 ibid
20 ibid
21 Quote from Austin (2007), p.73
22 Mackay (1932), p.87
23 Chapman (1975)
24 Bean (1938)
25 ibid, p.513
26 Duke (1934), p.21
27 ibid
28 ibid
29 ibid
30 ibid
31 Lloyd (1932), p.45
32 ibid
33 ibid
34 ibid
35 Quote from Austin (2007), pp.75–76
36 Lloyd (1932), p.45
37 Lloyd (1932), p.45
38 Quote from Austin (2007), p.73
39 Anon (1934), p.18
40 Quote from Austin (2007), p.73
41 Goldenstedt (1932), p.26
42 ibid
43 ibid
44 Harrison (1995), p.28
45 Goldenstedt (1932), p.26
46 Quote from Wren (1935), p.101
47 Wren (1935), p.102
48 Bean (1938); Fewster, K., Baüsarın, V.

& Baüsarın, H. (2003) *Gallipoli: The Turkish Story*, Allen & Unwin, Sydney

49 *The Daily Advertiser*, Wagga, 25 April, 1987
50 War Diary, 1st Australian Division, August 1915 (AWM4 1/42/7 Part 11), White's message to Birdwood Headquarters, 050 hours, 7 August
51 Wren (1935), p.104
52 Lone Pine (AWM38 3DRL/8042 item 19), MacDonald letter
53 ibid
54 ibid
55 ibid
56 ibid
57 Bean (1938)
58 MacDonald R. Service Record, Series B2455: First Australian Imperial Force Personnel Dossiers, 1914–1920 (SERN 560)
59 Goldenstedt (1932), p.26
60 Bean (1938)
61 ibid
62 Wren (1935), p.103
63 Goldenstedt (1932), p.26
64 Bean (1938), pp.504–05
65 Lecky (1932), p.29
66 Taylor & Cusack (1942), p.130
67 ibid
68 Bean (1938), p.508
69 Lone Pine (AWM38 3DRL/8042 item 19), Cook
70 Taylor & Cusack (1942), pp.131–32; also see Lone Pine (AWM38 3DRL/8042 item 19), Cook
71 Taylor & Cusack (1942)

CHAPTER 11

1   Bean (1938), p.518
2   Quote from Oral (2007), pp.244–45
3   Bean (1938), p.518
4   Bean (1952), pp.185–87; see also Erickson, E.J. (2010)
5   Bean, (1952), pp.185–87
6   ibid
7   ibid
8   ibid, pp.187–88
9   Bean (1952); Erickson (2010)
10 Quote from Oral (2007), pp.246–47
11 Bean (1952), p.188
12 ibid
13 ibid, pp.188–89
14 ibid, p.189
15 ibid
16 ibid
17 ibid

18 Bean (1952); Erickson (2010)
19 Bean (1952), p.189
20 ibid, pp.190–91
21 ibid
22 ibid, pp.189–90
23 ibid, pp.190–91
24 ibid
25 ibid
26 ibid
27 Bean (1952); Erickson (2010)

CHAPTER 12

1   Bean (1938), p.519
2   Bean, C., Diary (AWM38, 3DRL/606, item 11/2)
3   War Diary, 1st Australian Division, August 1915 (AWM4 1/42/7 Part 11), Note from 1st Brigade to 1st Australian Division Headquarters, 1020 hours, 6 August
4   War Diary, 1st Australian Division, August 1915 (AWM4 1/42/7 Part 11), Note from 1st Brigade to 1st Australian Division Headquarters, 006 hours, 7 August
5   Bean (1938), p.518
6   Quoted from Chapman (1975), p.53 & p.55
7   ibid, p.55
8   Bean, C., Diary (AWM38, 3DRL/606, item 14/2); also see Fewster (2007), pp.183–94
9   Cherry, F., Papers (AWM 2DRL/0302)
10 ibid
11 Schuler (1916), p.232
12 McKinley (1995), p.36
13 Adam-Smith (1991), p.121
14 Humphreys, A., Service Record, Series B2455: First Australian Imperial Force Personnel Dossiers, 1914-1920 (SERN 2259)
15 Cherry, F., Papers (AWM 2DRL/0302)
16 Rule, E. (1933) *Jacka's Mob*, Angus & Robertson, Sydney, p.6
17 Schuler (1916), p.231
18 ibid, p.232
19 Lone Pine (AWM38 3DRL/8042 item 19) Elliott letter dated 25 January 1916
20 Bean (1952), pp.191–92
21 ibid
22 Austin & Austin (1995)
23 Taylor & Cusack (1942), p.132
24 ibid
25 See Cameron (2007); Taylor & Cusack (1942)
26 Bean (1938)

27 Jacobs letter in AWM38 3DRL/8042 item 19
28 Quote from Gammage (1974), p.103
29 Lone Pine (AWM38 3DRL/8042 item 19) Jacobs letter
30 ibid
31 War Diary, 1st Australian Infantry Brigade, April – August 1915 (AWM4 23/1/2 Part 1)
32 War Diary, 2nd Australian Infantry Battalion (AWM4 23/19/6)
33 Taylor & Cusack (1942), p.130
34 ibid
35 Lane (1932), p.43
36 Gammage, B. (1974)
37 Gammage, J., Papers (AWM PR82/003)
38 ibid
39 Chapman (1975)
40 Quote from Maitland (2000), p.64
41 Lawrence, C., Diary (AWM PR86/266)
42 ibid
43 ibid
44 Quote taken from Stevenson, R. C. (2010) 'The Anatomy of a Division: the 1st Australian Division in the Great War, 1914–1919', PhD dissertation, University College of New South Wales, Australian Defence Force Academy
45 Cavill (1916) *Imperishable ANZACs: A Story of Australia's Famous First Brigade from the Diary of Pte Harold Walter Cavill N. 27 1 Bn.*, William Brooks & Co, pp.90–91
46 ibid
47 ibid
48 Talbot, D. (1932), p32
49 Reynolds, H.V. Diary (AWM PR00039)
50 ibid
51 ibid
52 Quoted from Chapman (1975), p.56
53 ibid

CHAPTER 13

1 Bean (1952), pp.192–93
2 ibid
3 ibid
4 Erickson (2010)
5 Bean (1938); Erickson (2010)
6 Bean (1938)
7 Donkin, R., Diary typed manuscript (AWM 2DRL/0069)
8 Lawrence diary (AWM AWM PR86/266)
9 AMM (1920) Journal of the Royal Military College of Australia, p.17
10 ibid
11 Graham (1967), p.28
12 AMM (1920), pp.17–18
13 ibid
14 ibid
15 Bean (1938) Official History Vol 2
16 AMM (1920) Journal of the Royal Military College of Australia, p.18
17 Taylor & Cusack (1942), p.131
18 Bean (1938), pp.532–33
19 Lawrence, C., Diary (AWM PR86/266)
20 Lane (1932), p.43
21 ibid
22 ibid
23 Broadbent (1990), p.94
24 ibid
25 War Diary, 2nd Australian Infantry Battalion (AWM4 23/19/6)
26 Taylor & Cusack (1942), p.134
27 Quote from Austin, R. (2012) *Wounds and Scars: From Gallipoli to France, the History of the 2nd Australian Field Ambulance, 1914–1919*, Slouch Hat Publications, Victoria, p.54.
28 Elliott, H.E., Personal Papers (AWM, 2DRL/3328)
29 Lone Pine (AWM38 3DRL/8042 item 19) Elliott letter dated 25 January 1916
30 Austin (2004) *Our Dear Old Battalion: The story of the 7th Battalion AIF, 1914–1919*, A Slouch Hat Publication, Rosebud, Victoria
31 Coombes (2007)
32 ibid
33 Erickson (2010)
34 Aylward (1937), p.43
35 ibid
36 Bean (1938)
37 Mackay (1932), p.87
38 Besanko, C., Service Record, Series B2455: First Australian Imperial Force Personnel Dossiers, 1914–1920 (SERN 6)
39 Bean (1938), p.534
40 Mackay (1932), p.87
41 ibid
42 ibid
43 Bean (1938); Mackay (1932)
44 Goldenstedt (1932), p.26
45 Taylor & Cusack (1942), p.134
46 War Diary, 1st Australian Division, August 1915 (AWM4 1/42/7 Part II) White's message to Birdwood, 0603 hours, 7 August

47 Newton (1925), p.62
48 Wren (1935), p.104
49 ibid
50 ibid
51 Bean (1938)
52 Quote from Austin (2007), p.72
53 Smyth (1932)
54 Barrett diary quoted from Maitland, G.
    (2000) *The Battle History of the Royal
    New South Wales Regiment, Volume
    1: 1885–1918*, Simon and Schuster,
    Australia, p.61
55 Quote from Derham (2000), p.17
56 Bean (1938); Pugsley (1997); Cameron
    (2011)
57 ibid
58 ibid
59 Aspinall-Oglander (1929), p.181

CHAPTER 14
1   Erickson (2010)
2   Bean (1938)
3   Bean (1952), p.193
4   ibid p.193
5   Bean (1952), p.197
6   Quote from Oral (2007), p.247
7   Quote from Wren (1935), p.105–06
8   ibid
9   Taylor & Cusack (1942), p.134
10 Newton (1925), p.62
11 Bean (1938); Pugsley (1997); Cameron
    (2011)
12 ibid
13 ibid
14 Pugsley (1997)

CHAPTER 15
1   Erickson (2010), p.147
2   Bean (1952), p.194
3   Bean (1938), pp.536–37
4   Bean (1952), pp.194–95
5   Bean, C., Diary (AWM38,
    3DRL606/195)
6   Bean, C., Diary (AWM38,
    3DRL606/192)
7   ibid
8   Aylward (1937); Bean (1938)
9   Bean (1938), p.538
10 Quote from Chapman (1975) *Iven G.
    Mackay: Citizen and soldier*, p.58
11 ibid
12 Graham (1967), p.28
13 Lloyd (1932), p.45
14 ibid
15 Austin (2007), p.75

16 Lloyd (1932), p.45
17 ibid
18 Austin (2007), p.75
19 Taylor & Cusack (1941), p.135
20 War Diary, 1st Australian Division,
    August 1915 (AWM4 1/42/7 Part 11)
    White's message to 1st Battalion, 0623
    hours, 7 August
21 War Diary, 1st Australian Division,
    August 1915 (AWM4 1/42/7 Part 11)
    White's message to 1st Battalion, 0709
    hours, 7 August
22 Lone Pine (AWM38 3DRL/8042, item 20)
23 Data of battalion strength taken from
    Bean (1938), p.566
24 See Crawley R. (2010), p.161
25 Lloyd (1932), p.45
26 ibid
27 Duke (1934), p.21
28 ibid
29 ibid
30 Lloyd (1932) p.45
31 Bean (1938)
32 ibid, p.540
33 Bean (1938)
34 ibid, p.541
35 Bean (1938)

CHAPTER 16
1   Bean (1938)
2   Lone Pine (AWM38 3DRL/8042 item
    19), Youden letter
3   ibid
4   ibid
5   Lecky (1932), p.29
6   Bean (1938), p.543
7   War Diary, 2nd Australian Infantry
    Battalion (AWM4 23/19/6)
8   Bean (1938), p.544
9   Bean (1938)
10 Taylor & Cusack (1942), p.135
11 ibid
12 Lone Pine (AWM38 3DRL/8042 item
    19) Cook letter
13 ibid
14 Bean (1938)
15 Lone Pine (AWM38 3DRL/8042 item
    19) Cook letter
16 Bean (1938), pp.545–46; Taylor &
    Cusack (1942), p.137
17 Lecky (1932); Taylor & Cusack (1942)
18 Lecky (1932), p.70
19 Taylor & Cusack (1942), p.137
20 Bean (1938), pp.547–46
21 Taylor & Cusack (1942), pp.137–38

22 Bean (1938)
23 ibid
24 Taylor & Cusack (1942)
25 Lane (1932), p.43
26 ibid
27 ibid
28 ibid
29 Newton (1925), p.62
30 Hale, E. (AWM 2 DRL/0103)
31 Bean (1938); Austin (2004)
32 Goldenstedt (1932), p.26
33 ibid
34 Lawrence, C., Diary (AWM PR86/266)
35 ibid
36 ibid
37 Lane (1932), p.43
38 ibid
39 Quote from Austin (2012), p.55
40 AMM (1920), p.18
41 ibid
42 Talbot, D. (1932), p.32
43 ibid
44 Lawrence, C., Diary (AWM PR86/266)
45 ibid
46 ibid
47 ibid
48 ibid
49 ibid
50 ibid
51 ibid
52. ibid
53 ibid
54 ibid
55 ibid
56 ibid
57 ibid
58 ibid
59 ibid
60 ibid
61 ibid
62 ibid

CHAPTER 17
1 Bean (1952), pp.195–96
2 Bean (1938), p.550
3 Quote from Taylor & Cusack (1942), p.139
4 Austin & Austin (1995)
5 See Tyquin (1999), p.62
6 Bean, C.E.W. Diary entry 26 September 1915 (AWM38 3DRL 606, item 17). Also see Fewster (2007), p.206
7 Austin and Austin (1995)
8 Bean (1938)
9 War Diary, 2nd Australian Infantry Battalion (AWM4 23/19/6), Lone Pine
10 Dando-Collins, S. (2011) *Crack Hardy: From Gallipoli to Flanders to the Somme, the true Story of Three Australian Brothers at War*, Vintage Books, Sydney
11 Lecky (1932), p.70
12 Graham (1967), p.28
13 Quote from McKernan (1986), pp.117–18; McKernan (2010), p.166
14 Lawrence, C., Diary (AWM PR86/266)
15 ibid
16 Graham (1967), p.28
17 Quote from Durham (2000), p.17

CHAPTER 18
1 Goldenstedt (1932), p.26
2 Bean (1952), p.198
3 Goldenstedt (1932), p.26
4 Taylor & Cusack (1942)
5 Bean (1938)
6 Taylor & Cusack (1942), p.140
7 Taylor & Cusack (1942) p.141
8 Elliott, H.E., Personal Papers (AWM, 2DRL/0513), item 1/1
9 Quote from Travers (2001), p.117
10 Quote from Olson (2006), p.252
11 Sergeant Les de Vine (AWM 1 DRL240)
12 Quote from Gammage (1972), p.71
13 Quote from Fallon, O. (2006) Colonel H.F.N. Jourdain and the Connaught Rangers on Gallipoli, *The Gallipolian: The Journal of the Gallipoli Association*, Vol. 110, p.8
14 Donkin, R., Diary typed manuscript (AWM 2DRL/0069)
15 Crawley (2010)
16 Sadler, P. (2000) *The Paladin: A life of Major-General Sir John Gellibrand*, Oxford University Press, Melbourne
17 Bean (1938), p.732; for additional details on the battle for Hill 60 see Cameron, D.W. (2011) *Gallipoli: the Final Battles and the Evacuation of Anzac*, Big Sky Publishing, NSW
18 Bean (1938); Pugsley (1997); Cameron (2011)
19 See Crawley (2010)
20 Bean (1938); Pugsley (1997); Cameron (2011); Kerr, G. (1998) *Lost Anzacs: The Story of Two Brothers*, Oxford University Press, Melbourne
21 Bean (1938); Pugsley (1997); Cameron (2011)
22 ibid

23 McAnulty, C., Diary (AWM 1DRL042)

CHAPTER 19

1   Quote from Harris (2011), p.81
2   ibid
3   See Rees (2008); and Harris (2011)
4   Butler (1938), p.308
5   Quote from Tyquin, M. (1993)
    *Gallipoli: The Medical War, The
    Australian Army Medical Services in
    the Dardanelles Campaign of 1915*,
    University of New South Wales Press,
    Sydney
6   Butler (1938)
7   ibid, p.165
8   Quote from Broadbent (1994), p.94
9   Rees (2008), p.106
10. Quote from Chapman (1975), pp.59–60
11 ibid
12 ibid
13 ibid
14 ibid
15 Quote from Oppenheimer, M. (2006)
    *Oceans of Love: Narelle – An Australian
    Nurse in World War 1*, ABC Books
    Australia, pp.67–68
16 Cook, E., Diaries (AWM PR 82/135),
    August 13
17 Rees (2008)
18 Cook, E., Diaries (AWM PR 82/135),
    August 15
19 ibid, August 18
20 ibid, August 19

CHAPTER 20

1   Bean (1952), p.198
2   Bean (1938), p.554
3   Bean (1938)
4   Quote from Coombs (2007), p.81
5   Lawrence, C., Diary (AWM PR86/266)
6   ibid
7   ibid
8   ibid
9   ibid
10 Donkin, R., Diary typed manuscript
    (AWM 2DRL/0069)
11 ibid
12 ibid
13 War Diary, 1st Australian Infantry
    Brigade, April–August 1915 (AWM4
    23/1/2 Part 1)
14 Bean, C., Diary (AWM38, 3DRL/606,
    item 14/2); also see Foster (2007),
    pp.189–90
15 Austin (2004)

16 Lone Pine (AWM38 3DRL/8042 item
    19), Elliott letter dated 25 January 1916
17 Elliott, H.E., Personal Papers, (AWM,
    3DRL/0513, item 3/3)
18 ibid
19 Bean (1938); McMullin (2002); Austin
    (2004)
20 Elliott, H.E., Personal Papers, (AWM
    2DRL/0513, items 7–9), Elliott letter to
    Kate dated 8 August 1915 (Note: likely
    written on 9 August)
21 Quote from Austin (2004), p.92
22 Lone Pine (AWM38 3DRL/8042, item
    20), Elliott letter to Bean
23 Elliott, H.E., Personal Papers, (AWM
    2DRL/0513, items 7–9), Elliott letter to
    Kate dated 8 August 1915 (Note: likely
    written on 9 August)
24 Elliott, H.E., Personal Papers, (AWM
    2DRL/0513, item 4–6)
25 Bean (1938); McMullin (2002)
26 Quote from Austin (2004), p93
27 ibid
28 War Diary, 1st Australian Infantry
    Brigade, April–August 1915 (AWM4
    23/1/2 Part 1)
29 See McMullen (2002)
30 Bean (1938); Cameron (2009)
31 Elliott, H.E., Personal Papers (AWM
    2DRL/0513, items 7–9), letter to Kate
    dated 8 August 1915 (Note: likely
    written on 9 August)
32 Graham (1967), p.28
33 Quote from Broadbent (1990), p.92
34 Quote from Coombs (2001), p.34
35 Bean (1952), pp.198–99
36 Quote from Pugsley (1997), p.298
37 Bean (1938)
38 quote from Stowers, (2005), p.172
39 Bean (1938); Pugsley (1997); Cameron
    (2011)
40 ibid

CHAPTER 21

1   Lawrence, C., Diary (AWM PR86/266)
2   War Diary, 3rd Australian Infantry
    Battalion (AWM4 23/20/6)
3   Reynolds, H.V., Diary (AWM
    PR00039)
4   Bean (1938)
5   Elliott, H.E., Personal Papers, (AWM
    2DRL/0513, items 7–9), Elliott letter to
    Kate dated 8 August 1915 (Note: likely
    written on 9 August)
6   Quote from Snelling, S. (1995)

Gallipoli: VCs of the First World War, Wrens Park, Gloucestershire, UK, p.54

7 Quote from Austin (2004) *Gallipoli: VCs of the first World War,* Wrens Park. Gloucestershire, UK, p.93

8 ibid

9 War Diary, 1st Australian Infantry Brigade, April–August 1915 (AWM4 23/1/2 Part 1)

10 Wren (1935), p.108

11 ibid, pp.106–07

12 ibid

13 Goldenstedt (1932), pp.26–27

14 Woods, P.W., Papers (AWM, PR00050), letter

15 Goldenstedt (1932), pp.26–27

16 Wren (1935), p.106–07

17 Bean (1938); Snelling (1995)

18 Quote from Wren (1935), p.106

19 ibid

20 Bean (1938); Pugsley (1997); Cameron (2011)

21 ibid

22 Quote from Broadbent (1990), p.94

23 Austin (2004), p.94

24 Elliott, H.E., Personal Papers (AWM, 2DRL/3328)

25 Austin (2004)

26 Quote from Snelling (1995), p.158; Austin (2004), p.94

27 Elliott, H.E., Personal Papers (AWM, 2DRL/3328)

28 ibid

29 ibid

30 Quote from Austin (2004), p.93

31 ibid, p.95

32 *Albany Advertiser,* 15 September 1915

33 Newton (1925); Bean (1938)

34 Elliott, H.E., Personal Papers (AWM, 2DRL/3328)

35 Bean (1938), p.862

36 Austin (2004)

37 Quote from Snelling (1999), p.153

CHAPTER 22

1 Donkin, R., Diary typed manuscript (AWM 2DRL/0069)

2 Gammage, J., Papers (AWM PR82/003)

3 Coombes (2007), p.81

4 Wren (1935), p.109

5 ibid

6 War Diary, 1st Australian Infantry Battalion, August 1915 (AWM4 23/18/3)

7 Bean (1938), p 565

8 Quote from Snelling (1999), p.164

9 Quote from Adam-Smith (1985), p.121

10 Reynolds, H.V., Diary (AWM PR00039)

11 Richardson, J.D. (1923) *The 7th Light Horse Regiment, 1914–1919,* Radcliff Press, Sydney (Facsimile Edition [2009] A. Green, Brisbane), p.16

12 Talbot (1932), p.32

13 Quote from Austin (2007), p.80

14 Sergeant Les de Vine (AWM 1 DRL240)

15 Graham (1967), p.29

16 Quote from McMullin (2002), pp.163–64

17 ibid

18 Margetts, Papers (AWM 1DRL/0478)

19 Gammage, J., Papers (AWM PR82/003)

20 Quote from Austin and Austin (1995), p.56

21 Bean (1938)

22 Lawrence, C., Diary (AWM PR86/266)

23 ibid

24 Donkin, R., Diary typed manuscript (AWM 2DRL/0069)

25 Bean, C.E.W. (1952) *Gallipoli Mission,* Australian War Memorial, Canberra

26 War Diary, 7th Australian Infantry Battalion, August 1915 (AWM4, item 23/24/6)

27 Elliott, H.E., Personal Papers (AWM 3DRL 3328)

28 ibid

29 Elliott, H.E., Personal Papers, (AWM 2DRL/0513, items 7–9), Elliott letter to Kate dated 8 August 1915 (Note: likely written on 9 August)

30 Gammage, J., Papers (AWM PR82/003)

31 Donkin, R., Diary typed manuscript (AWM 2DRL/0069)

32 ibid

33 Goldenstedt (1932), p.27

34 ibid

35 Bean quoted in Foster (2005), p.190

36 Data from Bean (1938); also see Erickson (2010)

37 Quote from Maitland (2000), p.65

AFTERMATH

1 Idriess (1932), p.41

2 Danisman, H.B. (2007) *Gallipoli 1915: Day One Plus... 27th Ottoman Inf. Regt. Vs. ANZACS based on Account of Lt. Col. Sefik Aker Commander of 27th Inf. Regt.,* Danizer Kitabevi, Istanbul, p.47

3 Donkin, R., Diary typed manuscript (AWM 2DRL/0069)

4 ibid

5 Dexter, E., Papers (AWM PR 00248)

6 Austin (2004), p.105

7 Austin, R. (1998) *Forward Undeterred: The History of the 23rd Battalion 1915–1918*, Slouch Hat Publication, Victoria, p.22

8 ibid, p.34

9 ibid, p.22

10 Danisman (2007), p.203

11 Bean (1938), p.842

12 Edmonds, A.H. (1936) 'The evacuation of Anzac', *Reveille*, December, p.39

13 McIlroy, G.S. (1932) Silent Stunts: Turks Outwitted, *Reveille*, p.54

14 ibid

15 Longmore, G. (1929) *The Old Sixteenth: Being the Record of the 16th Battalion, A.I.F., During the Great War, 1914–1919*, Perth (Facsimile [2007] Hesperian Press, Western Australia), p.89

16 Likeman, R. (2010) *Gallipoli Doctors: The Australian Doctors at War Series Volume 1*, Slouch Hat Publications, Victoria, p.181

17 ibid

18 Lawrence, C., Diary (AWM PR86/266)

19 Savige, S.G. (1932) 'Lone Pine Sector: 24th Battalion's Goodbye', *Reveille*, December, p.9

20 Quote from McKernan (2010), p.195

21 Savige (1932), p.9

22 McIlroy (1932), p.54

23 ibid

24 ibid

25 ibid

26 Savige (1932), p.60.

27 McIlroy (1932), p.54

28 ibid

29 ibid

30 Danisman (2007), p.204

EPILOGUE

1 See Crawley, R. (2006) *Perspectives of Battle: Lone Pine, August 1915*, Honours Thesis, University of Wollongong

2 Hamilton, I. (1915) 'Have Done Splendidly: Brave Australian Infantry, Capture of Trenches', *The Sun*, Wednesday 18 August 1915, p.5

3 Crawley (2006)

4 *The Sun*, Monday 23 August 1915, p.6

5 See: the *Hobart Mercury*, Wednesday 25 August 1915, p.5; Adelaide Advertiser, Wednesday 5 August 1915, p.9; *The Age*, Wednesday 25 August 1915, p.9; *The Daily Telegraph*, Wednesday 25 August 1915, p.9; *The Sun*, Wednesday 25 August 1915, p.6; also see also Crawley (2006)

6 'The Australian Casualties – Dead 2925, Wounded 11,334', *The Age*, Monday 30 August 1915, p.6

7 Scott, E. (1936) *Official History of Australia in the War of 1914–18, Vol XI: Australia during the War*. Angus & Robertson, Sydney; Robson, L.L. (1970) *The First A.I.F. A study of its recruitment 1914–1918*, Melbourne University Press, Melbourne

8 Crawley (2009), p.76

9 Crawley (2006)

10 See Ziino, B. (2007) *A Distant Grief: Australians, War Graves and the Great War*, University of Western Australia Press, Perth, p.30

11 Irwin, G.R., Service Record, Series B2455: First Australian Imperial Force Personnel Dossiers, 1914–1920 (SERN 2145)

12 ibid; Ziino (2007)

13 Goldenstedt (1929), p.7

14 Lone Pine (AWM38 3DRL/8042 item 19), Jacobs letter

15 Elliott (1929), p.7

16 Lone Pine (AWM38 3DRL/8042 item 19), Elliott letter, dated 25 January 1916

17 Goldenstedt (1929), p.7

18 Bean, C.E.W. (1952) *Gallipoli Mission*, Australian War Memorial, Canberra, pp.50–51 and 58–59

19 Bean (1952), p.325

20 ibid

21 *Treaty of Lausanne*, 1923

22 Bademli, R. (1997) *Gallipoli Peninsula Peace Park International Ideas and Design Competition Volumes: 1 & 2*, Gallipoli Peninsula Peace Park Office, Ankara, Turkey

23 Austin (2005), pp.152–153

24 Cameron & Donlon (2005) 'A Preliminary Archaeological Survey of the Anzac Gallipoli Battlefields of 1915', *Australasian Journal of Historical Archaeology*, Vol 23:131–138

25 Back, L. and Webster, L. (2008) *Moments in Time: Dioramas at the Australian War Memorial*, New Holland Publishing

WHAT HAPPENED TO...

1   Rees (2008)
2   Carlyon (2002)
3   Snelling (1999), p176
4   McMullin (2002), p.655
5   McKernan (1986)
6   ibid
7   Howell (1934); Hurst (2005)
8   McKernan (1986)
9   Quote from Snelling (1999), p.172
10 Bean (1957); also see Australian
    Dictionary of Biography, Australian
    National University; Derham (1998)
11 Bean (1957), p.206
12 Menzies, R.G. (1967) *Afternoon Light*,
    Cassell, Australia, p.18

Bibliography

AUSTRALIAN WAR MEMORIAL, CANBERRA

Charles Bean collection

Bean, C., Diary (AWM38, 3DRL/606, item 11/2) – Lone Pine and Chunuk Bair
Bean, C., Diary (AWM38, 3DRL/606, item 14/2) – August fighting
Bean, C., Diary (AWM38, 3DRL606/192) – Lone Pine and Captain Milson's death
Bean, C., Diary (AWM38 3DRL 606, item 17) – Censorship
Lone Pine (AWM38 3DRL/8042 item 19)
Lone Pine (AWM38 3DRL/8042, item 20)

Personal diaries and letters

Aarons J., Papers (AWM 3DRL8042 item, 15)
Birdwood, W., Papers (AWM 3DL/3376 item 11/5)
Champion, B.W., Diary (AWM 2 RL 512)
Cherry, F., Papers (AWM 2DRL/0302)
Cook, E., Diaries (AWM PR 82/135)
Darnell, A.H., Letter dated 27 May, 1915 (AWM 1DRL233, 8042, item 7)
de Vine, L. (AWM 1 DRL240)
Dexter, E., Papers (AWM PR 00248)
Donkin, R., Diary typed manuscript (AWM 2DRL/0069)
Elliott, H.E., Personal Papers (AWM, 2DRL/3328)
(AWM, 3DRL/0513, item 3/3)
(AWM 2DRL/0513, items 7–9)
(AWM 2DRL/0513, item 4–6)
Gammage, J., Papers (AWM PR82/003)
Hale, E. (AWM 2 DRL/0103)
Hobbs, J., Papers/Diary (AWM PR82/153, 1/3)
Lawrence, C., Diary (AWM PR86/266)

Litchfield, E.N 'A Prelude to Lone Pine' (AWM 3DRL3520, item 131)
McAnulty, C., Diary (AWM 1DRL042)
McLarty, H.R., Papers (AWM, 1DRL 0452)
McLennan, J.H., Diary (AWM 1 DRL 454)
Margetts, I.S., Papers (AWM 1DRL/0478)
Reynolds, H.V., Diary (AWM PR00039)
Shaw, G., Papers (AWM PR 83/027)
Turkish Machine gun officer in Lone Pine's diary, translation (AWM 3DRL/8042, item 15)
White, C., Papers 'Some Recollections on the Great War', (AWM, 3DRL6549, item 66)
Woods, P.W., Papers (AWM, PR00050)

Unit diaries

War Diary, General Staff, GHQ MEF (AWM4 1/4/5 Part 2)
War Diary, HQ ANZAC (AWM 4/1/25/4, Part 3)
War Diary, HQ ANZAC (AWM 4/1/25/5, Part 3)
War Diary, HQ ANZAC (AWM 4/1/25/9, Part 12)
War Diary, 1st Australian Division, July 1915 (AWM4 1/42/6 Parts 2 to 10)
War Diary, 1st Australian Division, August 1915 (AWM4 1/42/7 Part 3)
War Diary, 1st Australian Division, August 1915 (AWM4 1/42/7 Part 4)
War Diary, 1st Australian Division, August 1915 (AWM4 1/42/7 Part 11)
War Diary, 1st Australian Infantry Brigade, July–December 1915 (AWM4 23/1/8 Part 2)
War Diary, 1st Australian Infantry Brigade, April–August 1915 (AWM4 23/1/2 Part 1)

War Diary, 1st Australian Infantry Battalion, August 1915 (AWM4 23/18/3)

War Diary, 2nd Australian Infantry Brigade, April–August 1915 (AWM4 23/2/6)

War Diary, 2nd Australian Infantry Battalion (AWM4 23/19/6)

War Diary, 3rd Australian Infantry Battalion (AWM4 23/20/6)

War Diary, 3rd Australian Light Horse Brigade (AWM4 10/3/7)

War Diary, 4th Australian Infantry Battalion, August 1915 (AWM4 23/21/6)

War Diary, 5th Australian Infantry Battalion, August 1915 (AWM4 23/22/6)

War Diary, 6th Australian Infantry Battalion, August 1915 (AWM4 23/23/6)

War Diary, 7th Australian Infantry Battalion, August 1915 (AWM4, item 23/24/6)

LA TROBE STATE LIBRARY

Love, A. (1915) Diary, La Trobe State Library Reading Room (MS9603 MSB422)

NATIONAL ARCHIVES AUSTRALIA (SERVICE RECORDS 1914–1920 – SERIES B2455)

Aylward, J. (SERN 507)

Besanko, C. (SERN 6)

Brims, A. (SERN 137)

Clogstoun, H. (officer at enlistment)

Donkin, R. (SERN 817)

Elliott, H. (officer at enlistment)

Flemming, G. (SERN 1874)

Flemming, V. (SERN 104/2262)

Clogstoun, H. (officer at enlistment)

Goldenstedt, P. (SERN 1281)

Graham, W. (SERN 1363)

Hayward, G. (SERN 489)

Humphreys, A. (SERN 2259)

Irwin, G.R. (SERN 2145)

Jacobs, H. (officer at enlistment)

Lecky, C. (officer at enlistment)

Lloyd, E.A. (officer at enlistment)

McAnulty, C. (SERN 1406 1803)

MacDonald, R. (SERN 560)

Morris, E. (officer at enlistment)

Priestman, T. (SERN 396)

Reynolds, H.V. (SERN 622)

Roper, D. (SERN 2437)

Scott, C. (SERN 832)

Shadbolt, L. (SERN 649)

Smith, R. (SERN 232)

Tope, W. (SERN 280)

Wallish, A. (SERN 1186)

Wass, W. (SERN 239)

Winzar, B. (SERN 739)

ACADEMIC JOURNALS

Cameron, D.W. & Donlon, D. (2005) 'A Preliminary Archaeological Survey of the Anzac Gallipoli Battlefields of 1915', *Australasian Journal of Historical Archaeology*, Vol. 23:131–138

Erickson, E.J. (2001) 'Strength Against Weakness: Ottoman Military Effectiveness at Gallipoli, 1915', *Journal of Military History*, Vol. 65(4): 981–1011

Lee, J. (2004) 'Sir Ian Hamilton, Walter Braithwaite and the Dardanelles', *Journal of the Centre for First World War Studies*, Vol. 1(1): 39–64

Travers, T. (2001) 'The Ottoman Crisis of May 1915 at Gallipoli', *War in History* Vol. 8(1): 72–86

Travers, T. (2007) 'One More Push: Forcing the Dardanelles in March 1915', *Journal of Strategic Studies*, Vol. 24(3):158–176

UNIT HISTORY

Austin, R. (1992) *As Rough as Bags: The History of the 6th Battalion, 1st AIF 1914–1919* Slouch Hat Publications, Victoria

Austin, R. (1997) *Cobbers in Khaki: The History of the 8th Battalion, 1914–1918*, Slouch Hat Publications, Victoria

Austin, R. (1998) *Forward Undeterred: The History of the 23rd Battalion 1915–1918*, Slouch Hat Publications, Victoria

Austin, R. (2004) *Our Dear Old Battalion: The story of the 7th Battalion AIF, 1914–1919*, Slouch Hat Publications, Victoria

Austin, R. (2007) *The Fighting Fourth: A History of Sydney's 4th Battalion 1914–1919*, Slouch Hat Publications, Victoria

Austin, R. (2012) *Wounds and Scars: From Gallipoli to France, the History of the 2nd Australian Field Ambulance, 1914–1919*, Slouch Hat Publications, Victoria

Austin, S. & Austin, R. (1995) *The Body Snatchers: The History of the 3rd Field Ambulance, 1914–1918*, Slouch Hat Publications, Victoria

Belford, W. (1940) *'Legs-eleven': Being the Story of the 11th Battalion (A.I.F.) in* the Great War of 1914–1918, Imperial Printing, Perth

Browning, N. and Gill, I. (2011) Gallipoli to Tripoli: History of the 10th Light Horse Regiment AIF 1914–1919, Quality Books, Western Australia

Byrne, J.R. (1922) New Zealand Artillery in the Field, 1914–18, Whitcombe and Tombs Ltd, Auckland, New Zealand

Cubis, R.M.C. (1978) A History of a Battery, Royal Australian Artillery, Elizabethan Press, Sydney

Emery, M. (2008) They Rode into History: The Story of the 8th Light Horse Regiment Australian Imperial Force 1914–1919, Slouch Hat Publications, Victoria

Holloway, D (2011) Endure and Fight: A Detailed History of the 4th Light Horse Regiment, AIF, 1914–1919, Gallipoli, Sinai and Palestine, France and Belgium, The 4th Light Horse Regiment Memorial Association, Victoria

Keown, A.W. (1921) Forward with the Fifth: The Story of 5 Years' War Service, Speciality Press, Melbourne

Longmore, G. (1929) The Old Sixteenth: Being A Record of the 16th Battalion, A.I.F., during the Great War, 1914–1918, (2007 edition), Hesperian Press

Maitland, G. (2000) The Battle History of the Royal New South Wales Regiment, Volume 1: 1885–1918, Simon and Schuster, Australia

Newton, L.M. (1925) The Story of the Twelve: A Record of the 12th Battalion, A.I.F. during the Great War of 1914–1918, 12th Battalion Association, Hobart

Norman, H. (1941) From Anzac to the Hindenburg Line: The History of the 9th Battalion, A.I.F., 9th Battalion A.I.F. Association, Brisbane

Olden, A. (1921) Westralian Cavalry in the War: The Story of the 10th Light Horse Regiment, A.I.F., in the Great War, 1914–1918, Alexander McCubbin, Melbourne

Richardson, J.D. (1923) The 7th Light Horse Regiment, 1914–1919, Radcliff Press, Sydney (Facsimile Edition [2009] A. Green, Brisbane)

Rule, E. (1933) Jacka's Mob, Angus & Robertson, Sydney

Stacy, B., Kindon, F. & Chedgey, H. (1931) The History of the First Battalion, A.I.F., 1914–1919, 10th Battalion A.I.F. Association, Sydney

Taylor, F.W. & Cusack, T.A. (1942) Nulli Secundus: A History of the Second Battalion, A.I.F., 1914–1919, Sydney

Wren, E. (1935) Randwick to Hargicourt: History of the Third Battalion A.I.F., Ronald G. McDonald, Sydney

OFFICIAL HISTORY

Aspinall-Oglander, C.F. (1929) Military Operations, Gallipoli: Inception of the Campaign to May 1915, Vol. 1, Imperial War Museum, London

Aspinall-Oglander, C.F. (1932) Military Operations, Gallipoli: May 1915 to Evacuation, Vol. 2, Imperial War Museum, London

Bean, C.E.W. (1937) Official History of Australia in the War of 1914–18. Vol. I: The Story of Anzac – from the outbreak of war to the end of the first phase of the Gallipoli Campaign, May 4 1915, 7th ed., Angus & Robertson, Sydney

Bean, C.E.W. (1938) Official History of Australia in the War of 1914–18. Vol. II: The Story of Anzac – From 4 May, 1915, to the Evacuation of the Gallipoli Peninsula, 6th ed., Angus & Robertson, Sydney

Butler, A.G. (1938) Official History of the Australian Army Medical Services 1914–1918, Vol. 1, Australian War Memorial, Canberra

Scott, E. (1936) Official History of Australia in the War of 1914–18, Vol XI: Australia during the War. Angus & Robertson, Sydney

Waite, F. (1921) The New Zealanders at Gallipoli, Whitcombe and Tombs Ltd, Auckland

OFFICIAL INQUIRIES

The Dardanelles Commission, 1915–16, The Stationary Office, London (published later as Defeat at Gallipoli: The Dardanelles Part II/1915–16, The Stationary Office Publishing, 2000)

The Mitchell Report: Report of the Committee appointed to investigate the attacks delivered on the enemy defences of the Dardanelles Straits, CB1550 (1919) AWM51

DISSERTATIONS

Bentley, J. (2003) 'Champion of Anzac: General Sir Brudenell White, the

First Australian Imperial Force and the Emergence of Australian Military Culture, 1914–18', PhD Dissertation, University of Wollongong

Crawley, R. (2006) 'Perspectives of Battle: Lone Pine, August 1915', Honours Thesis, University of Wollongong

Crawley, R. (2010) 'Our Second Great [Mis]adventure: A critical re-evaluation of the August Offensive, Gallipoli, 1915', PhD dissertation, University College University of New South Wales, Australian Defence Force Academy

Mallet, R. (1999) 'The Interplay Between Technology, Tactics and Organisation in the First AIF', MA dissertation, University College, University of New South Wales, Australian Defence Force Academy

Stevenson, R. C. (2010) 'The Anatomy of a Division: the 1st Australian Division in the Great War, 1914–1919', PhD dissertation, University College of New South Wales, Australian Defence Force Academy

JOURNALS/MANUSCRIPTS/ NEWSPAPERS

AMM [Athelstan Markham Martyn] (1920) 'Lone Pine', *Journal of the Royal Military College of Australia*, Issue 7, Number 13 pp.13–18

Anon., (1934) 'August on Gallipoli', *The Listening Post*, August, pp.18–19

Anon., from Glen Innes (1930) 'All Misery: Soldiering at Gallipoli', *Reveille*, May p.25

Aylward, J. (1937) 'With the 4th at the Pine', *Reveille*, August, p.66

Barrett, L.H. (1930) 'The "Ghost": Terrors', *Reveille*, June, p.24

Barrett, L.H. (1932) 'Lone Pine: Tin Can Defences', *Reveille*, August, p.37 & p.43

Bennett, G.H'. (1930) 'Orgy of Death: German Officers' Trench', *Reveille*, March, p.24

Celik, K. (2000) 'Gallipoli: The August Offensive: A Turkish view of the August Offensive', (unpublished), AWM

Collingwood, J.J. (1931) 'Lone Pine: 1st Brigade in Epic Fight', *Reveille* July, p.13

Crawley, R. (2007) 'Was Lone Pine Worth it?', *Wartime: Official Magazine of the Australian War Memorial* Vol. 38, pp.14–17

Dix, C.C. (1932) 'Efficient Navy: How troops were landed', *Reveille*, March p.20 & pp.63–64

Duke, C.R. (1934) 'Reminiscences of Gallipoli', *Reveille*, May, p.20

Edmonds, A.H. (1936) 'The evacuation of Anzac', *Reveille*, December, pp.38–39 & p.44

Elliott, H. (1929) '7th Battalions VCs' *Reveille*, August, p.7

Fallon, O. (2006) 'Colonel H.F.N. Jourdain and the Connaught Rangers on Gallipoli', *The Gallipolian: The Journal of the Gallipoli Association*, Vol. 110, pp.8–13

Fenwick, P.C. (1932) 'Reminiscences of Anzac', *Reveille*, March p.39 & pp.70–71

Gellibrand, J. (1931) 'Humorous Interludes: Anzac Campaign', *Reveille*, March, p.20.

Goldenstedt, P. (1929)' 7th Bn. V.C.'s: Congratulations', *Reveille*, September, p.7

Goldenstedt, P. (1932) 'Attack and Defence: 3rd at the Pine', *Reveille*, August, pp.26–27

Graham, W.A. (1967) 'Lone Pine', *Stand-To*, October–December, pp.26–29

Hamilton, I. (1915) 'Gallipoli positions stormed: Sir Ian Hamilton's report', *The Sun*, Wednesday 11 August 1915, p.1

Hamilton, I. (1915) 'Have Done Splendidly: Brave Australian Infantry, Capture of Trenches', *The Sun*, Wednesday 18 August 1915, p.5

Howe, H.V. (1934) 'The Senior Private of the A.I.F.', *Reveille*, February, p.7 and pp.30–31

Kemal. M. (un-dated) *Atatürk's Memoirs of the Anafartalar Battles*, Imperial War Museum (undated), K35413 (Copy supplied to the AWM by DWC)

Lane, D.A. (1932)' Holding On: 12th Bn. at Lone Pine', *Reveille*, August, p.43

Lecky, C.S. (1932) 'Inferno of Death: 2nd Bn. Losses', *Reveille*, August, p.29 & p.70

Lloyd, E. (1932) 'Played Possum: In Turkish Trench', *Reveille*, August, p.45

McIlroy, G.S. (1932) 'Silent Stunts: Turks Outwitted', *Reveille*, p.34 & p.54

McKinlay, J. (1995) *Bring Decent Signallers*. Royal Australian Corps of Signals Committee, Watsonia, Western Australia

McNamara, T. (1936) 'Memories of Gallipoli' *Reveille*, June, p.28

Mackay, I.G. (1932) 'Lonesome Pine: Called After Song', *Reveille*, August, p.14

Orchard, M. (2008) 'I Ducked!' *The Gallipolian*, Vol. 116, p.47

Orchard, M. (2008) 'The Digger's Tenner' *The Gallipolian*, Vol. 116, p.47

Savige, S.G. (1932) 'Lone Pine Sector: 24th Battalion's Goodbye', *Reveille*, December, pp.8–9 & p.60

Smyth, N. (1932) T'he Storming of Lone Pine', *Reveille*, August, p.7

Stanley, P. (1984) 'A Note on a Lone Pine Uniform', *Sabretache*, Vol. 25, pp.23–24

Talbot, A.E. (1932) 'Lone Pine: A Padre's Memoirs', *Reveille*, August, p.32 & p.87

BOOKS/BOOK CHAPTERS

Adam-Smith, P. (1991) *The Anzacs*, Claremont, Camberwell

Ashmead-Bartlett, E. (1928) *The Uncensored Dardanelles*, Hutchinson & Co., London

Austin, R. (2005) *Gallipoli: an Australian Encyclopedia of the 1915 Dardanelles Campaign*, Slouch Hat Publications, Victoria

Back, L. and L. (2008) *Moments in Time: Dioramas at the Australian War Memorial*, New Holland Publishing

Bademli, R. (1997) *Gallipoli Peninsula Peace Park International Ideas and Design Competition, Volumes 1 & 2*, Gallipoli Peninsula Peace Park Office, Ankara, Turkey

Bean, C.E.W. (1948) *Anzac to Amiens*, Australian War Memorial, Canberra

Bean, C.E.W. (1952) *Gallipoli Mission*, Australian War Memorial, Canberra

Bean, C.E.W. (1957) *Two Men I knew: William Bridges and Brudenell White – Founders of the A.I.F.*, Angus & Robertson, Sydney

Bennett, S. (2011) *Poziers: The Anzac Story*, Scribe Publishing, Melbourne

Benson, I. (1965) *The Man with the Donkey: John Simpson Kirkpatrick the Good Samaritan of Gallipoli*, Hodder and Stoughton, UK

Birdwood, W. (1941) *Khaki and Gown*, Ward, Lock & Co. Ltd., London

Blair, D. (2001) *Dinkum Diggers: An Australian Battalion at War*, Melbourne University Press, Melbourne

Braga, S. (2000) *Anzac Doctor: the Life of Sir Neville Howse VC*, Hale & Iremonger, Australia

Brenchley, F. & Brenchley, E. (2005) *Myth Maker: Ellis Ashmead-Bartlett, the Englishman Who Sparked Australia's Gallipoli Legend*, Wiley & Sons Australia

Broadbent, H. (1990) *The Boys Who Came Home: Recollections of Gallipoli*, ABC Books, Sydney

Broadbent, H. (2005) *Gallipoli: The Fatal Shore*, Penguin Books, Australia

Burness, P. (1996) *The Nek: The tragic charge of the Light Horse at Gallipoli*, Kangaroo Press

Bush, E.W. (1975) *Gallipoli*, Allen & Unwin, London

Cameron, D.W. (2007) *25 April 1915: The day the Anzac legend was born*, Allen & Unwin, Sydney

Cameron, D.W. (2009) *'Sorry lads, but the order is to go': The August Offensive, Gallipoli, 1915*, University of New South Wales Press, Sydney

Cameron, D.W. (2011) *Gallipoli: the Final Battles and the Evacuation of Anzac*, Big Sky Publishing, NSW

Cameron, D.W. (2011) *The August Offensive at Anzac*, Australian Army Campaign Series, No. 11, Australian Army History Unit, Canberra

Carlyon, L. (2001) *Gallipoli*, Pan Macmillan, Australia

Cavill, H.W. (1916) *Imperishable Anzacs: A Story of Australia's Famous First Brigade from the Diary of Pte Harold Walter Cavill N. 27 1 Bn.*, William Brooks & Co, Sydney

Chapman, I. (1975) *Iven G. Mackay: Citizen and soldier*, Melway Publishing Pty Ltd, Melbourne

Chasseaud, P. & Doyle, P. (2005) *Grasping Gallipoli: Terrain, Maps and Failure at the Dardanelles, 1915*, Spellmount, Staplehurst

Clark, C. (2010) *The Encyclopaedia of Australia's Battles*, Allen & Unwin, Sydney

Connor, J. (2011) *ANZAC and Empire: George Foster Pearce and the Foundations of Australian Defence*, Cambridge University Press, Australia

Coombes, D. (2001) *Morsehead: Hero of Tobruk and el Alamein*, Oxford

University Press, Melbourne

Coombes, D. (2007) *The Lion Heart – Lieutenant General Sir Talbot Hobbs: An Australian Commander in World War One*, Australian Military history Publications, Victoria

Crawley, R. (2010) 'The Myths of August at Gallipoli', in Stockings, C. (ed.) *Zombie Myths of Australian Military History: the 10 Myths That Will Not Die*, New South, Australia, pp.50–69

Curran, T. (1994) *Across the Bar: The Story of 'Simpson', the Man with the Donkey, Australia and Tyneside's Great Military Hero*, Ogmios Publications, Brisbane

Dando-Collins, S. (2011) *Crack Hardy: From Gallipoli to Flanders to the Somme, the True Story of Three Australian Brothers at War*, Vintage Books, Sydney

Danisman, H.B. (2001) *Gallipoli 1915: Bloody Ridge (Lone Pine) Diary – Lt. Mehmed Fasih 5th Imperial Ottoman Army Gallipoli 1915*, Danizer Kitabevi, Istanbul

Danisman, H.B. (2007) *Gallipoli 1915: Day One Plus... 27th Ottoman Inf. Regt. Vs. ANZACS based on Account of Lt. Col. Sefik Aker Commander of 27th Inf. Regt.*, Danizer Kitabevi, Istanbul

Derham, R. (2000) *Silent Ruse: Escape from Gallipoli: A record and memories of the life of General Sir Brudenell White KCB KCMG KCVO DSO*, Oryx Publishing, St Kilda

East, R. [ed] (1981) *The Gallipoli Diary of Sergeant Lawrence of the Australian Engineers – 1ˢᵗ A.I.F. 1915*, Melbourne University Press, Carlton

Erickson, E.J. (2001) *Ordered to Die: A History of the Ottoman Army in the First World War*, Greenwood Press, Connecticut

Erickson, E.J. (2010) *Gallipoli: The Ottoman Campaign*, Pen and Sword, UK

Facey, A.B. (1981) *A Fortunate Life*, Penguin, Australia

Farmer, G. (1993) *A Letter to Norah on the Death of an Anzac at Lone Pine*, The Escutcheon Press, NSW

Fewster, K. (1983) *Gallipoli Correspondent: The frontline diary of C.E.W. Bean*, Allen & Unwin, Sydney

Fewster, K. (2007) *Bean's Gallipoli*, Allen & Unwin, Sydney

Fewster, K., Basarın, V. & Basarın, H.

(2003) *Gallipoli: The Turkish Story*, Allen & Unwin, Sydney

Ford, R. (2010) *Eden to Armageddon: World War I in the Middle East*, Pegasus Books, New York

Gammage, B. (1972) *The Broken Years: Australian Soldiers in the Great War*, Penguin, Australia

Glen, F. (2004) *Bowler of Gallipoli: Witness to the Anzac Legend*, Australian Military History Publications, Australia

Griffith, P. (1994) *Battle Tactics of the Western Front: the British Army's Art of Attack 1916–18*, Yale University Press, United States

Griffith, P. (2010) *The Great War on the Western Front: a Brief History*, Sword and Pen, UK

Hall, R.C. (2000) *The Balkan Wars 1912–1913: Prelude to the First World War*, Routledge, New York

Hamilton, I. (1920) *Gallipoli Diary*, Vol. 1 & Vol. 2, Edward Arnold, London

Hamilton, J. (2004) *Goodbye Cobber, God Bless You: The Fatal Charge of the Light Horse, Gallipoli, August 7ᵗʰ 1915*, MacMillan, Sydney, p.309

Harper, G. (2011) *Letters from Gallipoli: New Zealand Soldiers Write Home*, Auckland University Press, New Zealand

Harris, K. (2011) *More than Bombs and Bandages: Australian Army Nurses in World War 1*, Big Sky Publishing, NSW

Harrison, L. (1995) *Dear Da...* Dubbo, NSW

Hart, P. (2011) *Gallipoli*, Profile Books, London

Herbert, A. (1919) *Mons, Anzac and Kut*, Arnold, London

Hickey, M. (1995) *Gallipoli*, John Murray, London

Hill, A.J. (1978) *Chauvel of the Light Horse*, Melbourne University Press, Australia

Hogue, O. (1916) *Love Letters of An Anzac*, Melrose, London

Hurst, J. (2005) *Game to the Last: The 11th Australian Infantry Battalion at Gallipoli*, Oxford University Press

Idreiss, I. (1932) *The Desert Column*, Angus and Robertson, Sydney

James, R.R. (1999) *Gallipoli*, Pimlico, London

Kannengiesser, H. (1927) *The Campaign in Gallipoli*, Hutchison, London

Keegan, J. (1976) *The Face of Battle: a Study of Agincourt, Waterloo and the Somme*, Jonathan Cape, UK

Kenneally, T. (2011) *Australians: Eureka to the Diggers*, Vol. 2, Allen & Unwin, Sydney

Kerr, G. (1998) *Lost Anzacs: The Story of Two Brothers*, Oxford University Press, Melbourne

Kynvett, H. (1918) *Over There with the Australians*, Charles Scribner's Sons, New York

Laffin, J. (1989) *Damn the Dardanelles! The Agony of Gallipoli*, Alan Sutton, UK

Larsson, M. (2009) *Shattered Anzacs: Living With the Scars of War*, University of New South Wales Press, Australia

Lee, J. (2000) *A Soldier's Life: General Sir Ian Hamilton 1853 – 1947*, Pan Books, London

Legg, F. (1965) *The Gordon Bennett Story: from Gallipoli to Singapore*, Angus and Robertson, Sydney

Liddle, P. (1976) *Men of Gallipoli: The Dardanelles and the Gallipoli Experience August 1914 to January 1916*, Penguin Books, London

Likeman, R. (2010) *Gallipoli Doctors: The Australian Doctors at War Series, Vol. 1*, Slouch Hat Publications, Victoria

Lowndes, C. (2011) *Ordinary Men, Extraordinary Services: The World War One experiences of the 9th Battalion (Queensland) AIF and reflections on the Gallipoli Campaign*, Boolarong Press, Brisbane

McCarthy, D. (1983) *Gallipoli to the Somme: The story of C.E.W. Bean*, John Ferguson, Sydney

McKernan, M. (1986) *Padre: Australian Chaplains in Gallipoli and France*, Allen & Unwin, Sydney

McKernan, M. (2010) *Gallipoli: A Short History*, Allen & Unwin, Sydney

McMeekin, S. (2010) *The Berlin–Baghdad Express: The Ottoman Empire and Germany's Bid for World Power*, The Belknap Press of Harvard University, Massachusetts

McMullin, R. (2002) *Pompey Elliott*, Scribe Publications, Melbourne

Mackenzie, C. (1921) *The Tale of a Trooper*, John Lane, London

Mackenzie, C. (1929) *Gallipoli Memories*, Cassell and Company, London

Macleod, J. (2004) *Reconsidering Gallipoli*, Manchester University Press, UK

Mango, A. (1999) *Ataturk*, John Murray, London

Menzies, R.G. (1967) *Afternoon Light*, Cassell, Australia

Moorehead, A. (1956) *Gallipoli*, Ballantine Books, New York

Newman, S. (2000) *Gallipoli – Then and Now*, After the Battle Publications, London

Olson, W. (2006) *Gallipoli: The Western Australian Story*, University of Western Australia Press, Perth

Oppenheimer, M. (2006) *Oceans of Love: Narelle – An Australian Nurse in World War 1*, ABC Books Australia

Keown Orrnek, T. & Toker, F. (2005) *Gallipoli: Companion to the feature length documentary*, Ekip Film, Turkey

Passingham, I. (2003) *All the Kaiser's Men: The life and death of the German Army on the Western Front 1914–1918*, Sutton Publishing, United Kingdom

Pederson, P.A. (1985) *Monash as Military Commander*, Melbourne University Press, Melbourne

Pederson, P.A. (2007) *The ANZACS: Gallipoli to the Western Front*, Penguin Books, Australia

Perry, A. (1916) 'The Men of Anzac', *The Anzac Book*, Cassell & Company Ltd., London

Pugsley, C. (1998) *Gallipoli: The New Zealand Story*, Reed Publishing, Auckland

Pugsley, C. (2004) *The ANZAC Experience: New Zealand, Australia and Empire in the First World War*, Reed Publishing, Auckland

Rawson, A. (2006) *British Army Handbook 1914–1918*, Sutton Publishing, United Kingdom

Rees, P. (2008) *The Other Anzacs: the Extraordinary Story of our World War One Nurses*, Allen & Unwin, Sydney

Robertson, J. (1990) *Anzac and Empire: The Tragedy & Glory of Gallipoli*, Hamlyn, Australia

Robson, L.L. (1970) *The First A.I.F.: A study of its recruitment 1914–1918*, Melbourne University Press, Melbourne

Rodge, H. & Rodge, J. (2003) *Helles Landing: Gallipoli*, Pen and Sword, South Yorkshire

Sadler, P. (2000) *The Paladin: A life of Major-General Sir John Gellibrand*, Oxford University Press, Melbourne

Von Sanders, L. (1927) *Five Years in Turkey*, 1st English edition, Bailliere, Tindall & Cox, London

Schuler, P. (1916) *Australia in Arms*, Fisher Unwin, London

Smith, A.H. (2011) *Do Unto Others: Counter Bombardment in Australia's Military Campaigns*, Bigsky Publishing, Australia

Smith, D.J. (2008) *One Morning in Sarajevo, 28 June 1914*, Weidenfeld & Nicolson, London

Snelling, S. (1995) *Gallipoli: VCs of the First World War*, Wrens Park, Gloucestershire, UK

Souter, G. (1976) *Lion and Kangaroo: Australia 1901–1919, The Rise of a Nation*, Collins, Australia

Stanley, P. (2005) *Quinn's Post, Anzac, Gallipoli*, Allen & Unwin, Sydney

Stanley, P. (2010) *Bad Characters: Sex, Crime, Mutiny, Murder and the Australian Imperial Force*, Pier 9, Australia

Steel, N. (1994) *Gallipoli*, Battleground Europe Series, Leo Cooper, Yorkshire

Steel, N. & Hart, P. (1994) *Defeat at Gallipoli*, Papermac, London

Stowers, R. (2005) *Bloody Gallipoli: The New Zealanders' Story*, David Bateman Ltd., Auckland

Strachan, H. (2001) *The First World War Volume I: To Arms*, Oxford University Press

Strachan, H. (2003) *The First World War*, Simon & Schuster, London

Throssell, R. (1989) *My Father's Son*, William Heinemann, Melbourne

Travers, T. (2001) *Gallipoli, 1915*, Tempus, South Carolina

Tyquin, M. (1993) *Gallipoli: The Medical War, The Australian Army Medical Services in the Dardanelles Campaign of 1915*, University of New South Wales Press, Sydney

Tyquin, M. (1999) *Neville Howse: Australia's First Victoria Cross Winner*, Oxford University Press, Melbourne

Tyquin, M. (2006) *Madness and the Military: Australia's Experience of the Great War*, Australian Military History Publications, Sydney

Zjino, B. (2007) *A Distant Grief: Australians, War Graves and the Great War*, University of Western Australia Press, Perth

Index